Sanatorium

A Novel

Sanatorium

A Novel

Satsvarupa dasa Goswami

GN Press, Inc

Persons interested in the subject matter of this book are invited to correspond with our secretary, c/o GN Press, Inc., P.O. Box 30, Philo, CA 95466, www.gnpress.org.

ISBN: 0–911233–19–9

Library of Congress Cataloging-in-Publication Data

Gosvāmī, Satsvarūpa Dāsa, 1939-
Sanatorium / Satsvarupa Dasa Goswami.
p. cm. -- (Sanatorium / Gosvāmī, Satsvarūpa Dāsa, 1939- ; v.2)
ISBN 0-911233-19-9
1. Spiritual life--International Society for Krishna Consciousness.
2. Spiritual healing. I. Title.
BL1285.852.G664 2004
294.5'512--dc22

2003023770

Cover art by Kṛṣṇa-kīrtana dāsa.
Cover design by Madana-mohana dāsa.

To my beloved spiritual master,
His Divine Grace
A.C. Bhaktivendanta Swami Prabhupada

Table Of Contents

Chapter Eighteen	365
Chapter Nineteen	384
Chapter Twenty	395
Chapter Twenty-One	408
Chapter Twenty-Two	418
Chapter Twenty-Three	431
Chapter Twenty-Four	448
Chapter Twenty-Five	463
Chapter Twenty-Six	478
Chapter Twenty-Seven	493
Notes	507
Glossary	524

Preface

Welcome to a loving world of heart and mind and beloved characters slugging it out with Māyā to discover authenticity in a rehabilitation clinic in upstate New York. There's Swami Swims—the "retired" but searching leader, who's driven by love to care for and protect the other patients; Jane—the hardcore karate biker, who is at heart a fierce heroine moving to pure love of God; Junior—the quintessential teen rebel that everyone loves to hate but who melts away your resistance; and of course, Tim—me, you, and everyone who has ever come up against our own fragility and courage on the way to enlightenment. Finally, there's Sandy—the survivor of an automobile accident, left paraplegic, who, absorbed in love in separation, carries the crew upward on her heart and beauty, the real soul of the sanatorium and the friend we could all use. In *Sanatorium*, the inmates reach out to each other and confront their personal paths to recovery and relationship. To fulfill the promise of spiritual authenticity, each must face the challenges, hopes, blessings, and finally, fear of life and death itself that lead them on their ultimate journey to find the way back home.

Chapter One

What do you want to be when you grow up? A fireman. She told me, “Pick up your *sādhana* and we may meet in the spiritual world.” “What’s it like there?” They are released from quotas. I hear they naturally love Kṛṣṇa, *crazy* about Him. Disdain the impersonal void and even the formal worship of Vaikuṇṭha. Ask yourself, honestly, how could a fallen person like me make it in one jump after this patched, faulty lifetime? A friend said he realized it can and *likely will* happen because Śrīla Prabhupāda will be there at our death and take us. I believe he could do it. Maybe, though, he’ll consider we need some intermediate *loka* for further purification in devotional service. He may want us to help with the preaching in the material worlds. We should accept that gratefully.

The soul is in the body and it doesn’t die but flies off to its next destination perfectly arranged by one’s deeds, reactions and mercy of guru and Kṛṣṇa.

The preceding paragraph was written by Junior Barks, an offspring of Hare Kṛṣṇa devotees and a twenty-year-old student at the Rudolf Steiner[1]–inspired Waldorf School. I showed him the manuscript of this book and he was appalled by its lack of straight *śāstra* and orderliness. I tried to convey to him the impression

Swami Swims was trying to make in his writing, but Junior couldn't comprehend. Too young and straight. He didn't understand why I "jumped like a frog" and said it's not directly Kṛṣṇa conscious. I told him how Kṛṣṇa likes indirect Kṛṣṇa consciousness, but he'd never heard of that and guessed it wouldn't apply to what I was doing. So I accepted his sentence because he's right, a book of sober theology is required. But I like it the way I do it, and there are plenty of straight theological students and teachers to fill that need. Perhaps I'll let Junior Barks add some more here and there when I get overcome with digression, laughing gas, attachment to the "truth" of what my senses perceive, and other disorders. It's too late for me to go back in time and get the right parents and attend the right school. If you could, would you?

All the things you are
a mixture of granola and
bread and rice cakes with
spreads, too heavy a breakfast
for me. But I eats it.

Junior Barks' critique on the brain?
Not really, regard him as a square.
Pray to my Lord as all-encompassing
and taking my offering too. Know it
comes from joy of being alive,
gratitude of His allowing me
to do anything at all.

Somehow it comes out this way
whales and porpoises, Iraq war
for nothing, an ayatollah in charge,
Muslims, Hindus, Christians,
Prabhupāda said they're just nominal.
Kṛṣṇa consciousness teaches the science of God.

Whoever lives with uninterrupted devotion is a lover
of the one God Allah, Christ, Kṛṣṇa, Buddha.
All the things you are,
revisited, seen anew, the actual objects,
the real people with their flaws.

Come to see this man and see
how bad he is physically by examination,
inquire of each member of the family
how they are doing,
downside reported by me, upside reported
by Śacī to Dr. Ravi Singh.

I say they're consistent, chronic, several-a-day,
Śacī says "but we're not using the more
        powerful meds,
a head bath often works."

This is cable TV, the smallest
world for a family who are
interested.

Junior Barks phoned Swami Swims. Junior said he was talking to a representative of Torchlight Press. He showed them one of his little essays. They said if he gathered a manuscript, they would print a book for him. So he would not write for Swami Swims anymore, and he wanted back the one paragraph he'd written.

"That's okay," said the Swami, "I wish you luck in your career." Swims hung up the phone thinking, "But I won't give up that one paragraph he gave me. I never signed a contract or anything. Besides, I can write like that too. It's just my memory. And I don't have any books here except Śrīla Prabhupāda's *ślokas*."

The invocation praises the spiritual master. You can't attain spiritual advancement without him. He's the direct representative of God and should be treated as good as God. He never makes mistakes or eats ice cream cones or looks at pretty women or goes to non-ISKCON movies. Even if his complexion isn't perfect or he has a broken nose from his previous life, or if he's ill now, these shouldn't be seen as disqualifications. His disciples shouldn't attempt to instruct him, neither should anyone else attempt to instruct him. He's humble as pie and always wears his *tilaka* and brahminical thread. Go to him and inquire from him, "What is cloning?" "Was the U.S. right in bombing Iraq?," and be willing to serve him. The critical student of the spiritual master becomes the next spiritual master. Ecumenical red tape is involved in the institution, but you can't have an institution without the laws and cops. This applies too for making spiritual masters. The invocation is called *maṅgalācaraṇa* when you pray to the gurus generically, then your own guru, then Śrīla Prabhupāda and the gurus in the Gauḍīya-sampradāya, and then the Vaiṣṇavas, Lord Gauranga, the Pañca-tattva, and Śrī Kṛṣṇa Himself:

he kṛṣṇa karuṇā-sindho
dīna-bandho jagat-pate
gopeśa gopikā-kānta
rādhā-kānta namo 'stu te

> Oh my dear Kṛṣṇa, oh ocean of mercy, oh friend of the distressed and the source of the creation, oh master of the cowherd men and the lover of the *gopīs*, especially Rādhārāṇī, I offer my respectful obeisances unto You.

Swami Swims thought, "I wish I had a better, more *rasikā* name. But Swims is Śyāma, right? Okay, don't complain. Whatever name the guru gave. I can remember if I have a book and read a few verses." It's like drinking whisky, as Father Jack does. Once you get a few shots, you get warmed up. Get going with a few verses, be confident the memory will open and connect to other subjects spiritual and to personal anecdotes. Gun the accelerator, know you've only got to go thirty minutes. Are you actually convinced, and do you want the people in the audience to become Kṛṣṇa conscious? Pray for that, just do it and it will come. If Junior Barks and well studied, much blessed heroes, can do it, I can too, even though I've been out of practice for so long. It's something you never forget. You're unique, although simple ABC. The soul, a bright shining star, an actual person one ten thousandth the tip of the hair, resides in the heart. When he's liberated he assumes his spiritual body. Don't bother me with technical terms. Be confident in what you first learned and admit you never heard the rest. Come to our house and speak, they ask. You promise you will. You have no home, which is proper for a *sannyāsī*.

He said, "There are mice in the shed."

"Which shed?"

"The art shed."

"What? Do you think I'm going in there dancing around mice while I paint?"

What then? Kill them? Don't paint? Just get in ecstasy and imagine you don't see them skitter by? That's the world. I wonder if Torchlight would take me on. I could write on the "I" in Walt Whitman's *Song of Myself*, and how we Kṛṣṇa conscious people don't believe what he's saying, that he's the locomotive and the mother and the elm tree and the mice in the art shed. Literary view from the Hare Kṛṣṇa viewpoint. Write them and see what they think.

Dear old Stockholm, I was
there where midnight is

sunny, the chiropractor is
not coming tonight, you are
free to relax and count up your
beads, *just hear.*

Let the subpersons relax.
My favorite songs in an album
offered to Lord Kṛṣṇa.
Don't be disappointed, Prabhupāda
says. Get up and try again.
The Lord will accept your
sincere effort. I'm not
forgetting and neither is He
the attempts in Boston
to overcome your timidity and
cowardice.

The artist in me is the
best devotee because he's
most joyous. They didn't
give him enough time to stretch
out. Cut him down. Didn't understand his approach,
"too long and inept"—what rubbish. He's our man.

Swami Prabhupāda is the
founder-*ācārya* and that's it.
Anything else is distasteful.

Now I have to go, they'll be in
to administer pills and
crack your back. Test
your blood and genitals.
"Are you sexually active?"
"No sir, I'm celibate,
don't you know what saffron means?"

All these fools don't know
God rules, they want to enjoy
forever and make money—
we want the songs and praise
of God but they don't sell.

I asked a traveling preacher what he lectures on, since he doesn't use consecutive verses of *Śrīmad-Bhāgavatam* as they do in the temple. He said he speaks from whatever he's personally studying. That seemed to be a sensible, inspiring and non–labor-intensive way.

Swami Swims then thought, "What do I study?" Nothing. Yeah, I'm talking about the invalids in the New York sanatorium. They wave their ISKCON flags when the preachers go by. They climb the stairs slowly (and out of duty only) to attend the evening lecture. They say things they don't mean just to get along. "Yes, I thought the *kīrtana* was great." But they don't study because they can't read due to some malady or other. It hurts too much to read, their arthritis prevents it, or poor eyesight, the volunteer who agreed to read to them had to run out to do errands. And most of the day they are—valiantly let's say—licking their wounds and surviving.

They study the chiropractor's beard. The stunning smile of a worker at the dentist's office, even when she smiles with her mouth closed. Of course, none are saints, so they self-absorbably study their pain's intensity. They think about the visitors in anxiety. So you can't lecture on that stuff. They think, "Lecturing is Prabhupāda's mood. So if I get well again I can do it and speak on what I'm studying."

The fat groundhog, big as a large cat. The kitten is afraid to go outdoors. The children get really upset, run indoors crying. What happened? Pushes her father aside hysterically and runs to her mother. Study the schedule the host gives them. Remember to be grateful. Looking for a good night's sleep. They are not so eager to go into the gymnasium to build their muscles because it may exacerbate their pain, and they are lazy too, but the doctor says no, go to exercise even if you are reluctant. The caretakers encourage them. They're doing much better, but if that's true, it's by baby steps.

He said do it your way.
Reclusive or meeting people,
but what you want,
who you are.

I've got to stay close to the meds
and the bed and a caretaker as
sweet as Śacī. As sweet as
you are, he imitates the birds,
what's wrong with that?

I'm starting to tell you about
the subpersons in this sanatorium
and what they lack and how
they're growing up and becoming more alert.

They're chanting their prescribed *japa.*
Melancholic? I wouldn't say so but
a touch of that in the horn
of the fated Booker Little[2]
was prophetic. If he could
have lived much longer, Eric[3] too,
to celebrate the Lord as they strongly desired.
I've been given some time
so don't waste in "poor quality
of life," lying around on couches
in beds, watching the time go
by.

Don't die premature. Study
Bṛhad-bhāgavatāmṛta. Hear your
master's lectures. "Everything is
in Prabhupāda's books because
he teaches humility and humility
is everything."

Take me on a ride with You.
Even if I'm reluctant, I'll
go out and exercise. But if
it hurts too much I'll have
to back out. I am not made
of sterner stuff.

Dependent. Whoa. Joy in
words. And seeing friends.
Be grateful for every mouthful,
an opportunity to be kind
and render service. The
bonesetter wouldn't
take a fee. "Pass it on," he
said. So here is my payment
Dr. Michael, tall bearded man,

although you may not understand
my language. Don't go too long or
you'll be unwanted, the babies will
cry, and boredom will pervade the
hall. You can come back
tomorrow or even this evening.
Go now and drink your
two quarts of H_2O and remember
Kṛṣṇa is the taste of water.

The inmates are in beds early after a rough day. It's an open dorm with a few private rooms. How long will this go on? Even when lights go out they talk and listen to noises in the walls. Some stay up completing their *japa* quotas. No more visitors, at last. Darkness. Will the *siṁhāsana* arrive without cracks in it from transit? I don't want to write goofy so I won't order a new book by a poet they said was goofy. War on pain. Be religious and meet you in the spiritual world.

Humorous description of Gopal in Prayāg. He's dumb, yet he goes on chanting his Gopal mantra, given by Kāmyaka. Therefore he makes advancement. Other forms of God don't attract him. He needs a guru and better association, however, to attain the lotus feet of the object of the sixteen-syllable mantra. I like hearing how he is dumb and even offensive, yet he makes advancement because he's so determined to chant—until he much enjoys chanting—this highest mantra. What a lucky fellow. If he just persists he'll make it.

Take that as a lesson, my friends. Monitor comes through dorm and asks the *japa* chanter and the chatterers to cease all sound. It's time for needed sleep so the body can serve Kṛṣṇa. Let's get to know the individuals. An all-male ward. They'll play and pray in the morning. Some have special friends. But in the eating times, all hear about Gopal. That's their study. This scribe is too wounded to do more this evening. Shouldn't have written a certain letter, should write other letters. Oh Lord, help me to persevere and take whatever comes. And may I remove all blockages in devotion to my master, understand his love for me and accept his individuality.

Take it easy. I'll sneak in a
lullaby. Hurt eye he's telling
his friend. Shouldn't write
then. People aren't quiet as

they should be. It's too late
to meet. I'll see you tomorrow.

Rest in Kṛṣṇa's arms
figuratively and real someday. Eons away but your
spiritual master is for this lifetime.
Don't throw it away. Make it grow.

Your strategies. He told me
not to be so risky, because I
live in an institution. We
know what they did but
some are still hiding out.

The secret police can wreak havoc.

So many friends are coming and I
try to meet them. They sit
by your bed in the ward (have you a private room?)
and talk only an hour.

Tell some laid-back tales
but try not to forget you are
bhaktas and should chant
and hear. Run out of gas, why push it?
Tomorrow is another day. A day
of up and down. I can't
take any more tonight.

Each subperson on his own now,
own dreams and troubles,
but one God and that's why we are
in the Prabhupāda ward.
Don't kick us out even if we
never recover. We are grateful.

Up early in the morning and saying their *japa*. Some sitting up in bed, some sitting in their chairs, some walking back and forth. Some were allowed to use clickers because their minds couldn't concentrate using the beads and they didn't know which way they were going to count properly. But most had beads in the *japa-mālā*. The monitor didn't allow the chanting to get too loud because some inmates were disturbed. Lucky ones in the private rooms. And how the minds went all over the universe. Picking up trivia, dwelling on troubles, going blank and falling asleep. And those small periods of yearning to actually hear, to actually understand that this was the most important thing in the day. Not embarrassed in front of the others because we all know it's a struggle. If someone was actually advanced and tuned into the value of the Holy Name, well good for him, we're not envious. We want his association. Hare Kṛṣṇa, Hare Kṛṣṇa, Kṛṣṇa Kṛṣṇa, Hare Hare/ Hare Rāma, Hare Rāma, Rāma Rāma, Hare Hare. That's all there is to it, the simple repetition of those names. Lord Caitanya made it as easy as can be, so a fool can do it, can handle the precious gem and get benefit. What to speak of a learned *brāhmaṇa?*

An hour goes by. Some have chanted more than others. All are encouraged. And then they take a break.

Spaced-out. Reviewing a Laurel and Hardy plot. Faces float by. Something someone said. Drink water and pee. Just hear, just hear. Look over at another inmate and see how he's doing. He has allergy and the pollen count is record high; he's scratching his eye, which makes it worse. "I can't help it." One nods out and becomes aware others are looking at him so he picks up his head and chants loudly and distinctively for awhile. Where is the inner experience of the mantra? Gopal sometimes *saw* the Deity of his mantra. We mostly just see heads and feet, some have decorative bead bags, ink-stained, and the clickers. Everyone is making at least some progress.

The Holy Name is absolute. Even if you chant mockingly or by accident or the sounds aren't spaced—words like "Ramada"—still, it has the effect of chanting the Holy Name. The inmates knew this and so they chanted, knowing even a poor recitation was the most important thing to accomplish in a day. The numerical strength is also important. So don't excuse yourself. Meet you in the spiritual world. Don't fall behind.

The sun began to pour through the window blinds. Another day had begun. They filed into the temple room to watch a few *brāhmaṇas* undress and bathe and redress Rādhā-Govinda. Then they went down for breakfast. There was an early-morning guest so they got prepared to see him and embrace him, half-regretful that it would take away some *japa* time. But they tried for it later. Hare Kṛṣṇa, Hare Kṛṣṇa, Kṛṣṇa Kṛṣṇa, Hare Hare/ Hare Rāma, Hare Rāma, Rāma Rāma, Hare Hare.

Inmates recover in this way. They live in harmony under the shelter of the Holy Name.

Light blue, chipped teeth,
mashed hand, my good friend
brings an unbroken *siṁhāsana*
across the sea and now
Rādhā-Govinda and Prabhupāda
are joined happily on the little
altar in Rādhā's barn.

We can climb the stairs and
sit on our rockers and
listen to Swami sing a half-
hour and join in the chorus.

We can bathe them in the morning.
No time to do Prabhupāda in
weakened condition. Pray to him
early in the morning even
if it takes a walk upstairs,
you can do it. Hare Kṛṣṇa
music and art.

Light blue means
he's not outgoing but he's happy
he gets to go near the
japa quota and he's so
dependent on dear friends
who don't mind taking care of
him even though he's
a grownup man.

He's making it up, he
never loved and read
like he said in his
younger days. He's making up
everything as he goes along
praying to keep a decent reputation.

He's keeping to the outskirts but
meeting famous people as they
come through. They lecture to
crowds and give him a little
private time in his private
room of the sanatorium.

Keep the tune. To a friend
who does not mind he plays
"Coming on the Hudson"[4] and
says "I just like it always
even though now I'm an

enrolled renunciate for
my whole life."

I dig it says A.
and they don't let the others hear
because they couldn't understand a monk
loving God in his own
way each one, and God accepts them all.

"I got an astrology reading," said Bhakta Tim on his bed, "and it said if I could handle it, a pilgrimage would be good for me for a few weeks in October and November this year. But I'd have to have someone help me administer my medicines and so on."

Some of the other subpersons gave their different opinions that he probably wasn't up to it but some said it was an excellent idea and he ought to get off his duff and go and get the mercy.

One of them quoted from the *Bṛhad-bhāgavatāmṛta* which had just been read to them at lunchtime where it said that the highest goal can be attained by chanting the Holy Names of God *and* visiting holy places.

Another remarked, "But it's such a strain to go to India, so austere for a weak fellow like you, Bhakta Tim. You have to take astrology with a grain of salt. It could turn out to be a nightmare. You know you'd meet up with all kinds of people you don't like. And your regulated life like we have in the sanatorium wouldn't be possible. But what do I know? There's great benefit in going to the *dhāma* they say, and that's an absolute truth."

"Maybe if some of you guys went with me," Tim said, "you could help me get through it."

"I ain't going nowhere," said Anuttamā dāsa. "We have a very good deal right here for being with good people, being taken care of, and there's no shortage of hearing and chanting. We're in the best circumstances. So don't throw that away in a premature trip to wild India."

"But it's not 'India,'" said another. "That's just the covering. If Bhakta Tim goes, he'll have to suffer the covering to get to the inside. He'll have to be prepared for that. Good things don't come so easily."

"You're getting your pains every day right here, in the best situation for an invalid. How can we fly off and act like a rigorous renunciate? And look, Swami Swims has a cane, and he has to wear those orthopedic shoes. He wouldn't even be allowed in the temple."

"Don't put Tim down. Encourage the idea. If not this year, then the next."

There was an important statement for me when Gopa-kumāra was about to tell his own life story to the *brāhmaṇa*, when they were together in Vṛndāvana. One might think to talk about oneself is not bona fide. Gopa-kumāra didn't want to appear puffed up talking about himself. But he knew talking about what he had gone through to reach the goal of perfection was the best way to instruct the *brāhmaṇa.* So he was confident and went ahead. The commentator says, "Experience is the best form of proof." There may be other statements about the best form of proof, but there it is in *Bṛhad-bhāgavatāmṛta*, and I rejoiced to see it and present it to you now. Even if your experience is not the experience of one who has reached the goal of truth, describing it is the best way of instructing someone or telling them what is real, what is true. Mary Oliver entitles her latest poetry book, *What Do We Know?* We know what we have experienced, that's for sure. It may be faulty knowledge, but we know it happened. The person who hears from us will get authentic stuff. Even if it is a tale of woe, an uncouth tale, a tale of what we should *not* do. Of course, the experience of a perfect person is perfect proof in the very best sense. But I have taken it to mean that the experience of a struggler is also the best way to get a particular kind of truth. He's not bluffing, and you can learn from him. In other words, one form of teaching by experience means, "Do as I did," and the other is, "Don't do as I did," and both are instructive and even inspiring.

Bhakta Tim had so many worries, and now a new one to add to the others. He was in the sanatorium—and not on the front lines in the battle against *māyā*—because he was a Worrier and it caused him diabetes and arthritis and other diseases. He was thinking he'd let a friend run a horoscope on him, and the news came back that Rāhu, the dark, evil planet that covers the sun, would often visit him. If he could live past age thirty, lots of good things would manifest, but it was unlikely he'd live that long because of something about Jupiter mixing with another planet at a bad time and Rāhu moving in again. Tim worried like anything. His pro-astrology friend said, "Ask the astrologer if there's something you can do to offset this shortened longevity."

"It's just bullshit," said Swami Swims. "If you start listening to those guys, you won't be able to make a bowel movement unless they tell you it's okay. Chant Hare Kṛṣṇa and all the palm lines in your hands will change. And if you're going to die at twenty-two, so what? Get on the move and chant your beads and step up your advancement. Anyone of us may go at any moment, regardless of the stars' prediction. Remember from Shakespeare,

'The fault, dear Brutus, is not in our stars,

But in ourselves that we are thus or thus.'" (from *Julius Caesar*)

When is snack time? When is rest time? When do the babies play in the backyard? A friend writes and says, "It was in Hawaii (ISKCON) that I found I was Prabhupāda's son (after depression from a divorce) but in Māyāpur I found my heart," cried tears there every day and wants to make yearly visits. But you can't enter the temple with shoes on. You are expected to stand a lot and hear the class. He could do it and he loved it. Don't exile yourself. The sanatorium is also a sacred place, and they're getting a bigger altar for Prabhupāda and Rādhā-Govinda, with drawers for all their clothes. Go up there and chant. Discursive prayer, mantra meditation with an unsteady mind. Humble and grateful. Stay out of the firing line.

Why don't you visit our house? Why don't you look forward to the next dentist's visit? The subpersons get the call from the monitor. They have to go to the gym and exercise, like it or not. Drill time, visitors' time. Don't take a pill unless you absolutely need it. Left, right, left, right, left, right, oblique march, about face, left, right . . .

They just had a little difference,
and it spoiled their performance.
You've got to play as lovers and
good humble friends to
discover the best in the group.

Looking for Kṛṣṇa. He's everywhere.
Some place is concentrated. Make your
own temple in the heart. I
don't have time to read a
Christian book, *Difficulties in*
Mental Prayer, sent
in the mail, but they said you can
talk to God even at awkward times

when you can't sleep
or you're in the
doctor's waiting room.

All those magazines in waiting
rooms. All the fits you can
get from worries and threats.
Take it to God. A friend advises
you often write in your books
use everything for Kṛṣṇa so
why not try psychic path
and pray to the Lord
"Could you please relieve me
from these pains?" Remember
Rūpa Gosvāmī said material things
unused in the Lord's service
are *phalgu-vairāgya.*
Higher is to use everything for the Lord.

I'll write to him and tell him I
am, to a limit. Except I don't
know how to pray. But I do
talk to a counselor and we
hash it out and he's very
good.

I blew it again. Should have
let the authorities enjoy
having the upper hand. I
wrote back pushing the envelope,
reminding them of their own
wrongs and stating that compassion
is best.

Counselor said it was a mistake.
"But that's you. You take risks,

you're innovative." Just be
careful it doesn't get you hanged
at the gallows.

Be more legalistic and cool and
that you have just been
given the "Get Out of
Jail Free"[5] card. There's no more
to say then. Not like Sgt. Bilko.
When he's defeated, he touches
his authority on the shoulder and
says, "Two for flinching."

I'm okay I think but I must learn
to seek legal advice before
I move so fast into blabbing
about compassion to those
who seem more concerned
with judgment and fines.

Under dark stars, said Bhakta Tim, I've been under dark stars and dangerous planets for a year and a half. I made it through by the skin of my teeth, the astrologer said. Death was in the sky. Does that mean bright skies and starry nights are ahead? I sure hope so. So much anxiety, worry, wrong on my part. Wondering how it would manifest in this material world. Because I want to be a good boy. "How I want to be loved!" said Charles Lamb,[6] "And what I will do to be loved!" But if Rāhu passes, a worse scenario . . . no, I shall not worry myself to death. Everything is under control of the Lord.

A life of peace
you can't have all the time.
Bumps in the road

they point you to the Lord,
even if you're unseated.
"Mahāprabhu's mercy is to
those in the field." What
about those in the sanatorium?

Those who are moms busy
with their kids? The *sannyāsīs*
have a special role to play.

He's calming us, assuring us,
but the sharp edge is warning us,
you live in an institution and
there are rules. Tote
them.

Peace is something deep.
Lord Rāma had it even when he was
exiled, Yudhiṣṭhira too and
Haridāsa Ṭhākura while being
whipped. They were under the
control of Kṛṣṇa and did not
care for the influences
of demons or in the case of a *sādhaka*,
reactions to their own wrongs. "This was
coming to me. I am not suffering as an
orphan but under the protection
of my Father, who is righting me."

Peace.
So don't complain.
Cry. I don't deserve . . . but
now I see a light of dawning
Prabhupāda's son,
heart found in Nadia.

Kṛṣṇa is a living being and wants you back,
you are transcendental
to the influence of those
malefic planets. If you
just call out *hari-nāma*
and see the holy *dhāma* at
least in your mind's eye,
tomorrow?

Chapter Two

The sanatorium bought a new altar. Can't wait to see it assembled. Inmates are up at 1:00 A.M. aching instead of sleeping. Should they take that pill or see if they can subdue it by rest and positive thinking? It's another day and an important visitor is expected in the morning. I want to play "the wise one" for him. Tell him how it reminds me of Prabhupāda—transcendental, mountain-high, clear and peaceful, can give you that same peace even in material turmoil. But in return he wants you to give it to others.

Swami Swims received a "Get Out of Jail Free" card, so he should not push the envelope and try for the last word. The authorities like to think they went away with the candy. What are you trying to explain further? Go your new way free. "Oh, what a cute pussy cat!" "They call her Kṛṣṇa-Balarāma."

How are you feeling, Swami? Here's your snack. He always stays indoors. I am always feeling fuzzy. I can't work hard. I do a little work and then I have to stop. He wants the hosts to know where he's at. But doesn't mention how happy he is with the way his writing is going. Just fuzzy-headed, doesn't complain, thanks for the snack. The clear power is slowing down.

Recluse or learn coping skills? Why not both? Try cutting off all ties from the institutional stuff, wake up in the morning with nothing to do that you don't want to do. Find a place where you can try it, such as wild land in northwest California. See if it reduces anxiety headaches. Then come out and interact again. But you can never be alone in this world, nor is it desirable. *Difficulties in Mental Prayer*, tempting book lying on the floor. Talk with God or you're not a real Vaiṣṇava. Don't just recite the mantra dumbly. But I don't have time to read *Difficulties*. Priorities, first is sixteen rounds.

Who's talking? Another swami, this one in faded saffron. They get "perks" he said, but their lives must be transparent. No unauthorized CDs or books. March in step. Here they come marching, a long file, to attend a wedding. Travel to see your friend, imbibe his good qualities. They're coming but you don't know when, or if they're coming at all. You get to sit in a rocking chair and observe the beautiful Deities on their expanded altar. Are you still afraid? Is anyone watching? My friend who comes here to clean the room (another perk) has broken out with eczema. The basketball bouncing, the too-loud *mṛdaṅga*. Swami S. feels like saying as Prabhupāda did during a 1966 *kīrtana*, "Softly, softly," but Prabhupāda was the founder-*ācārya* and Swims is just a patient in the sanatorium.

Here comes the next wave. Mental prayer, you should be talking to God, "Please reveal Yourself to me, let me know my guru's mercy and give me clarity to serve him without grudge." It's discursive, does that mean He talks back right away? Atheists say it's all one-way imagination. Pious people talk and don't demand He answer, but they do listen and sometimes He answers in His own way and you're sure.

They go very fast, the young
ones, dance and leap. But

I sit back and enjoy it,
on social security.

Gray side hairs, he's afraid
and they say they can get
mouse traps or a cat.
Another swami is twenty-five miles away,
another two doors
away.

Who's doing the preaching?
So many ways, food for poor
in Vṛndāvana, hospices.

Selling used cars and using money
to save ISKCON in the courts,
tax your brain, give your
blood, at least behave.
Action without foundation
of rules is crumbling sooner
or later.

Behave, eat your snack
and keep chanting as long as
you can. Dentist's appointment?
Talk to God in the waiting
room and certainly when you are
in the chair and he's in your
mouth.
Just chat with Kṛṣṇa
and Prabhupāda as you know
them. Love thy neighbors.
Everyone's talking how great
the people are in upstate New York.

Better you meet them on
neutral ground, "nice day"

or if they agree to attend
a Kṛṣṇa function. Did
you phone that boy
who was angry and hurt by you?
I will. I'll ask his pardon.

Joe felt good and he would tell his friends. It's the present moment, each moment, that Zen-like statement from the fellow in prison. "Because you visited me when I was in prison." Don't forget to send him a book. This not answering letters has got to stop. They gathered for holy food and the primary saintly person would sit among them along with many children on Mother's Day. Swami Swims, properly dressed, preferred to sit alone in the barn. Could they please excuse him? He'd eat later.

Oh how happy the ones who are cooperating. So an average male lives seventy-four years, I hadn't heard that before. It was a bit of a surprise. I thought he might live forever. In Kali years to come, a man of thirty-five will be considered an old man and he'll be pygmy-sized. People will be too dull to appreciate snappy presentations or straight and simple discussions of Kṛṣṇa. So evil and animalistic, Kalki will come and simply kill them. But for the next 10,000 years, a Golden Age can flourish and Kṛṣṇa consciousness may be presented in many novel ways. Some are doing it in film and theater. He taught us that, outreach, and so we can invent our ways as long as they stick to the path.

The ice cream truck goes by playing "The Yellow Rose of Texas," and I wish I could pray or mourn for my lack. You don't take seriously how you have failed. It hasn't sunk in. Seek cheap redemption. Visit the grave where the flowers grow. "He keeps his lawn neat," said Śacī as we took a short walk. Everyone around here is keeping up appearances: trimmed lawns and American flags. Yeah, well I would too if I had property here. I have nothing against Old Glory, as flags go. It's one of the best designed of all nations. Will I be left alone today? "I"? I mean Harold. Too bad I don't know how to play the DVD and see Charlie. Need someone to help you with everything. Let him eat alone.

Grit teeth for lack of theme and inspiration. The reviewer said, "These gaps may be filled in with time, as the production plays itself in. If they are, this will be quite a remarkable piece. As it is, we have fabulous ingredients that have not yet been fully cooked."

Waiting for the theme, the title—the plot? Don't hold your breath. We were under dark stars. Now where will we go? Are there better predictions? Don't think of yourself but please Him and His.

All right, I don't hold
it against my Guru Mahārāja,
I told him straight.

I just feel sorry for the
distance. He said I was pure
though not a good manager
and he needed money.

I don't hold him to blame
for the faults committed in
ISKCON. He did what he
had to. Worked with the
monkeys who served him.

Now on the altar, Prabhupāda.
Wide new altar.
I'll keep him here in Stuyvesant Falls.
And they can worship

him daily. Even when
you're not with him?

Yes I'll let them do that.
But I must stay closer
to him in my deeds
and prayers. Hare
Kṛṣṇa Prabhupāda.

Śacī's band owes him $50,000. He told them he's coming to New York City, where they have a concert today. He'll come onto their tour bus and they should hand him $50,000 in a bag. He said he won't count it but will just leave. His seven-year-old daughter went with him. Meanwhile the Sunday gathering took place in this house. Rāma-Rāya was here fresh from six months in Vṛndāvana, and D. Swami told him to speak on "separation from Vṛndāvana." I asked to see him later. He said he read from the *Kṛṣṇa* book, end of chapter 81, where the *gopīs* meet Kṛṣṇa at Kurukṣetra but then say they will go back to Vṛndāvana while He returns to Dvārakā. Prabhupāda comments that actually Kṛṣṇa never takes a step out of Vṛndāvana.

Rāmarāya consoled me that not living in Vṛndāvana, India, was fine, was maybe even a better way to live in separation from Vṛndāvana than living there with all the noise and heat. He bought a harmonium and with great labor taught himself day after day to play it.

Swami Swims seemed okay in his glass enclosure. Too bad he didn't know how to operate the video or DVD. Have to write instead. "You write faster than I can read." Śacī called from Penn Station. He got the bag of money. It was thirty degrees in New York City, and he and his daughter were wearing shorts. "Did she complain?" "No, I bought her all new clothes." Father and daughter day. He will put the Deities to bed when he returns. Why not the Swami? Because it's too tedious for him. When is he going to lecture again? Will he be able to pick out a section like chapter 81 of the *Kṛṣṇa* book?

Remember the different periods of your life with Prabhupāda. He said I wasn't a good manager but he kept me on the GBC because I did what he said. Trouble started from jostling with his manipulative secretaries, best devotee collects most money. Trouble began after Prabhupāda passed away. I do not blame him. I beg he'll accept my new style of offerings, the new person I am.

It's cold but pain free
the plots and characters,
the beggar role on the Abbey Theater
stage as a Hare Kṛṣṇa devotee.

You can do it through the arts.
Even a little part chuffs
Śīlāvatī up. From across
the sea she wants me
to be well.

I'm on the boards too in
a little way, stick our
necks out. It will be
appreciated, the endnotes.
He didn't know
who Joe Louis was?
You want to know what's
the spiritual use of knowing who
the Brown Bomber is and the facts
of his life? I'll tell
you.

This is the experience of the
world we live in and we

saw it happen, *vibhūti*
to be such a champ.
They weren't saints. But
they were also holy saints.
I'm going to tell her about
Francis and Clare, and
Śikhi Māhiti's sister,
platonic friendships.

But I'll keep out of
trouble and follow the
mandate, just remind
them it's possible to
see it in a different way.

Music, music, you
needn't be so rigid that
it has to be the pumped
harmonium and the etiquette
of the *vyāsāsana*.

The times are a'changing
Kṛṣṇa is becoming the king of
West and East as never before.

The biggest gathering of the East Coast
June 14, NYC, down
Fifth Avenue. I will receive
the news. They sell a few
books and I will be glad.
Shallow? Nonsense!

I am not So-and-So. I am myself. But the others are good. When my picture comes up, I say, "Yes I do," as in marriage vows. I wish them well. They express their realizations about God and the path to love of God in their speeches, writings and actions. They inspire us or not. You either have it or not. But it always comes down as S.K. said, to the individual. He wanted those words, "That Individual," inscribed on his tombstone. But his relatives didn't grant the request. Just you, one at a time, face Kṛṣṇa and His agents at death. All masks removed. No wonder people speak of death as fearful. No wonder I left all gurus but the one I knew and who trusted me: "Although you are not a good manager, I keep you on the GBC because you do as I say." Did I live up to that? Do you? A big, infinite crowd surging toward the gate of death or heaven, as you want to look at it. But you cannot get carried in by the forward movement of the crowd. Each one is inspected. Your heart. Your attachment physically, historically, mentally and spiritually to a most powerful, pure *ācārya*. No bull at this stage. My analyzer looked briefly into my mouth and saw no cavities in my relationship with Prabhupāda. No major flaws: I don't resent him, I don't dwell on any "mistakes" he made, I don't feel he neglected me. The big sore in my heart is over the present distance. Apprehension whether he accepts my new writing style of offering. God knows I'm sore, sore lacking. Even my peers know, and some think I'm worth peeing on and not given a decent burial. "What did he actually do? He writes faster than I can read."

I did intend to write a *NY Times* editorial about other people and conditions. But I slipped back to the individual. I know it's certified by a great philosopher. Because when you read about him and his father and the girl (Regine) he never married, you are reading about everyone. Can I be a mirror for you?

Inspiration

We keep the titles nowadays,
we're more liberal. You

can go and research. We're
down to roots.

In the same way you talk
about God, the great unknown,
BB tells us about Gopa-
kumāra in the post of Indra
and so on but never satisfied.
It's the story of his own life.
But what a life!

Not just playing marbles in the street
and shy of girls. A simple cowherd
boy with utmost deliberation
to chant his Gopal mantra no
matter where he went. I'll
not be Indra but I may go
to jail. Then chant the mantra
in all places and times.

It will carry you to Madana-
gopal's lotus feet. Don't demand
they see you as a great soul.
Admit you like "Poinciana."[1]
We're going on and attending
"The Festival of Inspiration."

I gets turned on
by some people who play
a sweet tune they practice
a million times to develop
their skills—like Rāma-Rāya dāsa
"it's hard work" he was
guided and chastised by Aindra Prabhu.
He bought a good harmonium

"with the Vṛndāvana sound"
and after hours and hours every day
he learned to play different
tunes of Hare Kṛṣṇa mantra.

He's inspired and added to his
arsenal as a preacher.
We will inspire by rose growing,
baby caring, pure heart,
and I like the straight stuff too,
Ahmad Jamal.[2]

Give the examples of Saint Francis of Assisi and St. Clare of Assisi, of the Buddhist celibate poet Ryokan, and the nun with whom he exchanged poetry regularly and enjoyed a close nonsexual friendship, of Kierkegaard, who backed out of his engagement with Regine to dedicate himself solely to Christ and theistic writing (although Regine was always on his mind). And Rilke, who sometimes wrote of the theme of unrequited lovers who kept close relationships but did not consummate them physically but rather dedicated themselves to separate paths of art, spirituality, solitude, etc., yet kept close bonds. (Such an example, of course, would be torn to pieces by the reductionist psychologists, but nevertheless it exists in literature and in reality.) There is also the example of the ideal woman whom the poet never loves physically but looks up to as an icon—for example, Beatrice,[3] who in Dante's *Divine Comedy* guided Virgil through Heaven and for whom the poem is a memorial.

Even Śrīla Prabhupāda, especially in ISKCON's early days, had close relationships with some of his lady disciples, like Yamunā, Mālatī, Govinda dāsī, and others before things got too institutional. There was nothing wrong in it. ISKCON will have to some day come to terms with the fact that we are not sexist and that too much rigidity in this matter of rules and regulations negates the possibility of chaste friendships, even between celibates. It may be one of the things we realize in generations to come. Just as so many old-time rigidities have passed away. Even when I joined ISKCON, there was an innocent give-and-take among boys and girls that rarely came to harm. And girls are of course just as intelligent and spiritual and capable as men, so they can encourage a male celibate and help him in intimate service, but all this has to be done by careful avoidance of *māyā*. Success comes by mutual sublimation of all desires in the mutual goal of service to guru (Prabhupāda and Kṛṣṇa). The complete rejection of this concept speaks of the prison bars of institutionalism and bureaucracy, and lacks all humanness and even spirituality.

Are you going to dare to write that, Swami Swims? Why not, it's plain reality. It's not for everyone, and most should settle for marriage. But those who have the vocation for celibacy may find fellow celibates in any body, male or female, who can become a like-minded friend. How else did Śikhi Māhiti's sister wind up in the *gambhīrā* sitting close to Lord Caitanya, along with Rāmānanda Rāya and Svarūpa Dāmodara, where she heard the most esoteric feelings of Mahāprabhu in His separation from Rādhā? Was Prabhupāda wrong to invite Yamunā dāsī to come in daily in the morning and hear him sing his songs on the harmonium in his private, spiritual mood?

These relationships I am talking of are not "illicit sex."

He's playing from the heart. A
lot of head went into it too.
Don't tell us about a visit
to the dentist's office costing

$1,600.

You are lucky. "Would you
like water for your
medication?" All the things
you are to me.

The sunrise, the gnats, too
cold in the deity room.
Śacī coming in to see how
Swami is doing. Treats him
like his ailing father and
son too.

You are my support. I'm doing
something too. Click *japa*
as a prayer. Encouraging a
new wave. "Equal Vision
is known for keeping ahead
of the next wave in
straightedge music."

That "message music"
against meat-eating is
dead. He's alert for the

next. How did I get on this
wave I'm riding with my
esteemed friends, the musicians
of jazz? What has it to do
with 500 years ago in
Nadia?

Because we're here now
and not everyone is tuned
to the harmonium and lecture.
The heart of a reluctant

short-timer sailor who
fell in love in NYC
with the best of the
golden age[4] and met

his Swami, now sees
them singing as one
like someone in love with Kṛṣṇa
from the only position available
to him and believes the Lord
will say, "I see your point,
my son, yes, they are praiseworthy too
and included in My *pāriṣads*.
But they'll have to clean up their
act. You first clean up yours.
And I'll be more inclined—
see if you shall love them
then."

Bhakta Joe came to me and said he was dreaming, a shocking one. I was back in the Navy. I was avoiding participation. They were having well-rehearsed but rough skits and games on an entertainment day. I was sneaking around trying to remain part of the audience and not be in any of the plays. The Navy seemed worse than it was the first time. I saw Kathy Swanson, a kind of "one of the boys" friend from high school days. She was wearing Navy dungarees and shirt like the rest of us. I placed my hands in *praṇāmas* to her and asked her how long she was in for. She said, "I don't know," then smiled and said, "I'm getting a taste of heaven."

Then I saw Śrīla Prabhupāda behind a counter. I'm not sure if this was a continuation of the same dream or not. But I was still sneaking around, not doing anything. (I think this was the unconscious telling me of my guilt.) Śrīla Prabhupāda looked at me and acknowledged that I was just sneaking around, but then he looked kindly and I felt very good.

But then I heard the disembodied voice of a deceased *sannyāsī* from wherever he was now. He warned me, "Bhakta Joe, you have lost your love and service desire for Śrīla Prabhupāda. He always loved you for it. And those hideous paintings you do, they are portraits of him! He saved you! I saw you once before you met Śrīla Prabhupāda. You were a freckle-faced boy, not bad, but not good."

The dream left me feeling that I'm failing terribly, not serving and loving him. The illness is an excuse. (This ain't Bhakta Joe but SDG.)

Afterward, I decided not to paint anymore. I *was* sneaking around in the dream, but it was to avoid *stupid* participation in the Navy's program.

I often disagreed with that deceased *sannyāsī*. He made big mistakes himself. I broke with him because he tried to control me too much.

I should not glibly dismiss this warning. Yet at the same time I should seek support for what I'm doing. It's true Prabhupāda always loved me and thought I was a good devotee while he was with us on the planet. I don't want to fail his expectation of me now. Yet I am very ill. And I do believe that service is ecstatic and there are new waves, new ways to preach to the new kind of people in the world. And I do believe there's a new freedom now to express yourself, not just like we did it in the marching days.

I have bad karma with machines.
"Bah!" they say, "you can learn."
But anyway it doesn't require
machine skill to please the Lord.
That's why it's so scary for Bhakta
Joe to hear this senior devotee
past say from the sky

you are just hiding away.
That's like sitting on your laurels
or not making the natural
effort to get up from your
wheelchair

and serve in a stronger way.
I don't want anyone to get
angry. That's not the point.
You can take your place in
the fifteen-minute lecture spot.

Get that look of mercy he
gives to everyone to encourage
them. Then why let the brother's
chastisement affect
me? He was always a put-
down artist.
Listen to *this* artist.
Oh but he's not listed
in the *Pāriṣad* book.
He *should* be. All God's
chillun . . . He wants to
make them happy too.

And I did too. Kṛṣṇa
people and new
ones. "Thanks."

As for the "hideous paintings"
who says so? A Hare Kṛṣṇa
did it, etc. Best I can
do. Relieves the yen of
a wounded soldier.

"All this 'I resign' is garbage."

He'd probably say, "You're just
as good as the rest. How much
does it *really* hurt?" He asked me
that once and I said *Damned bad!*

You do things your way—
I can't participate in the mudslinging
campaign, the boxing match,
the other stupid antics I saw
in that dream on the Navy
ship.

Some folks don't think it's hideous
and give me space and light.

Dear Guru Mahārāja, I do want to
offer a primitive dancer to
your glory.

There was an old popular song and the last repeated stanza was, "Anna doesn't live here anymore." One can just see the old suitor knocking on the door and a stranger telling him that his Anna is gone and left no forwarding address. A disciple of Swami Swims calls his Godbrother Kṛṣṇa dāsa and asks for some help in service. The devotee replies, "I don't do any service for Swami Swims anymore." If it's a matter of money, we can reimburse you. No, it's not money, it's a matter of the heart. I cannot serve him. I cannot see him as a spiritual master. I do not have that unconditioned love.

Ask a purehearted soul how to take it. When there's a stone wall, a stone heart, you just can't break through. Let it be. Walk around it. You're not being neglectful, "Anna doesn't live here anymore."

Walk on his grassy backyard. No kids in sight, very pleasant. No one on the trampoline. The grass freshly mowed. He wears his Brooklyn Dodgers cap against the sunlight. But it doesn't cure a headache. Oxy does. Why this stigma against headache medicine?

In the dream he fought hard against the mob. Always outwitting them as Billy the Kid in the Old West. Finally he was trapped by the biggest one with the knife. In desperation and sharp thinking he said, "If you come a step closer I'll wake up from this dream."

This is more important than *japa* quota and *gāyatrī*? What have they got to say? Yes, we have new friends and we live in the newly reconstructed, spotlessly clean Rādhā-Govinda Barn. It is very important in priorities to get in at least one a day. God wants me to do *everything*, but I can't. "Prioritize," they say (awkward, trendy word). Then *japa* must come first. Billie Holiday[5] had some sense: "If I don't have friends, then I ain't nothing." And, "You've got to have something to eat and a little love in your life before you can hold still for any damn body's sermon on how to behave."

Anna doesn't live here anymore. But there are others who want to work and play and serve and talk serious with you. Schubert's last piano sonatas, calming down the last of the H.A. as you eat an excellent supper. In gratitude, in gratitude, accept it as coming from His hands.

He'll be home soon and we
can talk. I forget the melody.
If he comes too early I'll hold
up five fingers indicating "give me
five more minutes."
You've got to get it done, to feel
satisfied in spiritual life. Lose
some and gain some. Got an e-mail address.
Send me your questions and
I'll reply as best I can.

I was hard core when he asked
how to get his *japa* done.
Is it all right on the subway? In driving? I don't know
how hard it is for them—
show unconditioned love.

But somehow it came
off hard core. Get them
done at best time. Is that
called hypocrisy? Is writing as
good as *japa?*

Loving your big baby who's just
cutting his teeth? Hefting him around.
Cooking for an extra
sannyāsī.

We're all funny valentines[6] and
deserve His love or rather
He loves us no matter how
we look or misbehaved.

But He tells us clear
"That was wrong so
rectify" while at the
same time not holding
back His love and showing it
too: I'm on your side,
I am not your enemy.

Junior Barks lost his contract with the big publisher. They placed his book in many bookstores but none of them sold. They only waited a week and then took them off the shelves, ripped off the front cover, and trashed them all. They didn't even give him a copy of his own. Ruthless dealings. So he came to Swami Swims in a humble mood and asked if he could write his straight Kṛṣṇa conscious pieces for his new book. He said it would be beneficial for everyone to have more straight preaching instead of …

"Now don't criticize what we're doing."

"No, I'm not criticizing, but I just mean there should be some *śabda-brahma,* some Sanskrit and teachings from *Bhagavad-gītā* and *Bhāgavatam.*"

"All right, but then put a lot of quotes in it."

"But I've been traveling and I don't have any of Prabhupāda's books with me. So I can't quote."

"Well then come back later when you get some books. If it's going to be straight, then make it real straight."

"*Ahaṁ brahmāsmi,*" said Junior, I know that. It means I am *brahman,* I am not this body. Everyone is under the false conception that they are the body. But those who meditate, take vows, and hear from their spiritual master can learn very quickly that they are spirit soul and not this body. And once you know that, then you can be on the path of liberation. Liberation means you won't take birth again in the material body and have to suffer birth, death, disease and old age. Real liberation means to go to Kṛṣṇa's planet. Any other liberation is temporary because you'll fall down again. The soul is safe at home only in Kṛṣṇa's planets in the spiritual world. They are the Vaikuṇṭhas. And the topmost one is Goloka Vṛndāvana, where Kṛṣṇa plays with his Vrajavāsī friends, parents and lovers. How's that for a start?"

"Very good. It's pretty much what you said the last time. But it's always good to hear. And it's true, our book may be lacking it. So go get some more material, more quotes, and not always the same thing about 'I'm not this body' and quickly going to liberation. Write some of what it means to really practice, struggle, associate with devotees, overcome obstacles, and—whatever you've experienced and whatever you've heard. Especially go get Prabhupāda's books." Exit Junior.

Junior did not have much realization and was a bit puffed up in his initial enthusiasm on discovering Kṛṣṇa consciousness, but the writing staff admitted he was right, there should be straight *śāstra* and teaching, like in a lecture, in any Kṛṣṇa conscious book. Not just saying you met Swami Swims and he looked swollen and his hands were trembling from his medicines. Really? Does he look like that? Would he rather watch a Charlie Chaplin DVD than a half-hour of live Sanskrit before the altar? Tell the truth. DVDs, at least sometimes. I'd even stay up late when everyone's gone to sleep and watch but I don't know how to play the machine. Śacī has to show me. I can't sit downstairs watching *The Tramp* while they're singing the Holy Names upstairs in the temple room. What's that a sign of? The visitor lamented that the Swami was so infirm. Too many visitors, says the housewife. She's getting worn down and even spoke of going to the hospital. I agree, too many visitors. And they're mostly mine. Let's say "No!," no, you can't come, we're all getting worn out. We can't speak the scriptures except for the one Vṛndāvana *sādhu*. Too much cooking. Children lose control and the next day they're still unwinding.

Get into the gym and work out! Oh no, do I have to? Yes, it's an integral part of your program. Don't just sit and lie down. *Difficulties in Mental Prayer* sits on the floor, ever unread; too Christian, probably. Tiny daily progress in *Bṛhad-bhāgavatāmṛta*. Now he's gone to the *loka* above Indra's. More opulence in worshiping the Lord. Deity worship? It's an ancient story.

Illusion above standards is
love? There is love. Love
of mother for child

guru for disciples, in some
cases. Craftsman for his work,
capitalist for money (illusion)

love of brother and sister
centered in Kṛṣṇa. The lover of the Lord
can teach us.

Don't say there's only
standards as in a prison.
You can be the dove who flies
out and experiences going higher and comes back
better for it while the
safe ones stay indoors.

Teach us. Learn for yourself
you'll get kicked out for
teaching that. We got
her that time. We won the quiz
when we cited
the higher authority.

When we acted human
when he said let's try again.
Don't reject me for a few
faults.

Explain what you mean
so abstractly about betrayal
and dishonor. I can't even
understand.

Kṛṣṇa's got His hand in His
mouth and scooping out yogurt
before His ma catches
up. He's the cute naughty
and that's all you need
to know.
He stole the butter,

the *gopīs'* clothes,
but it's all perfect.

He is the cheater
and the thief and the
perfect God of gods.

You have His picture
and look when you
can and catch the idea
to save your life.

Chapter Three

Cruel, Cruel Love, written and directed by Charles Chaplin. She rejects him, gives him back the ring and says, "I never want to see you again." He goes home and "poisons" himself, but it's only water. They comically reconcile, only after Charlie has a vision of his destiny—hell and being poked by devils. *Sannyāsīs* are not threatened by such love. They avoid it a day at a time, as they say in the Twelve Steps program.[1] Billie Holiday: "Don't threaten me with love, baby. Let's just go walking in the rain."

The doctor reminded Swami Swims, "It was just the anniversary of your taking *sannyāsa*."

"Yes, no one knew here. I am following it strictly." The traveling preacher mused, How can a devotee of his caliber be so infirm? It's his destiny, like Charlie Chaplin looking in the mirror and seeing the devils with pinchers around his neck.

Don't reduce me to the little bad. See the good. He's polishing his head to look good for the annual Pāṇihāṭi festival. When so many guests attended last year, they used the toilets and faucets up so that the well ran dry. He'll stay home in bed.

Why don't you write more, why only forty-five minutes a day? That's enough. I'm going satisfied with less. But sixteen rounds' *japa* is even more important than physical exercise. Spiritual exercise. Antidepressant is for anxiety, he explained. Oh.

Even the ladies are tired from all the cooking for guests. "You learn to tolerate them, and another good thing is we keep having to make the house clean, because the guests keep coming." Swami Swims doesn't look at it that way. He wakes and thinks, "Oh no. What *do I have to do* today?" They heard he gave a little lecture. Bravo. Fifteen minutes long. That's ideal for me. Eight minutes would be fine. But then he invited another to make a comment, and that went on twenty minutes, and another was invited . . . and he envied and rocked in his chair. Yet he writes in his letter, "I am working hard on my relationship with Śrīla Prabhupāda. I have not betrayed or dishonored him." Often says the wrong thing and it backfires. Stop the rapid flow of letters.

I don't like such spicy
foods. I want to be a man.
They're hammering,
they're playing pitch and catch,
the girl and her dad—not
a promising pair.

I want less spice. I have
the letters to read my counselor—
things seem under control,
but maybe underneath there is
a volcano I haven't discovered.

Too thick chocolate,
too spicy stuff—you're
always complaining.

You want something mild like
Mother Kaulini makes,
but what about the *japa?*

April in Paris. It's nice outside,
want to go for a walk?
Can you talk through a swollen
face and so much sleep?

No, they're wrong, they don't
know I'm actually much
better, can skip over stones,
have no intention of leaving.

Like the poem by Rilke of
the dove that flew out of
the dovecote and went high
and came back, was better
for it
than the timid ones, but I'll keep it
to myself. Poetry is
a secret from those
who are not moved
by sentiment.

Be glad you have
the concept of the
dove and the dovecote
and April in Paris and
have *sannyāsa* under
your belt sworn by
vow and helped by His
mercy to stay aloof.

Oh Jody and Jim, don't proselytize. Don't park too many cars on the street for your festival. Tonight's a fundraiser, a man from India will show slides. Will stay as long as the program doesn't take too long. "If it does, he'll be talking to the four walls," said the boss.

So "if you get one thousand of rupees, ten rupees is already there. If you get Kṛṣṇa, then you get all perfection." (Śrīla Prabhupāda, Hṛṣīkeśa, May 15, 1977.)

When we are spiritually perfect, we develop the spiritual form and go to live eternally in the spiritual world (even on the top *lokas* there is no bloated face and trembling hands from heavy medicine. No quarreling. Of course, in the end they must die, unless they can transfer beyond Brahmaloka to the spiritual planets). There are all varieties in the spiritual world, but they are *sat-cit-ānanda*, not material.

This is very good, but the children don't like to hear it. They get bored and start running around. They have not developed the higher taste. I also get restless and may limp out of the audience. The audience all may walk away. They are willing to make a donation but not sit through a long program.

Christopher Columbus, Magellan, Floyd Patterson,[2] what is the date when the Prussian War ended? How many died in World War II? in the Twin Towers crash? What nations did George W. Bush refer to when he named them "an axis of evil"? Who did he refer to when he said, "That guy tried to kill my dad"?

Why would you prefer to live in Jagannātha Purī than in Taos, New Mexico, U.S.A.? Why is Tapaloka better than Maharloka—is it? What planets remain at the time of devastation (the end of Brahmā's day)?

Is faith in God a sectarian thing? Among the conditioned souls, do Kṛṣṇaites have more than Christians? How does the verse *sa vai puṁsāṁ paro dharmo* in *Śrīmad-Bhāgavatam* disprove this?

Junior Barks was making spontaneous notes to submit to Mandala Press, Torchlight Press, and the *Sanatorium* writing staff simultaneously, along with *AF's* "Questions and Answers—Shooting From the Hip," and to five online journals on the Internet. Then he thought, why not start my own online column?—"Junior Barks Speaks"? I'll make an attractive Web page. I don't have to beg these other publishers. That's the beauty of the Net. I'll go on, he decided, and stooped over his laptop. I'll do my own illustrations too.

Two hookers were loudly talking shop talk while the *sādhu* tried to give his fundraiser speech. Frustrated, he finally took his microphone and placed it on a little table right in front of the tarts. He then went back to his pillow and continued speaking without amplification. Needless to say, the tarts went on with their converstion. The big blond man finally removed them and returned the mike to the speaker.

Yes, it was a good program, funding for the poor in Vṛndāvana. Each householder was only thinking, however, of how much he could afford to give. That was on everyone's mind, including the fundraiser. Swami Swims had decided beforehand on $108, and he fondled the check in his *kurta* pocket while trying not to anticipate pain or agoraphobia. "That swollen face, trembling hands from medicine probably didn't do me any good," he thought, "but maybe it will keep visitors away." But the meds nay-sayers will get the confirmation they seek. Anyway, it gets you back for the things you wrote teasingly about others. (The door is squeaking open. It is my man coming to tell me my obligations for today. Someday I'll live in a place where no one tells me what to do, what to wear, but they assimilate *Difficulties in Prayer* for me and send me back a synopsis.)

Oh it's too fast to run,
they had no horseless carriages
then, a few model T Fords.
Charles Chaplin speckled
films I watch a
short one with Śacī before

I go to bed. It's pure therapy,
friends.

It's funny stuff to save your
life which may go beyond
seventy-four. Aren't you too old
for migraine?

No *parikrama*, no shoes
in temple. Haven't seen
you in twenty-one years, you
look bloated in face and trembling
hands but speak with devotion
rare to find—

about Ahmad Jamal. How
dare you? We know of only one
other ISKCONite who shares such
tastes with you.

Well things are a'changing.
We're dovetailing our taste.
Moonlight in Vermont[3]
is a code for an aspiring devotee
praying indoors, learning to actually
talk to his Lord in a submissive
way. He just doesn't like the
talking tours and festivals.
Isn't there
another way? Stick it out
and learn to concentrate and believe,
"my dear Lord Kṛṣṇa, You
are my best friend. I've done
some preaching and intend to do
some more right now, as
soon as I get a new denture
with a suction in it."

Rādhā-Govinda upstairs,
sit and relax and cancel if you must
but never stop whispering His names.

Here is a beautiful poem by Ranier Maria Rilke:

To Erika, for the Festival of Praise

Dove that ventured outside,
flying far from the dovecote:
housed and protected again,
one with the day, the night,
knows what serenity is,
for she has felt her wings
pass through all distance and fear
in the course of her wanderings.

The doves that remained at home,
never exposed to loss,
innocent and secure,
cannot know tenderness;
only the won-back heart
can ever be satisfied: free,
through all it has given up,
to rejoice in its mastery.

Being arches itself
over the abyss.
Ah the ball that we dared,
that we hurled into infinite space,
doesn't it fill our hands
differently with its return:
heavier by the weight
of where it has been.

A guy gave the Swami this poem and subtitled it, "(Dove that ventured outside—this is Swami Swims' heart)."

Hold up, baby. Is the dove like Uncle Ralph's "flying the coop"? No, Ralph the elder DiMaggio never learned anything by his desertion of home responsibilities, just more drunkenness and womanizing. The dove Rilke talks of is one who dares to fly where conformists do not go, but he does so to . . . become closer to God in his self-endeavor. He wants to do *more*. Break the bonds of mechanical dryness, institutional forms of dovecote life. "It's risky," said a friend, Tim. "But you've always taken risks. You've created new spaces for us to follow." But notice, the dove is not a transgressor. He returns to the dovecote, but he's learned something he can share with those who need it.

Junior Barks showed up again at the writing staff's headquarters (a small room with a small desk and bed). He said he didn't know enough about the computer to get his own Web page. "Could *Among Friends* do it for me?" No, they said, we barely have enough money and time to do a thirty-three-page pamphlet each month. "Then," threatened the young man, "I will go to the anti-ISKCON people. I will write scathing pieces exposing scandals. I'll learn yellow journalism and attack you."

"Junior, how naughty of you. You should reconsider before taking such action. It will hurt Prabhupāda. It is anti-Kṛṣṇa."

Junior really just wanted some love, attention and recognition. That was why he was precocious.

"Could I write some sastric pieces you'd insert in your book?"

We told you we would. But vary them a little. Read Śrīla Prabhupāda's books and look in your own heart. Also, you are pretty young. Maybe you shouldn't be so ambitious. Come and join our *kīrtanas*, help cook and serve *prasādam*. Don't be so hung up on writing and publishing. Write a journal for yourself and pass it around here if you like. We *do* have our own plans and standards here. But we *love* you, Junior, we do. Where are your beads? How many rounds have you chanted?"

"How many rounds have *you* chanted?," he snapped back, ill-bred brat.

"I've chanted ten and I'll get the rest done by the end of the day."

"Okay, I'll help clean up in the kitchen and chant and keep a journal. But one day I'll show you."

You can't tell me it's wrong.
It's in the holy book. She
went to a mystic healer high
on a mountain in Russia

for her concussion. Served by
cleaning the candles. She
was accepted as a pilgrim.

He cured her of all impurities.
She wants me to go there for
my headaches. She showed him my
picture. He said, "It's too
complicated. He has to come here."
Another is in Brazil. One in Florida,
a woman who
touches you, Sufi healer.

I said I can't travel. I'll
have to do it from here,
whatever I can. "Someday
he'll come along, the
healer I love. He'll be big
and strong."[4] He'll vanish my
karma.

Someday maybe not. You
live with this "swollen face
and trembling hands" (poor
description). He stopped time.
We can't describe it, it's too
intimate, you have to be there
to believe it.

To be cured you need some
austerity. Travel to the White
Mountain in Russia or
dust and garbage plastic
of Vṛndāvana. They are doing
tremendous work to clean
it up. What do you think
of the anti-theme?

Grasping for a handle.
Someone to love, SK's
book dedication: "To that
one who is *my* reader."
The Individual.

A big muscle-bound guy with a T-shirt revealing many tattoos, tight leather pants, and a belt with many metal studs in it walked into our office about 7:00 P.M. We had finished our work for the day and were watching an early Keystone production of a Charlie Chaplin film.

He said, "I'm Junior Barks' father." We turned off the video because he was an interruption, and a threatening one too.

"Oh yes," said Tim the editor, "he's a nice boy, very very precocious. He's been working in our kitchen and we advised him to keep a journal."

"But how come you don't print his stuff in the book?"

"Well, we have already printed some of his things. But we thought they were a little basic and repetitious. So we asked him to practice some on his own."

"I read what he wrote and I think it's excellent. I'd like you to print whatever he writes right away."

"Is that an order, a threat?" said Jane our typist. She was the toughest of our bunch.

Mr. Barks backed down a little.

"Well what's the problem? The rest of the stuff I read in your book is kind of zookie. Like jokes and stuff. And I just caught you guys watching Charlie Chaplin. Why weren't you having *kīrtana*?"

We let Bhaktin Jane speak up for us. She also had tattoos, and when she stood, she was as tall as Mr. Barks, and she worked out daily in a local gym.

"Now look here, Mr. Barks," said Jane, "this is a free country, and there's freedom of the press. If you're so anxious to have your boy published, you can use some of your money from wherever you get it and print a real nice book of your own, and you can sell it in many ways. You can advertise on the Internet or sell it on the street corners. And we have a right to publish our own book without Junior Barks' stuff, or his stuff only occasionally. We're only doing him a favor by telling him how to write better."

"Hmm." Mr. Barks' father seemed to have nothing more to say. "I'll think about it," he said, "but I might come back later. You ought to give the kid a chance and not be hogging everything yourself."

Our staff waited for Jane to speak up. "We're not hogging. It's a free country. He can write as much as he likes and publish it. What's the big deal? There's not much prestige in getting into our book. We only print 1,000 copies, and hardly anybody buys it. And they don't buy it because of the very reason Junior Barks doesn't go over so well in our book. We like to write our way and he likes to write his way."

"Yeah, I seem to understand now," said Mr. Barks. "I think my son's a better writer than you. So why should he try so hard to get into your book? I'll work with the kid, and we'll make our own book, better than yours. It'll be more pleasing to Prabhupāda. What's your name?"

"Bhaktin Jane."

"And what's the Sanskrit tattoo around your wrist mean?"

She said, "Whom Kṛṣṇa wants to kill, no one can protect." She then raised her voice with emphasis, "Whom Kṛṣṇa wants to protect, no one can kill."

Mr. Barks seemed a bit cowed and exited the office, closing the door softly.

"That was great, Bhaktin Jane," we said in unison.

"Okay, turn on the video again and let's not worry about Mr. Barks."

The next day there was a note under the door of the writing office. It was from Junior Barks. It said, "Two days ago I attended a meeting of a visiting *ācārya*. He was speaking amazing realizations about Rādhā and Kṛṣṇa, far above anything I ever saw in your books, or even Prabhupāda's books. It was like a new opening of the heavens for me. I decided I'm going to write a commentary on Rūpa Gosvāmī's *Ujjvala-nīlamaṇi*. I don't know if you dopes even heard of the book. Compared to what I'm going to write, your stuff will look like *Mad* magazine. Don't expect to see me coming around doing menial tasks in your kitchen anymore. I've gone on to better things. My dad is satisfied too and says he'll put up the money. He was interested in your typist Jane, though, and asked if she'd like to go on a motorcycle ride with him. We live at 224 84th Street. My dad's e-mail is Tuff_Stuff@knucks.com. I also have a new e-mail, Rupa_Manjari_Barks@Radha_kunda.com. Goodbye, chumps, all glories to Rādhārāṇī.—Rasikā Barks, no longer Junior to you."

The man I love wears
saffron, didn't like to be
called "a man," he's a
spiritual master.

He changed the consciousness
of the world. I'd like to speak
about it. How can I leave
his *mūrti* behind? You've
got his books in early
editions.

Don't let the memories
fade. He sang the tunes and
they are all collected. Thousands
of statues. People who are devoted
to his mission.

He wants you to love Kṛṣṇa.
Not him? He never pointed
to himself. Said I may be
imperfect but Kṛṣṇa is perfect.

That way he humbly but lionlike
put down the nonbelievers.

It scared you how he cut them
off in conversation and Joe said
he seemed to lack some savvy
as to getting on in this world.

We overlook the mistakes.
The hurts he gave us because
we were tender. Some soldiers
understood it well.
He turned to them, "Get me
Tamāla."

But some can be his gentle
heart. And more than before
extend the ways and innovations.
Room for everyone
in that expansive heart that surely
connects you to the One and His *pāriṣads* of varied temperaments.

"I pray the emotional void in your heart can be filled with spiritual happiness." Hey, who's he to say I have an emotional void? So uppity, these top cops. They have no void? No, their sober guru fills it. Cane-users' instructions: "Canes are typically used on the strong side or opposite the injured extremity, providing a safe tripod stance. Keep this straight when using canes. When going upstairs (this is the hard part to remember), place uninjured foot upstairs first, followed by cane and injured foot. When going downstairs (Whew! This is harder to learn than *Nectar of Devotion*) place cane on stair first, followed by injured foot, then uninjured." Maybe you need to practice this slowly.

But it doesn't mean I have an emotional hole in my heart. I just like friends. As Billie Holiday was already quoted in this book, "If I don't have friends, then I ain't nothing."

"Turn back here or you'll be shot."

Animated cartoon of what happens to a person who illegally duplicates a video. Shows him in black-and-white striped prison clothes sadly entering the row of cells, into his own. He sits on a bench and places his head in his hands in misery. Don't do it!

"Oh, but in New York City you can buy an identity on the street." The FBI will track you down, or in Canada the Royal Mounted Police. Stop copying the videos and filling the void with unauthorized contacts. We'll tell you when to breathe. "Drill them until they're half dead, then give them shovels to dig, and then drill them some more."

He prays, I wonder if he really does or just writes that as a matter of speech for spiritualists. Really praying to fill Swims' emotional void in the way *they* think best. They are absolutely right. Left face, right face, about face. It's all in the books.

We very much thank Bhaktin Jane for her show of strength. Sorry I had not introduced you to her previously. She was our secret weapon so I kept her under wraps until needed—to confront Mr. Barks. Maybe she'll be needed again. She's a good typist, a loyal-to-us devotee (how much needed!) and fills the void of our hearts. She thinks of getting another tattoo, she's been giving it a lot of thought, where to place it and what it would be, although definitely Kṛṣṇa conscious. She was thinking of another Gaura-Nitāi but then thought that for fighting, a Nṛsiṁhadeva with Hiraṇyakaśipu on his lap might be more effective. Anyway, she's our Bhaktin Jane and we're glad she's on board. Some desert, some warn others to keep away from us, but Jane is solid. She likes this kind of writing.

I can't stay up so late
there are people talking.
There are mice crawling
electricians drilling.
I went through Frova.
But I feel good up here in
upstate with a happy
family. They care for
me.

I pray sixteen rounds, that's
good for a start.

Tim and Jim and initiated
giants all come together for
a festival.

No he's not getting better.
It's not true. But he's
getting his major chance
fulfilled. To say
God's names. It contains
the *mahā-vākya* instruction
from Prabhupāda.

Just hear. That will
lead to seeing and remembering
the pastimes and qualities
of Lord Kṛṣṇa and all His glories.

He's shouting them on.
All fisticuffs in the earliest
Mack Sennett films and
Charles didn't even have
a moustache.

John Handy[5] blowing us to
a good night fill up
void. I remember this
before. Go to bed. Rest thy head.
You've got a lineup of
pain preventers and
ten predicted years in
this body. I'm talking of amateur
Fred Turtle and the fisticuffs
at the masquerade. And he
left and started his own movement.
And I told him you can't do it
but he did and he was born.

Ants crawling as they were
made to. Humans doing what
they are meant to—gain
liberation from birth and
death.

I didn't do it on key but
I'm filling up the void and
they'll be no contact on the sly.
The bosses and the FBI will
track you down.

Don't copy them videos,
don't write those letters,
don't do anything beyond
the rules and versions of
the cops. But you can
paint and follow your doctor's
orders.

And they can't stop you
from living and dying.

Needless to say, Jane turned down the date offered by Biker Barks. All of the men on the writing staff have a platonic relationship with her. She's too tough for anything else. She's dedicated her life to just Kṛṣṇa and guru. "I love you," she'll say, "but not this body love." So she's one of the boys.

But even Jane won't go to a proposed retreat in California in the winter. A man is preparing a small house in the midst of real country land (they even have mice) and Swami Swims will go there with maybe only one male assistant and try to taste real seclusion and see if it helps headaches.

I even heard today another Swami may be coming through. You sit and talk and receive them and appreciate them. Is there one I could read the dove poem to? Only one guy I know. Others will read it in the book and I hope they'll understand.

Somebody says he's feeling better, but he's not really feeling better. The one who's coming through is a sick man. We can commiserate about that. Your back, my head, your psychological trouble and mine. How far can you go with that? We both know it's our fate. We don't want to embarrass each other. Then talk about Kṛṣṇa. Somebody tells what he lectured last night. I talked about the path from *śraddhā* to *prema* in four hours. I give a two-hour class every morning at my house. I force the attendance and make them sit through it. I like to talk. When New York City's Mayor Giuliani resigned, they asked him what he would do. He said he'd like to go around lecturing. "I love to lecture," he said, "I could do it ten times a day."

Most of the politicians' work is by words. They give the orders and the grunts fight the wars. They give the orders and money is withheld from the starving people of the world. They give the orders and their political party coaches them about how to stay in power. They give the word and it's written by their script men.

But devotees speak strictly according to Kṛṣṇa, and if they're realized, they do it in their own words and with their own wisdom and experience. They draw the big crowds. They have compassionate hearts. They've organized many, many programs for bringing new people to Kṛṣṇa consciousness. Collecting money, treating people personally. They bring tears to your eyes when they speak about the sweetness of the spiritual world. They've got terrific memories. They draw envy from people like Swami Swims. And when they speak where there are lots of children with their parents, the children get impatient after a little while. That's what's nice about Vasant Falls, as they call it. They try to restrict the speakers to short talks, on a plea that the children will go wild. The speakers say, yeah yeah, but then they go ahead anyway and speak overtime. Swami Swims sometimes gets out of his rocking chair, makes *daṇḍavats*, and exits.

He said he'd come in and check up on me, but he's an hour late. So I probably won't have time to finish this. He'll want to do something. He takes fastidious care of his big lawn. I asked if it's all right to walk on it. He said yes, so maybe we'll walk. I'm not up to another big gym exercise.

They'd prefer an important book like *Vaiṣṇava Compassion*, all neat and in order. Or the old *sādhana* books, a breakthrough on personal prayer. Sell out a first edition in two months. Poetry and diary sit on the shelf unbought. Too much competition. "He's a prolific author," as everyone says. Are you carping, baby? If all you can do is write, at least be a kind and nice guy. There are no naughty children at Vasant Falls. They share the swings and balls. The kitten ventured outside for the first time. A groundhog twice her size in the distance. I have affection for you and I hope you have for me. I inquire from others of your well-being. So there's no need to communicate further. That makes sense to me. Gimme space. I told you he'd be here any minute. The worst time is if you're in the middle of a poem—it's like being caught in the shower. They gasp, "But I thought you were a Vaiṣṇava. You don't even have genitals or tattoos." Put the sign on the door—"Writing poem, give me ten minutes." Dare?

Spring swing no doubt in
mid-May in your home state
minus the Twin Towers.
He spoke two hours with a two

hour slide show and I endured
it all.

Melodic. I admit he is.
Better unmuted. "Sounds
tinny," she said when she
heard Miles with his mute.
But I better not think about
that.

Inquire how you can sharpen
your wits. Rememorize the
ślokas you used to know.
"I like intellectual preaching."
"I prefer animated telling
of Vṛndāvana pastimes the
way Braji does it."

"I like a serious talk on
how to heal the wounds
with psychology in it."
"I prefer a Prabhupāda
symposium where everyone
gets to talk even if they
don't follow the rules."
"I come for the feasts,
the *bhajanas*, nothing less
than a one-hour *kīrtana* by
an awesome singer, the one
and only."
"I prefer a lecturer
who has studied with gurus
other than Prabhupāda
and who has a broader perspective."

The envious Swims has
no hope until he gives up his

surly nature. He wants to
be coddled, pampered. Got
this new persona, "official
disabled old man." It's
real neat, gets you out
of almost all work.

But Kṛṣṇa and Brahmā and Sūrya
and even mortals see through
what you're doing.
They forgive you or just
ignore you as a has-been,
broken-down hack.

He trembles so much his
face so fat he must be
taking too much med.
No one has stopped him yet
so he thinks he's free.
But you can't fool the Supreme.

He'll let you do your little
reclusive thing and you'll
dwindle into a non-
sastric fool.
I take it back. I love myself.
"Come to love yourself," she
said, "own your self enough
to be your own nurse and nurturer."
(Remember on your own what
pills to take.) You can do that,
I have always known that.

Gopa-kumāra couldn't understand
what Brahmā was saying to
the Kumāras because it was

over his head, so he couldn't
repeat it to his student.

Okay give us the simplified version.
I'm happy when I'm singing,
no hole in my heart and
the FBI at bay. Don't
copy them videos and
call on Big Jane when
bullies come and yes
don't mess with Māyā
in the form of wimmin'.

Chapter Four

Sleeping midday, Tim. The phone rings. A woman talking wants to sell children's books. "No," says Tim. She says, "I can understand your hesitation," and goes on talking so fast with a "no strings attached" offer, so he finally says, "Thanks but we're not interested," and hangs up while she's still talking. That's her job, but it's not Tim's obligation to buy baby books. He's had his *kicchari* for today. Waiting to hear whether a swami is coming, which means he'll have to change out of his sanatorium-lounging sweat pants into *brahmacārī* uniform. No final word yet. Why not call up Śacī?

But you can't say the Hare Kṛṣṇa prayer like that girl in Russia. She learned it from the Christian healer. I've read about it. You bow down and bring your mind to your heart. She right away experienced a burning in the heart and saw Kṛṣṇa, and it was revealed to her that she's been ignoring her feminine nature. She ought to get married and have children, she decided. Swami Swims wondered what would happen if he did that. Bring Hare Kṛṣṇa into the physical organ of the heart. Very hard. SS thought it was too much like yoga, never taught by Prabhupāda, so he wouldn't go for it. Starting to get the afternoon pressure. Sit alone and it won't be good. Go for another nap and a salesperson may phone.

"I can understand your hesitation not to try the Jesus prayer, bowing your head low to the ground. Please come to Russia. He has to see you in the flesh. He'll tell you the karma that brought you these migraines. You'll feel repentant, and then it will go away."

I can understand your hesitation not to fly on Russian airlines and climb the White Mountain, but please come. Also in Moscow you can talk to hundreds of devotees or try avoiding them, and that will surely exacerbate your headache.

Swims wears his sanatorium clothes until he hears a staunch *dhotī* person is coming. None today. Went for a walk with Śacī, Swims wearing his FDNY cap. Passed bald Baby Lakṣmaṇa in his mother's arms.

"Is he laughing at my funny hat?"

"He likes it," his mother says. Lakṣmaṇa wears a bonnet of his own, gives a toothless smile. We walk. These shoes feel too big. Polly noses drifting. Heavy bass music in cars passing. Some houses for sale.

"I'll just hang around and do some writing unless it gets worse."

"I'll be around if you need me."

Yes we will hang around
and do our service.
I never said you betrayed
Prabhupāda.
I've got some good news
for you.

No one is knocking on your
door for money. Save it
for when there's a settlement.

Curl in the arms of round midnight,
is this the same one? Yes,
the very one.

The busy persons on
the street don't know
I'm doing all right.

The other man turned
back. Too many ailments
to travel this far north.

I don't think Kṛṣṇa will
ever forget. She out-argues
you from her side but
He will accept you in
your One-to-one.

Whatever He does I must accept
and be glad
and ready to dance some more.

All right there's nothing to wait for. Cut down the cane, ladies, while the men play cards and drink cheap wine. The offspring of the marriage are neglected, especially the girls, sometimes just left lying on the ground all day with no food. The people are so poor. Born with anemia, diarrhea, poisoning from the water, tourist bus runs over a two-year-old girl and no one fixes her broken bones. Plastic rubbish everywhere. The cows try to eat it and die. ISKCON is trying to help. Clean the filth and garbage along the *parikrama* trail. Hire a policeman to stop people from dumping stuff in holy places. A reform movement: "Vṛndāvana is a holy place. Help keep it clean."

In some ways it is too late, too far gone. But they are making an effort and making a comeback. Donate for this cause.

The covering over the holy place drives away the insincere? Even those who would like to go, who are pious, cannot take it anymore. Cleaning it up, help the Vrajavāsīs to take care of themselves. He shows the two-hour slide show and says, "Now I'm going to blackmail you. I don't like showing these last pictures." One of the girl with a bent leg that was never treated. Some before and after shots when they were treated. Swims gave $108.

"It is the best-financed program in Vṛndāvana."

Grateful for your own *kicchari*, for your friends. Now use that good karma to benefit others and to elevate yourself.

American flags on most houses.
Upstate NY. Everyone has a
house, clean toilet, job.

But the country is led by a hawk
who bombs the countries
he suspects are making
bombs against the U.S.A.

Why doesn't he give some
rice and grains and fruit
and education to the underdeveloped?

No one cares. They want their
video, their meat. As others
are poor, the Americans
are ignorant. Born dumb
and no one can convince them
about the souls in animals
and the karma of next life.

Churchgoing is a farce.
Violence a common experience,
taught in the "extreme" video

games. A two-year-old knows
how to kill another
human being.

But there's some good left.
The Hare Kṛṣṇa movement,
fractured and strewn with garbage,
is still persisting and preachers
and *kīrtana* singers have not
given up.

They are infiltrating places
so outsiders ask, "What is
this? Please tell me about it."
That happens.

I am, I am. The new
writings. They've got to do
something before you break down,
leave a jolly heritage.

I don't care what they think.
I never said you are a
schmuck. I said you are a
schmo.

Attend the festival and buy
me a T-shirt of Lord
Jagannātha. Let's have
a nonalcoholic. Here's
the composer himself
playing his own tune.

Are you tired? No not yet,
it continues to sustain me.
Some better than others.

Pity the poor box, the
thief who steals it
the Keystone slapstick—
throwing garbage over the
fence on the man with
distinguished top hat and coat.

Call the huge butler and
he throws out the
man who came to steal
scientific secrets.

Time running out. Kṛṣṇa
in control. He taught us
and I have not learned much
more in forty years but
I want to keep *my*
Prabhupāda as close
as possible. This isn't
going to run on Broadway
or Barnes & Noble and
the book table at
Rathā-yātra doesn't sell out
but Bemsha swings.

Swami Swims got to talking about Prabhupāda when a disciple asked him what he wanted from him. He said Śrīla Prabhupāda wanted work and obedience; that pleased him.

Now there is more freedom.

At the dentist's office you could have been engaged in discursive prayer. Talking to Prabhupāda. Swami Swims, you thought you were a good disciple, huh? We could cut down that image. He was content. You've got a new offering now, and he's not here to say, "It's garbage, it doesn't remind me of Kṛṣṇa." So you assume it's okay to present a new wave to a new generation. If he's in your heart and dreams, giving you that approving smile. These *are* different times.

At the dentist's office, the radio was playing opera, a male tenor. The dentist was inserting a plastic fit as a new top denture. Nothing was expected of Swims but to sit there and think, "This is fun," so that he would prevent a headache. After the opera came a pop song, but he couldn't hear it as the dentist was fixing a metal thing over Swim's ears and asking him to press up on the new denture with his thumbs. Then came a white girl singing imitation black girl rock, it seemed. "Freedom, freedom," she kept shouting. Swims wasn't discoursing with Prabhupāda. He wondered why the pretty hygienist wasn't in the office but was replaced by a triple-chinned one. That other lady was so nice. The dentist is a gingerly oldster with curly white hair.

Swims didn't ask, "Śrīla Prabhupāda, now that I'm in a kind of privacy and need a little relief from all this poking and fitting in my mouth, why don't I talk to you? I wrote that person who always liked me as sincere. Good boy. It's true. Be blessed by remembering he loved you, he loves you. Don't imagine you're distant. Take his *mūrti* to California or get a new one. Have him near you. Put his *cādar* on. Get back into his books and appreciate especially the aspects of his personality that you can. The war commander may frighten you as he blasts away with his bazooka. Shoots, kills. You are not strong enough to pick up your own and lob hand grenades into the airports. You *did* lecture in colleges and take care of devotees in temples."

What is a good disciple of Prabhupāda? One who doesn't forget him, sticks to his mission in one way or another, even if you are changing as you grow older, bolder and infirm.

As Swims was leaving the dentist's office, the hygienist said goodbye and he turned his head and saw it *was* her, the pretty one! She'd been there all the time.

Olatunji[1] concert, giving his last public performance, spilling it all out. All forms of religions and feelings and pains and pleasures in the way only he can do it. Prabhupāda, do you like me liking him? I am my own man too, just as you are, just as Gaura-kiśora dāsa Bābājī was, and Bhaktivinoda Ṭhākura, and Bhaktisiddhānta Sarasvatī, and my Godbrothers.

"The guru is one." But we want Prabhupāda. That "guru is one" stuff can be spread around too loosely.

"Do you have a headache?"

"No" (not yet). Dear Śacī.

"You're the only house without an American flag."

Dentist: "It's going to be colder for a week."

Receptionist: "That will be $2,100."

Oh he's dressed like an American in a Banana Republic shirt and sweater with little alligator logo on it. Forgot his cane, phony. We will somehow chant the rounds and sing the songs. And stay in one place mostly. Listen to the books. Please don't spend so much money. Take the holiest essence. Chant with attention, hopeless one. At least chant the quota.

We've still got time so we're
going to use it in the best way
pressing the beads.

Thinking of Kṛṣṇa if you can.
He won't be here to read to
me at snack time from
BB. I do enjoy hearing
Gopa-kumāra always
dissatisfied with higher
planets because Madana-gopal
of his mantra isn't there.

He's a kind of funny character
in his persistence yet
he's being allured to places of great *yajña* to other
forms of God where he
gets less than perfect
information.

It's very good for me to "eat"
this *prasādam* from the
book but Śacī will be at
the office or at suppertime we'll
have to sit around the table
socializing.

Take one, take two,
"Where have you been?"
"Who's visiting next?"
"What is the latest
on the lecture tour
and court case?" It will take
seven years for the thing
to be over. So save your
money for the settlement.

Loose lips. I told them
what I think. They'll
defeat me and say what
their version of the
guru-disciple relationship
is and why I dishonored it.

Charlie threw the garbage
over the corrugated fence and it
hit a top-hatted
gentleman. I laughed so out loud
Śacī was surprised. I keep these little

comedy snapshots with me
during the day. But it
would be better to
talk to your master.

Faith in God, the most precious thing. He's always with you. The yogi is not afraid even living alone in the forest, because he knows Kṛṣṇa is in his heart. In the spiritual planets there is no death, disease or old age. Everyone is mad after Kṛṣṇa and they each get to exchange with Him, even the flowers and birds and bees, and of course the beloved cows of Vrajabhūmi, and His relatives, friends and *gopīs*, chiefmost Rādhārāṇī, the Queen of Vṛndāvana.

On earth we think of these things. We drain ourselves in quarrels. "I don't think anything is wrong with you," said his counselor, "except the battle fatigue of what you have been through and that's why you are ailing."

Of course there is karma from past lives. Go to the White Mountain and meet the white-bearded monk, he will cure you, but by the time you reach Moscow, scores of devotees will want to burden you with new karma. Swimji was thinking over why he wouldn't travel to Russia to meet the healer.

"A spiritual master is not a fashion," said Śrīla Prabhupāda, "if one is actually inquisitive to understand the highest perfectional stage, then he should search after a spiritual master."

Don't call me in for a chat. I can't take it, said Swami Swims. Bedtime not far away. Pajamas, dreams, only a few hours and then a new day. The disciple sees the guru falling asleep while chanting his *japa*. But he's understanding.

Make a shopping list. What kind of an art studio would you like? One with plenty of light and classical music and no one to disturb you. But you can't paint with pain. Some could. Paint simple image of Christ on the cross. Paint *rasa* dance. Don't dare. Big face. Let go.

I heard there are horses on that farm, and you can feed them apples in their barn. And mice in the houses. Could you make friends with them instead of killing them? Seclusion. Give your address? No, please don't bother him. But he must be fed Kṛṣṇa consciousness. The baby is bald and I am growing bald. He has no teeth. I have false ones. His will grow in.

They blew horns and *dundubhi* and *mṛdaṅga*, what a racket, and they threw flowers from the sky and played on kettledrums, that's the usual description when a great thing happens.

"Are you going further out?"

"Yes."

"Then you will lose the conservatives."

"But there are new ones." The minister cleared his throat and began to speak on loss and how to handle it in a Kṛṣṇa conscious way. Swims had to lie down. One of these days he'll do more and better, he thought to himself, or at least hang in there with Swamiji A. C. Bhaktivedanta.

Kṛṣṇa-kīrtana with bent peak on his baseball cap is an artist but gets no time to paint, "not yet." He has a two-car garage set aside for it. Sold paintings in galleries. Cleans Swamis' rooms on Wednesdays and Sundays. He said he could get more light when painting (if he had time) by opening the garage door, but then he'd lose privacy. Yes, blessed privacy to chant your 16 rounds, bring the mind to the heart.

The dove is still flying, hasn't returned to the dovecote. Going with the youngsters. "As soon as this batch grows old I'm going to get me a younger group. Yeah. I'm gonna stay with the youngsters. It keeps the mind active."

Swims would have liked to play longer with little no-teeth Lakṣmaṇa, who likes his cuddling him. But he had a headache. "I'll get a hold on him later, when I see him. I didn't know he liked to be handled, I thought he would cry. But he's like Prahlāda, cries when he's alone and Kṛṣṇa comes running. They are all some kind of devotees here. Don't have American flags out front, but Deity altars inside. Not a very good day. But it ended okay, this is fun," Swami kept telling himself in the dentist's chair, and finished up all alone watching W.C. Fields, no one to laugh with. Gopa-kumāra, burdened as Lord Brahmā, wanted to be with Kṛṣṇa in Vraja. Chanted his mantra to bring himself to his ultimate destination. Always remained a humble cowherd at heart, even when worshipped as Brahmā. "Get me out of here," he thought, "too much management and I can't concentrate on the Lord of my mantra."

Get to bed baby
Bud Powell[2] will touch you,
poor misguided geniuses,
all they needed was contact
with a bona fide guru.

But something prevented
them like sins from
bad association and past lives.

That guy always wants the
last word. Let him have it.
I stay safe and preserve that honor.

Kṛṣṇa, Kṛṣṇa, no contact
with dangerous electric open
wires. Do not play
on or in this garbage dumpster.

So many things to watch for,
flashing lights of cops, give
the guy a ticket for loose
hanging license plate.

You are risking another H.A.
when you write a poem.
The fat man went into
the steam bath and overstayed,
came out skinny as a rail,
promised to sue the barber.

It could happen to you.
You could miss the target
and the ball could hit your
head and knock you out.

You could be attracted.
But wrap it up in
the canon. I am
not fearless. I don't
tack on. The dove
isn't ready to come
down, not yet.

It could happen to you—
Lord's mercy suddenly
descends out of His
causeless desire to make
you happy.
Bhakta with no void
in the heart and smart enough to lecture
to intellectual minds
but not too long that babies
would cry.

It could, it could, and the one
who prays
and the one who is in the field
and the one who remembers
Swamiji is eligible to help
himself and others. Hold on
to those memories that he
loved you because you
worked and did what
he asked.

It could happen to you.

You said keep remembering those Prabhupāda memories. Read them, speak them to intimate friends, explain them. Ones that involved you—he always liked you, "perfect gentleman." Others' memoirs. Keep in touch. It is a good way. You have a precious treasure. Don't be a miser.

Tim was thinking of going to see Giovanni the "astrologer" café owner. It was three days before the New York City Rathā-yātra down Fifth Avenue.

"Giovanni, may I speak to you?" said timid Tim.

"Ah, my son. Sure, I got some time. Whad da'ya wan'ta know? You cumma to the Rathā-yātra? You know, there was a sage in India who used to hold a class every day. But on Rathā-yātra, he noticed nobody was in da'audience. The next day, they was all there with beaming faces. So he said to dem, 'You been to the Rathā-yātra, huh?'

"'Yes, Guru Mahārāja,' they replied.

"'You was'sa looking at da pretty girls and tastin' da sweets, huh?' He wasn't pleased.

"'But isn't it good to go to Rathā-yātra and see the Lord in His wooden form?'

"'Yeah, but are ya seein' Him or lookin' at 'da girls?'

"The *brahmacārīs* bowed their heads and considered what their renunciate Guru Mahārāja had said."

"It's funny that you said that, Giovanni, like you were reading my mind. I came to see you because, you know, I'm a *brahmacārī*, but sometimes I'm thinking I should get married. I know marriage is nothing but trouble. You have to pay bills, and it's just entangling. I can see it from the *gṛhasthas* that I know."

"Then?"

"The only trouble is my mind. I keep thinking maybe I could be happy if I was married."

"Well, *gṛhastha* is a good thing too. Potential Vaiṣṇavas are brought into da'world. But for yourself, it's better to stay *brahmacārī*. That'sa da fast lane, and you can help the bigger family of Kṛṣṇa. Dat sa'why I never become married."

Tim said, "My question is how to remain determined to be a *brahmacārī*."

Giovanni put his arm around his son. "If a'you go to the Rathā-yātra, then actually you'll look at the face of the Lord. Work. Take care of a table and sell books or give out *prasādam*. Don' just hang around talkin' *prajalpa* and glancin' at the faces and shapes uh duh women. Keep yourself engaged in the real stuff, service. And think a'what Śukadeva Gosvāmī and the other renounced sages said about marriage. You know . . . "

"They're fallible soldiers . . . "

"Yeah. And how the family are like different animals who send the husband out to work every day and then attack him when he comes home."

Tim beamed a boyish smile. "It's all in the *Bhāgavatam*, right Giovanni?"

"That's a'right, my son, and it's all in the eyes of wisdom. Hear from the right people. And be prepared to live simple."

Tim bowed down at Giovanni's feet.

Giovanni said, "Hey! What's sa'dis? Don't bow down at *my* feet. I'm just a low-class man. An' you gotta decide on this yourself, not because I say so or even Śukadeva. But I tink you got the right idea, so just hang in there. Keep a'da saffron. So are you goin' to da Rathā-yātra?"

"Yes . . . ," said Tim, "but I think I'll man a book table for my spiritual master. How are my stars?"

"Let's sa'try da palm," said Giovanni, and he took Tim's small hand in his big hairy one. "Hmm. I would say it'sa not so bad, but it's not so great either. You jus' passed through'a time of great danger. But aside for palmistry, there's always a danger in this material world. How about tryin' to increase the quality of your chanting *japa?*"

"I'll try," said Tim. "One last thing, Giovanni. Someone told me I had an emotional void in my heart."

"What's a void?"

"Emptiness."

"Kid, if there's emptiness, then fill it up with Kṛṣṇa consciousness. Chant, hear nice music, be—what's sa'da word?—proactive in some service. And come to my place for *prasādam.* I won't charge you 'cause you're a *brahmacārī*, and my son. So you can fill up da void even without a wife an' kids."

Tim's eyes filled with tears as they embraced and departed. "Can I see you again, Giovanni?"

"You know de answer to that, anytime. But not dis Sunday. The Rathā-yātra's gonna fill dis place up to the ceiling."

I'm old-fashioned means
he doesn't want the slick
shit they purvey now.

He wants it like it was.
Old partner says it can't
return to that. It's over.
I'm sorry if you don't understand
how the partnership is
dishonored and betrayed. It's
draining to even think of it.

Then go your separate ways
on the path of spiritual progress.

Old-fashioned plea
can be made by the individual splashing
his paint the way he used to.

Remember old days that cannot
be again. It's a limited
instrument, the trombone,
even in the hands of
Curtis Fuller.[3] Everything is
limited. Old-fashioned movies
are the best.
Downtown Swami (Lower East Side)
better than uptown.

Sit and read books if you
could, hot milk at night
for *sādhus* free at the
gate of Krishna-Balaram
Mandir.

Take care of the children,
girls especially. The old,
slow-player ballad.

Control, exercise, American
flag, front porch,
picnics, swim in the
pond.

Before the Hare
Kṛṣṇa movement appeared in the West?
No, not that! That was prehistoric.
I mean me sitting before
him and worshiping by
work typing, and selling some
mimeographed magazines and still
youthful, old-fashioned.

A fierce debate ensued on Satyaloka in the presence of Gopa-kumāra. The *śrutis, smṛtis, Upaniṣads* were all arguing about the means of liberation. The *jñānīs* said that only by knowledge could one get liberation. Other scriptures said that knowledge was required and it would lead to *bhakti,* which would lead to liberation. The more advanced *Purāṇas* like *Śrīmad-Bhāgavatam* and the *Gopāla-tāpani Upaniṣad* stayed silent with slight smiles on their faces. As the debate continued, the *Śrīmad-Bhāgavatam* put his hands over his ears and walked away from the assembly. Gopa-kumāra ran after the *Śrīmad-Bhāgavatam* and with polite and learned words begged that it please come back and teach what it knew. We read each morning before we go to work.

Tim became afraid of his imminent death because of what Giovanni said—"Hey kid, you'va got a short lifeline." Tim was a member of the writing staff, with menial tasks. The men there laughed at him for studying his palm and saying he had a short lifeline.

"Even Lord Brahmā was always afraid of his imminent death," said Swami Swims. "That's what Kṛṣṇa consciousness is all about. We've got to attain liberation through devotion to God, and then we either go to Kṛṣṇa's planet, where everything is immortal, or even if we come back, we render devotional service to the Lord in an eternal spirit."

Tim: "Yeah, but you weren't told you had a short lifeline."

Swami Swims: "Even if he told me I had a shorty, Prabhupāda said that if you clapped your hands while chanting, all the lines can get rearranged. I think even technically, astrologically, there are things those Bṛghu people could tell you to do to extend your lifeline. Some rituals like eating ghee on the black moon night. But Prabhupāda's method is best, just chant and clap. Anyway, we've all got to go sometime."

"Don't worry, Bhakta Tim," said Big Jane from her typing corner, where she was pounding at the rate of 120 words a minute. She spoke without stopping her typing. "I'll protect you. I'll chant Hare Kṛṣṇa so loud and fervently that death will run away." She gave a hearty laugh.

"I know what you're saying, but I'm just a *worrier*," Tim said candidly.

Swami Swims: "Well, it is a heavy topic. Everyone wants to live forever. But Mahārāja Yudhiṣṭhira said it was the most absurd idea to think that you could live forever in this material body, and yet everyone—even though they see everyone around them dying, and their family, and elsewhere—each person thinks he won't die. That's the most amazing thing. Let's not worry so much about death but about life, Kṛṣṇa consciousness. Let's do our work and chant the Holy Names. And when death comes, let's help each other, we'll chant like Bhaktin Jane says. And even if death doesn't run away, it'll be a Vaiṣṇava departure, no Yamadūtas but Viṣṇudūtas."

Tim said no more, but he thought he'd go back to Giovanni and talk some more about the "technical" things, as Swami Swims said. Maybe he could get some precious stone to wear, or give a black cow on a moonlit night, or something like that. He just felt shaky, and he worried. "What if I have to go before I'm not perfect, not ready? We all admit we're not perfect. But the Swami was right, the solution is not to worry but to work at it."

Nothing to worry about
when it's going smooth.
Don't begrudge the leader,
play your part.

I don't know much to give
advice, bluff mystic knowledge:
"I dreamt your daughter had
a lump on her head but it
was benign."

Guy said he apologizes, he
resented being forced to become
the zonal *śikṣā* of Swims. Says
he prayed two years for *nima*
wood Gaura-Nitāi Deities and has Them
now. Swami said I'm praying
for that myself.

Not easy to get.
"Going to California sounds
like going to the moon."
No, it's seclusion, and I like
to have Gaura-Nitāi and

Prabhupāda. You can leave
your "old" Prabhupāda here
and get a new one?

Oh Kṛṣṇa, they are so nice
to me, building a whole altar
room around my *mūrtis*.

How could I take away
lovable Prabhupāda? He seems
happy here and Śacī said "I
think night and day of
worshiping them."

He and Swims side by side,
pouring the water pitcher
together. Be grateful and
give Prabhupāda a New York
home.

I'm getting better, happier
there's nothing wrong with
you just a string of karma
from past lives and this
one.

Oh he came and went.
He left us the best.
When he's blazing his
submachine gun and not
cooperating in interfaith
talks with a cardinal, I
may wince, but I know the
lion must have his prey—

Kṛṣṇa sent him for that,
and planted a seed of it in each
of us according to capacity.

Make people happy if that's
your way. I can't stop *this*
way I like it so much.
Go get your snack and maybe
you'll sing better today
with an inspiration from
the Renounced Poet's
Society—for the New
Wave youth, ages twenty to ninety.

Chapter Five

God bless America. No one dies anywhere. Everyone shuffles off the mortal coil and speedily goes to get punished in the subtle body if he's a sinner. Or speedily back to the human species if that's his destiny, in a tight bag as an embryo. This is the subtle law that few are convinced of. The New Agers have increased the numbers who say they believe in reincarnation (a large percentage of Americans said so in a poll). But very few know what liberation from birth and death is. Gopa-kumāra hadn't heard about liberation until he reached Satyaloka. And there are so many beliefs on what it is. There was an argument of polite suggestions among the sages at to what Mahārāja Parīkṣit should do in his last seven days, until Śukadeva Gosvāmī arrived. There was a "fierce debate" on Satyaloka, until *Śrīmad-Bhāgavatam* blocked his ears and walked out, and Gopa-kumāra pursued him and asked him to come back and really explain.

Impersonalists, demigod worshipers, those who want to go to heavens where gods dwell in high material delights, Christian liberation, vague and sketchy in the activities of immortality—and Vaiṣṇava *siddhānta.*

God bless America. No one dies here? Well of course they do. But they try not to think about it. Live as long as possible and enjoy the highest standard of material life possible. "As long as it brings you peace of mind," the Irish dentist told me. (He also had a pretty dental assistant working with him—young, long stringy blonde hair. It was such a small-time place, they had no secretary and the blonde collected the money and gave you change. Swims is better off with D.D.S. Danz, in Hudson, New York.)

God bless America, where you can get medicine or plenty of alternate treatments and counselors. Where many live homeless on the street. Where sex titillation is shamelessly played on TV and accessible freely along with recreational drugs. Where might is right and the military power must be kept up at all costs. Where I live in this lifetime. Where the sound of powered lawn mowers is often heard, and basketballs bouncing and the flag (Old Glory) ubiquitous on almost every car and front yard, store building—we'll never forget the Twin Towers and never stop bombing with better bombs, and the increasing enemies of America will find new ways to topple buildings and poison the citizens of the second largest democracy on the earth (India being first). So the *mūḍhas* vote a big *mūḍha* into power because he promises we will be rich and on guard. Where thousands are homeless. Where the worst music sells the best. And poetry has no power. And the cow and bull are slaughtered with no qualms. And quarrel—this is the age of Kali—reigns supreme.

You can hear it again with me
and notice the art. Hope
you won't get interrupted.
Hope for the day you'll
get a *nima* wood pair
of Gaura-Nitāi from
Māyāpur, and privacy ("it sounds like living
on the moon—California") to paint again.
Is that proactive to helping
the hapless as Prabhupāda ordered?
Yes in a way. Patch up those

with loss, with quarrel.

But we have grown apart
and wish to stay apart.
And many are disabled.
I'm speaking of Hare Kṛṣṇas.
They loved too much not
knowing it's mostly a dream, Frank sang so
well, "in me you see a
man alone."
Footsteps in the night.
No chance to be left alone
to figure the secrets of the universe—
they're right in the book—
and how they tally
realistically with your
ability
capacity to surrender
more than usual.

Try again. Softer this time,
no ranting or trying to test
someone. All your Marx
Brothers videos can't play on
American VHS, so that
will soon fade from my
repertoire.

Don't demand. Accept
what's on your plate.
It could happen to you
that mice or rats
would
crawl on your chest at night.
Or some kind soul would
give you Gaura-Nitāi.
But liberation,

it is not possible until
one is pure and fully in
love—ready to do anything—
for pleasing Govinda.

They ask me what does
a guru expect of a disciple,
what does he get out of it?
Work, he wants them to
work, assumes surrender,
is not exploiting, and gives
their labors to the cause.

Ah but you don't
understand why it broke,
you are too dumb or
the *śikṣā* too evasive
to explain it.

Excuse me for wandering,
you wanted something from
the store, Staples?
Paper clips, you wanted
a haircut. Oh you
said you wanted Gaura-
Nitāi.

Well you are too damn
greedy in your demands
and don't listen and feel
the grievances of others.
That's why you're a dork,
said the majority.

We talked. Roundtable. Two swamis. The *kerelā* is good. "Good for digestion." "Sour." "Do you want more bread?" Talk about Baltimore preaching. Talk about a man visiting. Swims is a welcome boarder. "*Limelight*' is not funny." I like the funnies, not the "poignant story of the old passing on the torch to the young." You sit and watch twenty minutes of it. No pratfalls. Soon he'll come in to see the inmates (remember them? the sanatorium?). Give them their pills for the evening and make sure they're not about to do anything crazy.

Put the Deities to rest, do it together. Waiting for a phone call. "Are you the great comedian Calvero?"

"Used to be." Now if he performs, the theater is empty. He's finished. Time to become serious about life. Not so cynical about eternal life just because you heard it preached by pontifical, boring priests—people you would not like to be like. But *Limelight* is not going to tell that story, so it doesn't qualify as comedy therapy. A plot. A lovely young ballerina who tried to commit suicide because she thought life had no meaning.

The elderly Chaplin tells her don't look for "meaning," look for "desire." What kind of philosophy is that? Abandon it. It's not going to help me. I'm in the strict Vaiṣṇava path.

Tim walked out on the others. They turned off the movie because it wasn't funny. Take your pills and get ready for bed. But Tim was expecting a phone call. He phoned Giovanni, whose son answered and said the old man was putting one of the children to bed. He'd call when he was done. That was a half hour ago, forty-five minutes ago. Maybe he forgot or didn't want to bother with Tim and his problems. The devotees had explained adequately about "imminent death" and longevity and how he should not worry about it, or even consult palm readers or astrologers. But Tim was a worrier, and Giovanni had said, "I am your father." So he phoned, but no reply. Tim helped put the Deities to rest, put on his pajamas, sat on his bed and waited for the phone to ring.

Don't worry when you're in
the arms of your parents.
They put you to sleep.
Once when you were
young alone in your bed
you felt terror's presence
and ran downstairs to them.
What was it? You couldn't explain.
But they let you sleep between
them in their double bed.
That was bliss. Safety.

Your protection. But later you
have to learn no one can protect
you. Life *does* have meaning,
ballerina. Meaning must
be heard from the supreme eternal
not from a retired comedian.

Better get it right or
you'll try again to turn on
the gas and put a towel under
the door and die.

You're a dancer? Dance for
the Lord. Who are you telling?
Did you chant all sixteen?

"Waltz for Debbie" in his
ears. The lights are out.
Tim goes under the covers.
The heck with the call
from Giovanni, I'll
live as long as I will.
He'll take your breath away
at a precise instant whether

or not the stars predict in
their relative way with
loopholes for the embarrassed
astrologer to explain it if
it doesn't come out as he predicted.
It's time for me to take me own rest
with God Almighty there's no
terror, certainly no mortal
parents to sleep between.

Please hang onto this for the
next life too. I can't see you
succeeding in this one. But a
friend said, *Yes yes*
He'll be there to save us,
He loves us and He'll be there—
"I had a vision."

The people on the writing staff were patients in the sanatorium. But there're plenty of other patients there too. They were all allowed to sleep without being forced to get up early. But if they didn't get up by 7:00, a monitor would come to their bed and say, "Is everything okay?" Tim slept in until seven the next day. When he got up and headed for the shower, he thought, "I've got a short life expectancy." But Giovanni hadn't bothered to call back, and the devotees told him not to worry about it.

Preaching about death was always easy, up to a point. Who could deny that they wouldn't die? So you could stretch it out in a sermon. Old age, disease. People neglect you. Prabhupāda's example of how in Africa they have a feast by killing the old grandfather and eating him. Separation from loved ones in your house and car. Especially the fear of the unknown. What will happen next? "Aye, there's the rub." But when you try to convince them that there are higher planets, lower planets, and eternal planets, then they have to participate with their faith. The ease becomes difficulty, and it can turn into dogma.

In the film *Limelight*, Charles Chaplin, playing the has-been comedian (which he actually was by then, 1952), preached to the young ballerina who attempted suicide. He told her that the human consciousness had taken billions of years to evolve. The sun is so powerful, sending out its heat rays, and yet it has no consciousness. But the human being has this rare gift of consciousness, "and you just want to throw it away." That was pretty good preaching. But then he said, "Please forgive me." Maybe he thought he was getting too preachy. And his own consciousness wasn't so joyful either. Yet it's true, consciousness is the rare gift, especially elevated human consciousness, and it should never be thrown away or abused. Just to have consciousness and misuse it in drinking or anything material is wasteful.

My consciousness is alert. But it skitter skatters everywhere according to the state of my mind and body. There was an argument in *Śrīmad-Bhāgavatam*—was it Rahūgaṇa and Jaḍa Bharata?—in which King Rahūgaṇa kept insisting that the consciousness was dependent on the body. But Jaḍa "proved" otherwise by logic and insistence on the absolute truth. We don't know anything unless we read those books and hear from a spiritual master. "One must be very much inquisitive to know . . . what is the highest perfection of life. If one is actually inquisitive . . . then he should search after a spiritual master" (Śrīla Prabhupāda, May 22, 1969). The consciousness is a symptom of a soul. But the consciousness is covered by layers of material nature, *tamas*, *rajas*, and *sattva guṇas*. So we can't see with the eyes of the soul. We are blind. But the self-realized spiritual master can enable us to see with spiritual vision. It's called *śāstra-cakṣus*, seeing through the eyes of the scriptures. *Ahaṁ brahmāsmi*, I am not this body. Spirit is eternal, and all forms of matter are temporary. Also, pure spirit is not formless but has form, although this is inconceivable to the impersonalists.

I once had a silly doubt. We can't remember our past lives. So what does it matter that after death, we get a new body? We don't know whether we've gained or lost, we just know we're in another body. What's the point of striving if we lose all consciousness of what we were and we just *are* again? Another body. Don't know how I got here. It seemed to me I wanted a proof for the mind, to substantiate transmigration. You'd actually see yourself going from your old body to your new body, something like that. Now I can't even remember it clearly, one of those things that no longer bother me. I have enough faith in *śāstra-cakṣus* to know what I *should* be doing. I should be striving to get a better next body, whether or not I get to "see" what my loss or gain is next time around. Perhaps you do see at the time of death, with great regret, or great joy.

How many versions? It's all
one. One life expressing the
same thing in different ways:
he has an emotional void and
tries to fill it with the wrong stuff.

"May you be happy in Kṛṣṇa
consciousness," all filled up and
never empty. Unless you reach
the "void" of Lord Caitanya and
the *gopīs*, which is a feeling of
ecstatic joy in reverse—"Where
is my Kṛṣṇa?"

Do we have a touch of that
when we're looking for something
else to satisfy us and it doesn't
work? Once again,
"life has no meaning,"
can't find Kṛṣṇa
so even if you become a famous
ballerina you want
to kill yourself.

Lucky those who contact
the transcendental reps who
have enough courage and faith
to speak it, present it,
even thrust it in your face

or insist even this abstract painting
is my search for the Lord.
Some seekers will see
it too and even prefer it to the
straight Hindu *dharma* too
quickly shoved down their throats.

My romance: *my* way is His
pleasure. Lord, are you coming
with me?

"Death where is thy sting?"
sings the baritone in
The Messiah. She's sure
that her redeemer lives—
makes your hairs stand
on end.
Where is thy sorrow? Turn
it all to "I'm missing

the Lord of Sorrows, the
Lord who teaches us in
ways like loss, gain
and guru's teachings.

Giovanni finally phoned Tim and said it was a good time to come down to the café for a private talk. Tim went, and they sat in the corner at a quiet table. Giovanni was serious.

"Well, my little paisan," said Giovanni, placing his hand on Tim's, "I told you I'm a'notta real astrologer. But I went to a professional one with your birth date, and he gave a'me a horoscope." Giovanni's face was very grave.

"The astrologer told me that you actually should'a be dead," Giovanni said. "Yeah, you should'a be dead right now. You jus' been going through a period where death has been very prominent in your stars. That period lasted from a'last December up'a ta just last week. He said he's surprised you didn't pass on already."

"So then things are all right?" asked Tim. "I don't have to worry about longevity?"

"Well, you gotta look at'a bright side, no? At least you're still alive. But the stars, they could be better. You gotta be careful. The astrologer, he also told me he gotta some special divine medicine for you. You gotta take it two months from now at a special time, just after the sunrise. You take it with some warm water after he chants some mantras on it, and den you take a'some ghee. I dunno. What da ya think?"

Tim said, "I think the guys in the sanatorium would laugh at me if they saw me doing it."

"I tinks you got nothin' to lose. No?" Giovanni looked deeply into Tim's eyes. "You have'a disease, no?"

"Yes," Tim admitted.

"It'sa cancer, no? In da colon?"

"Yes," Tim answered in a quiet way, "the doctors think they have it under control."

"So you can just tell 'em it's some new medicine that you try, since you tried everything else for your maladies."

"Hmm. I'll think about it, Giovanni. Thanks for the advice, and I'll come back to talk some more about whether I should do that. Will it cost a lot of money?"

"It'll cost something. Maybe I can help you wid it, or get a reduction since you're there at Kṛṣṇa's sanatorium."

Back at the sanatorium, the inmates said they wanted to continue watching the movie *Limelight.*

The monitor said, "These movies are just comedy therapy. This was a film Charlie Chaplin made in 1952, so we thought it was a comedy. But it turned out to be not. So I don't want you guys watching any more of this *Limelight.* Jeeze, it began with a girl trying to commit suicide, and Chaplin doesn't look like he does as the Tramp. So I don't want you to go to bed with these kinds of impressions on your mind."

"Don't tell us what we can do and can't do," said Tim. "We're here to get better, and if we want to watch this movie, you can't stop us. It's two hours long, and we'll just watch it in short segments and then get back to the slapstick." The monitor said no more and walked out.

They watched and got headaches. The ballerina, who thought she couldn't walk, found she could walk when Calvero (Chaplin) preached to her to fight, fight, fight! Then he got a small part as a comedian, but they walked out on him. He was washed up. But she got back into the chorus as a dancer again. Then she came home from her first performance and found him drunk. He said he wasn't funny because he wasn't drunk. Nothing funny about the film, but it's thoughtful. His moral preaching about how you have to fight and overcome your weakness. I guess he's going to help her, is that the idea? He'll pass on the "torch" of creativity to a young girl, and what will he do? What's it got to do with Kṛṣṇa consciousness?

I too have to fight. The doctor said that she had just a psychological condition which made her think she couldn't dance or walk. She got cured from that by Charlie's preaching, especially when *she* turned and preached to him when he felt defeated. I have to fight too. Overcome these headaches. But without medicine? Anyway, stay alive and keep practicing. Don't give up.

He'll be true rain or shine,
not afraid of rubber 'gator on the path,
envious but that's a wart
Kṛṣṇa will overlook

if we can just love each other
and do our own work—
they're having a huge Pāṇihāṭi festival and I'm staying home,
nothing wrong with that.

I can't remember the stories,
but I can . . . rain or shine
remember my master and be
with him at all times.

Kṛṣṇa, Kṛṣṇa. Kṛṣṇa Lord
Caitanya made it so easy,
you just say those names
rain or shine

and it doesn't matter if
you have long hair or short

you can walk or not
be able to. So many minor faults

but we do expect you to
grow up and be mature,
and to be kind, be glad to see a Vaiṣṇava or
even a groundhog and hug
a baby every day.

Do I get my chance to hold
Lakṣmaṇa Dāmodara and see
his toothless smile
and his mom say, "He likes Mahārāja"?
Maybe he sees me as just
an object, but I hug
him nevertheless.

Some say I haven't taken
my responsibility for wrongs,
betrayed them, dishonored
them, am a walking
ingrate. They are astonished
at the superficial letters and
can't imagine how I
write them except it's
my serious emotional
blockage.

Others think I'm smart
for picking out that
Rilke poem for *Among Friends*
and I think I should
follow my guru—that's
what the stars say will
bring me spiritual success
but I ought to drink some

divine water too.

Two quarts a day, smack
is back, stick him full
of pins, Lee Morgan
welcome. They do it
not the same but
spiritual life is varied, and as
for me, I'm just writing
this as fast as I can because
that's how
I've been self-trained.

A higher authority in the sanatorium came to tell the inmates that they could watch no more of *Limelight.*

A spokesperson for the inmates said, "It is good for us to watch this film. We saw how Charlie saved a suicide and although his philosophy was not complete, he argued in favor of the existence of human consciousness and said it was the rarest thing in the world. Then he found out that the girl had been in the hospital for five months with rheumatic fever and said that for the last five years she couldn't walk! The doctor was called, and he said that her disease was all mental. She had different tragedies in her life and had transferred this into some psychological paralysis of her legs. When Charlie heard this, he began to preach to her to fight! fight! and not allow herself to succumb to defeat. He told of his own heart attack, which came from drinking alcohol when he saw that he was a has-been comedian. Then he finally got another show for his own comedy act. But the audience walked out on him! His contract was broken. Now he knew that he was finished. He walked home to the apartment where he lived with the girl and put his head on the table in utter sadness and defeat. She then began strongly speaking to him in the same way he had spoken to her. She said, "You have to fight! You're the great Calvero. Don't say it's all over. Do what you told me to do. Don't give up! Don't give up!" And in the course of her speech, she suddenly found that she could walk. In miraculous rapture, she repeated again and again, "I can walk! I can walk!" And it was true. She was perfectly healed.

So this kind of picture is very inspiring to us. We want to hear also that if we keep up our spirits and fight, we don't have to remain always invalids in this sanatorium. We can get well again and be able to leave here and do our spiritual master's work more actively.

The higher authority said, "I heard there's some skimpy dressing scenes with the dancer."

Spokesperson: "Oh come on! It doesn't bother us! She's a beautiful girl, so what?"

The higher authority turned to the next authority in *paramparā* and said, "You can let them watch it. But supervise it and report to me if there's anything unpalatable. I don't want my authorities to get down on me for this. After all, we were only told they could have comedy therapy."

Comedy, tragedy, gloomy, elated—what do the ants say? They silently crawl over the writing desk and up and down the writer's arm. No comment from them when they are flipped by the human hand onto the floor. They go on walking, uncrippled, searching, exploring.

The doctor came to give a quick examination and interview with each inmate. He asked the writing staff, "Are you getting your writing done?"

"Oh yes sir, sometimes two sessions a day. But when a visitor comes, our scribe Swami Swims gets a headache. We are low on Depakote and Gabitril." He asked about constipation and the usual things.

"Will you lower the titration on these heavy drugs?"

"No, let's wait another week."

"We spend much time with an onset of a headache or the headache itself."

"Yes, yes. But I think you're doing better."

When asked, Tim said he was fine, and mentioned nothing about his private investigations into longevity, the fact that he should have been dead, or his concern about marriage. He said, "We just want to write this book and that will be our way of spreading Kṛṣṇa consciousness."

"Very good boy," said the doctor, and he walked over to the next bed.

Upstate New York. A siren goes off at noon. Why? Testing for a future air raid. Painted on a wall: I ♥ New York. Regional illusion. But I identify with this upper state. A New York dentist named Danz. Small towns named Chatham, Hudson, Saratoga Springs, where is the mighty Hudson River? Laid-back devotees of Stuyvesant Falls, just as I like it. The doctor told Swims, "Tell them to leave you alone." "But when a senior devotee comes, I can't do that."

Pay the price, pray the price. But don't give up the fight. You can overcome.

Don't be sad lad,
things is gonna turn out fine.
When love is new it seems
best and then illusion and quarrels
set in.

The romantic revives it.
In Kṛṣṇa's planet it is always new
always young and everyone is
beautiful to look at.

Wouldn't you like to go there?
You can pray from here.
Don't be delayed for millions of eons.
When love is new in this

world you promise your lover
things that don't come true.
It's full of pain or just gets
worn down to partnership
in a struggle downhill.

When love is new can be
achieved by the romantic
touch of the artist who
knows pain and transforms
it into something beautiful

and you can look at it or
hear it and be revived again.
Don't sing prayers in an old
groove. New. What does it
mean?

It means the eternal hope
of contact with Kṛṣṇa and
you have to stay alive and fight
for it and make your own life
and art a new one.

Don't leave behind the
old friends and lovers but
find the new that first
brought you together.

It can be revived.
And you have a part to play.
New friends, new
farce, the same ones but
they always look different
in Kṛṣṇa's eyes when
love is new.

Chapter Six

He got out of *kīrtana* and obligatory social dinner because his malady acted up just before *kīrtana*. It wasn't a fake. Now he can eat alone. Maybe someone will read BB to him. How does money come in? Don't be only attached to keeping friends who keep abusing you. Don't need them. Work on yourself. You don't have to be so social. Can't eat salad. Can't eat alone, even with BB, but no tape recorder for hearing Prabhupāda. It would be good too. His voice and arguments against the *mūḍhās*. Ask Śacī, he'll fix up a way. I used to always listen to His Divine Grace while eating.

Take your time eating, don't have to compete with others or inquire, inquire. Don't be bitchy now. But the doctor said don't do anything that you don't want to do. A quiet rainy Saturday can be left at that. Just a small tape recorder will do. Listen to A. C. Bhaktivedanta Swami and you'll be able to give his examples. Better than quiet. My friend will accommodate.

Orders came down from a higher committee: "No films except ISKCON and committee-approved old-time (no later than 1930) *comedy* films." The inmates were disappointed. They were told by their doctors to do whatever they wanted, not what someone else told them to do. This was part of the therapy cure, self-assertion. No more burnout by following orders. And they *could* learn from this instructive film. They remained silent and sullen. But when "Lights Out" occurred and the monitors left, the only non-inmate around was the *chaukīdār*, who stood outside the front entrance guarding them with a rifle. They paid him $25 and told him not to tell anyone they were staying up late to watch a film, and if any big shot came, he should knock loudly on the door before letting them in so they'd be warned and get back into their beds. Then they set up the VCR in one of the private rooms and watched *Limelight*. It was up to the scene where Charlie was drunk.

The inmates hope it wouldn't get degraded but continue to give them instructions. I'm telling you this confidentially, so you too please don't pass it on to any naysayers. I don't want to get into trouble. Come on, you're invited to watch the film. If it's not Kṛṣṇa conscious or we can't make it so, I'll stop. I won't give you bad sensous impressions.

Tear-jerker, slow Trane,
live while you can in
your gifted profession.

She really loved him, the
young ballerina supreme and
although he was old and washed up they
held a gala benefit for him
and he was great. They clapped
and demanded an encore
but he died of a heart attack
and too much drinking even as
he finished the last laugh on stage.

His young beloved would have to marry
the young man who loved her
and she could learn to love but
she'd never forget Calvero
who gave her life and sweetness
and inspiration. Love doesn't
depend on young or old.

What lesson did they learn?
The inmates all shed tears
when Calvero died. They
felt. Where was he going
in the next life? He gave
his all.
BB teaches us
there are many higher planets and liberation
is a fig. Calvero would
come back (he sang in a
comic song) as a salmon
in the sea. But more likely
it would be as a human
comedian. And he hadn't
learned the evils of drink.

But we cried and went to our beds,
glad we defied the order not
to watch the all-too-human
Limelight.

She'll dance on as long as she can.
Stars and stand-ins.
He changed his name.
I believe in God and good
theater. Like to make my own
slow Trane. He's writing
twice a day, indifferent if
a stern one doesn't give
forgiveness.

Just want to pour my heart out
and write fast and slow
and see the movies we like.

The upper committee was right. We shouldn't have watched that movie in three installments. It left mundane impressions. In one scene, the lovely ballerina who was the star of the show was about to enter from the wings when suddenly she panicked and said her legs were paralyzed again. Calvero shouts at her and slaps her in the face. She snaps out of it and goes on to dance nicely. Then he falls down on his knees and with "folded palms" prays "to whoever You are" that she please dance successfully. But that's not much, is it? Other than that, all we really learn is that you shouldn't drink whiskey, we see some of the ins and outs of the theater, learn life is sad, and that a young girl falls in love with an old man because he saved her from suicide and taught her to walk again. But when he died of a heart attack, you knew the young man—the piano composer who is always chasing her—would become her husband. Doesn't add up to much. And leaves you the next day with mundane impressions. Wasted time, too, could have caught up on *japa*, could have gone to bed early and gotten up early. A chance to think more of Kṛṣṇa than of the elder Charles Chaplin and his passionate philosophy for life. Just before Calvero died, after his final performance as he lay on a stretcher waiting for the ambulance, his last desire was to see her again. But she was on the wings about to go out and couldn't be called over to him. He made no prayers. He shut his eyes. So the old artist had passed on the torch to the new artist. Poignant, yes, and that's how we got sucked in. And he had sang that night, although in jest, that in his next life he'd like to be a salmon. The inmates felt somewhat embarrassed with themselves when they got up in the morning, and they chanted their prayers more earnestly.

So things are pretty much the same. Inmates reformed. Monitors out today on errands. Workmen hammering on flagstones in the backyard. Someone suggested we have an art day and everyone draw pictures. This led to a discussion on individuation. One man said, "Each *jiva* is unique and Lord Kṛṣṇa enjoys infinite varities of offerings. We should not attempt a 'leveling' process, as Kierkegaard said, making everyone the same. If someone doesn't feel like drawing or painting, why should he be forced?" "Yeah," another said, "we are always opposed by people who don't want us to express our individuality in coming to Kṛṣṇa. It started with our parents, who didn't want us to become Hare Kṛṣṇas. But we defied them and we were individual. Then in the temple, the 'filtering' process continued. Some authorities tried to get us to walk exactly in step as everyone else. If our individuality survived, then we survived."

Another said, "Even in the *Kṛṣṇa* book you read that when Kṛṣṇa played His flute on the full-moon autumn night, all the *gopīs* wanted to go, but there was a filtering process. Many of their concerned fathers told them not to go. They said, 'Dear father, I love you and know you mean no harm in trying to stop me'—but by their mad desire to see Kṛṣṇa, they ran out of the house. Some *gopīs* were detained in the house, maybe because they didn't exert enough ingenuity in getting out. Not enough *bhāva* yet. Some were physically confined and gave up their bodies in feelings of separation. So there is always objection to our expressing our own heart's desire to serve the Lord in our unique way.

Those who persist in being individual and original *jīvas* succeed in devotional service."

"I think you're overdoing it," said another. "Devotional service is like the razor's edge. It might be the voice of Māyā encouraging you to act in an 'original' way. It might be false ego to be 'individual.' We do have a guru and a path of instructions to follow."

"Yeah, but it's not like in the army. And even in the army, you can express some individuality. For example, in college they having marching bands. Some are very stiff and formal, but some dance all over the place and play original tunes."

"But I don't feel like drawing today," said big Bhaktin Jane. "I'm going to type as usual. Anyone object?"

"I'd like to draw," said Tim. The monitors went down the rows and those who wished to paint accepted the paraphernalia, and others did something else.

"*Japa* comes first," piped up Swami Swims, who was far behind in his quota—a concession, he said, to his medication, which made him sleepy.

He was hip to T.S. Eliot's
Four Quartets. I said I can't
read difficult poetry.
Such long chatting on the
phone. The day gets
chewed on for Swims and
he's still got only three
rounds done.

What else was there to do?
Counting by the numbers.
Hammer them flagstones.
Keep from getting a headache.
I *should* have a concession—
"my legs are paralyzed!"

Oh lovely one, it's only in
your head. Slap her face and she goes, her gorgeous
legs and ballet movements
unafraid before a thousand people.

Try acupuncture, divine water,
living alone, but really
alone. *Four Quartets?* Not
me "chanting by the numbers."
Inmates doing their own things
and liking it. Tim drawing
a picture of death
and in the corner a couple
is getting married and producing
babies. Counting by the
numbers. Can't coordinate—
did you just cheat yourself and count
six rounds instead
or five? Why can't you count, man?

What's the problem? I think
there's nothing wrong with me
and I'll just mosey along.
Love Chaplin but the tragedian,
too bad. Too bad. Jean
Shepherd tapes I told her about. Make another
poetry book.

Nandi, put it into shape.
Seems we got the Rilke poem
wrong. Doing our own thing,
listen to John. The music that is so important to us.

Let's hear the scholar tell
the pastime of Pāṇihāṭi
and *Bhagavad-gītā.* We
hardly talk in public.
Keep it on the page.

Enough physical touch for now.
But he touched Prabhupāda *mūrti*
today, Sunday, massage and wash
him and new clothes. How can
I leave him behind?

Too many books for busy people
to read. "What good will your
prayer do?" They left a note
outside the nuns' barred convent.
A note came out, "Our song
to God may mitigate the
sufferings"—or something like
that, profound prayer they were
doing

not just counting by the numbers.
Asking for intercession.
Any kind of recitation of Kṛṣṇa,
in jest, by mistake can
bring liberation. Even
counting by the numbers.

Stay awake and hear that
prayer in your head Hare Kṛṣṇa
Hare Kṛṣṇa . . . the tragedian
doesn't take your soul to
hell but freedom.

Swims wanted to write. Bebop. Things are loosening up in ISKCON, they say. Depends who you speak to. What did he want? What can we do? Bring more people.

"Now that I have a chance to speak to you I can't think of anything to say."

"Silence is eloquence." He wanted to warm up to romantic talk but she had an old man she wanted to marry. But he made her remember the first time they met when he was a shy musical composer and she was a shy young shopgirl in the store where he bought his music sheets. Sometimes she gave him extra sheets or extra change. The boss found out and she got fired for it. Her first romance.

We're talking business but therapy is also getting to know one another. Preparing a secluded house in northern California. Will it be too secluded there? I am not so social.

Swims wanted to write but now that he had the pen he couldn't think of what to say. "Silence is eloquence."

"What will you order?"

"Bacon, eggs and toast."

"I'll have the same."

Where are these *Limelight* lines going to lead you? Calvero, the washed-up alcoholic comedian, once world famous, now can hardly get a job.

Kṛṣṇa-kīrtana came over and I suggested we paint together, but I felt a headache coming on. Maybe next time. He also had some of his paintings with him, but I said I'd better not look at them now. Said maybe we or I could work with a smaller notepad with colored pencils. Can't get to it. I want to get his phone number.

He said he's reading *Śrīmad-Bhāgavatam* again. Has a small-sized copy of Third Canto, chapter one, where Vidura gets kicked out of the palace. He's read it many times but enjoys it. And he chants a round before going to work. I listened, enlivened, glad for him. My counselor told me to not mistreat the holy names by resenting them or punishing myself with them when I can't chant the quota.

It's a hard quota for me nowadays. Rain or shine, Swims wanted to write. In between maladies, sneak it in.

I know that Third Canto beginning, how he wanders and meets Uddhava, who tells him Kṛṣṇa pastimes but then sends him to Maitreya. Lots of nectar. Tells how the Lord appeared when He was about to leave this planet and His intimate friend Uddhava was present. Maitreya was less intimate, but just happened to be there and heard all that the Lord said to Uddhava as He sat under a small banyan tree. Why was it small? I forget. A reason for everything. I forget more as I grow older.

Gaṇeśa club for relieving constipation, orthopedic foot insert club, dolors club, but don't complain. "Oh oh, oh, oh, oh you beautiful doll." All the things swimming in the mind ready to pop up when we don't need them anymore. We need Hare Kṛṣṇa. "Breathe through your nose," coached Śacī as I punched the heavy Everlast bag. "Ten more seconds," he said. I was flailing, no more stamina or force to my punches. Rowing, stretching, workout.

She said she's picking out
the cherries from a file
of 300 poems. I thought
they are all cherries but
some small, misshapen,
not so tasty, others full blown
and best ripe.

Talk your head off. In your
heart do you really want
to go into a medical leave
of absence? Can you explain
it to them?

Step from one room to the
other and write or paint
and the bed and toilet are
right nearby.

Tell them I'll write.
You write to me.
Tell the neighbor swami
I've come to be alone.
Come to try a seclusion
I claimed I wanted.

He has an unusual style and we
are all waiting for him to finish.
Waiting for someone to come.

Swims wanted to write but he was an unrealized punk and couldn't hold out for as long as these youngsters. Who was able to tell the truth in his own way?

Kṛṣṇa is the summit; we are trying to tell people to surrender to Him. On *parikrama*, make your wish and it will come true. Live in the *dhāma*, at least in your mind. Wish "I want pure devotional service." His last performance and then he dies. Leave it documented and we can hear it in our spare time. All part of the same poem. The imperfect looking for perfection. Leave them behind if they don't like your individual word.

Somebody gave me something to steal. "Hunger knows no shame" (shy musical composer).

Swims wanted to write but resisted restraint and training. Did it his way. Asked them to publish it. They said we can't understand it, we are from France. We want to hear of Rādhā-kuṇḍa. Why this stuff from Africa and U.S.A., ignorant countries, and you are making no attempt to take responsibility for your wrongs and your disoriented, disturbed mind.

Why should we listen? Why do you insist? Give us another player more straight who will quote lots of *śāstra*, stories, and ask for Food for Life.

Swims wants to write but he should get horse-trained, horsewhipped. Who is he writing for? Wants his book in the East West Bookstore in New York City, East Village. Five copies sold. He's an insider to the devotional service crowd. Not supposed to see any value in matter, not supposed to see what I see. No touch! No touch with matter. No more contact.

Die, Charlie, die, you have to so the plot works out because the young girl can't become a nun married to an old man and die because you're mortal and drank too much liquor. Die so we can end the movie and put the white sheet over your body and we can turn off the TV.

Die, Charlie, like you knew. "I think I'm dying. Can I see her one more time?" People grouped around him but no one with *tulasī* leaf or Ganges or holy name. Ignoble departure after a frivolous comedy act. Last burst of fame. They applauded and what good did it do him?

Die, Charlie, die. You will be remembered in the archives for your movie.

Live, Charlie. I identify with all *jivas* good and bad because they are all sons of God. Dostoevsky saw the potential of being saintly or demonic. He said humanity was like an anthill full of ants, all the same. The individual act is so rare.

Offer something to Kṛṣṇa. Is this it, Swims, the best you can do? It appears to be right now. All right, all right . . .

"I'll be gone for two hours," said
Śacī, definitely. There may have
been something I wanted him to do
for me but he was firm. I am
quiet, alone indoors on a steady
rainy Memorial Day. The flags
are all wet. Isn't this what
you wanted?

"Don't abuse the holy name."
I don't want to abuse Her,
I just want to stay awake
and alert and remember Swamiji and
all the many quotes that
this is the topmost act.

Maybe it's my illness or the
meds. Nothing to blame on my
side. Saturday rainy. Two
hours to myself. Make as much
progress as you can.

Like it here? Yes, pretty much, when
the obligation sense is dropped.
Leave him alone. He's finding
his own way to present something.
"Whew," he exhales.

"After all this, how can you be so
superficial, irresponsible and unredeemed?"
Who me? Show me another
short slapstick and I'll get out
of these blues or

Konitz with Marsh playing "Topsy."[1]
Come on, don't frown,
it's one way of serving Kṛṣṇa,
and not the worst by far
creates melodies
in the heart.

Swimsji likes to write, can you blame him? It's such a hurdy-gurdy, hurly-burly way. Even the best higher knowledge is contained in writings, the *Vedas*, the *āgamas*, the *smṛtis*, *tantras*, *Purāṇas*, etc. It appears from BB that these books are *persons* too.

Swimsji likes to write in a hundred acres. On a rainy Memorial Day with no parade. No Boy Scouts, no cheerleaders, no bands or drums. It's all rained out and the picnic will have to be indoors. The racetrack too muddy. Save your money for a worthy cause, not drink. The water rolls down the eaves and keeps the kiddies indoors, where it's harder for the moms to keep them from fighting and crying. Turn on the TV, the sucker tube, and put them in a daze.

Swims has a picture on his wall of a child praying. It's not sentimental. Beautiful. Should remind him to pray. God is on our side, but we're not too sure—in fact, we know our praying is poor. Not like those locked-up nuns, I bet. They pray for the sake of praising, gratitude, and for improvement of the world.

Saturday rain. It's perfect for prayer. You've got a chair (don't like the floor yogic pose), beads if you can learn to coordinate them backwards and forwards (gets that bad). Yes, a perfect time for prayer. And a perfect mantra blessed by a perfect guru in *paramparā*. Is that inviting enough for you, call to you again? Just the names, that's all that's asked of you at this point.

While it rains, save yourself and filter it out to all the worlds. Best welfare work, though it seems inactive. They say the sanatorium is for repair so you can go out and really preach, but the beads Prabhu, properly handled, are also as good as any mighty welfare work.

Swims likes to write, but he just wrote himself into a happy corner—so he'll put down his pen and pick up his awkward, thorny beads. She *really* thought he was waning when he said *japa* had become "exquisite torture." Broke her already-broken faith. Why did he say that? The Ramakrishna people tease, "*japa* is the Vaiṣṇavas' ordeal." Was I punning on them or did I mean it? It shouldn't have slipped out of my lips. It's no grind. We all love to practice it, don't we? Here I go.

Don't blame me for lying and
betraying. Why not? Why should
I let you off the hook?
Because I ask you to.
If this keeps up much longer,
we'll just have to let it go.

Said his sixteen rounds, well almost,
got confused at fifteen
whether he said it twice and just squeezed out
another. Preferred a phone call,
and laid back in bed.

So social in his virtual relationships
by mail, e-mail. Didn't take the
snack today. Well your letter
didn't admit what she wanted—
you haven't taken deep responsibility
for your wrongs and it's because you're
emotionally blocked, sick, can't
see the depth of human feelings.

Can't see how you hurt others. Maybe
but he's become a self-assertive
twirp and speaks up for his side.
In the rivalry between the Yankees
and the Brooklyn Dodgers you know
where his sympathies lie.

Pray but before you put
your offering on the altar go
make up a quarrel you had,
then God will accept it.
Don't be a fraud.

Yeah but I can't accept all
that shit they throw on my
head. It's got to stop or we
should stop and regard
each other as well-wishers
without fighting e-mails.
Just cool down and do your own
work. Say "we lack the broader
vision that would enable each
of us to see it as the other
sees it—and yet be true
to yourself. Not a person
created and possessed by another."
Both pray, everyone pray.
I think I did sixteen, I could go back
and try that one over
again. Where was your
mind? In Siberia, rabbits, a poem,
a magazine, a blank stare into
an empty video screen and the
long drag of hours alone on
this rainy day. You'd better
pray or such solitude is for
nuts.

Tough Mr. Barks strode into the sanatorium and into the writing staff's private room. He went over to Big Jane's desk and with his hands on his hips stood over her.

He said, "Hey Jane, let's take a spin on my motorcycle."

Jane looked up from her typewriter and said, "I already told you I prefer not to. Now leave me alone to work. Why don't you go into our temple room and chant Hare Kṛṣṇa?"

"I'm not interested in that mush," he said, "I want you." Jane stood up and stepped around the typewriter, facing him. She was wearing a Prabhupāda T-shirt, feeling tight on her big breasts and her big biceps also. Tough Barks wore a black T-shirt. He didn't have soft breasts but a massive, hard chest and bigger biceps than hers. But what he didn't know was that Jane was also a karate expert.

Swami Swims spoke up: "Didn't you hear what she said, Mr. Barks? She wants to be left alone. We've got important work to do."

Mr. Barks looked over at the Swami and said, "Shut up your face, cripple, or I'll break it for you and give you a *real* migraine."

On hearing those words, Bhaktin Jane swung her right arm and with the heel of her right hand hit Barks right under the bridge of his nose. In karate, there are three stages of force for this punch. The third force pushes the bridge of the nose into the brain and kills the opponent. Jane hit him to the second degree. She then swiftly lowered her hand and with the same punch, using the heel of the right hand, she hit him hard in the groin. Barks bent over and without any dignity cried with pain. He turned and stumbled out of the room. But before he left, Jane gave him a good boot in the ass.

The workers were silent. Jane said, "Vaiṣṇavas are peaceful and never hurt living entities, but when demons attack, they can attack back. Especially if a Vaiṣṇava is insulted. That's the worst offense," and she nodded toward Swami Swims.

Swami Swims stood and with folded palms politely said to Jane, "Thank you very much, Prabhu."

Tim then said, "It's getting late. Why don't we watch a comedy video?" A good idea to change the mood. They watched a short early film which began with Charlie being let out of jail. Immediately at the gate he's met by a bearded minister with a Bible. It's a silent movie, but the subtitle says, "You've got to go straight." Charlie looks very repentant and starts to cry and dries his eyes on the minister's long beard. He looks like he'll do good now and walks off resolute. But within minutes he sees that same minister preaching to a drunken man, and while he does so, the minister steals the man's watch. Charlie then returns to a life of crime. Twice during the film he meets religious people who give him the line, "You've got to go straight," and as soon as he hears the words, Charlie starts searching his pockets to see if they've stolen anything. All ends well as Charlie has a good heart that heals itself. He and an ex-cellmate are trying to rob a house. They steal what they can from the first floor, but beautiful Edna Purviance tells them please not to go upstairs, her mother is very ill and will die by the shock. The cellmate wants to go upstairs, but Charlie has already taken an affection to Edna and fights with his cellmate. When the cops finally come, the cellmate has escaped and they arrest Charlie, but Edna says, "He's my husband!" and the police leave him alone and leave. She then gives Charlie a golden coin, and he happily takes leave. Then with his back to the camera, he holds up his arms to heaven in a kind of "hallelujah" sign. He had gone straight in his own way by protecting the lovely girl from the more evil criminal.

"Lights Outs" was soon called. The boys went to their beds, and Jane to her separate room. Before she left, the boys all thanked her again. It hadn't been such a funny film. They had seen enough fisticuffs in real life just a few minutes before. The boys all tried to sleep, but all they could think of was the face of the chaste and kind Edna Purviance. Jane's was not as pretty. As if reading their minds, Swami Swims spoke out in the dark, "Don't forget Kṛṣṇa."

They've heard it
before, they play and I played
with Baby Lakṣmaṇa.

Maybe you shouldn't go so
solitary in California, at least
not for long. That's what
brought on your anxiety.

That's our opinion. It is nice
here in the sanatorium.
There you'd be on your own. But servants
are a factor. He is *in* your face.
Here you are surrounded by a family

but you're left alone. They don't want lectures
and you're not able to give them.
They empathize.

Empathic. Is that the word
she used? She said I'm failing
in many ways at this skill,
anxious only about my own
drives. Don't care about the people
enough.

Okay I'll call them up and try
to treat them better. He
writes empathically but doesn't
live that way. If they disagree
he drops them. Doesn't show,
tell I know what you've been
through for me.

I said you betrayed me just because
you spoke up with the voice of reason
to protect me.

Seabiscuit—an hour of horse
video. Come on, you're not
going to watch that are you? How
will it filter into a Kṛṣṇa conscious
book?

"Ysabel's Table Dance."[2]
I never watched a Charlie
Chaplin movie. Your baby
always wears overalls. Because he's too
fat for pants. I love to
see him every day.

So maybe this is better
for me than seclusion.
I still have this bullet-
proof room. And people
to see is good. You'll
get headaches wherever
you live. Don't try the all-seclusion
again. That's what she advised
me.

And she said you are mean and
harsh and never empathic.
I only spoke out against your
deeds for your own protection.

Okay, I'll have to decide for
myself and the subpersons.
Would it be best to stay
here mostly and just take
a two-month vacation there?

I'm talking about myself again.
Say it's someone else, why

fool around? I try to phone
the people I have hurt but they are
not home and I don't have
the right numbers. Tell
them I see their version and
here's my version so don't
depart from me.

"Can you take such seclusion?" a friend questions. Is that what brought you anxiety? You just had it in Ireland. No, it wasn't seclusion, it was all the crazy stuff that was going on. Give it a chance. With a painting loft. Swims was thinking of getting a medical discharge from the sanatorium for maybe six months to go for a medical retreat.

Don't hurt people. Be empathic. What's in that mail? Take what you need from a situation and leave the rest. Care for the people who work for you. But care for yourself. Leave the golden gift that maybe only comes in relaxed, meditative seclusion. Figure out how you can do it.

Birds chirp. He's gone to Jersey. Speak up at the table sometimes and say what *you* are doing. You have problems in human relationships. People have fried you. Mocked you. You don't trust. No open friendships. You're shy to show them a new book. Official philosophy. You are changing. You don't give spiritual guidance. "What do you mean, that I should speak more from the *śāstras?*"

Talking on the phone, hashing it out. Where do we go from here? I'm not sure. We invested a lot in this but maybe it's tailing out. I'll try to find a way to be empathic for what you have been through, how I neglected the health, love and service you offered. Tough case. Says I write mean letters, demanding too much. See it the other person's way, what they are going through. Acknowledge it.

"Give me three months of *real seclusion.*" It's good you also live around people. But institutional remnants . . . pick the right people to be on hand, to help you. He'll go back and forth to different modes of living. If he doesn't live up to expectations, I can leave. No one is forced.

"What did you think of Claire Bloom in *Limelight,*" asked Swims.

"She was gorgeous," said Tim. Why should a swami ask such a question?, he thought. Are they really going to watch that hour-long movie about a horse?

"How about W.C. Fields in a shorty, *The Fatal Glass of Beer*?" That sounds good, although I am also interested in horses. A package arrives, three homemade CDs of devotees chanting Hare Kṛṣṇa in Estonia. They describe how good it is there and ask for a donation. Can we afford to be so generous? Where is Estonia? Send them a book.

He said he had no time to read. Imagine. We go to all this trouble and they have no time to read it. The written word. But KK had a cookout at his house and he didn't attend it. He said, "I'd rather read." Doesn't like big crowds.

What do you want from them? To take this as gold. At least read some of it. It's not the best in the world, and I know you have pressing duties. Can you press my khakis? I don't need my swami uniform pressed, just fold it for when we have to go to marching practice and receive *pukka* guests. I've got a drawer full. Lots of underwear too. Thirteen *japa* rounds by 4:00 P.M. and a poem to go, if you don't get interrupted. Eat alone if you're lucky. It's a good Tuesday. He passed on someone's opinion that seclusion was not good, but the California patrons shot it down. "Good," he said, "that she's making you think about it." Can the dove leave the dovecote and do something worthy on her own and return better for it?

I want to hear the whole thing
but got cut off in the beginning.
Yes it's got me mesmerized,
left my door open.

Tricks. Requests. Be careful
you don't ask for too much.
Fix up that art room so it
will be more inviting. It's
important to you and some others.

Yes I'll ask. Go in and
see what's missing. How did
you used to do it? Was it
imitating anyone? Let's hear
the defense again for
free hand. Michelle Cassou,
Dattātreya said he'd been
blooped for fifteen years and
when he saw my paintings
at the New York Ratha-yātrā he
came completely alive and returned
to Kṛṣṇa consciousness.

Just get in there and try "for
Kṛṣṇa." Pave the way.
What's wrong with seclusion
in California? What's wrong
with having Lakṣmaṇa
every day?

No smoking in public.
No drinking while driving.
No picking up girls or even
dreaming of them or
reading books of men and women.

"I love you. I want to marry you.
I'd do anything for you."
Charlie: "No, it's impossible.
I'm an old man."

Don't indulge in that. She
went on dancing and he died
just outside the theater
after his last act.

I gained somehow and will
find a way to tell you why
the *New York Times* voted it
one of the ten best films and Chaplin
got an Oscar for Best
Dramatic Score (he wrote
the screenplay, was director, and
wrote the music).

They perform plays in Goloka.
Spontaneous, rehearsed.
Oh boy, this is walking a
thin line but we've got
to tell our story and get
through those forces who
try to "filter" us, hold
us back by citing the
rules. I'm not against.

Chapter Seven

Junior Barks dropped by. He said his father was thinking of bringing Bhaktin Jane to court for assault. She said, "I was merely acting in self-defense after his verbal assaults. If he wants to talk anymore about it, he can talk through our lawyer."

"He said he would drop his charges if you would write a letter of apology."

Bhaktin Jane inserted a fresh piece of paper in her typewriter and immediately wrote a note:

"Dear Mr. Barks, All glories to Kṛṣṇa! I apologize for being so rough with you. But you should not insult the Vaiṣṇavas or make proposals to ladies who don't want to associate with you. You are not welcome here when you come with that attitude. Sincerely, Bhaktin Jane."

She gave the note to Junior Barks, who glanced over it, folded it and put it in his pocket.

"I've come for another reason," he said. "Bhakta Tim told me that you watched a long nonfunny movie, *Limelight*." The writing staff looked disapprovingly at Tim.

Junior Barks continued. "So I can see your book is really going to the dogs. I'll give you another more Kṛṣṇa conscious paragraph now and then, if you'd like. My approaches to the big publishers and the anti-

ISKCON forces haven't been very successful. So I'm willing to help you."

"That's nice," said Swami Swims. "Bring something in and we'll see if we can insert it." Junior Barks nodded and left the room.

Two days later he submitted an essay under the door:

"Kṛṣṇa consciousness is the science of God. Other religions teach only vague concepts of God and eternal life. In the very beginning of the primary book of Kṛṣṇa consciousness, *Bhagavad-gītā,* we are taught what is not even found in advanced books of other scriptures and commentaries.

"Within the body of a living being there is an eternal spirit spark. Even when the body dies, the soul does not, *na hanyate hanyamāne śarīre.* According to his deeds, he goes on to take another body. Only in the human form of life does one have the developed consciousness to be aware of the chance to improve one's life so that in the next life, the soul will inhabit a superior body. The best body, of course, is one that will not suffer the miseries of birth, death, disease and old age, which are common to all mortal beings. When the soul is liberated, he can attain a body of eternity, bliss and knowledge. This is the goal of Kṛṣṇa consciousness. Formerly it was very difficult to achieve this. In the present age (the age of Kali), it is even more difficult because people are so fallen.

"So the Supreme Lord Kṛṣṇa appeared in the form of His own pure devotee, Lord Caitanya, and taught the easiest possible method, the chanting of His holy names, 'Hare Kṛṣṇa, Hare Kṛṣṇa, Kṛṣṇa Kṛṣṇa, Hare Hare, /Hare Rāma, Hare Rāma, Rāma Rāma, Hare Hare.' Just by chanting this name, especially if one does it under the guidance of the spiritual master and under regulations, he has a good opportunity to attain liberation and ascension to the spiritual world. Signed, Junior Barks."

Swami Swims had read the note out loud. "Any objections?," he asked the other staff members.

"No," they said in unison. "Let's use it, even though it's the same thing he said before. He put it nicely."

"And unlike his father," said Jane, "he's cooperative and wants to work with us. Maybe it will have a good effect on his dad."

"But don't forget to tell him," said a copy editor, "that there's no money or contracts involved. He freely submitted it, and we'll freely accept it. You have to be careful when dealing with these Barks people."

"And Tim," said Swami Swims, "why are you blabbing to Junior Barks about our private affairs here and what movies we watch?"

Tim hung his head regretfully and said, "I won't do it anymore."

Bhaktin Jane typed another note:

"Dear Junior Barks, we are honored to accept your essay and have included it in our book *Sanatorium.* None of us accept any royalties for what we are doing. It is pure devotional service. So please don't hassle us about payments or anything like that. We welcome more writing by you."

She gave it to Tim to mail.

Lament (Apply to Anyone You Loved)

Sorry he's gone, take time
to lament even though you know
the soul doesn't die. You
lament maybe that he didn't

make his life better although he
was brilliant in so many ways
and compassionate and sweet and funny.

And you lament he's been taken
from your company.

It's your tears shedding, he's
gone off somewhere else but
a rare-to-find good friend
is not around.

You go about your business,
the world spins and no one much
notices—many never knew
him or heard his name and
don't care.

All right, pick up your life,
remember his good qualities
and keep them with you,
tell others how good he was,
feel the pain.

I don't want to drain this,
even a lament can be too
long when there are children
who don't know
death only their *annamaya*
needs.

And adults too get sore
buttocks sitting on the floor,
swatting flies in the heat.

Goodbye dear friend, at least
we have your legacy,
and that's plenty.

Swims likes to write and he likes to edit. He likes his friends and tries to help his guru. His guru told him his name means "the inner form of truth." So why lie to protect his butt? It's not like him. Tell the truth and pay the consequences. And it will be done. There will be nothing left to say, nothing to hide. "I don't know you intimately enough to tell you about it"—try that one. But not before the Supreme Court.

Punitive measures. You can't paint. Cut off his hands or just his thumbs. Don't be so afraid, where there's smoke there's fire, but I didn't hear the bell go off yet. Let's enjoy the picnic while we can and construct a bomb shelter where it doesn't matter. Don't copy your own paintings. What you paint comes from God. Wonderful sayings of the artists who never grew up.

They have pet horses on that farm, and the trainer lets them out daily to run around. Don't let them trample you. A friend recommended I get pet rabbits and let them out to roam around the house. When they get friendly, they jump in the air, turn somersaults, and ease your anxiety, while the cats hunt the mice. I think it would be nice.

You wouldn't have to be alone so long. You have no place to live, they can always kick you out. Death finally does. Up the stairs. You can live alone, anywhere, and don't get dreary. It's the rainy season. Do you have enough canvasses? Any desire to paint? After your sixteenth round, you go speaking of Michelangelo. Is there any energy left? Not such a good day, my friend. Why did "Joe" (we gave the right-eye pain that name) act up so? He knew what was coming.

Can I come and see you? Yes, you'd better, before it's too late. But don't stay long. The writing staff are serious to turn out as many volumes as possible in between disturbances and the regimentation of the house rules.

You can't see with the ointment of love. You sat before the altar and noticed the varnish stain in the shapely *siṁhāsana*. In blurry vision, not with your heart. "Don't make it [Deity worship] a farce," said Śrīla Prabhupāda. When you're ready for it, then it is required.

He made a list of those he wounded. Try to attend to each one and demonstrate, "I know what it's like to be in your shoes." I'm sorry I abused you so much and did so much damage. I'm sorry for the mistakes I made. I can't "edit" them out. Guilty as accused. Walks in chains. No, that's not in store for me, but many folks are subjected to that, to prison life. I know a few. His external life was "paltry" (almost blind, confined), but his prayer life sounded more active than anyone I know. And the locked-in nuns, almost like prison, they chose.

You think you can get some release. Live true to your God and conscience. Isn't that the point?

The Kṛṣṇa conscious boy
went home and made his
prayers sincere. His parents
were also devotees.

We're rooted to this earth
and all the worries about
what may happen.

That's the anxiety reform
he seeks. Just live a day
at a time and take this
with truth and consultation.

See a lawyer who knows
how to do it. When the
time comes, and it may never.

The great theater star died
penniless. No one cared
for him. But a steady
devotee knows no fame
he wishes to be with
his Lord in *kīrtana* and
smaraṇam, in service
with hand and foot.

Jumping rabbits? Fly
to California? Are you
up to that? I dunno.
Give me the medicine
before I go and a password
and something like Bud Powell
and Bach CDs. And *bhajanas?*

I must have friends. I
must go and try out
the flexible attempt he's
offering me and not think a
little seclusion will ruin
me. Seeing people is
also nice.

Swims has got so much paperwork, e-mails and phone calls—he instigates some and some come in, and so that he hasn't written in two days. They're building a flower garden just outside this window, moms and loud kids. No wonder W.C. Fields didn't like kids. But I like them, sure. I hold Lakṣmaṇa for five minutes and I love it, says Swims. But then you've got to hand him back to his mom or he breaks your neck beads or bends your eyeglasses out of shape, all in gleeful, toothless spirit.

So much paperwork. There are three more Chaplin films that we're allowed to order. But don't watch *Seabiscuit*, which he sent unsolicited. "Are you interested in horses?," Swami asked two inmates and they both said, "No." But he's curious because the man who sent it said, "It's a great comeback story."

"Yeah, but if we watch it, it will go into the book. And I don't want to be writing all about horses." Rain suddenly starts to pour and the garden work is over. Kids scream in protest. It must be a hard life to be a mother. They'll be even more ill-tempered indoors. Local dogs barking.

The sanatorium provides many facilities. There's a prospect of an acupuncturist coming. And a counselor who goes bed to bed tending to each patient from the psychological point of view. There are several counselors with different viewpoints. One tries to find out the *varṇa* and *āśrama* of the patient and guide him toward a suitable occupation. Remember, however, in this sanatorium almost all the inmates have serious physical illnesses, and that's the main reason they're there. So doctors of all shapes and sizes and approaches visit. Some say the root of the physical disease is the mind and use depth psychology to try and find out what has brought on this condition, whether it is anxiety disorder or paralysis of the legs, concussion or whatever. Healers come for that. And pure spiritualist healers who teach to pray and don't even worry whether your body recovers.

Chant your rounds and the health will follow. Some of the inmates who have been in the sanatorium for years switch regimens, with no success. The caretakers are kind and determine that the inmates are actually ill, not loafers and freeloaders. They may have intractable diseases.

But Swims has been receiving letters from a friend saying he should not occupy himself so much with crisis (immediate troubles and worries and fears), but he and his steady counselor should go down to the roots of psychosis and only then will he be cured. What does she mean? He's got to go a step at a time. So many letters to answer, he can't stop publishing.

Someone accused him of making publishing too high a priority in life, above care of others, above reciprocating love, above daily *sādhana*, above health care. It's a passion. SK had it too, and published at his own expense. He collapsed in the street carrying home the last of his inheritance from his father, and he was taken home, where he died. Was it worth it, giving up Regina, being the object of mockery from cruel citizens of Copenhagen? Yes, many in the world today, centuries later, will say, "We have his books, which change the whole current of the world's philosophy from objective to subjective, exalted the individual and give great hope to the theists against the intellectual atheist philosophers."

It's his passion. How far can you tell truth? He worries. "Don't be so afraid, ISKCON isn't like that anymore. They'll have compassion, but not if you lie."

Headache Journal arrives with the same old feature story: "The Problem May Be in Your Medicine Chest." Yeah, Charlie, I heard it before, lie down beside me and feel this pain. Hail Mary full of grace. Holy face of Gaura-Nitāi. The human race has received the mercy of the mantra method, so go and do your bit, if nothing else.

That's not what I thought
was coming. My heart stood
still when I discovered
my friend had come back
to serve with me.

Ask her to travel with you
everywhere and be your secretary

and cook and private
typist. She can teach you
empathy. Don't let her
get away again.

"Hey guys, Swims wants us
to watch a horse film!"
They guffawed. He was
getting too liberal for some.

But they respected him and
loved him, although his
ratings in those areas were
lowering because of his
lack of empathy for
fellow workers.

"I learned my lesson.
I'm going to be kinder.
I just want a little freedom
and solitude."

Wouldn't it be nice if we
were fit for solicitude
and could do *tapasya* and
gain direct sight of Kṛṣṇa?

Third-class devotees see God
in temple and say, "Okay
He's God." *Madhyama-*
adhikārīs hear of Govardhana lifting
and say "Maybe. It's in the
śāstras after all." But first-class know
Him directly with
full conviction.

The rain has stopped. The
gardeners are going out.
I'm supposed to be a
guru and answer questions
"shooting from the hip" (shooting bull?) for
our magazine.

The problem is in the stars,
the medicine chest,
my karma, I accept,
I accept and don't give up
affection for the Vaiṣṇavas.

How's that for a little testimony?
Not as good as
Bags Groove?[1]

It's a Saturday and all the sanatorium officers have taken the day off. So two workers who are banging flagstones into place just outside the sanatorium's front door have taken the liberty to turn their radio on for rock music while they work. The inmates feel shy and powerless to tell them to turn their radio off (Jane would do it but Swims told her not to).

"Does that mean all day we have to put up with this 'mood' music and racket?"

"Well, they're laborers and they feel it's their right to get a little entertainment while they work. They probably see us as sickies."

"People should care more for each others' feelings."

"Yes, I want to write an essay on that," said Swami Swims, "on empathy. I'm just beginning to learn about it."

Some inmates put in ear plugs and shut the windows—although it was a nice spring day—and those with private rooms shut their doors.

"Listen to this," said Swamiji, "Nitai is disappointed in me because I said if he visits me I can only see him for an hour." Just see it from his point of view. He writes: "Oh! I wish I did not have to write this but I can't hide anything from you. When I first read that I could only meet you for one hour during my visit to the U.S., my nonsensical mind made me feel somewhat like you felt when you visited Prabhupāda at 26 Second Avenue after the very first initiation in ISKCON and were served some grapes by Śrīla Prabhupāda. You felt that you had done so much work and all you got were a few grapes. So when I read that I could visit you for one hour—my mind made me think—I am trying somewhat hard to serve my Guru Mahārāja and I'll be traveling thousands of miles, and all I will get is one hour. Hare Kṛṣṇa!"

I'll have to phone him and show empathy. But he needs to know I'm in this sanatorium because if I talk to someone intensely—someone with high expectations—I'll get a headache pretty soon. Empathy.

"Is that the same as sympathy?"

"No, it's a little different," said Swami. "It means you not only pity someone but you really identify with them. You don't have to agree with them, but you are able to get inside their skin, in their shoes and see the world as they do. Just the opposite of being totally self-absorbed. And you know what? They say most sick people tend to be self-absorbed. Like we have no empathy for these flagstone workers with their radio.

"Let's stop talking so much," said Swims. "Look at Janey's example. She's typing, not talking. I've got to concentrate to write."

When he tried to concentrate, Swami remembered the short walk he had yesterday with Śacī. The neighborhood is generally peaceful. Swamiji felt his ankle ache and said, "I forgot my cane." Then suddenly they saw three or four scowly-faced young guys and one young woman come out of a house and get into their car. No friendly exchanges with Śacī. Tattoo on the bare arm of the driver. After they disappeared, Swamiji asked, "Do you know them?"

"No," he said, "but they were definitely sizing me up." Śacī has bigger muscles and more tattoos than any of them. But Swims is obviously what Bukowski[2] called himself in his later books, "an old fart." Śacī said a few years ago he saw a young tough in the neighborhood wearing one of the T-shirts they make at their factory, with the name of a straightedge band, Breed Hate. He greeted the guy, "Do you like Breed Hate?"

"Whatever, old man," the ruffian replied.

"He called me an old man."

"How did you feel?"

"I just laughed to myself. It showed me how out of touch I am with the younger kids."

The Swami somehow kept thinking of that phrase, "Whatever, old man," and he didn't like that it was directed at Śacī. When they worked out in the gym that morning and Swims took his turn at the heavy punching bag, he imagined that guy who said, "Whatever, old man," and he hit harder and harder, as if right in his face.

Come on now, concentrate. Write something Kṛṣṇa conscious. This is. Do I have empathy for that young punk? No. But I'll laugh it off, like Śacī. Kṛṣṇa is so kind he lets everyone come to this world and act out their little role for awhile. Concentrate on your own *japa*. Be tolerant. Our family is mending. Kaiśori is back.

Just be yourself. "I can only see you for one hour." These guys are working hard with the flagstones and charging a high price. Śacī has been too busy to read BB to me. Can I read it myself? Seems not. I listen to Prabhupāda. Don't doubt, he said. Don't attend phony *bhāgavata-saptāha* meetings. Be a good student of a bona fide spiritual master and it will be potent.

Oh complainin'. I'm so glad
I'm back on good terms.
Wear your regular clothes,
be yourself.

Be yourself, don't put on
an act for me. That's not
what I need now. Maybe
I'll wear my "Cleveland
Rathā-yātrā" T-shirt and
khakis. Back and forth
from the dentist's and seeing
visiting heroes and friends.

And Śacī watching that I
take my meds. When are
you going to learn to take
care of yourself?

They are performing pretty well.
I claim it's for God if it's
done from the heart.

That's why I want to
be among their number.
They are dedicated and even
if their lives are very
faulty, they dedicate
to the art

and I claim that's a way
of pleasing people
for God. Yeah they don't
know better.

But in a way they do
know the universal need
of we sad humans with
our selfish needs and cutthroat
deeds.

We need our hearts softened
to cry and laugh.
God? No hypocrites
as they see in so many priests.

But there are true holy men
of course who give the
straight instructions we
need best from the *Vedas*
like BG up to BB.

So we're showing them
all humans are capable
of approaching
and we devotees are capable
of approaching them
and we are both ordinary *jīvas*

but there's something special
in our Deity room, come and
see Gaura-Nitāi and the words
we sing, eat our *prasāda.*

We are like you but there's
something different,
you've got it too.

By midday it began to rain and the flagstone workers went home, thank God. But many of the inmates were manifesting their illnesses from the anxiety of the morning. They felt they couldn't do the little jobs or amusements they usually did, or take a walk or do exercise.

Swami Swims forced himself to keep writing, although a top-head headache was bothering him all morning. "I'll write a little, take Ambien and go to bed. Can't answer letters. Can't show empathy right now. Forgive myself. At least sixteen rounds done." Push the pen like a *japa* bead—Hare Kṛṣṇa. "I've gone beyond wondering why I have this or why You have sent it. Thy will be done, not mine. And I'll meet the visitors and take what med I need. Each sentence is a mantra in disguise. A poem is a prayer, in my language. I couldn't watch *Seabiscuit*, or even a short Charlie, even if I wanted to."

"Have you ever loved?" someone asked him once, and added, "that's a rascal question." Emotional blockage, selfish fellow. In his anxiety illness lies his bastardliness some say. But his counseling friend says, "I don't think there's anything wrong with you. Prabhupāda and Kṛṣṇa are in your heart."

For some "good" reason the inmates have to suffer a little. Emerson: "When the sky is dark the stars are brighter." Can they see better or just become self-absorbed and addicted to pain relief? "The problem may be in your medicine chest."

The problem is no problem, it's just what it is. Consider the millions in Africa and Eastern countries or even American ghettoes who don't know where their next meal is coming from or whether they'll be killed by a mugger on their walk. The severe, hopeless cases who are not in "sanatoriums" but intensive care units, oxygen tanks, plugged in alive. And lower planets.

Pray for them, not just yourself. Consider the cheaters, the killers, the defiant Godless.

Consider yourself lucky and don't complain. With empathy I cannot stretch myself that far—to identify with a starving, crippled babe in India, with a runover dog. But at least remember to pray in a broadened way, intercessionary.

Give them sense. Don't question God the Unknowable, who is the salvation and Lover of all. Take your Ambien and lie down. One of these days you may paint again and sing again. Time is running out, clear the *anarthas*—ask a friend how he does it. Not fault-finding, but attention in *hari-nāma*. A man, not a mouse. Look into their hearts with compassion. Try.

What is there to say?
They say I am tortured and
full of ambivalence and
many people aren't.

Why don't you go deep
and accept who you are? Don't you
have deep emotional needs?
Don't you accept yourself?

What good will it do to
go to CA if you bring the
same troubled person?

Swims said I like my writing.
"You got deeply impressed by
the hard commands of His
Divine Grace because you're
so sensitive."

Swims was trying to tell her
he's pretty okay but he will
press the doctor again tomorrow
on rebound headache.

What is there to say and what
is there to do, I'm caught
in a deadlock.

That bad? Work it out.
A place a person to go
to who would hear you
out like a pillow in
my tortured ambivalence.

Really that bad
and the writing is churning without
resolution. Helping
him?

Help people, people
you want in your life.
I want you all but
I've got these pains
and won't go for cold turkey or
the rebound challenge.
Floating around, doing my
work. Run out of energy.

The inmates in bed. No
time for a film. Go to
bed nonambivalent.

Your spiritual desires will
come more close when
you feel more who you
are. You'll even get into
the art shed. Maybe ignore
a headache. I can't.

You've come home.
I'm glad to see you,
I'm proud you raced
well. Hare Kṛṣṇa.
I thought it was only
for girls. No, boys
raced too, but
Śacī's girls outran
all the thousands of girls.
Good night.

Swims, here's a crevice. Go for it. They say you are ambivalent! You're torturing yourself. You don't know what you want, after all these years. Huh? Is that true? You still haven't found a way to fulfill your deep emotions. Jesus. Do you want to be a Christian or a Kṛṣṇa? I thought that was settled long ago, said Swims. Are you for sex or renounced? Renounced, even though I'm human and "a pretty girl is like a melody that haunts you night and day."[3] I like Sarah Vaughan singing "April in Paris."

Isn't painting and writing fulfilling emotions? The questioner says I don't know. It rather seems to reveal more ambivalence. Your paintings and writing do more churning up than peacefully resolving.

Prabhupāda. You going to tell me I'm ambivalent about him? Well, I've heard it from your own lips. I think it's settled: "I just plain like the guy."

Yeah, he's distant, so is Kṛṣṇa, I admit. Heal, heal, how do you do that? Don't tell me rebound cold turkey, says Swims. He just doesn't want to hear it again.

You want to live up to death with headaches?

No, no pain.

But when you first started with the tranquilizers, there was no pain, how come now?

I don't know. Maybe it's rebound. Is that ambivalent? I'm just too chicken for the cold turkey or any detox, and I tried it twice or so and then came back to pills again. They want you to go three months without any analgesics. I've had enough of that pain and my current doctor agrees. He says, "Mahārāja, for you there's more damage in the side effects of pain than the side effects of meds." So put that in your pipe and smoke it. And don't sermonize to me about quality of life. I get it where there's a crevice. I've got a cross to bear and I am carrying it, okay?

They speak against the California plan. It won't work. They speak in circles. They say take care of your disciples or—

"No, what we say is be yourself and live with it. Stop torturing yourself."

But I want both as much seclusion as I can get (for part of the year—it's a California experiment) and at the same time, I can exchange mail even there. Say no when I need to. Live as I am. What if that adds up to (in somebody's book) neglect of disciples? At least it won't be ambivalent.

And you've got to have some tension in life, he added. Be yourself. You guys, when you talk to me you confuse me, but I appreciate it too. It challenges me and makes me think.

Śacī asked Swims if it was too loud during the night—it rained all night. "Oh no, I *like* the sound of rain," said Swamiji. And he felt the truth of it for him. Remember Wicklow on the skylight? And here on the roof too. No winds here so it comes straight down. Hope they let me return to take possession of the place like I have now. But you're a beggar. Stay away too long and someone may sell the place or give it to someone else. A *sannyāsī* has to take his chances because he owns nothing. He spends donors' money on Charlie Chaplin films; not a very good investment for the future. (But good comedy therapy.)

You put your emotions in your writing? they asked, the battery of counselors.

"Yeah, what's it to ya?"

"What's special about it? Where is your writing going?"

"More innovative. Even a touch of the territory I dreamed of as a youngster, fiction."

"Yeah," they say, "but for spirituality we'll have to go elsewhere."

Gosh, there's a big festival happening next Sunday and plenty of swamis are going to speak, and then some will go northward past this territory, and it's likely some will stop here. It will be hectic. "Why don't you open your heart to so-and-so?"

"How much?"

"As much as you want."

Rather stay home and hear the rain on the roof and go to Dr. Danz and his female assistant, along with Śacī. Get new dentures. Wear nice clothes to go there. Just me and the chair and the dentist giving me all attention.

I knelt and genuinely prayed a little before Rādhā-Govinda, thought Swims. I really did. To come close to Them, to heal.

He gives a good report.
Well how do you feel?
Too many people talking at once.
I can't understand why they
aren't more attentive when
Bill is playing "I Love's You Porgy."
It's like chanting God's name
and letting your mind go wherever
it wants. It must be most
annoying to God. Shut up
and listen. Why did you come

here and pay money to hear
the divine sounds? You're
most offensive.

I loves you Porgy,
they are so dumb, they are more
interested in touching
their girlfriends' legs under the
table and drinking down the
required liquor. It's partly
not their fault but
the rule that you must
drink booze while
listening.

Let's give our chanting a chance.
Do it in a sacred studio,
a chapel of the mind where
there are as few interruptions
as possible.

And you can taste and please
the giver of *nāma* and hope
to get passed the worst *aparādha*,
"madness."

I loves you Kṛṣṇa,
mahā-mantra given by
Prabhupāda. Don't let them
handle you with their
hot hands. I am
your woman, I am
your lover. Don't let
them laugh while
I pray.

I'll clear the house
of those rascals, best I can.

Chapter Eight

Sunday newspaper local region *Kaleidoscope:* Catherine Miller stumbles in national spelling bee when she misspells the word pallescent (to look pale). The winner, Sai Gunturi, thirteen, an eighth-grader from Dallas, beat the other 250 contestants to win the national contest, correctly spelling the word pococurante, which means caring little or indifferent. Senator Hillary Rodham Clinton is facing mounting criticism from an unlikely quarter: liberals. "Now, Clinton seems to be going out of the way to convince Republicans that she is someone with whom they can work."

"Retired firefighter, ex-cop admit embezzling $216,000 . . . each faces up to 30 months in jail."

Swims had to rest after the counselor phone call. Both counselor and doctor said he's doing great. But he's in conflict. Fighting is spiritual advancement. He forgets what they said after a short nap, just relieved he's at peace. Be yourself. But you have to answer a stack of mail. *Japa.* Drawing you never get to. "He should have started drawing earlier in his life." No, it doesn't matter when you start. Real rest. Wet blankets on the CA plan, turn deaf ear. Didn't get to see Lakṣmaṇa yet today.

If you take to the lectern, waving your arms, you are expected to teach the expectant audience. They didn't want an off-the-wall personal talk in the name of a *Bhagavad-gītā* class. Then shut up. That's my privilege. You're doing fine, just hang in there kid.

"Your ankle seems better."

"No it isn't."

"I'm hard of hearing."

"Oh. I'm up here because it's a good place to chant." But he can't chant long. When Śrīmatī Rādhārāṇī with her beautiful golden complexion wears a lovely blue sari, she may be compared to the blue sky with streaks of lightning. We couldn't find it in a book so Swims made it up for a front piece for a book. We won't tell you the book title. "How are you feeling?" Okay. Rosemary headwash and a nap did the trick. I heard you're in rebound. Get off my back. Just help me write this essay. Let's keep boundaries. Warm voice. Didn't follow it up. Everyone knows you're a flip-flop, but resilient too. Make reality check.

Sing in the choir. Kicked off the football team. Out of 250 contestants, the Dallas boy won and celebrated. He'd get $12,000. Why do we always have to compete? It gets our juices up.

I outran you. I was innovative. But you were more enthusiastic and popular and inspiring—so I salute you. You must be tired from all your preaching. Would you like a glass of water? Thank you for stopping by to visit me. I don't have much to offer. Swims rehearsed his lines. But if you go spontaneous, it may be trivial. "I loved your book." "You are doing good work." "Where do you go from here?" "My spiritual journey is taking me to a discovery of the self." "Pretty nice layout you have here." "Yes, Śacī is very generous." "You watch movies?" "No, I meant to hide them. But they are recommended as therapy. You know the story of Norman Cousins?"[1] "Is this title *Seabiscuit* a comedy?" "No, I forgot to hide it." "What is this thick book, *Penguin Guide to Jazz in CDs?*" "Oh, someone must have left it here." "Schubert? Can I look around your private room?" "I'd rather you didn't."

Is there some spiritual topic? What were the lectures on at the Pāṇihāṭi festival? (God, am I going to get through this? Am I going to be able to open my heart and his? Am I so closed?) Tell him you're in conflict. No, I can't, I can't even explain it. Just hanging around the sanatorium. Prabhupāda is great. Come upstairs and see our altar.

Contemplate. There must be something profound he can say to his
friend. "Would you like to
hear this 'Contemplation' by
McCoy Tyner?"[2]

No, I don't think so. I want
Indian *bhajanas* with the
name Kṛṣṇa and Rādhā or
Gaura-Nitāi. What's become
of you?

Oh it's this anxiety disorder.
And I've loved this since I was
a kid and find it still in
my heart.

We think how to serve
Lord Kṛṣṇa. The way we're
meant to in our genes,
want to from our heart,
not as told by Master
Sergeant Johnson of the
Fifth Platoon.

Laurel and Hardy joined the
Foreign Legion and after one day
didn't like it, changed back
into their civvies and headed
for the gate. Stop!

Deserters. You can't leave
once you're in. You'll
be killed at dawn.
We didn't know we
thought it was a voluntary
unit.

Contemplate. Dig a
tunnel in your cell and
run away. How to become
your own free man untrapped.

We may not be able to satisfy
all these people. Throw
them crumbs. Isn't the
work enough?

Think about it in bed at
night. No, better sleep.
Sleep soundly and paint
a picture you want. You
are not too late to find
a safe place in yourself.

You yourself—
well it's a tough world.
But I do love him and proving
it my way.

Take what you need
and leave the rest.
Kṛṣṇa, take, give
Kṛṣṇa learn,
remember the one.

The lady said she wanted an essay, not free writing. Funny, I don't even think of it as "free writing," thought Swims. It's *Sanatorium.* They've never even read it. But they want "essays." He said, "What you want is linear writing." What he really meant is this book is better than an essay, but he knows most people want that essay. They want one paragraph to follow another with transitions on a topic like "Self-Forgiveness" or "Loss" or "Equanimity."

He could write a confession on "how I watched *Seabiscuit* by myself and liked it." But they certainly don't like that. "We've got to weave it into Kṛṣṇa consciousness."

It's a comeback story and all the people in the sanatorium are trying to make a comeback. Billie Holiday said, "I'm always making a comeback but nobody ever tells me where I've been." Yeah, you've been here all along excellently, baby, but they didn't notice you. You got into some trouble with the law so you were persona non grata for awhile, but you kept doing your work, recovering maybe, healing, and now they call it a comeback.

If this is free writing, then everything is. Or like Charles Bukowski said, "Everything is subjective, even a synapse." They told him his writing was too subjective. They don't want those topics jumping around. If it's announced that you're to give a lecture on "loss" or the opera *Madame Butterfly,* then they don't want something else. Or even if your work has its own steady canon, if it's too odd, they kick you out. Cecil Taylor auditioned for a nightclub, and after two bars at the piano, the mafia manager said, "Get out." Do you think that stopped Cecil? Kept playing his way and folks eventually came around to see it. Who told me this story about a painter? I can't remember, but he did very original stuff. He showed a painting to Salvador Dali, who said, "This is nails." He meant, "You'll never sell it," and Dali ought to know because he was the most self-promoting artist in the world. Painted "weird," but what he knew would go over—and promoted it with publicity stunts. Dali the surrealist weirdo with the long waxed moustaches. Anyway, he couldn't have been that bad because he was often approached in Manhattan by Hare Kṛṣṇa book distributors, and he always gave a donation.

They're opening a new headache center nearby. "I felt my head was going to explode," a migrainer said, trying to explain what it's like. But they charge lots of bucks.

Yes, Swims watched about the first twenty-five minutes of *Seabiscuit*. Pure black-and-white documentary of the actual races, Pollard the one-eyed jockey, the people in the stands and the way they dressed in the '30s. Now they've just made a Hollywood movie of Seabiscuit, about to be released in a few days. They have to spend millions of dollars to duplicate the 1930s dress and scenes, and come up with a false Seabiscuit and a false Pollard. Śacī said, "They've probably dumbed it up with a romance." Nothing could match those newsreel shots of Pollard whipping Seabiscuit to a four-length victory over War Admiral, whose sire was Man o' War. Each gesture of the hand and face genuine. You can't match it now. Let's go for the authentic.

That's what we're saying here. This is the authentic Kṛṣṇa conscious life of an already-dumbed-up (but actually so) aspiring devotee. A group of them. Doing what they should. Partly? Trying to be themselves.

Disciple to his guru: "When I chant a round or two before I go to work, I feel so much better." For years he didn't chant at all and left the Kṛṣṇa consciousness movement and broke off contact with his guru, and felt guilty about it. Now he's back doing what he can with his family and his art, and his "feel good" *japa* rounds. I'm not approving it or recommending it, but I like him and I like honesty rather than putting up a front.

This has been an essay on "Loss," but they won't accept it. They need an essay? Maybe I'll get Junior Barks to ghostwrite one for me. He'd probably want to be given credit for authorship, and I don't blame him. At least he sticks to a lecture topic and plows right ahead, a hundred percent *paramparā*. I seem to be off skelter. But I don't call it "free writing."

News came that Junior Barks' father had a bad motorcycle accident. He hurt his head and lost his memory. They didn't have any more beds for patients in this sanatorium, but by the influence of Swami Swims, they squeezed the beds a little closer, added one, and he has been admitted. Swims' motive was that he might be a good candidate for Kṛṣṇa consciousness. And guess who's giving him special attention and trying to bring his memory back? You guessed it. Bhaktin Jane.

Certainly I'm searching for peace.
Not dead body, R.I.P.
but lively with
no big disorder.

Who wrote "Peace"? Lots
of people. Who works
for it? Guy going around lecturing.
Bush created a quagmire
by war on Iraq when
they never had any
atomic weapons anyway.

Not just absence of war.
Dalai Lama says it starts in
yourself. Prabhupāda said
we want much more than
that peace.

Seems he equated it with
"liberation" when a guy asked
him a question about peace.
Prabhupāda was at war with
Māyā. "The whole world
will be against you."

But we need some peace.
I said, "Keli is worried,
Baby Lakṣmaṇa is sick.
She's taking him to the doctor."
Śacī: "He's always so happy it's
a shame to see him lying there
in a daze." Kaiśori: "Babies
do get sick."
I don't want any special
act by you. Don't get anxious
on my account.
But what if I'm too small or
contentious for you?

I'm not so peaceful with
all these swamis coming
and the newsletter articles
on rebound: "We've got to get the word out.
Doctors don't know.
This is real."

Peaceful corner to compose
his sonata. That's all.

Then all hell breaks loose
after he dies.

When a phone rings, you're at its mercy. It could be a worked-up guy accusing you of lying, keeping secrets. He tells you to stop publishing books, accuses you of cutting yourself off, hiding, not associating with Godbrothers. You try to tell him something about "posttraumatic anticipatory anxiety migraine." Quote from the headache newsletter, where a lady says, "It feels like my head is being blown off."

But he doesn't want to hear it. You stopped chanting sixteen rounds for awhile. You try to explain why. Then you understand he's treating you as a person incapable of speaking truth or that anything you say is "public relations." So you stop talking and listen. He rants on. There must be a resolution. Stop being a guru? Tell everyone all your faults. All the disciples—he's been calling them—are upset with you. He vents for an hour, laughs "now I've given you a headache. I want to be completely frank. I don't consider you my spiritual master." Love-hate. But he loves you anyway. But you're a hypocrite. He's repeating himself. You help him finds the words he's seeking when he gropes and cannot find them.

So-and-so said, "He left ISKCON years ago." Finally he ends.

You phone a trusted Godbrother. He advises you what to do. Another caller phones and advises you what to do. Another call comes in from someone who already heard about the attack. "I was advised to write a group letter." Tell them you're making progress. Enjoying the association of devotees in a sanatorium in New York. Let me get back to bed.

"I advise you to change your phone number."

"Well if that guy calls again, I won't talk with him. Tell him to write."

Back to bed. Not feeling so bad that you couldn't get up and write something before supper in fifteen minutes. Watch end of *Seabiscuit* tonight. We're up to the part where the 'Biscuit has a serious injury and they say his racing career is over. They said that twice about Pollard, his jockey, but he fought back and got back in the saddle. Maybe Śacī will watch it with me.

Lakṣmaṇa's fever has broken. But he's still coughing and not smiling his usual irrepressible way. Don't let it get you down. The detractor will marginalize himself. Just what we don't need. But more flack will come. That's life. Babies get sick, jockeys thrown, champion horses hurt badly, guys under dark stars get into trouble. "He's in conflict." "He's getting better." Poor Tough Barks can't even remember.

I want to be happy,
flaggery aint the way.
U.S. made a big mistake
in taking your taxes.

These aren't good days but
the home is where I want
to be.

Who loves you? You don't
have to take three guesses
who loves you sweetheart.

The American flag on every damned
pole and house but the dentist lab
made a dumb mistake and
I have to go back again. At least
get to see the pretty

assistant. Who loves you?
It's Kṛṣṇa, fell for you from
the start and trying to bring
you back.

But you're so stubborn.
I don't know what to do.
Lie around anticipating
swamis falling from heaven
and each one a different
tweak. Got your meds
in case.

"You'll find your fortune
falling all over town.
Be sure your umbrella
is upside down,"[3] sang Billie.

"If you want the
things you love you
must have showers."

Don't run from the thunder.
Go back to the dentist in good mood.
Minimize the stress of that guy who
chewed you out—
you're still a Prabhupāda man.

There's going to be a big festival for devotees quite close to the sanatorium. At least six or seven swamis will stop here after the festival. It's going to be high pressure. Get your smiles ready, keep in uniform. You don't think of what to say beforehand, but you might hide a few books. Don't talk of *Seabiscuit,* although he's a great comeback hero, and don't talk of Sid Caesar.

Hang in there. This is your chance to be yourself, be sociable, prove you *are into* ISKCON and making your own contribution. He writes to disciples, tries to heal, can sit in a rocking chair and sing in *kīrtana*. Ask intelligent questions. Search your mind. Don't be afraid. Relax. Be who you are. Ah, when the swamis come marching through, or when the Godbrothers come marching through, I want to still have some control of my time, when the swamis come marching through.

Haribol. Here is the address and e-mail of my spokesperson. If you have any complaints or dirt you don't want to tell to Swims' face, then write to this man. He'll collect it and we'll investigate the things. Did I do wrong? Please let some yay-sayers write on my behalf. "We're lucky to serve Swami Swims." That's life, I guess, that we don't get to see him much. He's got this affliction and the monitors try to keep even the sanatorium off-limits to visitors.

Hang tough. As War Admiral was sired by Man o' War, Swims was sired by Prabhupāda. Hare Kṛṣṇa. You can talk to animals and birds; that's one of the things Kṛṣṇa and Balarāma learned at Sāndīpani Muni's *āśrama*. And They learned how to tell stories by drawing pictures. How to kill demons.

Okay, hang up the phone, man. One rang today: "Hi! This is Jerry Downson! I can tell you how to cut down your telephone bills . . ."

Cut him off: "I have to get to work right away!" He was still talking as the phone disconnected. Be empathetic that he's go this job as a telephone marketer, but it's intrusive. As someone said, "There is some shit I won't eat."

It will be good. Talk with genuine traveling preachers. And don't be apologetic, but try to say something about Kṛṣṇa. We're reading BB sometimes. We try to say our rounds. I don't know you well enough to tell you everything.

Well if you really want to
race I can do it too but
our passion is for Kṛṣṇa.

We want to celebrate it at
Rathā-yātrās. Are *you* going?
No, you can't expect that.

He said I love the way you
smile and passion dance.
"What's the word on Swami Swims?"
"Why don't you ask him yourself?"
Good answer.

McCoy up and down the keys
as he used to with John, fast
yet "classical." Are you
waning? You seem to be
doing better to me.

The pain threshold is higher.
He resists running for a med.
Toughing it. Listen to
his favorites and dedication
to the Supreme.

On the car radio he was
playing Amala, telling
how Kṛṣṇa killed Kaṁsa
with Indian music in the background.
I could hardly hear it for all
the American flags and our
conversation, dear Śacī.

Plug a hole in that guy's mouth.
If he calls again

I want to tell him sorry I've got
a medical leave of absence
and don't have to subject myself
to your tirades.

Even my friends were upset.
Blow, blow for the Lord
and we have so many friends
when the truth is out I
can live in a camp
in Vermont (in the summer)

and stay right here in my
glass-enclosed place.
Rādhā and Kṛṣṇa on the cover of
books he publishes, *Every
Day, Just Write.*

That's a lot of self-
absorbed advertisement and
self-defense. He's in
conflict. Don't listen
to them. That's just what
we don't need. Calm down.
I want one of those.

Give me a funny film.
Give me a resolution to say
my *japa.* I've fallen
low but don't push
me lower.

I've got a lot to learn so
listen to the critics and
go on with the only way
you know how to be
a Kṛṣṇa conscious individual.

What's an individual?
Not all leveled like ants in an anthill
or other similes. Each
one is different to Kṛṣṇa.
I know you've heard
this but it's funny no
one believes it or allows it. Is that
true?

As the time for the big festival drew nearer, single swamis and visitors dropped by the sanatorium to inspect it and say hello. The monitors were proud to show them the big hall with all the beds and patients, who were being treated mostly gratis. One tall swami entered the hall and stopped at the first bed, where Tough Barks lay with a blank look in his eyes.

"Will you be going to the festival?," the tall swami asked, but Tough Barks just looked back at him blankly. "What's a festival?," he asked. Jane, who was sitting by his bed, said to Barks, "A festival is a kind of celebration for Kṛṣṇa. Devotees get together and sing and increase their happiness for love of God. I don't think you can go until you get better." She was trying to help bring Tough Bark's memory back, but not the memory of his old life. "I want you to gain your memory as an original spiritual soul," she said. "That's why I'm taking so much time with you, Mr. Barks. I want you to learn everything in the original way." Jane patted his hand and he smiled. The tall swami walked down the middle row toward the other beds. He asked a cripple if he was going to the festival and the man grumpily replied, "No." In fact, none of them were going. They didn't appreciate being asked. The swami didn't seem to understand their condition. Many of them had bad backs, agoraphobia, anxiety disorders, rheumatism, and some undiagnosed illnesses.

They looked forward to the festival only because it would mean people would be gone and they could be alone. Almost every one of them had a little CD player with earphones. They could listen to their favorite music, or write their memoirs, or read favorite scriptures. Some were just in too much pain to do anything, but tried to enjoy the stillness, the quietness. But they knew that after the festival, many swamis, like this single tall one, would be coming to visit them with the same misunderstandings and proddings and greetings, and they just couldn't rise to the occasion and reciprocate. Of course, the monitors wanted to protect them, but they couldn't completely bar the visitors, what with their curious desire to see the patients and offer them "cheer" and have deep talks with them in hopes of reviving their preaching spirit in Kṛṣṇa consciousness. Some of this was presumptuous. The patients felt the extra pressure and braced themselves for the week ahead.

Peace. Piece. After a rough
night he's calmed down.
We call this a crevice
and run into the poetry shack.

Big scandal in baseball.
Champion used a cork-
lined bat. Suspended.
America's favorite sport
defamed.

Taking steroids to make
big muscles. "I didn't
do it."

Scandal. Confess it.
I just wanted to be the top

home run hitter so
I cheated, what's wrong
with that?

You try cheating on the
Lord. He'll split your
bat open for all to see.

Stand before him naked.
Ashamed. Never the
same.
Did you take an Advil?
Are you going to get off rebound?
I didn't answer her.

They don't know what
it means. What pain is—
"felt like it was going to
blow my head off."

Boy, they didn't tell me
how many visitors were
coming through. I'll hide
if I can. Feel better today.
Catch up on your homework.

I can answer letters like
lightning, Swims said, but
not if I have a blockage.
No time for sergeants.

Lay me down. Let's hear
some mantras, boy, there's
nothing of higher priority than
that.

Worse scandal than a
cork-lined bat.

Swims' counselor sent him a long quote from Rilke's *Notebooks of Malte Laurids Brigge.* He said this applies especially to you. Swims couldn't identify with much of it except the following:

"For though he had wanted to hold himself back forever, he was now once again moved by the growing urgency of his heart. At this time, he hoped to be answered. His whole being, which during his long solitude had become prescient and imperturbable, promised him that the One he was now turning to would be capable of loving him with a penetrating, radiant love. But even while he longed to be loved in so masterful a way, his emotion, which had grown accustomed to great distances, realized how extremely remote God was."

The book then goes on to say that he did sometimes experience "hours full of disclosure" toward God and that he was like someone who learned a glorious language and decided to write poetry in it but found that it was very, very difficult. And so he needed great patience.

"He who had adapted himself to infinite space had now become like a worm crawling through crooked passageways, without exit or direction. Now that he was learning to love, learning so laboriously and with so much pain, he could see how careless and trivial all the love had been which he thought he had achieved; how nothing could come of it, because he had not begun to devote to it the work necessary to make it real.

"During those years, the great transformations were taking place inside him. He almost forgot God in the difficult work of approaching Him, and all that he hoped to perhaps attain within him in time was *sa patience de soppoter une ame*—'His patience in enduring soul.'"

Yes, may Kṛṣṇa be patient with me and may I be patient. He does seem very remote. I have lived in solitude, which seems good for creativity—"Rilke seems to have needed, desperately, the feeling of freedom which he found only in open, windy spaces, Duino, Muzot"—but I have not made spiritual cash out of such places. Some tell me it's not good for me to stay alone, I should learn coping skills for socializing. My counselor guesses that for me to realize myself in my offering to God, I will need freedom to write and paint. Yes, said Swims, these are major drives of my offering. Other wells have dried up. And if I again have wide acres, I shall try to fulfill myself in my unique offering to God and others.

Tell again the painful occurrences in your life, with Godbrothers, GBC, traveling. Doing what you didn't want to do. A secretary of Swims recalls him saying on a GBC visit to Chicago, where the temple president didn't really need him, "I feel like a prisoner here."

You're my everything I wish
I could feel honestly and simply
God and nothing else counts
where only in connection to
serving Him. Fly higher with
Gopa-kumāra. Hear the
learned discussions which may
even deviate or be over
your head.

But stick to your
Gopāla mantra.
From time to time your
guru will visit you and
encourage you—keep on
the path to Vraja and nowhere
else.

I don't know why I haven't
been returning letters to
certain friendly folks. It just
doesn't give me juice.

Pull the donkey cart.
Punch in your card
at work and do what
you may not want to
because you have to.

"The last time I was here
I answered a hundred e-mails."
I lay in bed instead

and charted the ups and downs.
He's even planning to watch
the Belmont Stakes on TV.
This kind of fellow should be
investigated.

He wants to be happy and
regain his memory before
it's too late—like an
underdog racehorse making
a fast burst in the home stretch
for a great comeback
in ISKCON history.

I think we should straighten out something. It is very intense. You want to lecture on the *Bhāgavatam* with a modern slideshow video machine? Who is the longest lecturer? He said Śrīla Prabhupāda usually clocked in at twenty-five to thirty minutes. So why are they doing marathons? A little at a time, especially when there are children and old men and total newcomers present.

I could do it too. Phone someone up and apologize. You were right about the names of the Seven Dwarfs.[4] There was no Weepy, but Bashful. The names of the four Kumāras are Sanaka, Sananda, Sanātana, and Sanat? Have a quiz and find out the most learned devotee. No cheaters who put cork in the middle of their baseball bats and drugs in their arms. It's a great scandal. He shall be suspended. Imagine, a cork lining in his bat. An *ācārya* should not do anything that is forbidden or hidden from his disciples.

I believe you. Another baseball pitcher had sandpaper and a razor hidden in his glove, and he scratched the ball so it would produce an extra curve. He was caught. You'll get caught. Sun, moon, and Viṣṇu see everything.

He was forging checks, stealing cars. Not speaking from the heart. Now I have to stop writing because my monitor has come. He'll let me write a little longer. What have I got to say anyway? It's near Lights Out. A letter home to mom? No mom or home. Dear disciples, forgive me. If you have any complaints, write to my spokesperson.

Whew. Small talk. I'm not interested in the lecture of the *asura* who was actually a *mahā-bhāgavata*. I can't explain why.

Boy what a night.
You never know when it's
going to turn out nightmarish.

I don't suddenly see God
and discover a new language
too hard to apprentice. I keep
the one I learned from
mother and father.

Oh boy what a night,
in the morning I hope to wake
and be able to chant
without falling asleep.

But that's not possible.
Bringing complaints to my
friend. He'll mediate.
I'm set up.

Take the burden off me.
Let the sax player take
it for awhile and
then Lee Morgan.[5]

They're playing some person
and we're remembering Prabhupāda.
Some fool is envious. He didn't
know him and he has no memories
to tell.

I was too proud to contribute to *Memories*.
Why the hell did I behave
like that, thinking I was too
good to be heard, thinking
"this is all in my books,
why don't they read them?"

No stopping the swarm of
visitors or anxiety influx.
Śacī's place is too unsecluded
for me. I want seclusion
in California, northwest.

Take it from right here, tell
the pains you remember.

I like his technique. I won't
tell others. We work open.
He trusts and I trust.

Do we get forgiven? Head
figure with no potency.
Thirty-four years old but a child,
can't manage his way out
of a paper bag.

Became too much and he
broke down, "Jim" the
right-eye migraine came
to the rescue and pulled him off
the GBC.

"Jim," go away now, but he
aint. Needed my prayers and healing,
got to paint.

Swims thought of what he might say to a visiting swami (there'll be at least three or more who will stop by his bed, or he'll get out of bed to sit with them). Maybe, he thought, I could say, So this is your first visit to America? I suppose you noticed all the American flags on every house in this town except the devotees' houses. They call it flaggery. The present leader of this country is such a hawk. The country went to war against Iraq and in two months probably destroyed the country and killed the demon-tyrant Hussein. But now they're in even worse trouble than they were before. You see, the people will want to elect a religious leader, an ayatollah. And he'll hate America even worse than the other guy. And for all this, the people in the United States are going to have to pay higher taxes for all the bombs and tanks and everything.

That would show him I'm up-to-date, thought Swims. And then he could get into spiritual topics. Show him you're alert, bright-eyed, heavy-bodied.

Say to him, "So I hear your presentations are being well-received. You are either the first- or second-most loved preacher in ISKCON." I'm very happy for this. Keep people from going outside Prabhupāda's movement." Swims knows he should not talk about "tranquilizers." Call it medication. The swami is living here right now, and Swims walks to the dinner table to sit with this swami who has not mentioned Swims' cane once. So just be yourself. Swims asked the monitor today, "Could I have a pair of shorts? It's getting a little warm for my sweat pants. But something conservative for an old man."

Listen to them. "I heard you gave a seminar on *japa* reform. Could you please tell me just a little bit of it, especially about paying attention? And even how to give it priority so you always get your quota done?" Let it flow. They are each kind in their own way. But don't let them get too deep into your heart. That's just how I feel about it. Deep would mean to show them the Rilke "Dove" poem. What would they make of that?

Be yourself. You think it's a beautiful poem and expresses your heart and what you wish would be his heart? Then show it.

Bow at his feet. Smile to show you're not depressed. Be genuine. You benefit by these visits. But you don't need their permission to be sidelined. Don't be ashamed of yourself. Since there's going to be an extra influx of visitors, don't be afraid of taking required meds. Take what you need, leave the rest. Say, "Excuse me," when you've had enough.

Yes, he'll try to give the impression that he's okay, nothing wrong with that, but be real. Real. Real. Nothing to prove. Wearing my uniform and shoes. What'cha wanna know about me? How close are you to me that I should tell you? Why are you asking that question, and what are you trying to lead to? Flop back on the bed. "Nothing as nice as clean sheets." I agree. And goodnight. Lights out. We inmates know how sweet that is, provided there's not a lot of noise outside or scurrying of rodents in the dorm. Someone is sobbing. "Calm down, dear, say God's name." "Someone go and show her some empathy."

Why did you confuse your mind by looking at the month's news in review? Prabhupāda said devotees are always thinking of Kṛṣṇa. In the evening in the villages, they used to gather and hear *Mahābhārata* and *Rāmāyaṇa*, because those books were popular with the ordinary man. They didn't speak on Vedānta. So then the people would go home talking about *Rāmāyaṇa* and *Mahābhārata*, and then they would sleep thinking of *Rāmāyaṇa* and *Mahābhārata*, and they would dream of the same topics. You also should always be doing something Kṛṣṇa conscious—typing, writing, editing, cooking, going on *saṅkīrtana*, distributing books, always being engaged in some Kṛṣṇa conscious activity. So you see, it's not very narrow-minded, there are many, many things you can do and still be included in ISKCON. Yes, I said ISKCON.

This totem pole I built in
Ireland, it will be shipped
to California. I will go
there in the rainy season
and write and paint,
said Swimmy.

But will they let him?
You cut yourself off
too much, some say.

Try to be yourself in
no conflict and yet in touch
with those who want
to help you and don't
think you are crazy
for building totem poles
and pictures like children
but not children.

Hey Kṛṣṇa people I
may get in galleries all
over NYC. And in
the New York–Puerto Rican
cafes—get this—
I'll be reading a poem—
on video and behind me
will be a live band and then
live devotees
will read some of
my poems.

I like the idea very
much. Way up here
in Flagville where Bush
is popular and I'm
talking "she said you're hip"
and a band playing behind
it.

Oh thank you for trying
it. A model and our editor.
Oh man I like
clean stuff not Mars
bars. Christians make
chocolate crucifixes
but say don't eat Jesus but

you can eat the crucifix.
We don't eat Kṛṣṇa but
want to eat with Him.

I don't mean to criticize.
But God should be treated
with all reverence and be
bathed in the morning,
new dress, and night
dress by 8:00 P.M. and tucked
into bed by 9:00 P.M.

He accused, "You said
you are a bankrupt *sannyāsī*
but you are spending too
much money to get your
ankle and teeth fixed
and your paint brushes."

Tears you to pieces.
Hare Kṛṣṇa. Let them
complain to my spokesperson.

I'll build more totems
to the One God, Kṛṣṇa,
from whom all comes.
I'm sorry. I'm glad
you gave me some pain-free time.
We're going to
hear some BB I hope when
Śacī is not too busy or
else I'll hear Prabhupāda.

Tough week. At least it's something
to write about—the
best compliment: hip,

Lee Morgan and his friends.
I say they mean to praise
God and make Him less
remote. It's mystic but
with a 4/4 beat. He's
right here in your body,
and your soul, your
totem pole.

Chapter Nine

It was 8:00 in the morning and the birds were chirping. But many of the inmates were still trying to sleep. They were the ones who had hard nights due to pain. They had been up during the night in the backroom quarters, applying various remedies like aroma therapy, massage, and acupuncture. Some had resorted to extra-strong allopathic pills and gone back to their beds to calm down. Other members were awake but mindful of their suffering bedfellows and tried not to make much noise. They all remembered the main doctor's instructions, which they had posted on a sign: "Take only medicines I prescribe. Rest sufficiently. Do only what you want and not what others tell you."

At 6:00 A.M. the door opened and the head of the dormitory turned on the lights. The chief of the county dormitories was with him, and behind them, entering the room, was a pack of about twenty Boy Scouts and their Boy Scout master. They wore their customary dark khaki clothes, short pants and multicolored scarves. Many of them wore caps, some even had knives in sheathes at their belts, and some carried small American flags. When they all had entered the room and shut the door, the chief county sanatorium master made an announcement. He usually never came by and had nothing personally to do with any of the inmates. He was a local politician who tried to cash in on the magnanimous work being done by the sanatoriums in order to get more votes. In a loud voice he said, "My dear inmates, I realize it's a little early, but we have some special visitors this morning. This is Boy Scout Troop 34, from Nashville, Tennessee. They are an award-winning pack who have been touring the country to see as many natural spots and places of interest in our grand country, America. Someone suggested that they visit our successful sanatorium in Hudson County, and I was happy to agree. They'll only be here a short while, as their bus is due to leave in five minutes to take them to see Stuyvesant Falls, and then go up to Albany, and then to Niagara Falls." At the word "Niagara Falls," the Boy Scouts started to smile and look excited. Otherwise, they seemed quite bored and a little put off by being in this "sick place." It was not their idea to visit. As the Boy Scouts looked around with disdain at the sickies, some of the more cynical inmates surveyed the Boy Scouts as silly assholes and truly resented their visit. Others saw it as a possible opportunity for preaching.

The county politician then said, "As they go down the row, please greet them and answer any questions they have." The inmates began pushing their urine bottles under their beds, as well as their CD players and ear plugs. They placed holy books on their laps and tried to look peaceful and smiling, even though some of them were in pain at that very moment.

The adult Boy Scout master said, "Does this sanatorium belong to a certain religion?"

The county dormitory chief hesitated and then said, "Yes, this was built by the Hare Kṛṣṇa religion." Some of the Boy Scouts began to titter and sing the Hare Kṛṣṇa mantra. The inmates joined in with them and sustained a *kīrtana* for about one minute.

The Boy Scout master said, "Well, it's a free country, and everyone is entitled to their own religion. But I remember these fellows used to be quite aggressive in selling their books."

"We don't do that anymore," said Bhaktin Jane. "We spread the word of God in the most palatable way possible, and give shelter to many people, as well as cows, by our various programs."

"Shelter the cows?," asked one of the boys, and the others laughed. The boys didn't have any questions and walked around the dorm without much curiosity. They looked to their Boy Scout master, and one of them said, "I think we'd better go." And so he ushered them all out and shut the door, with the politician at the head. After they had left, the Hare Kṛṣṇa monitor shut the door and turned to his inmates. "I'm terribly sorry at this interruption. This was really an intrusion, going too far. I'll try to talk to the county manager and other people to see that this doesn't happen again."

One of the inmates spoke up, "Yeah, and this is just the beginning. Next week all those folks are going to be coming in an overflow after the festival. Please give us some protection. We're not a freak show or some local entertainment. We're here to heal ourselves, and we're doing it fine without interruption."

"You say you'll talk to your men. We're also going to talk to our Hare Kṛṣṇa authorities. We built this place with certain laws and intentions, and we don't want them broached."

"Yes, yes," the local monitor said. As he was about to leave, Swims asked, "Can we sleep late this morning?"

"Okay," and so they ached, and they baked, and they waked the morning through, even as the sun rose. Some of the inmates began to groan and tried to rest, but for some it was too late to rest. Those with anxiety disorders calmed down and tried their various tricks to think optimistically about the situation. But they all thought that this was going to be a tough week, and they attempted to tolerate in Kṛṣṇa consciousness.

Waiting for the acupuncturist
to turn you into a pincushion.
Are you extra sensitive to pain?

I don't think so. But I don't
want to be thrown into hell.
Don't hesitate. Your fate is sealed:
lifelong celibate
man asked me how his wife
can show more affection to him—
she's always so down. I feel
like telling him I agree—
what's wrong with holding hands
on a long walk, man and wife,
a hug, she touches you on the shoulder
as she passes your chair,
you tell her she looks attractive in
her new sārī. But she's so staunch
and he's so down he's resorted to
you know what.

What can I say? That's not my territory.
One *gṛhastha* said even a hug is
"the royal road to sex intercourse."

Tell him to keep a mile away from
her and finger his beads and take care
of their new baby. Yes it's a
mismatch. Maybe he can learn
something from it. But as for me
I must have nothing to do with
wimmin' and so I may have
to tell him "ask some more successful
gṛhastha."

I'm on the sidewinder finding
my pleasure in human
poems where sex drive
is sublimated and reaching for that
Savior, assembling an essay on
individualism another on innovation

and trying to be myself
in the Kṛṣṇa conscious
movement. They would prefer I would
live closer to my disciples. Maybe I
should have. Ireland. New York.

The wilds of California where only one
sannyāsī and his men live in the next
valley and could spoil everything if we
get chummy. Because I'm going there
to paint big canvasses.

This sounds like old SDG of
EJW, I lost my writerly craft.
Where's the sanatorium,
where's the plot I'll be buried in?
You'll be burned,
sidewinder,
Śacī will teach you how to
punch and lift weights.

Sixty-four years old.
Figure out *what you want*
to do for the Lord
and live in harmony.

Their morning was so disturbed that when the three acupuncturists came, the inmates weren't in the mood and found their questions silly, not deep.

What is your favorite color?

Uh . . . blue . . . green. They stuck the stainless steel pins in and they hurt but didn't hurt.

Does this come from China? Did you study Chinese philosophy?

Actually no one knows where acupuncture came from. But in China they have made pure acupuncture illegal because it has spiritual origins and inclinations and their government is now Communist. So they teach a Western version of acupuncture.

Oh, only in the West you can get the pure version?

Yes, and actually some say it comes from the Tao masters. That's my particular interest.

Oh yeah? I like ancient Taoist poems. They're beautiful. Stick. Stick. Maybe they make up this talk so you don't notice. Breathe in—*stick*—now breathe out. Do you have a craving for a certain food?

No, but there are some foods I like. Stick.

Then he says for a few days your headaches and other aches will be worse and you'll sleep more. Stick. I'll come back next Friday. Stick. Swims realized that he should have cut his toenails; they were jagged and too long. Stick. Then suddenly the man said he had taken all the pins out and it was all over.

Can we just get up and do what we want?

Do you feel woozy?

No I just need my eyeglasses so I can see the world.

Soon after that, Keli-lalitā brought in Lakṣmaṇa the Great and said, "Hold him while I get your snack." Swims loved to hold the baby because he was always so happy, but all of a sudden he began to bawl. Swims patted him, turned him in different positions, placed him on the couch beside him, but he bawled even louder. The magic was over. He was alone with a heavy kid who didn't like him. Finally his mother came in and the crestfallen Swims handed him back. Swims and Keli had been playing this game that the baby had a special attraction for Swims. Later she came back with Lakṣmaṇa smiling and said, "He was just hungry, he still likes you." "I don't know," Swims muttered; he'd lost his confidence to be alone with that smiler again.

"I've been falling behind in my *japa*," said a man in a wheelchair. "Ever since this talk about the festival visitors, I've started worrying. I worry beforehand like many of you. And now that it's actually begun with that Boy Scout invasion, I'm getting shaky. Please give me some support."

"Don't worry, Baldy," said one of the volunteer Hare Kṛṣṇa visitors. "Let's all just concentrate on the holy names while we can. You know you can still chant even if a visitor comes."

"I can't," said Swami Swims, "not if he's a VIP."

"You could set a better example and not watch videos and make unimportant phone calls," said Baldy.

"How observant you are," said Swims. "Why don't you just mind your own *hari-nāma*? Look at all this time we're wasting."

Jane and Tough Barks were chanting *japa* together, oblivious to the arguments. Almost all the other inmates seized their beads or clickers and went to work chanting.

"Even if it's mechanical, the Lord gives credit." Do what you can. Numerical strength.

"Better than lifting barbells"—another dig at Swims and others who worked out in the gym.

'Hare Kṛṣṇa, Hare Kṛṣṇa, Kṛṣṇa Kṛṣṇa, Hare Hare, / Hare Rāma, Hare Rāma, Rāma Rāma, Hare Hare.'

"Chanting sometimes brings on my arthritis pain even worse," admitted an old one-time *pūjārī mātājī*.

"Shh, shh," said the Hare Kṛṣṇa nurse.

"But she's right," said the man beside her bed. "My counselor told me not to bash myself if I can't chant all sixteen rounds. Be self-forgiving."

"He said that because you're a helpless case."

"Stop the arguing," said Jane loudly so *all* could hear. "Just do the best you can."

"It's so dry," said the arthritic ex-*pūjārī*. "And that pinsticker just said it would get worse. I feel it. But I can't sleep either."

"Please, please everyone, calm down. The visitors haven't even arrived and we're all in a disunited uproar. Let's have some harmony and love for the less fortunate. If you can't chant just now, if it makes you feel worse, then lie back quietly and think of Kṛṣṇa."

Outside the power lawn mower moved close around the outside of the sanatorium. They heard a landscape man yell, "Who do you like in the Belmont Stakes?"

"Oh no," said Tim, "and tomorrow the flagstone workers will arrive."

Jane urged, "Chant, chant, chant."

A man with a headache echoed back, "Can't, can't, can't."

The *chaukīdār* who had been fingering the small white *japa-mālā* bag the whole time poked his head in the door of the dormitory and said, "'Umpossible is a word in the fool's dictionary,' Prabhupāda said."

But some of the irritated tempers continued as neighboring children screamed on the lawns outside. It was an unseasonably cold June day.

A few inmates queued up outside the bathroom, complaining about breakfast.

"Goddamn Boy Scouts."

"Goddamn pinstickers."

The peacemakers remained silent and made no more attempts at unanimous peace. You can't please everyone. Blessed are the steady. 'Hare Kṛṣṇa, Hare Kṛṣṇa, Kṛṣṇa Kṛṣṇa, Hare Hare.'

I don't complain, lie down
and think of another gig
for my Lord. He is so
kind even to younger players.

He asked me, "Did you get
anything to eat? How's your
essay coming? Are you going
to take your med without shame?
And don't listen to those who
say you're on rebound."

But chronic everyday? Isn't
that rebound? Go rebound
yourself. I'm alive right
now, the result of pain
is worse than the side results
of med.

We will persevere until the
last day. We're not just
another anonymous ant
in the anthill.

If this disturbance continues, people
will disenroll from the sanatorium.
No they won't. It's mostly quiet
and they have nowhere else to go.

Mow your lawn. A blind man climbed
Mt. Everest. A blind woman
won the women's footrace
two years in a row.

People learn to play saxophone
with their toes. Even Charlie

Parker practiced sixteen hours a day
to reach his God-gifted technique.

Don't complain. I gets me writing
in. I don't mind your chewing
at my heels. Go deeper means . . .
two different opinions. I'll ask
him his on Sunday.

Something about be yourself.
Not whether you had an anal
problem on the toilet or
wanted to go to bed with both
your mom and dad and Sigmund Freud,
the libido hunter. Why
did you take to Kṛṣṇa consciousness,
and what were you like
before you did? I told
the pinsticker I was a beatnik
and was very skinny and smoking,
taking dope, so my health became
much better right away.

What made you spiritually search?
It was personal, the guru himself.
That Swami and his teachings
attracted me so I went at
great risk. Stick. Stick.

They asked Swims to add an endnote on SK. He hadn't read him in fifteen years, never read him with a professor or in a systemized way, and never could grasp the whole. But he was intrigued by the great Dane and treasured many of his paragraphs. He said the day St. Peter converted 300 (or was it 3,000?) people to Christianity, that day the religion died. It wasn't so easy to become a follower of Christ. In Denmark, the state religion was Lutheranism. (SK was basically a Lutheran also.) But he said there was not a single Christian in Denmark, including the ministers. He said it would be better if the so-called Christians would be *truthful* and admit, "I can't do it, I can't believe and follow Christ," rather than pretend they were on the road to heaven. Imagine applying these standards to ISKCON? He would say no one is Kṛṣṇa conscious!

Oh how he thumped them, the hypocrites and atheists, too, with such wit and intellectual acumen. Swims wanted to say something of SK's teaching about how the subjective is more important than the objective. The big question is not whether God exists. That's an insult, not a question. The question is, What is *your* relation to Him? But Swims didn't get into that because he wasn't expert enough at it, and he didn't have any of SK's books or books about him. So he wrote a few touching anecdotes he remembered from the biography of "little Kierkegaard," the passionate author who died in his forties, who wrote a book, *Attack on Christendom*, although he himself was a devoted preacher and even gave sermons in church, and gave up his fiancé to lead a life dedicated to the One. He will always haunt me favorably, and I'll never understand him. But he's certainly a friend, and maybe someday a Kṛṣṇa conscious scholar will write a wonderful book proving it. He's already written of in a book called *Passion for Truth*. And the titles of his own books! *Fear and Trembling*, *Sickness Unto Death*, *The Concept of Dread*, *Purity of Heart Is to Will One Thing*. I could only lick the outside of the bottle of SK's thought, but it was sweet. Especially his dedication to authorship *and* publication. Go, Soren, go! They depict you as a tortured one, the first existentialist, but you flew on ecstatic wings when you stood and wrote at your 45-degree wooden desk (I saw it in Copenhagen). Even though so few read you at first, and eventually, in your lifetime, you became the object of mockery to the people in the streets. Now your books are read in practically all the languages of the world, and you are not an object of mockery but praised as a world-class philosopher/theist.

Stick, stick them pins, he's coming every Friday. He asked if we'd be here. Yes, we're always here. Where else would we go? We can sit on the veranda, but there are always wasps and other flying bugs and intense sunlight. We could go for a walk, but many of us can't walk long, like Seabiscuit. We *could* take a car ride and go swimming in the river, but cars make many of us sick. We don't want to attend a big festival, even if it's fifty miles away, because we would soon want to lie down in bed. Imagine asking for that at a festival. We will be occupied, indoors, pale for it. But we get some exercise in the gym next door. We hear Prabhupāda on tape saying that in Yudhiṣṭhira's time, all the elements of nature cooperated. Not too little or too much rain. We are allowed to watch funny films to perk up our spirits. Yes, Mr. Pin Man, we'll be here next week, and maybe ask you more about the Tao. How much do you charge per visit?

We'll be here, at least through the summer, not forever. Oh them golden slippers, how will we answer all that mail?

You have to hurry sometimes
because people walk in on you.
There's no flashing light on
your door saying, "Stay out!"

Boy we want to ride with Sonny,
he's so inventive. "I'm home."

Are you doing all right? Yes
as long as the boss comes up
and lines us up with meds for
the night.

Rilke wrote that sometimes in the
night (although God was
normally remote to him), he'd
fly up like in a dream
and come close to Him and learn
a glorious new language
and want to write in it.

But the apprenticeship in this
new language was hard and
very humiliating. I don't understand
this at all. My language
comes free as William Stafford[1] said
it should.

You don't wait twenty years
for a sonnet but lower your
standards and say
"there's a telephone,
I'm a boy sixty-four years old and I
want to go to God but He's remote
but I like His champions."

How come I don't go to Vṛndāvana
where His superstars love to go?
All these blockages people tell
me about. Advise him to
go where he can write and
paint.

But in California you can't write
"I just met a *sādhu*
pouring sugar down an anthill."

Yeah, yeah, I heard that.
I'm a wimp. Pampered.
In a certain kind of solitude.

Phew. If this is the homestretch you'd better beat me harder,
I'm sweating and can't
go any faster dear jock,

I'll give my heart to win
but don't feel I'm able to compete
on that ground.

Please give me back those pins you
left two standing in my arm. Please
let me see Sid Caesar. Why not
the story of Kṛṣṇa or just sit
and sing *bhajanas* and extra rounds?

I don't understand you, you are
really under average, you've
become a Kali-yuga pygmy.

All these superlatives he threw at
me and I didn't know what to
make of them. Is the painting
worth a damn?

Listen to the different drum.
Follow the path less trodden.
Go where your Father said to.
I don't believe you misbehaved *that* much

but you'll be lucky to get out
of this morass called
Iraq with a live pulse and
as far as I'm concerned

you are mind and body conscious
too much and will not go to
the lotus feet—shut up.

You don't know nuthin' 'bout me
so don't predict.
If the Swami wants to collar
me he will under Lord's order
and throw me across the pond or
like a tiger set me up
to guard some gates or
get the anxiety out of my system
by a simple measure.

Now that's enough.

Rained out festival. Rained out flagstone workers with their radio. We sit up in bed or nap or pace and hear the gentle patter on the roof. Most monitors have gone to the festival. They have a tent but it's on a hill and the rain has run down and muddied the ground. It may rain out the Belmont Stakes, which the inmates intended to watch on TV with no censors to restrain them.

What's the last Kṛṣṇa conscious thing you heard that touched you? That everything is meant to be in harmony in an ecosystem. God would like to have it that way and He'll give it if everyone—trees, animals, and especially people—cooperate. But they don't. *īśāvāsyam idaṁ sarvam.* Pitter-patter.

Jane was not trying to restore Tough's actual memory—as a tough—but teach him Kṛṣṇa consciousness from the start—as a child with a clean slate he would learn about life. She was very patient about it, although she didn't neglect her typing. She just typed faster.

"We are playing the big *mṛdaṅga*," said Swami Swims, looking out the window at the rain. Prabhupāda at the end of his life said, They are wondering where that old man is but I am (in Vṛndāvana) beating on this drum and it is going out all over the world. Our hopes are not so ambitious, but something. A girl in Bavaria, a desperate man who lives in an apartment in the Bronx and savors every word. And guru and Kṛṣṇa, for them we beat this drum. When it rains this drum doesn't go slack. It stays tight. Oh, but now he has to lie down and wait for a crevice. It will come. Another wave.

Wave. Has the rain stopped? It's a sandy track and all the horses are good at running in the mud. No one allowed in unless they can prove they chanted their sixteen rounds. A headache can't be proven; you have to take the patient's word for it. But we have ways of detecting if you've chanted your rounds. Your face doesn't look cherubic if you do less. Lie detector! Can we afford one? Bomb in his shoe. Why should I lie about that? Because you are a liar and want people to think you're better than you are. "I like the 'normalcy,' here" said a visitor, "so many people are on a trip." Well stay around here awhile, honey, and you'll see through our normalcy. Why do you think we're sick if we're normal? We've even heard Śrīla Prabhupāda lecturing and he said if you have anxiety or shock, it will result in physical illness.

An innocent person asked, How would anxiety, I mean what's the connection? I don't know, said Swims, until I heard about it two years ago. Maybe it's just a fairy tale. But *Bhagavad-gītā* is 5,000 years old, and so is *Śrīmad-Bhāgavatam,* and we're sticking with that and they're sticking us with pins. We are open to it even if we never get out of here. Anxiety. Jeez. Can't you understand? There is a connection between the mind and body and stars and mostly biology and the effects of medicine and karma and too much dairy—it could be anything, like overwork in the 1980s, somehow your transmission drops in the road.

"Is it contagious?" one of the Boy Scouts asked early that morning as they were ushered in. Yes, very contagious, so stay away, you little fart. Let us endure in peace. The rain *has* stopped, visitors *will* come, we *will* get anxious, and we'll all feel gay when Johnny comes marching home.

You better believe us we
are innocent of major crimes.
We are campaigning for an
appeal. The cork in our bat
was in one used only for
batting practice.

They cheered the guy as if he'd
done something great. Two other
guys caught with cork in their
bats and steroid in their forearms

and horseshoes in his boxing glove
and hand under the table,
false confessions, learn the art.
You might use it someday
if you are really sparring:
"Don't keep your neck
so stiff, weave and bob
and hit harder."

Yeah he gave a course on
japa reform and I hope it

will help. How can I get
a copy of the tape?
You've given them yourself—
don't you remember?

I have forgotten like
Tough Barks and can't seem
to relearn the art of
attentive loving numerical
strength.

Retake. Take two,
take five million.
I never get it right. Pie in
the face, shoes too big,
fall on your face to get
the laugh, anything for
the laugh: "He really
knew now!" poor Clown.

He'd never make the top ten
of the alumni emeritus of
demoted. Should we be
confidential? No he and she
said but our man
stood passionate and emotional and
said, "We've got to love fast!"

It was past Lights Out when one of the head monitors opened the door and shouted in, "You guys didn't watch the Belmont Stakes did you?"

"No sir," some of them answered in unison, although some were already asleep.

Tim said, "But we heard that the favorite, Funny Cide, came in third and didn't win the Triple Crown."

"How did you hear that?" asked the monitor.

"The *chaukīdār* told us. And some other visitors who came by. Everybody was talking about it."

"Hmm," the monitor mused doubtfully. "You all chant your sixteen rounds?"

"Yes sir!" in unison.

Tim added, "I didn't. I only did fifteen, but I'll catch up tomorrow if I can."

"We're going back to the festival again tomorrow," said the monitor. "So you people will be mostly alone. So no monkey business, all right?"

"No sir. Hare Kṛṣṇa."

"Tim," said Swami Swims, who slept in the bed next to Tim's, "why do you say such queer stuff?"

"I'm trying to be honest."

"Well that wasn't honest about hearing from the *chaukīdār*."

"It was better than all of you guys, who shouted out, 'No,' that you didn't watch the Belmont Stakes. I at least told a half-truth."

Swims said, "There are some situations where you can lie."

"Where? Who said that?"

"It's in the *Bhāgavatam*. It was said by Śukrācārya, the guru of the demons. He said it when Bali wanted to give away everything to Viṣṇu."

"Swamiji! How am I supposed to learn from your association?"

"Well, at least you learned that I'm human. I'm not a perfect person on a pedestal."

"Yeah . . . ," said Tim as he was falling back asleep. "I love you, even if you don't always say your quota of *japa*. You're an inspiration."

"I love you too, Tim," said Swamiji. "Why the hell did he have to stick his head in the door and shout after lights out? Let's try to sleep. I think I'm starting to get a headache."

"I think he was intoxicated from eating too many sweets."

"Pulling rank."

"Forgive, forgive," said Jane, and they all fell silent.

Oh the winner is the loser
and the jockey's young Mexican
son is crying big tears and his
mother is comforting but broken-
hearted too. Santos
did what he could
but his horse could not pass
Empire Maker
or even Ten Most Wanted.

I knew that grief at ten years old
when the Brooklyn Dodgers lost the
pennant playoff to the New York Giants
in the ninth inning
when Bobby Thomson homered.
Big bulging tears from a little boy.

But Santos, you are still so lucky, son,
your dad won two out of three
and you have plenty of money and
fame and victories ahead.

We should cry for our lack
of love for Kṛṣṇa not the
girl who could give us so much
love and feeling in return.

Tears stream because we cannot
reach Govinda—"when will
my eyes fill with tears at
Your absence?"

You remote One, I deserve it,
I know, under dark stars for
Your reasons. But I pray
please let me improve. I
wish I could cry for that
love and really sacrifice
the world of images.

There is no joy in Mudville, Funny Cide has struck out. Now it's really going to happen tomorrow. Devotees and VIPs will be coming from the festival for a tour of Stuyvesant Falls, and many will want to drop in on the sanatorium. There's no stopping it. The inmates are lining up their meds and phoning their doctors what to do if it gets really bad.

"You don't actually have to see them."

"Oh come on, these are VIPs and friends."

"Yeah, but what can you do if your head is blowing off?"

"Stay on rebound another week and we'll quit next week. Increase your dosage. Be a living sacrifice. Smile. Look good."

Junior Barks came to visit his dad.

"Dad, mom and me want to know when you're coming home."

"I had a real bad accident and lost my memory. I don't think I know who you are. Bhaktin Jane is helping me to revive my memory."

"Why take help from her? She beat you up. Don't you remember?"

"Junior, you should leave this to me. It's a spiritual revival we want, not a revival of material memories."

Junior: "What are you trying to do, deprogram him? We can get some authorities to stop you."

"Hey kid, why don't you just get out of here? I'm recovering. I'm healing. I'm learning that the original soul is pure of birth, death, disese and old age."

Junior Barks: "I know that stuff too, even more than you do, Dad. I studied the *Bhagavad-gītā* before you did."

Father Barks said, "Well if you want to study *Bhagavad-gītā* and remember your original self, why don't you stay here? You can get some service in the sanatorium or in the big house. Learn to chant Hare Kṛṣṇa instead of just talking about it."

"Dad! Are you my real dad!?"

"Nobody is dad and nobody is son," said Barks Sr. "These are all coverings. They're temporary. Maybe I was your son in the last life, and you've come to give me a bad time. Just let me alone to recover my spiritual memory, my spiritual self."

Junior Barks looked astounded. What should he do? Go home to his mother, who mostly drank and had other men in the house? Maybe his "new" dad was right.

"Now run along, sonny," said Sr. Barks, "and think over what you want to do. Don't disturb me."

Junior Barks went outside and sat on the front stoop of the sanatorium for awhile with his head in his hands. Then he walked back to the writing staff's office and asked Swami Swims if there was any service he could do.

"Yes, you can keep this place clean. Empty the waste-baskets, clean the bathroom, and help out with the cooking. But right now it's going to be a really busy week, so we can't give you much attention. Just be well-mannered and don't come out with all that egoistic stuff, and I'm sure you can fit into our family."

"Where will I sleep?"

"We'll find a bunk. That's no problem. The only problem is your free will. Surrender it to Kṛṣṇa."

Junior Barks went out for another walk around the grounds to think things over, as much as he could. He thought he'd take a little time and watch what happened when all these visitors came through and then decide afterwards. For the time being he'd go home to his mom.

This one will surely be
interrupted. Your eye will
pop open. Your request
to see Lakṣmaṇa will be
fulfilled in the midst
of a poem—
he'll grab at your eyeglasses,
and dribble on your chest,
and smile with one white tooth.

"We could make beautiful
music together." Who wrote
that? Are you going to
read Rilke to the swami
from Germany? For sure
and give him my ISKCON
interpretation of it:
we flew high at first on
meeting Swami, new worlds,
easy, God seemed close,
we learned a new
glorious language.

But years later we learned
it was very difficult to
write in this language.

It was a humiliating apprenticeship.
No more taste for *Śrīmad-Bhāgavatam* and *japa*.
Like a worm crawling with
no direction or exit.

All he had was "the soul
enduring his own patience."
He endures himself, that's
all he's got. The once
remote, once close Kṛṣṇa
is again remote.

Sigh about that one and
better quit now because your
eye is acting up and if you are
going to see the German well-
wisher at all you'll have
to be pain free.

Dentist tomorrow too
and Kaiśori's arrival.
"Don't be anxious on my
account."

Read him that excerpt from *Malte Laurids*
Brigge and your explanation—
it will be a good way
to reveal yourself and make
open friendship.
Will if I can.

Chapter Ten

Junior entered his house and saw his mother's bedroom door open. She was completely drunk, with whiskey bottles on the floor, lying naked in bed with a naked man he'd never seen before. He walked quietly to his room and began to cry. He had a little altar there with Jagannātha and Nṛsiṁhadeva Deities. He prayed to Them for guidance what to do. I can't live here anymore, he thought. But those people in the dormitory are strange too. They don't teach you anything that you can use in the world. Maybe Swami Swims will let me live with them. I could do some chores for them. He got into bed and took a sleeping pill, decisive as to what he would attempt. He prayed to God to protect him.

"Yes, it's all right with me," said Swami Swims the next day. "But this is a sanatorium. I'll have to ask permission from the higher authorities for you to live here. And you'll have to get your father's permission."

"Oh I'm sure Dad would give it."

Junior Barks went back to his home to get his belongings. When he opened the door he saw his mother sitting on the lap of yet another man, who had his hand up her dress. "What do you want now? Where's your ole pop?" she said with disdain.

"He's still very ill in the hospital," said Junior.

"Well tell that bastard that if he's not going to come back and bring some money, I've got my own sources of income, so he can just stay away from this door." The strange man's hand went further up her dress and she giggled. Junior went to his room, packed all his belongings in a duffle bag and came out again, starting for the front door.

"Where do you think you're going?" she asked.

"I'm leaving home."

"That's all right with me. But before you go let me tell you a secret. I'm not your natural mom. Your dad fucked some other woman and you came from her. I think she's in the loony bin now. So if you step out this door, I don't want to see you come back again. You understand?"

Junior was too shocked to make a reply, but he felt relieved too. He shouldered his duffle bag and started for the door. He slammed it hard behind him. Now he was an orphan in the world with no one to turn to but Kṛṣṇa.

"Like Nārada Muni," Junior said to himself out loud, and he went down the porch stairs and started walking to Stuyvesant Falls, ten miles.

As he passed the houses with their American flags out front, the people sitting on their porches still seemed downcast after yesterday's race. "Somewhere birds are singing / and somewhere children shout / but there is no joy in Mudville / Funny Cide has struck out." But Junior Barks was feeling differently.

"Look out! Look out!
Pink elephants on parade!
Here they come
Hippety hoppety
They're here and there,
Pink elephants ev'rywhere!

. . . but technicolor pachyderms
Is really much for me."[1]

Oh come on, it's not that bad!
It's nice to see your Godbrothers
and show off your snappy
good health and remind them
you can get a head bust at
any second so they shouldn't
expect you to be on time or
even attend the *kīrtana* and
certainly no lectures.

"Swami, lots of people
know you." Yeah I used to
live here. I told the *grāmya-
kathā* of Funny Cide and
"there is no joy in Mudville."

The New Yorkers . . . yeah, they
caught your story and saw your
poetry book *Can a White
Man Be a Haribol?* You were
a lively one like Sid Caesar.
Admitted to watching the Belmont
Stakes on TV with Śacī.

But I'll try to escape without them
seeing me wear khakis when I go
to the dentist. "You're not
a khaki," he said to me, "after
your seclusion, who knows what
you'll come out."

Change so much? Endure my
own soul. But will I still

love Beethoven quartets?
You chant all your rounds.

HBV kept telling me he
thinks he's going to die soon,
a palmist told him he has
a short lifeline. "Me too,"
said Swims, "but Prabhupāda
says you clap in *kīrtana*
and the lines all go away."

"Go to India."
"Can I take shelter of Mahānidhi Swami?"
"Sure." "But he does so many
austerities." "You don't have to
imitate them. Rāma-Rāya doesn't
imitate Aindra Prabhu, just
wants him as a friend
and to play harmonium
like him and stay
in Vṛndāvana.
You talked all that?
No but I was lively. Maybe
I overdid it. Tell them
how sick you are.
Will they all be coming
to the sanatorium?
Don't worry, said Swims. It will
all be over in a few days.
I told them there's a jazz
composition, "Oh What
a Night," and it was like
that for me last night. I
had a splitting migraine until I
took my H-bomb pill to
be with you.

Oh goody. You told them
both the good and bad.
And wore your New York City
Fire Department
sweat shirt but *dhotī*
bottom. You are yourself.

"What did you tell them at breakfast," asked Jane.

"I said while you were not even in New York but transcendental to it, lecturing on *Bṛhad-bhāgavatāmṛta* and chanting, the vast majority of New Yorkers had their minds and hearts fixed on a racehorse named Funny Cide."

"Did they like it?"

"I think so. I began by saying, 'May I indulge you in some *grāmya-kathā?*'"

"The swami from Germany said, 'You kept us in suspense about Funny Cide.' I wished I had the actual newspaper with the story, 'There Is No Joy in Mudville.'"

"But then one of the swamis said, 'In the *Mahābhārata* it says that competitive sports are a form of intoxication. People get puffed up."

"Uh oh," said Tim.

I turned to Śacī and said, "Is that true?"

Śacī said, "I just get nervous."

They were kind. I said, "There's a jazz composition called, 'Oh What a Night,' and I felt like that last night."

"You just told us that."

"Yeah, well, I'm a little nervous. I feel like I'm putting on some showbiz act to prove to them I'm not a depressed, overmedicated hermit. One of them even said, 'Hermit,' and I overheard another say, 'Expatriate.' There's a lot to go for me today—dentist Danz, the transcendental German swami, and maybe Kaiśori."

"Well don't push it."

"It's good to see devotees and especially to read that deep quote from Rilke's notebooks. Would you like to hear it and my ISKCON interpretation?"

"For though he had wanted to hold himself back forever, he was now once again overcome by the growing urgency of his heart. And this time, he hoped to be answered. His whole being, which during his long solitude had become prescient and imperturbable, promised him that the One he was now turning to would be capable of loving with a penetrating, radiant love. But even while he longed to be loved in so masterful a way, his emotion, which had grown accustomed to great distances, realized how extremely remote God was. There were nights when he thought he would be able to fling himself into space, toward God; hours full of disclosure, when he felt strong enough to dive back to earth and pull it up with him on the tidal wave of his heart. He was like someone who hears a glorious language and feverishly decides to write poetry in it. Before long he would, to his dismay, find out how very difficult this language was; at first he was unwilling to believe that a person might spend a whole life putting together the words of the first short meaningless sentences. He threw himself into this learning like a runner into a race; but the density of what had to be mastered slowed him down. It would be hard to imagine anything more humiliating than this apprenticeship. He had found the philosopher's stone, and now he was being forced to ceaselessly transform the quickly produced gold of his happiness into the gross lead of patience. He, who had adapted himself to infinite space, had now become like a worm crawling through crooked passageways, without exit or direction. Now that he was learning to love, learning so laboriously and with so much pain, he could see how careless and trivial all the love had been which he thought he had achieved; how nothing could have come of it, because he had not begun to devote to it the work necessary to make it real.

"During those years, the great transformations were taking place inside him. He almost forgot God in a difficult work of approaching Him, and all that he hoped to perhaps attain with him in time was *sa patience de soppoter une ame* (his patience in enduring soul)."

"I don't understand it," said several of the inmates.

"Here's my explanation," said Swami Swims. "When we first come to Kṛṣṇa consciousness, we're soaring. It's easy. We're near Prabhupāda, near Kṛṣṇa, and it seems so easy. But then—at least this happened to me, probably because of the illness, as well as other reasons—it became very difficult. The gold that we first discovered turned into a lead of patience that we have now to wait for. We have to endure. That's all the soul can do. We discovered something wonderful, and God was close. And now he may be remote. It's hard to chant *japa*, it's hard to read Prabhupāda's books. But God is good. We have to stick to that patience. That's my interpretation."

"So how many more VIP meetings do you have?"

"One tomorrow, and some soul talk with an old friend who's here for a week. I've been holding up well so far. But when I read that Rilke to the swami and told him it was a *confession* that my *japa* and reading were down, he was empathetic. But I'm so stubborn. I'm not trying enough."

I think you'll get better if
not, so what? I am already getting
better. He saw him out the door.
He gave him a present of a candle
and a book but Swims had no presents.
Couldn't teach a *japa* technique

or a revelation he had that
he should preach and love
everyone. Confess he was low
on *sādhana*. His brother gave
him his own prayers to say
but they didn't seem to fit.
Each person has to have his own,
I guess.

"What do you want from me?"
"That you return to your old
self with me but that's not
possible. Can we be something
nice that's new? I don't
see why not."

Too much betrayal?
Ah let's just sing, it's late
and we've heard all this before
how you can't try enough
just open your heart a little
and not too much.

There's no one here *that* confidante.
Try to strike deep quick but
not phony. Old friend how
are you?
Everyone is
mellow talking on the back lawn.

Give me an Ambien
and two short old slapstick
Chaplin films, then I'll be able
to sleep I think.

The lead of patience,
the gold he gave us to start with
our Swami. Our beloved.
Jumpin' pumpkins it was
so easy. Weren't it?
Aint it still in its own
way? Your God
is kind and these friends so
mellow.

Even without *tilaka* or
dhotīs or *saris* and chant as
much as they can.
They don't drag
me down. "Apologize?"
Too late.

"She saluted me!" said Swami Swims on entering the sanatorium after his visit to the dentist.

"Hmm?"

"The dentist's assistant. She was wearing all pink today. Pink pants and shirt. When I was leaving I turned to smile and she saluted and smiled back. I think it was because I was wearing my FDNY sweat shirt."

"Did the dentures fit?" asked Tim.

"Yeah, but I have to go back two days in a row next week. And on the first day I'll leave without my bottom dentures for a day."

"Sounds like you like your visits," said Jane.

"Yeah, as long as he can get a smile from a pretty girl," said one of the monitors whom Swamiji hadn't noticed and who had overheard.

Swims became serious and hitched his *dhotī* up. "I have to get ready for Deity worship, then breakfast with a VIP, and at 10:30 another VIP visit." There was some things he liked sharing with the inmates but didn't like the monitors to overhear. He went solemnly into his private room.

In the dentist's office he had seen three copies of *TV Guide*, showing a picture of a woman with bulging, exposed breasts and the headline: "Sex Is Back!" Had it ever left? Well, I can stay steady, said Swims to himself. I don't read *TV Guide* or watch TV, and I only smile once a week at my favorite dentist's assistant. It's just a friendly thing. I smile at Dr. Danz too, although he's not as charming, but much more important than she is.

He flopped on his bed.

"Visitors over?"

"No, I just spoke with the last VIP. Our meeting was supposed to be one hour. He went way overtime, and then on leaving he said he'd like to come back in a month. And there are still others here who are not VIPs but I've got to meet with."

"Did you confess to him that you use a clicker and sometimes don't finish your daily quota?" asked Tim.

"Don't be so nosy," said Swami. "Just leave me alone."

Then Junior Barks came in carrying his duffle bag. He went into the writing staff's room and started to cry. Jane came in to hear. When he finally finished his story, in between gasps and weeps he said, "And my mom isn't even my mom. Is there really a God?" They calmed him down with empathy and assured him he could live there. Swims was conniving in the back of his mind how he'd get permission for that. Well, he *was* a sick kid, Kṛṣṇa conscious, in bad trouble and in need of care. He was an orphan! They couldn't throw him out. Jane brought in a little cot and pillow and catty-cornered it in the available space in their room. "You've lugged that duffle bag all the way from your home. You should rest now. We'll talk later," said Swims.

"And don't worry about moms," said Jane. "You have plenty of them. I'll be your mom, and the *Vedas* are your mom, and Śrīmatī Rādhārāṇī is the Mother of all devotees." Junior smiled through his tears.

"Could I have a new spiritual name?" he asked.

"Yes, yes," said Swims, "just give me some time to get this straightened out with the authorities."

"I'd like to be called Śukadeva," Junior said.

"Let the Swami pick the name and the time when you get it," said Tim. "Even I don't have a spiritual name yet. The main thing is to be patient and humble and grateful that you've got shelter in this excellent sanatorium."

What do you want from me?
I forgot that you love
me. But it's too late for
that. You're the one
who changed.
"You changed too." Can
we talk about Kṛṣṇa?
People are listening and
they want that.

I told him you lecture
a lot and that compensates
for not reading a lot.
Swims did confess to the
clicker and subpar quota.

Don't tell that. Vicious
ones pick it up and smear
you. They have no empathy.
They just slice through on the
philosophy without caring what
the other person is going
through.

After his car accident Gobhaṭa
Prabhu was permanently paralyzed.
He lies on his back and
presses a button
and a number flashes
on the wall. That way he
chants his Hare Kṛṣṇa mantras.
No *tulasī-mālā*.

Do your best. It's the heart
that counts. We agreed we
don't want to read the
higher rasa *aṣṭa-kālīya-līlā*
eight daily pastimes of Rādhā
and Kṛṣṇa. Agreed on many
things. He said I was surviving but
doesn't know how poor I really
am. Where is my cat?
Where is my Wicklow home?
How can I possibly answer
all this mail?

Cut the medication.
Would you like to learn
hypnosis? I've tried a
lot, said Swims.

Have you listened to
very slow piano
and mysterious cymbals and
a bow over a double bass?
Oh no, that's an airplane
passing in the sky.

June 14, Flag Day and
fireworks. I asked Śacī Swami

(first time in America) if
they had such display of
flags in Deutschland.
No he said, such nationalism
would remind people of Hitler.

"Ever since September 11, 2001,"
he waved his finger, "they're saying
you can't do this to
America and bombing
all the countries."

Don't get hung up. You don't need to be someone's spiritual master. Just be their friend. I did a lot of service for ISKCON, Swims wrote to people he heard who complained that he did not. He apologized for not endorsing their own ISKCON work when he had to live in a sanatorium. Give people credit.

Reaching out to the offended, the insulted, the wounded, the complaining. So that they don't get outraged with you. "I'm thrilled that you are doing such important proactive work."

Then back to bed with two Advils. Quit that med in a few days. Stigma against inmates. They resent it.

Reading aloud two hours from Prabhupāda memories with two *mātājīs*. Time went by so fast I didn't notice it, said Swamiji. How Prabhupāda gave up the name Swamiji and accepted Prabhupāda. Girls allowed to receive brahminical initiation when Govinda dāsī threw a tantrum. "Because he is softhearted." And he took the name Prabhupāda (used by many, like Rūpa, Sanātana, Viśvanātha, etc.) to protect his disciples. Trading stories.

Are you really doing what you want by going to California? I don't know for sure, he thought. How can you know anything ahead of time? Before I was initiated by Prabhupāda in 1966 I didn't know if it was right. Rāya Rāma said, "Take a chance, a gamble." It was a good one. Never leave him.

The acres have quieted down. Do you have social skills? Will you get out of the world alive? In one memory, Śrīla Prabhupāda said in his lecture, "You have to be a hundred percent Kṛṣṇa conscious" to go back to Godhead. Then as he stepped down from the four-foot-high *vyāsāsana* he said, "If you are ninety percent Kṛṣṇa conscious, Kṛṣṇa will take you." Then he said eighty percent, while his long *cādar* dragged along the ground. "Even if you are seventy percent Kṛṣṇa conscious, Kṛṣṇa will take you back to Godhead," he said, flung his *cādar* over his shoulder and walked off with his head held high. Pradyumna's story of starting the transliterations for *Brahma-saṁhitā*. "That was the beginning."

Two hours and ten minutes and no one complained. Please stay in my life. Lakṣmaṇa enters the sanatorium carried by his mother, who wants to change bedsheets. "There's nothing as nice as new bedsheets." While she changes, each inmate is delighted to hold one-year-old Lakṣmaṇa, even though he pulls on eyeglasses, noses, and leaves saliva on shirts. One old man pretends he doesn't like babies and refuses to hold him.

Another: "Look! He's just like baby Kṛṣṇa. Look at him as Mother Yaśodā would."

Grumpy: "Kṛṣṇa was blue."

Another: "Let me hold him. He's Kṛṣṇa's devotee."

Mother Keli was halfway done changing the sheets when Lakṣmaṇa changed his mood and didn't like being handed around. He cried, and only his mother could pacify him. "I'll have to do the other sheets later."

"Oh we can do them. We just wanted our daily *darśana* with Lakṣmaṇa."

Grumpy: "Bah. Humbug. I agree with W.C. Fields, who said that anyone who doesn't like children and dogs can't be all bad."

"Chant, chant, chant, everybody," said a monitor who happened to be passing the open door. "If you people spent more time praying and less time quarreling, you'd be healthy and out of here in no time—and do more service to the Lord."

"Did you catch that? Doing more service to the Lord?" said Tim after the monitor passed. "Same stigma. Doesn't know we can do as much in here as anyone out there."

"Yeah, but chant, chant, chant was good advice."

"How many rounds have you got done, Tim? It's 1:30 P.M."

"Five only," he confessed, "and I think I have to take a nap now."

You think you can get away
with this? Your old-time
bop will just bring you
back as another bopster
or the next-life version
of it.

I'm listening, I don't understand
why that man wouldn't
hold the delightful baby.
I want to hold him until
he cries.

I'm a pampered slob.
I'm a bona fide guru.
A resilient recluse,
a person who cuts off
telemarketers when they

phone and ask, "Do you
want to keep drunken drivers
off the streets?"
"No!" says Śacī.
"Horrible! Horrible!"
the telemarketer shouts.

So intrusive. Put her
on your list of devotees
you wounded by your
mistreatment. What did
I do wrong? You are Dopey
of the Seven Dwarfs who
doesn't know anything except
he likes to get a goodbye
kiss from Snow White
before he goes to work.

Enough *grāmya-kathā!*
But I saw the swamis
liked it when I told
all about the Belmont Stakes.

Just can't believe he's
so peppy. Well you ought
to see him after the lights
go out. Surely I've done
something wrong.

Told my friend my recurring dream
of buying something
and having only false currency.
He told me his, that he's done
something *horrible* and the authorities
are trying to find out what it is.

Kṛṣṇa was a baby like Lakṣmaṇa.
He crawled and reached His hand
forward for a *lāḍḍu*.
He upset the yogurt pot,
He grew up to be the darling
of the young *gopīs* and necked
with them at night.

We can talk about that too
in the right company. Don't
go into areas where even
Śukadeva didn't go because
he'd get too ecstatic mentioning
the names of the *gopīs*.
You are better than Śuka?

No but we want some nectar.
Tomorrow is Friday the 14th
but I don't care.

Yeah well you should go to bed now. The crone is sleeping. The dog is barking. The maiden is gone from his life. The mother is himself! Feminine soft in nature, unlike many of the men he was forced to associate with.

This is the Celtic sign: 

Swims was able to paint for the first time in eight months, and these signs come out and the words "Hare Kṛṣṇa." But they have not provided him enough paint. You're not supposed to spend a lot of money on things, you beggar. You could use house paint, but it's runny. Artists about. You could get in a gallery, "but don't think that while you're painting." Most of the inmates can't relate to it unless it's explicit Hare Kṛṣṇa. Why draw a Druid sign or a star? And funny men. At least they wear *tilaka.*

New meds, dispose of the old ones. It was too late to talk on the phone. They had already gone to bed. *Oṁkāra.* Sky, land and sea. Maybe like the three modes of nature. "But *japa* is most important," said Tim. Mr. Barks' Kṛṣṇa conscious memory was returning, and he was bonding with Junior on that basis. Swims told Junior to be humble and just live with the name "Junior" for awhile. Things could be much better, but they were okay. "Just no stigmas against us," said Tim. "It's a sickness like any other. Backache, arthritis, diabetes, anxiety disorder."

"Okay, lights out."

Wish that damn dog would stop barking. At least no basketballs, and two new paintings drying in the other room. And loving friends. Wonder what tomorrow will be like. They're chanting thirty-two rounds, thought Swamiji, but I mustn't feel guilty. I just had to paint today. After eight months. And I had to read two hours with them to salvage a friendship. Oh, the pin sticker man comes tomorrow, 9:00 A.M. Seems to do no good. Who knows? I had a good day.

Dirge to Django

I already told you
fire captain didn't
like the slow start. But
it's the best part. To
mourn the departed.

No the upbeat is better,
life. But you have to
die before you live.
Born again? What do
you mean? he asked Christ.

Jesus the hunted said you
have to completely revive
your Kṛṣṇa consciousness,
"at least seventy percent."

Some say Prabhupāda will
be there for us. He won't
forget you, she said,
he loves you and you had
so much personal association.
She seemed to know.

Certainly he could do it.
But "during those years the
great transformations were
taking place within him.
He almost forgot God and
the difficult work of
approaching Him." (Rilke)

I'm passing around to all my friends:
"He who was used to infinite space found
himself at the worm without
direction or exit." Why are
you attracted to such
difficulty and sorrow?
"Easily obtained gold
now transformed into the lead
of patience."

Because I read it long ago,
because he was my friend
in the Navy.

Because I know that
difficulty and that waning,

I almost fell, I'm fallen
now and people complaining.
Heal, heal they say.
I say "Just give me
gallons of paint."
Dirge and upbeat,
Prabhupāda, be there.

We talked a little about Taoism because he mentioned it last time. He said he likes Lao-tzu because he's so simple and things tend to be complicated. Mao wiped out all the pure acupuncturists in China, but one escaped to Japan, and the line is still going. He asked if I followed Rajneesh! (Swims is telling all this to his buddies instead of *japa* and after an hour nap.) Imagine while I was filled with pins for twenty-five minutes, Rajneesh! I answered politely no and said he made things up. He asked about our line. I told him people think Hinduism is polytheistic. There are minor gods, but One Supreme, Viṣṇu or Kṛṣṇa.

He asked about holy places. I said yes, wherever the *avatāras* from higher planets visit, they are holy places. And rivers, Ganges and Yamunā. It was a good way to pass twenty-five minutes with "sedative" pins in you. One kind of pins are stimulating, and this week I got the sedative ones. When I ask for explanations, I don't understand what he tells me, but he seems to have full answers. He said my pulse was very good. I admitted I was improving a little it seemed from last week.

I said the *dhāmas* were covered with filth and commercialism and said you had to see beneath the coverings. (Some of the inmates started fingering their beads or walked away from Swims, not interested in his tiny preaching to the pin sticker, which he seemed so proud of. Inmates rarely get a chance to talk to outsiders.)

I was really mild with him. I mean I kept leaning to things spiritual *he* might like, and he kept coming back to Hinduism. I tried to paraphrase the Li Po poem, "People ask why I live in the mountains / and I smile to myself / the peach trees are blooming, / the rivers are flowing, / and I live in a world beyond this one."

"Why didn't you preach more directly about Hare Kṛṣṇa?"

Well, it came to that naturally. I told him my guru's name and the kind of meditation we do, on beads or singing. (Some of the inmates walked out to the front porch and sat in rockers and chairs and fingered their beads, out of hearing range.)

Yeah, I got it all in, but gently, said Swims.

"Did you say the mantra?"

No. I was shy to come out and say, "Hare Kṛṣṇa movement." But I talked a lot about my spiritual master and monotheism. Then he asked me about celibacy. I said there were temptations but it was the fast way to God. You give up all other attachments and are free to preach. All over the world there are saintly celibates. He was hinting we must yearn for sex. I said sometimes you may, but you get over it. You're more satisfied without it. Anyway, there was no *prajalpa*. I asked a little more about acupuncture. I mean you can't just lie there silent for twenty-five minutes, and I didn't want to say, "Today is Friday the 13th," or "Too bad about Funny Cide." He asked if I liked my stay in Ireland . . .

"Maybe you'd better get back to your own *japa*."

Swims was a little annoyed. I try. I will. I get sleepy. I'll chant now. He said he'll come back four more Fridays. I said, well, I'll be here.

"Yeah, we're always here."

You sing your song I
told him, that's one kind
of meditation. You sing.

"Did you say the names
of God?" No. I assumed
he knew I meant prayer.
And I said we chant
on beads, we pray.
But he asked about "meditation."
He meant that deep breathing
kind of stuff. I couldn't
imagine he'd realize
the power of the name.

Maybe because I don't
realize. You know, when
they say *meditation*
they mean sitting in the
yogic pose and breathing and
going off nowhere
"deep."

So to say we utter
out loud names of God
seems a hard jump for
them.

"But you should make
that jump of faith."
Next week I may tell
him the actual mantra and
the power of the sound

but I don't like bluffing and
I did feel a bit guilty,
like that disciple who
called me a hypocrite
for saying "I chant sixteen
rounds" in a lecture.

I meant I've been
doing it for thirty years
but just now I "can't."

Tell him what you can.
"Take what you need
and leave the rest,"
your friend says.
And God is kind.
But let's go work on it now
that you've got a little spare
clear-headed time.
'Hare Kṛṣṇa, Hare Kṛṣṇa, Kṛṣṇa Kṛṣṇa, Hare Hare,
/Hare Rāma, Hare Rāma, Rāma Rāma, Hare Hare.'

Chapter Eleven

Swami Swims came back from the telephone and sat glumly in his chair in the writing staff's room.

"I had heard there was some dissatisfaction in the last place I was actively serving. So I wrote a general letter to them and asked them what they really thought. I just got two letters back from two men there, and they said that I didn't endorse ISKCON projects. I'm going to write them back and tell them how I burned the candle at both ends for thirty years on ISKCON projects, but when I was struck down with migraine, it became impossible for me to do all that I was doing before. But I'll apologize for not endorsing *their* continued efforts and admit that I should show interest, even if I can't do it myself. I remember I had a disciple on the farm who used to walk behind the oxen. I heard he was angry with me, and so we had a one-to-one talk. His complaint was that I didn't also walk behind the oxen and so I didn't inspire him. I told him the spiritual master's duty is not to do exactly what a disciple is doing but to encourage him in his service. Anyway, now I'm not endorsing ISKCON projects."

"Stigma," seethed Tim.

Barks Senior was recovering very nicely. Jane's unorthodox approach to his therapy was to allow him to remain a blank slate about everything that occurred before his accident and make him remember only Kṛṣṇa consciousness, as if he had just come out of the womb and was being introduced to *bhakti* by Vaiṣṇava parents. It was actually working. Sometimes he'd remember some of the old days, but she would tell him they were like dreams, illusions, and he should put them aside.

Actually, he aspired to become a devotee, and he spent all his time reading Prabhupāda's books and chanting and taking his instructions from his new *śikṣā* guru, Bhaktin Jane.

One day, she took a break from her typing and came and sat beside him. He asked, "Bhaktin Jane, would you marry me?"

She hadn't been expecting this. In psychiatry, this phenomenon is known as "transference"—the client falls in love with the psychologist or vice versa. It is not helpful for the counseling process.

"No," said Jane. "That wouldn't be good for either of us. Although I don't want you to remember your past, I know from your history that you have been with so many prostitutes and so-called wives and lovers and you have shacked up with so many women over the years. Your son doesn't even know who his mother is. And his heart was broken several times when he walked in and saw you with one of your paramours. You were a drunk and a junkie. I'm not saying getting married is going to bring you back to all that, but what I mean to say is you've had enough of married life and living with women. I'm trying to tell you that you have a life ahead where you can live pure of material attachments.

"And Mr. Barks, I can tell you that I too have had a sinful past. I was a female biker and consorted with many men, winding up in fights, drunkenness, addiction. I was lucky I didn't die but came to Kṛṣṇa consciousness by the Lord's grace and the guru's grace.

So why should either of us, even though we're now cleansed, go back to *gṛhastha* life? You're reading Prabhupāda's *Bhāgavatam*. Look in the second chapter in the First Canto and see what Śukadeva Gosvāmī says about married life. It's all right if you're young and want to raise a family in an ideal way. But we're both a little over the hill and our pasts are too sullied for that. We should just make it straight back to home, back to Godhead. I'll still be your friend and help you in any way I can."

"You're probably right," said Mr. Barks, "I just wanted to express how indebted to you I am. I love you."

"I love you too," said Jane. "Śrīla Prabhupāda was once talking to a yogi, and the yogi said, 'I love you, Prabhupāda.'" Prabhupāda replied, 'I love you too. But not this skin love.'"

"And what about my son, Junior?" said Mr. Barks.

"He's still your son. But now he's part of our whole family. He's everyone's son. And he's doing great. He has given up his puffed up notions which he had when he first came here. He's just happy to serve the Vaiṣṇavas. And he's healing from all those horrible things he saw and felt when growing up in your house.

"You guys and girls are building a wall around yourself and hiding there. You should come out and meet the grounded ISKCON. Why are you so afraid of your Godbrothers? I don't believe in your crutches. You are not invalids. It is not true. You shouldn't accept it. You're paranoiacs. You are much more than this stuff. Why don't you release yourself from this decline and anxiety? Crack the wall you've built around yourself. Center yourselves and live your actual truths with integrity—whatever that turns out to be." These words were delivered in a loud voice at the open door of the sanatorium for all the inmates to hear by a preacher VIP who was just stopping by on a five-minute tour of the grounds before heading off on a vigorous world tour of the States and then to India.

The inmates were stunned and hurt. He left without another comment.

"Should we run after him or write him a note before he goes?"

"He's already in his car."

"Don't they know pain is real, illness is real? That it's slow to heal?"

"One day they'll be here too, or worse."

"I'd like to give him a piece of my mind, or boot," said Jane.

In the backs of the minds, some inmates were doubtful: "We *are* wimps. We *are* hiding behind a wall."

"Don't think like that," said Swims, as if he read their minds. "Many of us are slowly getting better. There is more than one way to be a member of grounded ISKCON and to preach. He's just one swellhead. Even if there's a tad of truth in what he says, we know our illnesses are authentic—diabetes, arthritis, pains and disabilities that prevent us from more active service."

"Stigma." Tim repeated his mantra.

"I don't understand why they think we're fakers," said Swims. "We all know that if any one of us tried to march in the Rathā-yātrā down Fifth Avenue, New York, today, we'd quickly exacerbate our weak conditions and have to retire from the action. I'm getting a headache just thinking about his spite."

"Chant quietly," said Mr. Barks, and they all looked at him and his calm leadership with surprise. They tried chanting, but some could not keep it up.

Oh well what the hell,
you've got people who
believe in you.

You've got the flagstone
workers pounding and not
helping things. You've got
people starving in India so
they fight off dogs to
get the remnants from
people who just feasted.

You've got the Oval
Office and one dunce after another.
The rebels, the opinions,
the advice that you're
sick and have to find
yourself.

Deep souls like Rilke
on their own. Poems.
A *sampradāya* truth
you follow somehow,
a guru who wishes you well.

"Delaunay's Dilemma."[1] "What
a revoltin' development this is,"
said William Bendix,[2]
the simple comedies.

Even at this moment I hope
they're marching down the Avenue
"the most important street in
the world" with their colorful carts.

Seven-month-old Lakṣmaṇa watches
for the first time in his life
and upstate a group . . .

listen, if you go alone and
paint without all this tormenting
input of put-downers
you'll be better
and can paint
your passion on canvas.

See a friend tomorrow a
nay-sayer today. Throw
in the towel after too
many attempts.

The dilemma is can he reach God
without a bona fide
guru? That's not true here,
so take it on the chin and
rise on the next wave.

Comeback kid never had
it better in one sense.

Inmates talk:

"Are we going to stay here forever?"

"What do you mean? No one lives forever."

"No, I mean for the rest of our lives."

"Some of us. Some may get shifted to old age homes. Some may recover and lead more normal lives. Some may move to California."

"I've been thinking about that," said Swami S. "Someone advised me not to go. They said it's really nice here with the children and occasional visits. Better association than in California. But as a writer, it could be good to get a different environment."

"You can change your inner environment while staying here."

"Everything can change."

"Yeah, but slowly."

"Or fast."

"He's a writer, and that's what he thinks of first—the world of objects and how to get sense impressions."

"Yeah, but if you can heal here, then that's best. Who advised you not to move?"

"Nevermind. They told me to think for myself. I have so many people ready to accommodate me. But it's true I could do everything here."

"You mean as a writer you'd feel stagnant with the same people?" asked Jane.

"No, I'm not saying that."

"Because we're all changing too. Look at Mr. Barks and how he asserted himself today. Different people could move in. You could tell more about the monitors. So many things. In a week summer begins. Tell how he found where the groundhogs are sneaking into the garden. Read us more memories from the *Prabhupāda Memories* books. Some are surprising."

"Don't be in a rush, Swims. You've got a good spot here, even if it's a little crowded, and there are visitors, and it's noisy."

"But the man has already spent so much money in California."

Things. Things on the desk. Lots of pens and cups. Revving up to do painting here. Don't be guilty you don't chant your full rounds. Just set them on your side. Mail in and out. Did you ever watch Ernie Kovacs?[3] He was well ahead of his time. She said she did not like Chaplin slapstick because it reminded her of how her parents beat her as a child.

Things. But beyond things. On the way out of the door, a friend caught the acupuncturist and asked, "Is he okay?" He said, "His energy is splayed all over. It's not concentrated in one place. That's not good." But he wants to be a writer and painter. Nevermind what they think. Dinner. Usually too much to eat. Hide it in a paper towel. Talking things out.

"Goodbye, pal."

"Trust that I am on your side and I will be confidential."

Maybe we won't communicate so much. She has secrets too? Really. I thought only I had secrets. Do the groundhogs have secrets? Yes, but we found out today their entrance to the fenced-in garden.

Everyone has God in their heart. It's an open secret. Kṛṣṇa is calling for us.

"Hey, listen to this," an inmate called out without considering whether the others wanted to hear or not what he had to read. "Listen to this Rilke poem from *Love Poems to God*. I like it."

You, God, who live next door—
If at times, through the long night, I trouble you
with my urgent knocking—
this is why: I hear you breathe so seldom.
I know you are all alone in that room.
If you should be thirsty, there's no one
to get you a glass of water.
I wait listening, always. Just give me a sign!
I'm right here.

As it happens, the wall between us
is very thin. Why couldn't a cry
from one of us
break it down? It would crumble
easily,

it would barely make a sound.

It was near time for supper. Is anyone really hungry? We don't so much like what they cook. Hear Prabhupāda lecture. Take it in. Ask someone to read BB to you when you eat. No. They'd see us sneak the food we don't want and hide it in the garbage.

Noise is not so bad, she said. I would miss my daily hugs with Laksi. What to speak of the mixture of solitude and people. "The hidden swami," the grandma called me. KR said he'd buy me conservative shorts. I don't need the seclusion.

But you need to go deeper, like Rilke, waiting and waiting for the first lines of *Duino Elegies*, and finally they were dictated to him in, as he said, a divine revelation: "But who among the hierarchies of angels would answer if I called?" Then he had to wait a long time before more came. We can't wait. Dentists, pins, letters, tattooed close friend. Disciple. What does it mean? I will not get a tattoo. I will get a bamboo flute. I will break down the paranoiac walls and meet people without fear. Many people can see that I am fearful of people. Like what, a deer? Please don't hurt me. Tender heart. Hit the heavy punching bag, harder and harder, row faster and faster. I am not a wimp. I shall stay in New York or California as I desire.

I didn't expect this to happen,
that Hawk[4] would play. I
thought we were on a different
track

but I'm open to new impressions.
A writer wants to see the different
sights. Use the big desk.
So change again, get me out
West.

With trepidation he can
move in any clothes he wants
and find his self. Get new
people to work for you.
Can you edit? No smoking.
Here, Śrīla Prabhupāda told
Miss Mexico, "Why did you say
you will come back?
Why? Do you want to learn?"
She fluttered her eyelashes
and didn't know what to say.
Suddenly she was no longer
Miss Mexico but a soul.

The guru is not for trivialities.
Approach him when you need
to know the absolute truth

and you are ready to surrender.
Eat breakfast early and clean
your mouth, always thinking
of God.

As you move in the toilet,
the truck, tomorrow to DDS Danz, don't forget
Kṛṣṇa in favor of
"sex is back."

He may want to go to California so Swims and company can get new sense impressions, but that place isn't going to be ready for months. Swims phoned the California patron yesterday and said he didn't want to go to California. Swims had been talking with an influential friend who said it wasn't a good idea and that he should really think on his own what he wanted to do.

He thought on his own and concluded that New York was just fine, a good balance between seeing people and being alone. The patron said, "Fine, I'll agree with whatever you want." So he hung up the phone and then thought about it some more. He began to change his mind. He said what I really am is a writer. And so the most important thing is that Swims and company have stimulation. It hasn't happened yet, but it might get stagnant here in New York for them. The same sanatorium, the same situations. They'll be great changes if we go to California! So he phoned back his patron and said, "This is Mr. Flip-Flop. I thought about it some more and I decided that I do want to go to California." The patron said, "Fine, we'll get the place ready for you in any event and if you change your mind, you won't have to use it."

Today is the scheduled day for Swims to talk to his counselor (who is also the patron in California). He's going to start off with a whole rap about California, how in '49 so much gold was discovered there, and people were saying, "There's gold in dem dar hills." Then comes the famous statement by the journalist in the 1800s, "Go West, young man!"[5] Americans began to migrate West because they heard there were better chances for homesteading, making money and living in better conditions. So the West was "won." Then he'll say to his patron that California became ruined, that carbon dioxide from the cars fills the skies around Los Angeles with yellow haze. Hollywood, Hollywood. Ruined the environment. San Francisco had its own life, and there was a writers' renaissance there in the 1960s, with the Beats. But now as a footnote to this, in 2003, there's a little author, Satsvarūpa, who's writing some fiction about some characters living in upstate New York. It's going well, but he's thinking it might be good if they had a break, a change, and went to California. In this way he'll make it clear he wants to go there.

But it can't happen overnight. A lot of work has to be done on the little funky house that he's supposed to move into. It'll take months. So we've got to keep rolling here in New York and not feel we're bogged down. Don't be afraid. New York, New York. All the wonderful people here, and my Rādhā-Govinda Deities and Prabhupāda *mūrti*, all of whom I'm going to leave behind when I go! This is really my home, as much as California could become. And I love seeing Laksi every day, and Śacī's care, and the fact that I'm in close contact by phone and mail to New Yorkers who do my editing work and enthuse me, sending me comedy videos and so on. Yes, stick it out in New York. There's plenty to do and say here.

Whose opinion? Why are you asking?

"My eyes are burning." No more meds; try Radox. What did you want to say? Those old writing sessions. Now is a good time for drinking water. Your eyes are burning. Then you should take a nap. They don't understand. We must keep moving. Do you have funny ones? I gave him the wrong name for the girl in Russia. It's Himavati, not Pārvatī. She wants to help translate my books. Are they worth it? Yes. He talked two hours with a woman who had hardly any clothes on. Then he spoke two hours with a man with a big beard. I realized he wasn't recognizing the body but the soul. He's an *avadūta*. But a bookseller doesn't have that much time. You have a small window of time, four or five hours, in which to sell all the books." Rathā-yātrā report. They sold all the books they had brought with them. Made $2,000. Sold many art catalogs. Keep painting. Keep painting.

It rained at the end. But many people came. It was good. They didn't have time to talk to people. He was a little spaced out, couldn't concentrate. Yeah, well, he's getting older, and all these stressors hit him at once.

Interviewing servants. Must chant *japa*. Must serve guru and not be offended by his paintings. Must agree with his madness. What she calls his "paranoia" may be his fear of letting go his full artistic charge, which he has been holding back so the institution won't be offended.

We haven't even begun to tell you the e-mail life and phone life of Swami Swims. For example, here's a letter he wrote but was advised not to send: "So-and-so told me that So-and-so Mahārāja phoned you and for two hours told you how to live your life. Don't you know how to hang up the phone? When X dāsī and her husband were visiting Vṛndāvana, he wanted them to live there. She disagreed. Mātājīs came up to her, pressuring her to obey her husband and stay. In her vulgar way she said, 'Mind your own f_ _ _ _ _ _ business.'

"You taught me self-assertion. Now use it yourself.

"They advised me it's too early to try to be just friendly. But I'm so fried to hear you stayed on the phone so long being told what to do.

"PS – Listen to your inner voice and what's revealed in your meditations. As you have told me to become my own person, you have to do that to."

How long can a man keep running
as fast as he could at twenty-five
years old? Money in the bank.
He's planning to go all over the
world and get the books translated.
I gave him Rilke's *Love Songs to God.*
"Is this excellent?" I don't know,
I haven't read it.

I'd preferred to give him
Buckowski but didn't dare.
Don't know what he's looking
for. The devoted poet.

Said he saw a biography of
Rilke and it was horrible.
He made such pretty poems
but his life . . .

Rahsaan's Run.[6] They hit
the high note. The limits
of the instrument. A human
being can talk with God.
Can get response.
Living in Vṛndāvana *sādhus*
used to and still can bathe
in the Yamunā and lose
all sins
don't you
realize the advantage?

I have lost all control.
He was
spaced out. I've seen crazy people,
been in the van with them, and
my mother was an alcoholic.

You see people at their worst
and learn how to handle
yourself.

But it's not peaceful atmosphere
to tell the beauties of California.

Oh God, oh God, he used that
word in German, said
the wall between us
is very thin and I think
we should be able to break
through.

Which one of the angels
would answer my call,
was how he interpreted it.
I thought it meant none of
them would answer and he
was in despair. That's why
I thought he was such a
sad person and I should
avoid ultimate intimacy with
him.

Learn from a more straight-
forward American. Radox
on the head and lie down. I'm going
out West, I confirmed. He gave
me a Jungian chart. Haven't read
it yet. I'm hard put, my voice
is tired. Please *you guys* handle
it for me. I can't do it
myself.

All I can do is rally the wounded
with virtual relationships and
cuddle Laksi and explain a
few more e-mails outgoing.

Ask opinion and you'll get
smacked on the head.
No I am not ready to
deal again with the tigress,
stay on the safe path
of religion, although you
like to reach out and
help a friend.
Sacrifice that.

Swims was thinking. He wanted freedom. This is too often called *the golden mean*, which Madeline had learned in an ancient Greek history course at Hunter College. When Swims was a teenager he began to think his sister used the golden mean as an excuse for mediocrity. She abandoned poetry and married a man who from his earliest age meditated on what he wanted to be when he grew up. He decided that money was certainly the most important thing in the world and that he should seek out a job that brought the most money. He gave his life to that and eventually entered Wall Street and became a stock analyst. Swims lost touch with them after some time, but it looked like the money was rolling in. They scoffed at Swims' "beatnik" irresponsible nature, and they rejected him when he discovered the East and Swami Bhaktivedanta.

But that was ancient history. Now Swims had to decide for himself who he really was and what he wanted. He had surrendered himself wholly to the mission of his spiritual master for many years, even though he was put into positions that were ill-suited to his psychophysical nature. Śrīla Prabhupāda had written him, "You are not a good manager but I keep you on the GBC because you do what I say." That sentence was like a double-edged sword; he wasn't a good manager—that was admitted by his guru—and yet he was obedient, like a slave, doing something that was against his nature.

Now more and more he sought freedom of expression. And that meant a turning toward art. He had been devoted to art (which mostly meant writing) since he was seventeen years old and was living the life of the "starving artist" in a cold flat on the Lower East Side. Writing was his religion, and he was influenced by dedicated persons like Rilke, Kafka, and others who despite moral deficiencies considered writing to be their religion and put all morality aside to devote themselves to perfecting the art. It was a "religion," not just in a mundane sense but in a truly spiritual sense, because it was their very best attempt to serve God, even though in most cases they didn't know guru or God through an enlightened *paramparā* system. That opportunity simply wasn't open to them.

Swami Swims *had* the opportunity to know God in a bona fide way, and he knew God's desires through a great *ācārya*, A.C. Bhaktivedanta Swami Prabhupāda. And he knew the method as taught by Lord Caitanya, to call on God's names, to live a pure life, and—the special emphasis of his own guru—to spread Kṛṣṇa consciousness to the suffering masses who are in ignorance of their real need. But Swims always did it the institution's way, and in many ways that squelched his own personal tendencies. Now, in broken health, despite the risks, more and more he was expressing his real tendencies. He had to do it before it was too late. So he found himself writing "a novel with poems" for the first time, and painting primitive, wild, vibrant canvasses. His counselor told him this was definitely the way for his personal health and fulfillment, but that he'd have to expect resistance from the conservative element in the movement. Swims had long tried to live *the golden mean*, as Madeline did, but now he was drifting more toward bringing it all out, as his life duration raced toward the final turn and into the homestretch. There were people who liked it, as well as those who didn't.

One older devotee who had been a sculptor from an early age and who pleased Prabhupāda very much with his creations saw Swamiji's paintings and said, "Too bad he didn't start painting at an early age." Swims took that as a challenge. He didn't need to start early, he thought. I shall do it my way. And I already know that people like it.

So how to find more freedom? The headaches prevented him, visitors, e-mails, the tight quarters of the sanatorium. California promised more freedom. But since he had arrived at these realizations now while in New York, he wanted to hit the accelerator right away and "let freedom ring." He prayed to God to let him do it, and to let it be an acceptable offering to the *saṅkīrtana* movement.

He read in an introduction to Rilke's poems that Rilke felt deeply for suffering living entities, but his poems were not aimed to change social conditions, as the novels of Emile Zola, who actually tried to bring about political and social reform in his time. Rilke went about it in his own way, expressing the pain and suffering of all *jivas* and pointing the way to love and a God consciousness. And although Rilke's poetry is not as clear as Gauḍīya Vaiṣṇavism, and although it certainly contained dark elements, which the Vaiṣṇavas are free of, it is a sincere offering for all living beings. And some have taken in that way.

Certainly, therefore, one who possesses the knowledge of *Bhagavad-gītā* can do so much more. And if he lets himself do it with full freedom, what is the harm? Even if his contemporaries do not understand it, he must do it, because he is an artist, a writer, and he has the call. At least that is how Swims was thinking at 11:00 at night in the middle of June '03 in his small New York room, with a pain in his right eye. Freedom, and for this he would require more renunciation and less influence from others.

Two days in a row to Dr. Danz. He said if you want to remove the new upper denture (now that the bottom is removed for one day), "blow your cheeks out like Dizzy Gillespie." Swims was so stunned by the Novocaine—

tooth pulled and pained as the upper denture touched the skin—that he had no composure to smile. The pretty assistant didn't smile either. He staggered out. But he kept thinking how cool Dr. Danz was and how he'd tell him tomorrow, "You know, I'm just the man for you to mention Dizzy Gillespie to, whereas one of those young rockers might not have related to it. Dizzy, Charlie Parker, Thelonious Monk, Coltrane, Bud Powell and the musicians of that era are my favorite."

It didn't hurt Diz but it hurt Swims. "Only tourists hear the doves, residents don't notice," a friend said. He's right. We fail to notice. They want *sannyāsīs* to regard everything they are given as belonging to ISKCON. They have to stand on line and ask, "May I have $10 for gasoline for a drive to a lecture I gave at Saratoga? I'm now going to be giving one at Albany." Yes, the institution man says, we must be on the up and up. If you are "renounced," you shouldn't get what those who live in the temple can't get. Swims wrote back, "I don't take a big piece of the pie. Forgive me for not thanking you for what you did." They claim he only encourages "artists." He is an artist himself, doesn't praise managers. Doesn't praise preachers. Doesn't praise anyone. Doesn't give shelter. "I've got to do some damage control and make up for this bad reputation," thought Swims. But freedom calls. "Why should they always tell me what to do and expect to control me?" Leave the *brāhmaṇa* to go free and he'll do better work for you. Put him under no control. If his right hand and arm is always connected in fear to the brain—"will they censor me?"—then how can he break new ground? Aspiration and patience both will produce the breakthrough.

Can you go that deep? Is that art or management or just plain Kṛṣṇa conscious prayer? BVT said only the *kaniṣṭha-adhikārīs* can't taste Kṛṣṇa's pastimes because they have doubts as they argue and preach.

The *madhyamas* and *uttamas* are free to see and enjoy God. Work on, *madhyama-adhikārīs*, work on. God sees you and will reward you. Be real, be better, aspire and work. I don't see you working so hard. Lord knows it better than your counseling friends, girls, boys. Guru too. They know. And you know, so why don't you improve?

I've got to write a poem and watch a film. Got to.

Got to be nutty?
I think you have to be serious.
Little lions and angels
imagined by Braji in
the back yard.
Two-year-old nudie making
pancakes for her dad
on Father's Day.
The nutty hidden swami
received new safari shorts.
He's far-out to wear non-
sannyāsī clothes. Do you
think it's wrong to be
a *kaniṣṭha?* It's all we've
got.

Nutty. *Grāmya* aspiration,
it's a kind of play. You have
to be happy to serve the Lord
and sometimes a little nutty
in a lecture to wake up
the sleepers—I wish you
would not be so far behind.

It seems like real
rebound. They love you
but don't see you
doing much better.

Five minutes and twenty-five seconds
isn't enough time to cure
anxiety disorder. But
it helps to wear
a black bio-band around your head
and get acupuncture pins.

Headaches every day.
"Really?" said Dr. Danz.
Honey, you could have
smiled and it would have
made my day. But at least
he mentioned the
bulging cheeks of
Diz and there was good
deep Kṛṣṇa consciousness in her
letter which I sent
out to another.

Chapter Twelve

Swami Swims returned to the house. Before entering the sanatorium he saw some friendly monitors in their house. He said, "The doctor botched it again. He didn't make the bottom denture properly, and I have to go back again tomorrow for a refitting." Then he thought about what he hadn't said, that he and Dr. Danz had talked about Dizzy Gillespie and John Coltrane. Dr. Danz said he saw Thelonious Monk at the Five Spot,[1] and Swims said he also saw him there, and saw John Coltrane several times. But Swims couldn't see the pretty assistant anywhere. Maybe she was somewhere in the background, but he couldn't spot her. So when the botched job was over, Swims' face was still dirty, according to their standards. Dr. Danz said, "We have to wash your face, we don't want you to leave dirty." So then suddenly she came forward with a wet tissue and began to dampen his face.

Swims said to her, "Oh, I didn't think I'd get a chance to see you today."

"Well here I am," she said.

He felt like saying, "Seeing you makes my day," but he didn't. But she said, "You'll see me again tomorrow too." That made up for the botched job, and she knew it. Thought Swims, I could tell her, "If the dental lab keeps botching up my dentures, then I'll get to see you every day." And even as he went to the front desk to get his appointment time for tomorrow, he caught a last glimpse of her, just a teeny glimpse, as she went around the corner, and she looked his way, and he looked her way.

No use telling the monitors all about that, or even the inmates. They'd get the wrong idea. There's nothing really wrong with it. It's just harmless flirtation. It's just brightening your day with a pretty assistant. And in fact, this day was even more brightened by old white-haired Dr. Danz and their exchange about Coltrane. Danz said he belongs to a spiritual group that meets once a week, and they're suppose to bring spiritual gifts, so last week he brought the album *A Love Supreme* and presented it.

Swims told him, "That album converted me from an atheist to a theist."

On returning, Swims strode into the sanatorium wearing his civilian clothes. He liked wearing his civvies and mixing with the ordinary people, instead of always wearing his uniform.

"How'd it go?" asked one of the inmates cheerfully.

"Not so good," said Swims, "they botched it again. They made the bottom denture too high and they have to fix it again overnight. I have to go back tomorrow."

"Boy, that's two botches. Are they charging you for it?"

"No. But it's a twenty minute ride each way, a trigger for my illness. And sitting in that waiting room with all the shiny magazines and the lousy music. It makes me appreciate the peace of the sanatorium. You should also. You've got this nice backyard with the grass, and you can walk on it and use the swings if you want. Sit in the lawn chairs, read a good book, chant your rounds in peace. We don't really have to do anything, that's how our doctors advise us. So I get impressed with that when I have to go into town and see this doctor. Especially when he keeps botching things. But we did get to talk about jazz. He told me to remove my new dentures by glowing out my cheeks like Dizzy Gillespie. That led to a long conversation about our favorites. He's pretty hip."

"Didn't you mention something about his dental assistant too?"

Swims was reticent. "I didn't notice her today." Then he went back to his room, thinking he could use a little nap. Dentists are a pain in the ass, even if they do like John Coltrane. In his room, Swims turned to Tim and said, "I told him the liner notes on Coltrane's *A Love Supreme* converted me to theism. But I didn't tell him they converted me to the Hare Kṛṣṇa movement, or that they at least helped me to accept the Hare Kṛṣṇa movement."

"Doesn't he know you're a devotee?"

"I don't think so."

"Well why don't you tell him, or what's the use of dressing up in those civilian clothes and acting so cool?"

"You're right. I'll try to find a spot and tell him. I already told the acupuncturist, so it shouldn't be so hard."

From the corner, Junior said, "*yāre dekha, tāre kaha 'kṛṣṇa'-upadeśa / āmāra ājñāya guru hañā tāra' ei deśa*, tell whoever you meet about Kṛṣṇa and you will be with Me soon."

Yeah Danz and I were rapping about
Monk, imagine if we ever met
"Five Spot Blues" at the bar,
a dental student and an
aspiring out-of-work writer.

What would we have said?
He couldn't have known

we would meet in
'03 at his office in
Hudson, New York, and I'd
have only one tooth and
say to his daisylike assistant
when he was out of range,
"I didn't think I'd get to see you today."

You've gotten more uninhibited in
the last year and a half, an
advisor said. Well is that a
bad thing? I think it's healthy.
I forgot to carry my cane. I'm
very careful now how I dress
when I go there.

When Danz went to the
Five Spot was Johnny Griffin
on sax? I boasted I'd seen
Trane "a number of times."

"Blues Five Spot" he plays
not with arced fingers but
flat on the keys.

You ought to concentrate on
your *sādhana* and more on
your health or your sleep
or your movies or you
clemency, answering letters.

I want you to find yourself
and heal yourself.

New teeth. Birds chirping. This is
cold country. Bicoastal writer.

Give me permission and things will
change. Those canvasses
will roll out and you'll be
unashamed. Plenty of paint,
quick time and don't care what
they think.

Report how much money
you spend. Be accountable.
The infamous statement
he said your secretary made:
"He left ISKCON ten years
ago." No, she said *I* said
it in a book.
Where? Show me the page.
"Blues Five Spot," me and
Danz drinking away and
digging monk and not knowing
the wonderful future
I would inherit.

Hey, there's nothing wrong with the first person singular. You can pop "I" in there when you like.

Three times W.C. Fields tried to hit his golf ball across a little pond onto an island where the golf hole was. He failed each time. Then in a rage, he grabbed his whole bag of clubs and threw it in the water.

"You can't do that!" his friend said.

Fields replied, "I can do anything I want!" And so it is with this book. It doesn't have to be a novel. In fact, the doctor told me, Do what you want. Don't listen to others. Keep those people cooped up in the sanatorium, or let them all out. I am, however, attached to how things are going right now at Stuyvesant Falls and to the different personas, but I'm just alerting myself that there's no absolute rule as to persona, first person or second person or third person forms of address, and so on. We've got a fairly well-ordered thing with prose and poems and invalids who are aspiring for the absolute truth. Who found easy gold and are now finding a little lead to go further. They're aspiring and not giving up. This is our theme. And they are becoming themselves, even if it means dropping down a notch from the official behavior of a *pukka* Vaiṣṇava. Be who you are. Find Kṛṣṇa in your way.

Since I keep coming in every day to the dentists to do their botches, I thought he might ask me whether I have a job. But out of professional politeness he hasn't. I'd tell him that I used to be an active religious minister but now I'm living at the sanatorium.

After the difficulties of the drive into town, Swami Swims wanted to encourage the other devotees about living in the beautiful acres that they had, with nice grass and children playing, with their not being responsible for the children, the freedom of just watching them from a distance. Noises that they could bear. Doctors who they dealt with on the phone and who were sympathetic to them. The phone counselors, who were definitely sympathetic. And the monitors, who just overlook things for the maintenance of the place, although they are sometimes a little pesky but basically compassionate. They shouldn't feel guilty that they couldn't "go out."

"Everything you say is right, Swims," said one old man, "as long as we don't take it as a senior citizens' home, a nursing home, and just count our days till death playing checkers. I heard a tape where Prabhupāda said a devotee yogi is engaged twenty-four hours in Kṛṣṇa's service. I was trying to figure out how we can do that, but then he said simple things, like chanting Hare Kṛṣṇa or doing any task, seeing Kṛṣṇa and thinking of Kṛṣṇa, not like transcendental meditation, where it's something vague and you don't have the form of Kṛṣṇa. So this isn't a nursing home, because it's transcendental. But it's up to us to keep up those spirits and not let it become mundane."

"Does that mean we can't watch Charlie Chaplin tonight?" asked Junior.

"You know we can," said Swims, "and I'm into it. A new one just arrived."

Junior: "But you have to finish your rounds first."

Swims: "Uh, yeah. Unless you've got some disability that doesn't allow it."

It was a beautiful Chaplin film. At the beginning, for just a few moments Chaplin narrated and said this was going to be a silent film without the 'yakety-yak' of the human voice." And then he fell into his silent mode, and we saw the first of the three silent movies, *A Dog's Life*. It certainly qualified for comedy therapy. He was the poor tramp with no place to live except the junkyard, and the cops always on his trail, and he very feisty to fight them back. The co-star was a "thoroughbred mongrel dog" whom Charlie befriended and saved from a ferocious dogfight. They became great friends. Charlie walked into the Green Lantern dancing café with his dog and was kicked out because there were "no dogs allowed," but he reentered with the dog disguised in his pants. And there he met our darling of the silent films, Edna Purviance. She was a shy, beautiful girl who didn't really want to be a dancing girl. And so she was fired by the boss. She was fired, and Chaplin was homeless. They took a liking to each other. And unlike other films, it ended very happily, because through the good luck of the dog, he rescued a hefty sum of money from some thieves, and Charlie and Edna realized their dream of going to live on a farm in their own cottage. They were very much in love, and the final scene showed a little baby crib and a silly ending where the dog had given birth to puppies. Come to think of it, it's not a silly ending, because it was only because of the dog's heroics that they won all that money, which gave them their wonderful life together away from the sinful city.

No don't worry if it seems
the same every day, it's not—
you have to meet the chief.

New pains. Suddenly the
woodchuck appears.
Pharoah goes way off scale
in his "Greetings to Idris."[2]
I go further out on a limb,
health, *sādhana*, and preaching
was the order my brother said
was his priority because if
you don't have health you can't
do the others.

I told the inmates. Higher
and screechier, this is nothing.
Greetings and kisses and flirtations.

Edna Purviance was shy but sang
a sweet song and everyone cried
but she could not do the routine
where you wink, bump your
hip against the customer and
dance and then
sit at a table and he buys you a drink.

She was too chaste for that.
So she quit and joined Charlie
and his mongrel
and because of
the dog they came
into a huge amount of money
and at the end he is no longer
a tramp but building little
lumps to plant seeds for the
farm and after hard labor

returns to his cottage and hugs her
and the dog has puppies.
He'll have to answer to the
chief why he watched a
movie like that and why

he listened to Pharoah
of "Greetings to Idris" the drummer.
Don't know what to say,
admit "I'm errant."

Chief may ask, "I don't mind
so much if you do it *after*
all your *sādhana* is done,
but Junior Barks told me . . . "

"Damn that kid," Swims will
mutter under his breath
and admit he's errant.

Swims entered the sanatorium. "How'd it go?" Tim asked.

"Okay, but I again have to go back to the dentist tomorrow. This is the fourth day in a row. I got both the uppers and the lowers in, I just want to see if it creates any sores overnight."

"The chief is waiting to see you," said Tim.

"I'd rather take a nap just now," said Swims. "Coming back from the dentist is not a picnic."

"Yeah, but he's seeing everybody in order with their files, and you're next. He's been waiting."

Swims went back to his room and flopped on his bed. He thought about the gifts he was going to get the doctor and his assistant. His friend was FedExing them from New York, but Swims didn't think they'd arrive by tomorrow. He had his little poem all made up for the assistant, and now he knew her name, Karen. The poem read, "A trip to the dentist / is a dismay / but your pleasant presence / makes my day." He'd really rather say, "but a glance from you / makes my day," but that would be a little too high-tempered, sound like he was flirting. And today she didn't look to be flirting at all. No smiling, and her straight hair looked plain. It was a cold and rainy day, and so he just said, "What happened to your sun?" She said, "Oh, it'll be back. I'm hopeful." She didn't have anything else cheerful to say. Swims was thinking of Edna Purviance and thought she was much prettier and livelier. Of course, she was just a movie actress, inaccessible to him. Anyway, his friend in New York City said he sent the books by FedEx and they might even arrive tomorrow in time for him to bring them for his 1:30 appointment. She'd get a book of Emily Dickinson poems that were selected by Joyce Carol Oates. "Dr. Danz, expert dentist, spiritual jazz follower. Your patient, Stefan Lazzaro." And that was really a knockover, *The Making of A Love Supreme.* The doctor would love it. I didn't know if Karen had any taste for beautiful poetry. Emily wasn't so easy to read.

"Swamiji?" Tim came up to Swim's bed. "The chief really wants to see you."

"All right. All right." Swims changed back into his uniform and walked toward the main building. He didn't feel so good. He stopped and took an Oxy with water, and used his cane. Why do they have to bug us like this, he thought.

The chief was a high administrator in the religious hierarchy, and one of his duties was to oversee the sanatorium. He would come once a month or once every three months. Each patient had a file, made up by the monitors, doctors, and the other overseers. It contained their health records and reports on their behavior at the sanatorium and on their service in the institution since the very beginning of their joining.

Swims entered the chief's room without much thought of what he was going to say. He wasn't afraid.

The chief was a tall man with a rather bright orange *sannyāsī* cloth, compared to the rather faded saffron of Swims. They exchanged *praṇāmās*. The chief was taller and carried his *daṇḍa*. Swims had left his *daṇḍa* back at the sanatorium. You can't carry a *daṇḍa* and a cane at the same time.

"You're one of the first devotees to join this movement," said the chief with a genial smile. "You had a lot of association with Prabhupāda. You're almost everyone's older brother. So we all admire you, and at the same time we all expect you to keep a high profile and inspire us."

Swims didn't like the introduction. He said, "I was lucky to get in so early. At the time of death, I'll remember Swamiji, as we called him then, and how kind and accessible he was. I'll depend on his leniency. I remember the little things I did for him, like bringing him a mango every day. I was his typist. Through the years he was with us he always said kind things about me. I'm depending on him like anything."

"Yes, and you've done a lot of service too. But now you've been suffering for over twenty years with migraine. It's a pity that you can't be more on the front lines, pushing this movement. I think there's a tendency for invalids to get out of touch with what the movement really is. If I may say so, you had to drop out of the GBC because of your illness, at a time of great trauma. I mean trauma for the whole of ISKCON, when bad things were happening. You may have a tendency to think that ISKCON is still like that. You may have a tendency to fear devotees and not want to get back into it."

"I'm willing to do what I can if I can recover physically. But it's true, chief, my temperament has changed. I'm sixty-three years old. I don't have too much hope of getting rid of the chronic headaches, because I've tried every remedy possible, and I'm still trying new ones. Some of my Godbrothers also have very serious illnesses. You know, G. Swami has had a bad heart attack. He's such a trooper that he's tried to go out on tours, but he was driven back to a life of seclusion. It's either that or death for him."

"Yes," said the chief, "yes, I know."

"So we have to choose some service that is actually in tune with our physical capabilities. My migraines have shaped me more towards my writing. And that writing has served the society well. Devotees like my books. At the New York Rathā-yātrā they sold all the books that they had brought with them. They should have brought more. And they're being translated too."

"We have no complaint about your writing," said the chief. "There has been some question about the medication you've been taking. I've had a long discussion with your doctor, Nitāi-Gaurasundara, and I'm satisfied that you're not overdosing in any way. There was concern in the beginning, but you've reduced medications and your symptoms are good. I can see I'm talking to a clearheaded man, and recent liver function tests and other tests show that your system is holding these medicines well.

"Although we don't expect you to take part in the institution, in the GBC, in the meetings, we expect you to give full support. And some persons doubt that you do."

"I've heard that," said Swims, "but I don't believe it's true. I wrote two essays, one about how the *paramparā* would continue, and one about how we should read only Prabhupāda's book. And in Russia they put them together as a pamphlet and they distributed it against all ISKCON schisms. I'm an ISKCON Prabhupāda man."

"Hmm." The chief seemed stymied, and he turned the pages some more. It seemed he was thinking more of rumors than of anything he could find in his pages. "Do you chant your sixteen rounds every day?" he asked.

"Chief, I tell you honestly I can't always do it. I still do have side effects from the medicine that make me very sleepy when I chant. Other things I can do don't make me sleepy, but the chanting is such a meditative thing that it brings on sleep, and I have to take an extra nap. I'm working toward it, though. I had a chanting buddy, and when I worked with him, we would chant sixteen rounds a day. I'm looking forward to being with him again and getting up to that standard. The gold that was easily obtained years ago is now like the lead of patience as I wait to return to that standard. It's been hard for me, but I try not to feel guilty. I forgive myself, and I depend on the mercy of Kṛṣṇa and Prabhupāda."

"What do you mean?"

"I mean I don't bash myself with the holy name. Kṛṣṇa knows I want to be at that standard. And I know that you want me to show a good example to everyone. I always chant ten or twelve rounds before bedtime."

"This is one of my main points," said the chief, and he leaned forward. "You do things like watch comedy movies. You've picked up that this is good therapy for persons with anxiety and other disorders that tend to make them depressed. I haven't found this recommendation anywhere except in Norman Cousins' book, *Anatomy of an Illness as Perceived by the Patient.*"

"No, you'll find it in other places also. My doctor also recommends it."

"Anyway, it's a little unorthodox. They're not Kṛṣṇa conscious films. There's Charlie Chaplin, Laurel and Hardy, and others. And the main thing is it takes up time. Precious time. While you're spending thirty or forty minutes watching one of those, you could be finishing up your rounds."

"Chief, I can't explain to you what migraine headache is like. People who get it describe it like someone picking out their eye with an ice pick. They say they feel like jumping out the window, committing suicide, banging their head against the wall, or they feel like their head is just blown off by an explosive. Unless you've had this pain or some of the other pains that the sanatorium inmates are having, you really can't empathize. This little laughter that we have at the end of the night really does wipe away our absorption on our pains, our self-centeredness about it. And we go to sleep laughing. It may sound trivial and not Kṛṣṇa conscious, but it really is a lightener and helps us to go to sleep despite pain and to exchange little jokes and to think of little light things even in the midst of pain. So it's been approved by all the local monitors and Hare Kṛṣṇa doctors here."

"Yes, I know, but I just don't want you to overdo it. Don't watch full-length films, and don't watch films that don't fit into this category. I wish you wouldn't watch them at all. And I wish you would be very careful about your practices. You're putting time in almost every day now on painting. I know the arguments for it's being a form of preaching. You got a very good review in the *Washington Post*, and there are a lot of people in your spiritual family who buy the paintings, especially the ones of Rādhā and Kṛṣṇa, and say that it reminds them of you or Kṛṣṇa. They like your primitive style. I may be a little square on this because it's not my taste in painting. But I get the point. However, again, your painting takes time and money. Some other *sannyāsīs* raise their eyebrows about it. But you go ahead. You have a tendency to push the envelope. Maybe in the future you'll be more appreciated as an 'outsider' painter. You don't seem to care about your reputation in that regard, whether you become famous or not. You go for self-expression, and a lot of people are inspired by it. This is a time in ISKCON in which people are doing things that make them feel good, that give them self-expression. So you're going on that wave. But just be careful. Don't overdo it. I can't say I'm forbidding you, because you probably wouldn't obey. I don't want to push you to a confrontation. You're a senior man, and you're not doing something explicitly against the law. But I do know some senior devotees aren't so pleased with how you spend your time, even though they empathize with your migraine symptoms. I just want to emphasize that there's only so much time in the day, and *japa* is a priority."

"But it starts to bring on a headache, or I feel sleepy."

The chief said, "What can I say? Chanting the holy name is the only way to liberation and love of God. So many saintly persons in the past have chanted despite all their pains. I think you're really taking it a little easy on yourself in setting that example for others. I think you could cut it out a little more and not surround yourself with people who console you in your movie watching and support you in your painting, and even commiserate in your subpar *japa*. It's not good. I'll be back in three months, and I want to hear that no matter what, *you're chanting sixteen rounds*. That's the bottom line for me. All right, that's all I have to say. Dismissed."

Dismissed? thought Swims. What is this, the army? Anyway, what more can I tell him? I'm certainly not happy about my *japa*. I have nothing to say to defend it. I've gotten into bad habits. I'm overdependent on the Lord's lenient mercy. Bad habits. *Anarthas*. The chief is speaking fair, even though he's a bit square.

Swims went down to the floor and made *daṇḍavats* to the chief. "I'll do my very best to follow your instructions, as they are coming from Śrīla Prabhupāda, and give you a better report in three months." Swims then turned on his heel, with his cane, and slightly limped out the door, trying out his new dentures.

The film for tonight is Charles Chaplin in *Shoulder Arms*, produced during World War I, "the first comedic film about front line life, and hailed as one of Chaplin's best movies." How can I deny the inmates this fun? How can I ask them to pass muster of first chanting their rounds before they see it? How can I demand the same of myself, even though it's a bad habit?

You better think seriously
about your priorities.
Laughing yourself silly
with not so good aftertaste

or grinding through sixteen rounds
mechanically, not feeling particularly
great after the "duty" but
knowing it's duty and vow.

But to lapse away. You've lapsed
before. And then how can you
lecture or say to anyone, "we
chant sixteen rounds a day"? Some
gurus order sixty-four a day but our
spiritual master was lenient and said
"at least you can do sixteen."

You have no taste? What about when you
press your legs against
the exercise machine,
pull on the weights,
the rowing machine,
and finally punch
the heavy bag? You're exhausted.

But you do it because your doctor
said it was integral to your healing
and you *do* feel it's helping.

So do you think Lord Caitanya was
not all-wise spiritually and Śrīla Prabhupāda
did adapt it to our times,
at a lower quota? You think
spiritual "exercise" is less
important than physical?

I know you can't pray.
It's mechanical. It's lead
with little aspiration. But
it *does* feel good, obey.
It does make you feel
you're following and pleasing
the most important
selves.

Chapter Thirteen

He tricked us in the beginning. No, not tricked. He introduced us to the *mahā-mantra* and said it was the panacea. Three times a week for the public. One half-hour chanting, half-hour lecture, half-hour chanting with invitation to get up and dance, each alone, hands upraised, the Swami step, taught in his room. It is so easy. We *did* feel high. Sweating underarms. We are after the high of LSD. So this produced a high. No more coming down. He convinced us. Even if you can't understand the books. Because the names *are* Kṛṣṇa, it's absolute. *He* did it, we followed. He did it, eyes closed, playing the drum. He was in ecstasy and we followed.

Now can you honestly tell people it's nectar, you'll feel ecstasy? All those elaborate drumbeats and complicated dance steps. Boys and girls apart, 'Hare Kṛṣṇa, Hare Kṛṣṇa, Kṛṣṇa Kṛṣṇa, Hare Hare, /Hare Rāma, Hare Rāma, Rāma Rāma, Hare Hare.'

Singing together is better than *japa* alone. But he said, *Of all the orders of the spiritual master, the order to chant sixteen rounds is the most important.*

Lead of patience. The soul must endure itself. Go back and try some more. Yakety-yak of talking films. Charlie said it's not as good as the silent ones. Lone *japa* man. Get them done. Even advanced Godbrothers admit the mind wanders all over. The mind is Godlike in power and takes you where it wants, away from the syllables of Kṛṣṇa and Rādhā. You say, "If I pay attention to one mantra a day, I'd consider it a success." Seems like a stoned out person, a dummy, comatose, drunk. So naturally he switches to any activity that brings him clearer consciousness.

"Say Mississippi," said Dr. Danz.

I said it with pep and good enunciation.

Babies have a short attention span.

Lakṣmaṇa started crying on the way home, but then he fell asleep. No *japa* expected of him yet. Hare Kṛṣṇa Hare Kṛṣṇa. "It's not intellectual enough for me."

Lakṣmaṇa was babbling sounds like, "da-da," and I repeated them to him. It was fun. I was alarmed when he started to cry.

The new teeth seem to fit. There should be no bar to chanting. No time for painting. Eat normal food tonight. You won't make the quota, but I'll try some more. This is a terrible confession, but I don't seem to care. I'm not lying. I will overcome it.

Miles ahead[1] you once were?
Monkeys behind?

Oh he's wonderful but he didn't
do his homework. What will it gain
a man if he wins the whole world
but loses his immortal soul?

Clear unmuted horn of the
most melodic sounds like
coming from a hip heaven with
Gil Evans—music not race.

And yet, and yet
there's only one way in the
age of Kali to overcome,
to cross over the ocean of
vices, one *mahā-
guṇa.* You know
what it is and so I order you
to leave this heaven and go down
there to woodshed it.

You've forgotten who you are.
Yes sir, I'll try, I won't
make it today, but I
shall answer your call
and not prolong this pretty
waste.

Swims wanted to be kind to the inmates. Cheer them up. Someone was playing a tape of Prabhupāda, and Prabhupāda was emphasizing preaching. People don't know who God is and they're wasting their lives. So help them. Yes, that's what we have to do. But the inmates can't go out and do it yet. So there's nothing wrong with being kept cheerful in the meantime and being encouraged—yes, you should do like that more directly—they have to reach nondevotees, and devotees too, and show compassion and learning. Talk about Kṛṣṇa. Show how everything in the world is connected to Kṛṣṇa and is coming from Kṛṣṇa. All talent. All unhappiness is coming from forgetfulness of Kṛṣṇa. And so his act of kindness toward the inmates, this human touch, is something they appreciated. Showing them he wasn't just a rules and regulations man. "This is the army, Mr. Jones." They were friends, and they did things normal people did, as well as things normal people don't do. They had the precious gold of Kṛṣṇa consciousness, and unfortunately the lead of patience, especially those who had the lead of physical illness. So to be a role model for them meant not just stiff upper lip but relaxing and saying it's okay to be human. Don't feel guilty if right now you can't do the standard. We'll get there by baby steps. *And Kṛṣṇa is kind.*

What I didn't like about *Shoulder Arms* is that Charlie Chaplin had to very bravely go behind army lines and did wildly comic, brave things to make many Germans surrender. Finally, he captured the Kaiser himself in his own car and drove him back to the allied lines, along with his (my) favorite costar Edna Purviance, whom Charlie had put a charcoal moustache on and given German dress. The allies got the news by radio, and they all celebrated as they drove into the camp, and the Kaiser himself and his top brass surrendered. Everyone cheered, and the subtitle said, "Peace on earth, goodwill to men." It was a perfect ending. But the movie wasn't over. The next scene showed Pvt. Chaplin in boot camp sleeping in a tent after his first drill lesson. His going overseas, living in the trenches, going "over the top," succeeding in great underground heroics and capturing the Kaiser himself *were all a dream*. I think we would have all been perfectly satisfied to just leave it as a "true" story, that he had captured the Kaiser. Why make it a dream? We were willing to believe the fantastic, to suspend our disbelief. We have enough dreams, enough comedowns. So that little bit of ending, which they often do, left me disappointed with the whole production. And so we have to go to our beds thinking that the great things we want to achieve are only in our minds, just a fantasy.

Let's cool one, we don't
need to be told it was just
a dream. We'll live the
dream.

But if someone told you
you were a cowherd boy
in eternal Vraja, surely that
would be your fantasy and
you'd have to wake up to
reality.

We can't live on dreams
but in Charlie Chaplin
we can, that's why we go there.
Keep the "dream" a reality.
In the film as it is, he
never met Edna Purviance.
Who wants that? Sorry, not me.

I want a reality in my Kṛṣṇa
consciousness, to know where
I'm really at and not have a
puffed up idea I'm more advanced

but neither do I want some
upstart's opinion that I'm
oversick, overanxious according
to their view and just need to
do such and such.

Reality and dream, back and
forth, at night I dream
and go to the dentist with
some fantasy in mind.

I'm growing too old but may
still write the book
I anticipate—not end
it "this was just a
dream, we are back
to page 1 and the rest
never happened."

It *did* happen. Don't tell me I did
not meet the Swami. Don't tell me
the deep impressions didn't
take place and continue to take place,
not just gold but transformations.

Okay enough preaching. Enough to
say cool one, we drift from
dream to real. Five Spot.
How many times did you actually
go there? How many times did
you actually meet Trane? Do
you have a B.A.? Were you
recognized by Śrī Kṛṣṇa?

After his fourth daily visit in a row to the dentist, Swims walked back into the sanatorium. "How did it go?" His mind was bothered by the fact that his driver talked all the way and didn't give him a chance to savor the delicious kiss which dental assistant Karen Ressler had given him on the head when he gave her her gifts of a selection of Emily Dickinson's poems and a recent CD of Joni Mitchell singing jazz songs. He had written inside the Dickinson book that he didn't know her tastes so he picked something that he loved. Then he explained that as to Joni Mitchell, he really didn't know anything about her except that she was once a very popular folk singer and then had undergone a very serious period of withdrawal from that identity by living in solitude, and emerged as a jazz singer. As for this latest CD, a jazz critic wrote, "If ever Joni has made an effort to send someone a love letter it is to Holiday in her phrasing and smokey vocals . . . she sits perfectly with those that enjoy their personal torments and share the depth of the human condition with their listeners."

Wayne Shorter, Herbie Hancock, and Mark Isham perform solos on the album. That's when she kissed him on the hair of his head. It couldn't have been nicer. Dr. Danz said, "Is this to borrow?" referring to the book *The Making of A Love Supreme* that Swims Swami had given him.

"No," said Swims emphatically, "it's a gift for you to *keep*." They were like two people receiving Christmas gifts, and Swims was so happy, still sitting in the dentist's chair, to give away such prizes. He knew that Bob really would like the book, and Karen was at least touched by the gesture, even if she might not like ED's poetry or Joni Mitchell's singing. And I was thrilled with the kiss, although I didn't get a chance to savor it due to my driver yakety-yakking all the way home. Now I can try to recapture it in silence.

He has another appointment on Monday at 11:00 A.M. There may be more sores on the bottom. It's supposed to take another ten minutes. I won't have any gifts to bring them this time. No one made any comment about my Jagannātha T-shirt. It was the black one. I'll wear the white one next time. Then I can tell them that this is the symbol in Hinduism of the face of God. His name is Jagannātha because He's the controller of the universe. She won't kiss me on the head for that, but they'll hear the transcendental sound, which is even better.

Kiss you want, kiss. Kṛṣṇa will
kiss you little boy, I know
that's what you want and
so did Karen.

You forgot your cane and the
dentist brought it to the front
desk. I'm getting so used to that
place.
And so used to incomplete

rounds and not having energy
to set up and do my painting.

No shirt on. He's telling me in
the car trip home about Auckland and
New Zealand, and I get them
mixed up and mountain climbing
and Rushdie "the best writer,
he spins your head."

I felt like asking him if he
ever read SDG. He read
a book where a man practiced
three religions and the gurus of
each—Hindu, Islam,
and Christian—forbade him but he
continued.

He yacked and I was trying to
concentrate on peace and
quiet and what would
happen next. Sgt. Bilko
in the sanatorium and what
would happen next and what

is left of the afternoon and
that writer who does
Sanatorium typed so
fast by our Bhaktin Jane and
how she slugged out
Barks but now brings
him back to pure
devotional service and how
he himself could get
converted—
"Meditation on a Pair of

Wire Cutters"[2] sounds pretty right
to me.

The country is still full of hate.
Little sign on lawn: "War
is no good. Let's have
peace on earth." Odd for this
county. Most people are for
the eagle and missile and whatever
Bush says we ought to do,
get the raider before another
attack.

Teeth so painful you can't eat.
You may not like it but at
least you gave it out of love.
The Making of A Love Supreme
and *The Essential Dickinson*
and latest CD by Joni Mitchell.

Okay where is the latest *japa*
quota day done complete, where's
the latest homage to his
Swami, when is the last
time he wasn't a hypocrite?
Tell them that when you did something
good. I gave a gift. I ate
my toast in *tapasya*.

I sent a thank you note,
I played with Lakṣmaṇa. I'm
going back to work now. There's
no need to worry about Harry
Langdon, she'll find him and
if they don't like your paintings,
that's not important.
Do them, find time.

Gosh so much time.
The secretary said, "God."
She meant the month was slipping
by already June 23.
No time to finish
"Meditation on
a Pair of Wire Cutters."

He said I should study some writers who twist your head around by the time you come to the end of one of their sentences. He said one of the greatest writers is Salman Rushdie, and the other is Kurt Vonnegut, who he said is the greatest mixer of genres. So it seems I ought to read them to get some idea of what the best is.

The groundhog in our spacious backyard may think he's the best groundhog. He's wiped out the family's garden. Kaiśori, when visiting, saw where he entered the garden through the fence, but they didn't bother mending it.

I can't go deep like Rilke with my seriousness. I'm getting better, my counselor said, even though it hurts to eat. I stay away from women. It's the fault of the clicker that my rounds don't add up! I've simply got to go back to the bead bag, go back to the original red ones. Or maybe they won't add up either. "This is light talk," said the counselor. I didn't want to go deeper. Not headache deep. I just want to relive my moment in the dentist's chair in my Jagannātha T-shirt, giving out presents and getting a kiss on the head.

"They are your guests," I wrote, I don't want to see them. And when your guests are gone, I want to paint. So sometimes—if you want to hold *kīrtana,* don't depend on me. Be yourself, even in New York. The hiding swami, perfectly all right. This writer and that writer are very accessible reading, he says, and reads on while

I'm in the dentist's chair. The silent movies were better because there was no yakety-yak. Splits up your available time. Learn the art so you an give something better to the devotees.

Wee waa dippy doo. Children learn to speak. If you imitate their sounds, it helps them. Da da, ma ma, growly, rowl, roww. And give them the pacification nipple to suck on when they cry. I hope he'll fall asleep. I have no sleep, I mean I have no children. The triskelion that I draw represents, among other things, the maiden, the crone, and the mother. In my life there is a female maiden and crone, but I am the mother. Rilke often spoke of the artist as the mother. I once wrote a letter to my sister when she was giving birth, saying that I too was a mother because I was coming to the end of a book or long poem. I too was giving birth. She must have taken me as a preposterous weirdo. Stevie, the pretender, the pseudoartist. He should get married to a flesh-and-blood woman of German descent (more maternal) and work at a regular job and produce flesh-and-blood children. He shouldn't presume he's a great poet who can leave the company of women and substitute writing for sex. She thought I was nuts to imitate those crazy ones.

But now that I've had a few dealings with actual women, I see it as a siphoning from the real-life energy of my "motherhood," my capacity to give birth to art, without the complication of influential, womanly entanglements.

Can you make that true, old man? Clint Eastwood, on his Charlie Parker film: "Others might not think this is a great film, but I do."

With your imagination you can fly. He and his wife do those temporary tattoos that women wear in India. So they got a chance to do it at a stint in a nightclub. It was a horrible atmosphere. A gay man came up and she showed him the booklet of designs she could do. "What's this?" he asked. "It's a palanquin," she said. "What's it for?" "For carrying queens." "Queens!" he said, "oh, I must have one! Put it on my arm." They made several hundred dollars that night but did not return.

Oh Kṛṣṇa. My poor mind keeps going to those mundane grooves. The desperate cry doesn't go up. The *rasikā* crowd said Prabhupāda didn't leave us with enough and we should have gone to the real *ācārya*. I don't accept it because that other guru attacks and steals from our movement, says he's our leader. But it's true the cry does not come out desperate. "And who among the hierarchies of angels would answer if I called?" Would Rūpa? Nitāi? Prabhupāda! Am I crying? Just coasting?

I will take the inmates into our video room. Some of us have had a hard day. The lady with cancer, the man with a bad lung, the depressed girl who no one can seem to reach except Chaplin. I take it as a duty. I don't really like the films so much myself. Maybe we'll watch Sid Caesar instead, it's a shorter one.

You owe me a poem.
Don't be ridiculous, I
don't owe you anything and
you owe me for all
my Machados.[3]

The pin man was a
fan of *The Book of Miracles*
and Rajneesh. He left
with a copy of EJW Vol. 15.
I dare say I could
teach him a thing or
two.

He asked, "What do you write
about?" while I had seven new pins
in my back. I said, "Me and
my spiritual search.
I don't write very scholarly
as I used to. I'm far out."
Anything for a laugh when
you're pinned.

Before sticking me he
tried psychology. He
asked when did the migraines
first come. I said what they told
me: I have an anxiety
disorder. They came when
the GBC blew up in 1986
and I resigned. "Did you
feel you'd done wrong?"
"Yes," I admitted.

"That and the sheer
pain of the migraine
and I worry too much
and I've learned to be
more self-assertive."

He was happy about my
pulse which reflects the
inner organs. He told
me about a place in Scotland
which is supposed to be very
spiritual.

I just learned that Sid Caesar
will be "live" on *Larry
King Live* tonight but

it's 10 P.M. I have to
pee now and chant *japa*
in that order. The
main thing is *japa*.
Harer nāma harer nāma.

I wish my urge to chant
was like my urge to pee—
I'd be a *mahātmā*.

Somehow they made room for another inmate in the sanatorium. She was in a wheelchair, paralyzed. She was young—only nineteen years old—and very pretty, with straight blonde hair and blue eyes. She would be attractive to any man, except that she was a paraplegic. She was from Australia and had been visiting America with two friends, but the car she was in got into an accident on New York's West Side Highway, and she had been injured. She was allowed entrance into the crowded sanatorium on the recommendation of her father, who was a highly placed Hare Kṛṣṇa leader in Australia and who knew of the good repute of the sanatorium. She was there for physical therapy, which she practiced very seriously. Her name was Sandy, another uninitiated one. She was very quiet, yet not cold. She humbly accepted whatever she was offered. She spent her time reading *Śrīmad-Bhāgavatam* by the hour and chanting many rounds. When asked how many, she said it wasn't good to tell how many you did over sixteen. Starting from the beginning, she politely deferred attending the comedy movies, which affected a few others. Some thought she was a snob, but others thought it was a good example. Sandy spent at least two hours every day writing a letter. She was very private, and when asked who she was writing to, she would only say, "A friend." She had an allowance from her father and used it on envelopes and postage. Each day she would ride her battery-run wheelchair to the mail box and drop in her letter. They were all addressed to BJD, in Sydney, Australia. She was cheerful and a good *sādhaka*. The inmates were compassionate or self-absorbed, so they didn't bug her about her letter writing (and letter receiving). The letters came in a few a week. Ms. Sandy King, Kṛṣṇa's Sanatorium, Hudson County, New York 12487. Everyone was glad to get mail, but no one as much as Sandy. You could see it in her eyes. She tried to hide it, didn't say anything exuberant, but couldn't restrain that "thanks," and when a day passed without a letter, she couldn't restrain from asking the postman, "Is there one for me?"

"Not today, Sandy, but I'm sure you'll get one soon."

There you go again letting
the afternoon slip by—pick
up the round, faded gems
from candies and count.

There's a big fly in the outside
room but if he bugs me
I'll retreat to this one

and stay awake. Don't interrupt me
now. It's just a drum.
A nice girl has entered
the sanatorium.

The place will have to turn on
its fans soon. Swims waiting
the day until he has to go back
to the dentist. "Blow your
cheeks out like Dizzy."
He's errant. Maybe Sandy

can help him if he could
ask her "What are you
reading? What is this *Śrīmad-
Bhāgavatam?*" How far he
has come from gold
to lead.

A youngster could
lead the way. Listen
to the quiet. Something
good is going to happen.

It will be written, it
will come out of a horn,
a torch singer. It will
be a touch.
It will be from Kṛṣṇa
the Supreme Person.
It will come from His abode
to my heart.

Not just me. If you get a drop
don't hog it, share it. The
pin man has my book.
I gave him Volume 15 and
said it doesn't matter
where you begin.

Kṛṣṇa is all-pervading.
Do you want a gift from
me? I did it myself I
cried to the hierarchy of angels
and the one just meant for
me answered and said,

Come on Stephen you've delayed
too long. Make some dramatic
moves. Get on the right
track. We've already met
and it's never too late. You
can leave behind something
romantic in epistolary
form. Two Hare Kṛṣṇas in
separation. And one who
lives alone and talks to God.

Don't be a hermit, be with friends
or you're nowhere. That's enough.
Follow it up. You've got
enough to last sixty years but
only twenty to do it in—
not counting the many lives ahead.

Dear Braja,

Please accept my humble obeisances. All glories to Śrīla Prabhupāda.

I have been in the sanatorium a few days and have not heard from you yet. It is a nice place. They're all Hare Kṛṣṇa devotees and follow the principles. There's a separate building where I am receiving physiotherapy for my broken arm and, of course, my legs. I do this faithfully, along with my reading Śrīmad-Bhāgavatam *and chanting. We have no other duties, so I have plenty of time for my* sādhana. *The devotees are friendly here, but I am new and somewhat shy. Most of all, however, I miss you dearly.*

Do you still love me?

When I was eighteen years old, I was considered a very pretty girl, and in the Sydney temple, many boys proposed to me. Of all those boys, I was attracted only to you. I was attracted to your Vaiṣṇava qualities. You were the best scholar of Prabhupāda's books. You had made several trips to Vṛndāvana and could talk about it with real feeling for the holy dhāma *and the* sādhus *in temples. You never talked* prajalpa. *You were kind to all of the devotees, men and women. Your classes were the most learned, not in a stiff way but with humor and humanness and compassion. Certainly you attracted everyone who heard. I admit I was also attracted to your handsome, masculine looks. I fell in love with you at first sight.*

By Kṛṣṇa's grace, we were allowed to associate with each other by the temple president, and the bud of attachment began. You proposed marriage, and I was thrilled to accept. We talked about our propensities and how we wanted to live. We both wanted to raise children, and although we wanted to preach, we wanted to live outside the temple and to influence people in Kṛṣṇa consciousness in a more normal way. We're both attracted to living near devotees, but somewhere where we can do a little farming, maybe even have a few cows. Everything seemed so blissful as we lived in the shelter of the temple and contemplated our future marriage.

But now this terrible car accident. I came out a scrap of a human being in many ways. I do not know what will become of me. Will I have to live forever without being able to walk? It may turn out that I will be a very awkward and ungainly looking person. And maybe I will never be able to get out of the wheelchair. I am very afraid that your affection for me will change. It is not wrong if it does change. I mean I will understand. Certainly much of our attraction was probably on the bodily platform. We would be naïve to say that it wasn't.

And so I want you to write to me very honestly how you feel about me now. I don't want you to pity me. I want truth. We could not sustain a marriage on pity. I am ready to go on with my chanting and hearing and live a Kṛṣṇa conscious life even if I do not have a husband.

But the truth is I cannot take love for you out of my heart. I hope that my body can recover into some semblance of humanness. But it will never be beautiful again, like the girl you knew, like the girl you once embraced and kissed that night after you walked me home to the brahmacārīnī āśrama *after the* kīrtana.

I am eagerly awaiting word from you, like the bird that drinks only rain from the thundercloud and is waiting for the cloud and the drops to appear. Your servant, Bhaktin Sandy.

Chapter Fourteen

When Sandy returned from mailing her letter, Swami Swims met her at the door. "Hare Kṛṣṇa, Sandy," he said, "I'd like to introduce myself. I'm Swami Swims."

She bowed her head and made *praṇāmās*. "Hare Kṛṣṇa." She smiled, but tears appeared in the corners of her eyes.

"Are you feeling pain?"

"Not too much in my back," she said, and then surprised herself by openly saying, "I'm missing a friend."

"Oh," Swims said. "They say you have a good chance of recovering normal function in your back by the therapy, and they have very good workers and equipment here. But you're going to have to be patient. And sometimes patience is very bitter. I've had a migraine condition for twenty years, but I'm still hopeful that it will go away. In the meantime, you can make friends here and take these fellow inmates as part of your spiritual family. We're very happy to have you here, because we see you're so serious about your *sādhana*. I personally am inspired and want to improve just by seeing how you chant."

Sandy lowered her head humbly. "I don't chant with attention," she said.

"If there's anything you need, just ask me," said Swims Swami, and they parted.

Call a friend, he's feeling rather broke,
ask a mom if she's afraid her seven-year-
old daughter is riding horses, she
says no. Her two-year-old daughter
has stomach virus.

Haven't decided what's wrong with
Bhaktin Sandy. They've got Swims
in a diagnosed box. Everything
coming from the cold rainy summer.

A man is really complaining about
people taking money from the
institution. Free-for-all or
maybe they'll put tight brakes
on the spending.

Make it worse than it is.
Black market, laundered
money, pet projects, guru
tax, let's just quit and do our
own thing for Kṛṣṇa.

Don't push too far
in the name of
control. People give freely.
Squeak. The weekend is coming.
You have no excuse. I didn't watch
the whole film,
maybe Sandy's influence.

Go back to *japa.* Got no
special friend to write to.
Most dutiful. "Our relationship
was at a peak and now when
I read your books I feel

they have almost nothing to do
with spiritual life." Does he mean
I don't have anything to do
with spiritual life?
Christ the Savior spoke through
Helen Jones in seven days in
Shakespearean pentameter with
heavy Freudian (not Jungian)
influence.

Too bad He couldn't speak
clear like Hemingway
or Salinger. Prabhupāda made
it clear what He wanted
and who was God but it's
very hard to accept.

They want something vague
and very permissive.

"This is a nonkosher synagogue
and the name of my son's
straightedge band is Zen Mafia.
Thanks for printing $1,000 worth
of T-shirts. You don't have to give
another present."

Oh sigh, that one big missing Part.

Bedtime. Flashback: Karen Ressler kissed me tenderly on the head, right in sight of her boss. A perfect moment. It will never happen again in this lifetime. Now if I could only have the spiritual equivalent.

"But if I called, who among the hierarchy of angels would answer me?" It would be Prabhupāda. Don't think he *wouldn't* answer if you called sincerely (even desperately, and acted on it). I don't think it would be another surprise angel. He is sufficient, and he has already come to you and knows you. The other angels may know me or not. He touched me, I have struggled with him. I hear his lectures still and I am inspired and struggle. Even the struggle is good, like "wrestling with God." My dearest friend and master, who has a soft spot in his heart for me (don't boast, he has that soft spot for everyone), please let ... what was that "affirmation"—"despite all my faults, he will take me back to Godhead." That was optimistic stuff taught to me by a teacher of anxiety disorder who said prayer was the main thing, but I kept saying I don't know how. And she said, "Practice the therapies," but I couldn't get into them, knowing how to "dig deeper" by that method. We're stumbling in the dark, and when we find something I pick it up and he asks, "What's that?" I say, "Oh, it's a book I read in college." "Is it resonating for you now?" "No." "Okay, let's go stumbling on." "What's this?" "Something I never told you about. It happened in Cannes, France."

Inmates each have secrets. They come out especially at night. Not necessarily. Even during *japa* and *kīrtana*. Sandy pours hers out into her letters. The *chaukīdār* stands at the front door with a firearm, and who knows what's on his mind? *Smartavyaḥ satataṁ viṣṇur / vismartavyo na jātucit:* "Above all the rules and regulations is this—to always remember Viṣṇu." I don't think many are doing that. Prabhupāda strongly emphasizes that this is the purpose of life, not to own "three dozen cars and work like an ass or live like a pig." Humans are wasting their lives by not always thinking of Kṛṣṇa or serving Him with devotion. Go to a *saṅga* group where there's a reading, and even if you fall asleep in the middle of it, you'll wake hearing "Kṛṣṇa." Same with your paltry *japa*, which you can't even count up properly;

you start with the round in one direction, and halfway through your hand is going in the other direction. Blame it on Paxil. At least some "Hares" and "Kṛṣṇas" are coming out.

"But who, among the hierarchy of angels, would answer *if I called?*" Don't make that a desperate, existential question. You know who would answer, but you've got to call.

Misterioso[1]
it's a mystery how for
some they love and some hate
I was surely surprised some
men went out to see
The Incredible Hulk and
came back and said
"it was fun."

But I love him just as much.
I wasn't doing much better.
I recall probably ten years ago
the *Downbeat* review
gave Monk's *Misterioso* only
three stars due to what he
said was Johnny Griffin's poor
sax playing almost like rock-
and-roll in some parts.

I don't agree. I think it's all
nice. They've gone to the
bar mitzvah today, leaving
us inmates alone, on our own.
I'd like to paint but
have to share the room with Mikey
and he might
not like Beethoven

quartets. So paint in
silence. It's not the
same.

Sandy prefers silence.
Always thinks of Kṛṣṇa
even when you're writing your
letter of separation to your boyfriend.

That's not rock-and-roll. It's spiritual
jazz. Silence is fine. Thinks of
the Lord, let the right hand move.

Get on some organized track.
"Will you marry me?" said
Mr. Barks. Jane reasoned
"for us it's different. We've
been through the mill.
Don't stir up the sex passion.
Marriage means sex, probably
children. We're not so young.

"I've tried so hard to deprogram
you from your life with whores and
drink and drugs
and restore you to a pure spiritual soul."

"We could be ideal *gṛhasthas.*" Jane couldn't buy it.
She was disappointed her unorthodox
method of changing his being
wasn't totally successful. But
she'd continue to try and she'd
certainly not enter marriage
farce.

Give *Misterioso* four stars or more—
the whole sky.

My Dear Braja,

Please accept my humble obeisances. All glories to Prabhupāda. I have been at Kṛṣṇa's sanatorium for several days but I've not received a letter from you. Nevertheless, I must express my heart to you. I'm thinking back to the car accident and the immediate events afterwards. Only some of it is returning to my memory. I recall that I was fortunate enough to be rushed right away by ambulance to the hospital. There they said that I had an incomplete injury to the cervical spine, C-4 and C-5. They said it was a reversible injury, but that I cannot use my legs. Some of these facts came back to my mind today because for the first time I went to the therapy building nearby the sanatorium. They told me these facts from the file sent from the hospital. Just because of this "incomplete injury" to the spine, I have lost the use of my legs, and therefore I cannot walk but must sit in my wheelchair. The main thing now is therapy.

My father sent me here because they have a very good, reputable team of experts to work on cases like mine. I went for my first therapy session today. I worked with weights and they did some stretching massage. Several people assisted the main person, who was a physiatrist. (I hope I spelled the name right.) He is a physician who specializes in physical medicine and rehabilitation and attends to pain. He does it partly with drugs. (And I am often in pain in the neck and spine.) But he said he would mostly not depend on drugs but on alleviation of the pain through physical therapy. He told me directly that a big factor in my recovery will be psychological, that I have to make a healthy adjustment. He says a healthy support group will help me. And therefore he wanted me to appreciate that the inmates in the sanatorium are an ideal group to live with. I am a Hare Kṛṣṇa devotee and they are too. For the most part they are optimistic and compassionate to the other inmates. I am focusing on that and trying to see the good in them and trying to imbibe their mercy and trying to give whatever mercy I can from my own little store of Kṛṣṇa consciousness.

The physiatrist said that psychologically, an accident like this can be very devastating, not only on the body but on the whole person, to the self-esteem. He didn't have to say it explicitly, but I knew what he meant. Before the accident, I was an attractive young girl with many male suitors, although I had chosen you. And you, the ideal suitor, had accepted me, and you loved me. Now my esteem has fallen so much, and I cannot help but wonder if you still love this cripple who cannot walk and who is—I must admit—depressed.

I feel great separation from you and doubt whether you can wait for me to recover. I spoke to one of the senior devotees here, a man they call Swami Swims. He's very sober and cheerful. But he was encouraging me that we have to be very, very patient when we suffer an injury. He said that he has had migraines for twenty years and it has put him out of all regular action for a preaching sannyāsī. *He has adjusted in his own way by writing books and painting, but he must live the life of an invalid. I thought, twenty years! Surely Braja and I cannot wait twenty years. We want to be married very soon, while we're still young, while I'm still attractive to him, and we want to have children. I want to get well as soon as possible, within a few months.*

But the doctor cannot promise this. I press him on it and he says it depends on various factors and it may take a couple of years or more before I can get out of the chair. I need psychological care, and I need to strengthen my muscles.

The main thing I want to cry out to you is, Do you love me? But I feel it is an unfair question.

On the other hand, I feel such low esteem that I don't feel I deserve to be loved by you. I am willing for you to let me go. Please speak honestly to me about this. You may not want to wait so long. I would not regard it as a betrayal if you honestly said that things have changed and that you yourself have found another girl and you want to go ahead in gṛhastha life as soon as possible. And that the girl you wanted to marry no longer exists. Who knows if I will ever recover? I myself don't think much of myself now and don't know whether I can even be attracted to you, whether I have the strength to look into your eyes and say I love you, because I feel so low.

Having said these painful but true words, I hunger for words of solace from you and wait for every mail delivery. Your suffering servant, Sandy

Swami Swims thought of calling his counselor because he had so much to talk about. He didn't know if he would be able to discuss everything during the regular call tomorrow. He sat on a lawn chair just outside the front door in the sunshine. An inmate came up to him and said that the physiatrist wanted to see him. Swims walked in and sat down in the man's office.

The man smiled and shook hands with Swims. "I am Dr. Jones, the physiatrist who's working with Sandy King. I wanted to talk with you privately about this person. One of the big factors in her recovery is going to be psychological. I even told her in general that the sanatorium is a good place for her to recover because there'll be cheerful friends here. I understand that you're sort of the unofficial leader among the sanatorium members, and they like you. So I would like you to have a meeting with them when Sandy wasn't present and tell them that she's liable to be very depressed and have low self-esteem. We know she's betrothed to a young man in Australia, and that may be working on her mind too. So you might even encourage some of the ladies to gain her intimacy about that. But in general, everyone should go out of their way a little and show her she's loved."

"We try to do that with all the inmates," said Swims.

"I know that, and I don't want you to do anything phony. But I think you know what I mean. A word from you to the others will inspire them to not ignore this girl and to understand her need to be recognized as a whole person, a potentially healthy girl, and an attractive person. By the way, she's really well-studied in the scriptures, and she's an exceptional devotee. I think there are different ways you could recognize that, and I just leave it up to you to spread the word among the inmates not to ignore her. She's also the new girl on the block, so bring her in warmly with a welcome. Will you do that for me, for her, for Kṛṣṇa?"

"Sure, Doctor, it's just the kind of thing we all need to improve our Kṛṣṇa consciousness. Thank you for the assignment."

As soon as possible, Swims arranged the meeting while Sandy was in for one of her therapy sessions. Everyone seemed to warm up to it, and nobody complained, except the old mom, who was always complaining about her arthritis and said she didn't get enough attention. She said, "Why shouldn't I get more attention also? Just because I'm not a good-looking young girl?"

"No, you're right," said Swims. "It's a good occasion for us to remember that we should be kind to everyone, and especially to you, mom. But the doctor asked me to be especially kind to this newcomer, who doesn't know the ways here. And I'll take it as a special reminder to be kinder to you, mom, because I know you go through a lot of suffering."

"Thank you, Swamiji," said mom.

Be kind remind
round midnight I think
there's no better way

than to remember the
Lord the oldies but goldies
the golden era of
Hare Kṛṣṇa when we chanted
with Swami in the morning,
"chant one round."
Bring it back. "Chant
one round." Did together.
Watch him. Do it with
attention. No bead bag
around your neck. Then I
cut up my best aquamarine
shirt which a pretty girl had
even said was a "nice shirt"
when I was flirting with her—
cut it up and handmade a
bead bag and tried to sew it
but it came out strange and
awkward. As soon as
he saw it Swamiji said
"get a proper bead bag."

Those golden days. Remember
and restore the simple *japa*.
We'll give you less

Klonopin next week
so you can coordinate in *japa*
he said. "I'm chanting Hare Kṛṣṇa
Hare Kṛṣṇa but it doesn't
tally up." That's all right,
Kṛṣṇa hears.
Oh who if I called among
the *sādhus* of *japa* would
give me credit and not kick
me out? I know of one.
He'd say those beads I
know are not *tulasī* but
red wood, but it's all
right.

It's an homage to me his guru
and he was a good
boy.

Jane decided to change her tactics. Rather than try for the clean slate approach, she decided to accept Mr. Barks as a more "normal" person and go on from there. She told him she wouldn't tolerate any drinking, smoking, cursing, or womanizing. But they could loosen up a little. She let him wear his old skinhead haircut and his regular clothes, a T-shirt revealing all his tattoos. After all, she also had a tattoo. Hers was an empty heart. She thought someday she'd fill it in with the name of the man she loved. But now she was thinking she would fill it in with the words, Gaura-Nitāi. She started rolling him in his wheelchair outside the sanatorium on sunny days and calm evenings, and playing a guitar to him and letting him sometimes play the guitar. They would sing old, old Bob Dylan songs and other folk songs and any songs they knew. Some of the inmates thought they were getting romantic, but she told them it was just a clinical approach. She knew what she was doing. It certainly made Mr. Barks cheer up. She told him he didn't have to use the name "Mr. Barks," and asked him what he would like to be called. He thought it over for a day and then said, "'Barks' would be all right."

One sunshiny day, she took him for a ride in his wheelchair into a nearby park. As they came into a woody, secluded part, they were approached by three tough-looking skinheads. Immediately the men became aggressive, without any cause. "Hey," one of them said, "look at this pseudoskinhead in a wheelchair and his phony tough dame." The middle man kicked Barks on the chest with his boot and knocked the wheelchair over. Barks hit his head on the ground. Jane became enraged. She ran around the back of the wheelchair and uprighted it. Barks then stood up, and with a haymaker punch slugged the middle man on the chin and knocked him to the ground unconscious. Jane then did her favorite karate move, the punch with the heel of the hand under the nose and then into the groin. That man then screamed and limped off into the woods. The third man didn't need any warning but ran off unharmed. Barks sat down heavily in the wheelchair. Almost immediately, a police car pulled up. The cop rolled down his window and said, "We saw what happened. You people are from the Hare Kṛṣṇa sanatorium, right?"

"Yes," said Jane, "and this man in the wheelchair had a bad motorcycle accident that made him lose his memory. Now he may have relapse." Barks sat slumped in the wheelchair. He looked dazed. The cop said, "We'll go round up those culprits. You just go back to the sanatorium. You did a pretty good job of self-defense. Congratulations." While Jane turned and guided Barks and his wheelchair back to the sanatorium, the cops drove into the woods, having already handcuffed the unconscious man and put him in the back of the car. It didn't take them long to find the man who had been karatied lying on the ground nursing his pains. But they had to drive far before they found the third man running fast down the street and finally ducking into a tavern. The police went into the tavern with their guns drawn and came out with another handcuffed culprit.

Jane brought Barks back to the sanatorium and put him into bed. He was a little disoriented. The cops dropped by and congratulated them on what they had done and said that all of the men would be charged with assault, and that they had nothing to worry about. They said that anytime they needed help, they should ask for it. As the cops were leaving, Barks looked up and asked, "Where am I?"

"You're here safe in the sanatorium," Jane said gently.

Barks began to smile. "We just had a good fight, huh?"

Jane smiled without speaking. Barks said, "Would you marry me?"

"If you're feeling that good, then I think you should be able to chant on your beads. Here they are," and she put them on his lap. "We can talk about other things later."

One time only and then you'll have
to abandon ship. Not too many repeats.
I painted while the family was
out, and tried to chant. Not try, you
just do it instead of answering
letters. Paintings have been completed. No
visitors expected. No excuses.
Took an oxy so you should
get through. I don't even
need a pass. I live here on

charity of a man and his
family. Do I have to get kicked
out? Some new fiduciary
laws? It better be free for all
or that's what it *will* be, a
disintegrated hole.

Oh no you've got to see it
from the other side.

They had their favorite projects.
Charlie the fake priest slips out
the window just as the sheriff
walks by. He pretends he did it
just to pick a rose and goes back inside
and sheriff lets it
pass.

But he's an escaped criminal.
Do you want him to play a
better role? He could be an
actual minister and not
try to steal the Sunday collection
or the pint of whisky from
the sexton's pocket or
make time with his daughter.

But that's the kind of guy he
is. Swims is not like that. He's a
a law and order gold heart
of the sanatorium, who'll give
attention to Sandy and to
Jane and Barks and arthritic mom
and Junior and everyone but himself.
Sometimes he doesn't take care of
going to the dentist every day.
"But your presence

makes my day."
Oh dismay, where is God,
speaker of the names? The
most advertised easy glory?
Where is he in these shoes?
He should be right here, lost
identity like Barks. I told
the doctor it started with Paxil
and Clonapin. I'll try to lower them
next week, he said. It seems as simple as
that and then the habit developed and
it's never stopped. She says she's
in limbo. I know, sister, I'm
there too.

But there's a way out and we must
learn it, 'tis as simple as counting on
an abacus. What child
or Chinaman can't do it?
Lost coordination? Gain it back.

Dearest Sandy,

Please accept my humble obeisances. All glories to Śrīla Prabhupāda.

Please excuse me for not writing earlier. I was caught up in the whirlwind of Rathā-yātrā in Sydney. There must have been ten sannyāsīs *here, and I had to arrange for accommodations for them. Then I was in charge of preparing the carts, seeing that they were properly put together and protected. Of course, many others were doing tremendous service, like cooking and decorating with flowers, and everyone wanted to make it the best Rathā-yātrā ever. And it was a wonderful group effort. The weather was very good, and we marched with thousands of people watching us. They were in a good mood, and there were no unfavorable incidents. They all got to see the*

Lord of the Universe, which is a great blessing for them. There were wonderful kīrtana *leaders, heard over good amplifiers, and that was a blessing on us and on the watchers. At the festival site, the bright tents were set up, and we had several stages, one with bands playing live music. We had two theater productions, and little booths with* sannyāsīs *answering questions, girls putting* gopī *dots on people, and of course free food, as well as food that was on sale. The lines went quickly and people loved the* prasādam. *Prabhupāda's books and books of other ISKCON devotees sold well from book tables, and the sun continued to shine with mercy on the beautiful day.*

After the day was over, many of us who really had participated in it without any layback were completely exhausted. I myself went two days without sleep, and I just crashed out on the night of Rathā-yātrā. I just couldn't push myself to do much on the cleanup crew, although I wanted to help all the way. Some devotees who didn't do as much earlier pitched in and made sure that everything was clean, and the Rathā-yātrā cart group, who are experienced, knew how to bring the carts back.

These are the external reasons why I did not write you. But even while the Rathā-yātrā events were going on, and even during the period when I was too exhausted to concentrate and compose a letter, I was always thinking of you. As a pure devotee always thinks of the name and form and qualities of Lord Kṛṣṇa, so I, as the lover of Sandy, always think of you, your name, your form, your qualities. Please, therefore, do not worry that I would abandon you because of your temporary condition. From the diagnosis you give in your own letter and from some research I have done, your condition is not as bad as it may sound at first. You write that you had a bad but incomplete *injury to your spine and that it is* reversible. *You are at a place where there is a first-class physiatrist who knows how to alleviate your pain and give you the physical therapy that will bring a normal condition and healthy adjustment to your body.*

I understand the psychological condition is very important here. First of all, you have to cooperate with this team of therapists and very steadily do the exercises, which is just as important as your chanting of the Holy Names or any other spiritual sādhana. *In fact, I would say that for the time being, this* "sādhana" *is the most important of all for you. And also you should not be* depressed. *Don't think that you are no longer an attractive woman. As I write this letter, I look at a photo of you from the night that I proposed to you. You are smiling and very beautiful, wearing a reddish sari. And your long blonde hair is very captivating to me. I am sure you will again be standing straight and walking and talking and smiling as before. You also have to keep in your mind this image of your returning to physical normalcy.*

If you think, "I am a worm, my husband is going to reject me," then that will really slow down your progress. As your well-wisher, I accept you as you are in your wheelchair, in your bent condition, and it doesn't lessen my attraction to you. As a Vaiṣṇava also, we are not just attracted to flesh and body forms. I am attracted to you on the soul-to-soul level. So I can be as patient as it takes, and you should be also.

You have to live with that patience day by day in order to be healed in all the parts of the body, which was shocked from the accident.

I don't know the devotees there in the sanatorium, but they are all devotees and you can tell me gradually about them. You should make friends with them and don't hold yourself aloof. They're all there from their own ill conditions, and they have probably learned how to become transcendental to them and not remain depressed. You can help them *with your own compassion, because some cases may be worse than yours. And you can receive from their advanced transcendental attitudes toward injury how to endure and be patient.*

Everything can be cured by mind over matter and by proper medical care. I am your lover waiting for you to become better.

Even if you did not have this accident, if for some reason we had to be separated, we would experience pain. Kṛṣṇa and the gopīs *were not separated because of a physical accident, but they felt a terrible pain because they could not be together. So we are experiencing an enforced separation. Let us continue to write these letters and tell each other in honesty how we are feeling toward each other, and we can support each other in our own attempts to practice Kṛṣṇa consciousness.*

I hope I have made it clear to you that I fully accept you now in your present condition with your injury, just as I did before. But I'm also praying and trusting that by prayer and medical science and our patience, we will be rejoined in normal, healthy, conjugal life. Hoping to hear from you soon.

Yours in love of Kṛṣṇa and service to Śrīla Prabhupāda, Braja

Chapter Fifteen

Sandy was very private about her letter, and the devotees respected her not wanting to talk about it. She already had a file to collect her letters in, and she placed them there in a drawer in her bed table. But they could see that she felt very peaceful and content. If she wanted to, she would talk with them about it. She thought about it and took the letter out and read it again. It was full of affirmation and love. She did notice a few loopholes where Braja dāsa had been so optimistic about her recovery, as if his love was conditional to her getting well real soon. What if she didn't get well that soon? What if she were another case like Swami Swims? Surely he could not wait that long. He really seemed to emphasize that her condition was minor and that she'd soon spring back.

She didn't want to pop his balloon, because that might be another way of manifesting depression and lack of self-esteem. But on the other hand, to be realistic, it might be a tiny revelation on his part that he couldn't wait forever. In his mind, he might be treating it as a minor event with regard to his personal plans, so that in his mind he could get on with his marriage to the beautiful girl who walked with a straight back and certainly did not have to be pushed in a wheelchair. He mentioned in one sentence that if she was in a wheelchair, he would still be true to her. But who knows what a man will do in the passage of time? She could have liked a little more unconditional love in the expression. But nevertheless, she thought those loopholes were the gentlest way he could find to express his honesty, and she appreciated it. He was certainly true to her, thinking of her and giving her the best advice. And he seemed to be crossing his fingers that she'd be well real soon, while she was still young and could still enjoy a full life in good health.

Why should she doubt her man for such hopes? He was giving her the best advice—stay optimistic, take inspiration from the devotees at the sanatorium, and work hard with the medical staff. And—did he pray to Kṛṣṇa? That was assumed.

And did she still love him? Did she remember him? She took out her pictures and felt her love for Braja dāsa. Why did the accident have to occur so far away from Australia? If she had to have an accident, couldn't it have occurred nearer to Braja? These things seemed to be in Kṛṣṇa's hands, and she was helpless. Yet she still loved Braja, and she needed him. She needed his letters also. In her next letter she would ask for some pictures of himself in activities in the temple, and she'd have to think more deeply of what to write to him, so that the letter exchange did not become trivial and repetitive.

Meanwhile, the sanatorium was buzzing about the fight that Jane and Barks had with the skinheads in the park. They were especially impressed that after Barks had been knocked down, he stood up and knocked a guy out with one punch.

"I used to be like that!" he said with vigour, "and I could be like that again if I could get my Kṛṣṇa conscious memory back. But I don't want to go around slugging people. That's not the way to live. It's just a measure of self-defense, the way Jane uses it. I want a peaceful life. It's just these people who step in your way and challenge you and insult you and threaten you. Otherwise a Vaiṣṇava wants peace. But it was thrilling to be there with Jane and see the way she acted and see the cops come over and commend us."

The inmates looked at him with awe. Usually he was so silent, not talking about such things. "Anyway, the real punch is in the Hare Kṛṣṇa mantra, and I'm behind on my rounds so I'd better go back—the way Popeye eats his spinach—and get some of my real strength for the next encounter with *Māyā*." He chuckled and began chanting vigorous *japa*. Jane smiled and went back to her typing room, eager to keep up with the writings of Swami Swims.

In the middle of the night, Barks woke up to find that his memory had fully returned. The return of his memory had started when his wheelchair was knocked over by the skinhead and he hit his head on the ground. But now it suddenly returned completely. He felt like his old self before he entered the sanatorium. All the work that Bhakta Jane had done on him vanished. He no longer had a taste for her and the Hare Kṛṣṇa stuff. He wanted to leave and go out and drink and whore and ride his bike. He wanted to start by going back to his house and seeing if his old lady was there. If there was no man with her, he'd stay there for a while, screw with her and see what happened. Otherwise, he'd have to take to the road and just see what turned up. He quickly wrote a note and left it on his bed: "Dear inmates, my memory has returned. I'm leaving you all. I'm returning to my old woman, if she'll have me. Junior Barks is my son, but neither of us really care much for each other. I'm going to leave the decision up to him whether he wants to stay here or join me.—Barks." He remembered seeing money in the drawer of the night table of the man in the bed next to his. He quietly opened it and filched out a couple of hundred dollar bills. His motorcycle was still parked outside from months ago. As far as he knew it was operable, so he put on his boots and went to the front door. He saw that the *chaukīdār* was fast asleep on his bench. Barks tried the starter on his motorcycle and the engine immediately turned over. He gunned it a few times and then immediately dug out, spattering pebbles behind him while the *chaukīdār* slept on. Barks sped into the night, past all the Kṛṣṇa buildings, until he was on the main road with only his headlight showing the way. He'd head for his house, and if the old lady was there, he'd screw her, maybe get drunk, and if she had a stash of some drugs, they could get stoned. If she wasn't there, he still had an address book in his back pocket with the names of a number of whores he knew who would put him up. He was still the man he used to be, and the ladies always liked him. Ah, it felt good to be on the bike again and not have to think of four rules. All he lacked was a helmet, and he could pick that up in the next town with the money had had filched.

As soon as she heard the motorcycle roar, Jane jumped up from bed and ran to Barks' bed. She read the note and looked out the front door. The *chaukīdār* was still asleep. There was nothing else to see except a few lights in the main house and the stars. She sighed and took it philosophically. Swami Swims also woke up. He approached Jane and asked her what happened. She showed him the note. "Let's try to get back to bed," he said, "so many things happen in one day. We'll talk about it tomorrow. Everything is in Kṛṣṇa's hands. But don't you be disappointed. You tried all you could."

"Yes," Jane said, "I tried. And maybe I was even getting a little attached to him at the end. A little Māyā, so Kṛṣṇa saved me. But in terms of saving his soul, it's a shame because it seemed like he was coming around, like Junior."

Do you like "Lotsa Patsa"?
Too much going on, the rain
every day. I'm sorry, it's just
like Ireland. "You talk too much."
I talked of foolish things to Śacī
while I undressed Prabhupāda
and almost forgot to bathe him.

Then I remembered and started talking
about *him*. How he saw
TKG and I talking and said, "What were you
talking about?" I said, "Making plans." He
asked, "What plans?" Knew we were
devious pirates. Tamāla wanted to
go to America and me too.

Poor Prabhupāda had to become GBC
of India and get a new personal
servant. Stories now in my
new freedom. "You've got a far-
out guru." Ha ha.
"Her now infamous remark:
'he left ISKCON ten years ago.'"

Who said that? It gets around.
Ask for an explanation. In
the Chaplin movie, the money
keeps getting passed around from
pocket to pocket from expert
thief Chaplin to the other
expert pickpocket.

Chap is passing as a minister
and when the other guy steals
the mortgage money of the deacon,

Charlie goes to the rescue,
"I'll get it back."

Oh boy. This is great stuff.
He walks into the bar and grabs the
money and runs back and hands it to—
damn it! I promised I'd never
forget her name—who's waiting at
the door. He gives it to her but
immediately behind him is the
marshal and says he still has
go to jail.

He takes him to the Mexican
border, the sheriff on horse
and Charlie on foot,
and releases him there.

Tell her the story of the minister.
Charlie is always a thief but always
has a heart of gold and a
romantic inclination for
a pretty girl for whom he'll
do gallant things.

I watched it through and chuckled
a few times. But the
audience had thinned.
Sandy's virtuous influence.
I bet the funnies and after
a while when she gets depressed
she'll come in here to laugh said
Swims to himself and his own
broken heart, his anxious heart
and his habit—hooked on the
funnies.

Going too long. Where's a great writer
in my genre? The neighbour gave
me two books in straight
novel genre. That's not going
to help.

Listen to that drum, that
Ludwig quartet, that rain,
that messed up canvas order.
Get it right, will you?

He didn't do it right. They
asked for only a hundred
feet. Man, I do a hundred
yards in a month. Send
me some canvas!

Here we go asshole. Dumb
Barks left, but Sandy joined.
And what do you think
Junior will do and what
will your Ouija board right
arm move to?

"It reminded me of India,"
he said of the bar mitzvah.
"That was the only good
thing about it." *India*, Swims
thought. India. India.
India. Is it really the same?
Do I have
the heart to see it?
Ten years ago
he left what?

Swami Swims broke the news to Junior Barks. At first he was very disappointed. He liked his new position as a humble servant of the sanatorium, without pretensions. He was also glad to see his father there and how he was changing, and how Jane was taking care of him. It was almost like she was part of his family, and of course all the inmates were. But his dad's presence and his comeback into a kind of devotee was a real security. He didn't mind so much finding out that his so-called "mom," who was really just a whore, was not his actual biological mother and that he'd probably never know who his mother was. That was all Māyā anyway. He had no curiosity about it. He just wanted to be a devotee. But he was confused.

Swami Swims said, "Mr. Barks said the choice is up to you about where you want to live. He's going back to the woman he was living with, although he didn't know whether she'd take him back. He wrote that he had no particular attachment for you and that he wasn't going to claim you were his son and try to have you live with him. If you want to stay with us, it was all right with me. If you didn't, if you wanted to go back and live in that so-called house, that was your choice too."

"Let me think about it for a while," said Junior. He knew the kind of person his father was, and he knew it wasn't likely that he would stay with his so-called mother for very long. Soon he'd be out whoring and drinking and having sex, if not with his so-called mom, then with some other babe. "On the one hand the choice is obvious," said Junior, "but it's a life decision, so I want a little time to myself."

"Of course," said Swami Swims.

Junior went over to Sandy's chair and asked her what she was reading. She said she was rereading the Third Canto of the *Śrīmad-Bhāgavatam*, where the sage Vidura is thrown out of the palace at Hastināpura and starts wandering like a mendicant.

"Is that a good section?" Junior asked.

"Oh it's a marvellous section. I love to read it again and again."

"I think I'll read it today too," said Junior. "Maybe I can talk with you about it later today. Is that all right?"

Sandy smiled. "Certainly, whenever you like."

Junior went out the back door with a library copy of the Third Canto and began reading to himself. The other devotees gave him his distance.

When sunset came, Junior came back and sat in the chair beside Sandy's desk. She was writing one of her letters. "Is this not a good time to interrupt you?" he asked.

Jane hesitated a moment before answering, then turned from her letter. "I can give you some time," she said.

"So what did you think of the chapter about Vidura being thrown out of the palace and what happened?"

Jane laughed a little. "I certainly haven't been thrown out of any palace or become entangled in any politics. That happened to Vidura, and he took advantage of it. He was a man of politics, a minister who was used to dealing with governments and giving that kind of advice. So he thought he was fortunate to be disengaged from it so he could live like a mendicant and travel and seek out wise men. He finally found Uddhava, who told him those wonderful pastimes of Kṛṣṇa, which are like a preview to the Tenth Canto. And then Uddhava advised him to seek the sage Maitreya for further instructions. Vidura's example is one of renunciation. Giving up the safety of the palace and wandering around like one who has no income or house. He just has to eat what roots he finds and be like a beggar. No wife or family. So while I liked what he heard from the sages, I don't think I'm at the stage of life where I could leave home and become a perpetual wanderer. I'm looking forward to a *gṛhastha* life, with a husband who can be my guide. I'm looking forward to recovering from my accident and leading a full life as a woman, raising children and helping them become Kṛṣṇa conscious. In that literal sense, I didn't feel it applied to me, but the wonderful Vaiṣṇava wisdom I took in eagerly as something to teach others about. And certainly when I get much older, I will have to leave family and home and just depend on Kṛṣṇa. Anyway, that's my first take on it. I loved it. What did you get out of it, Junior?"

"You say you're young, too young to think of wandering out like a mendicant. I'm 'bout as young as you, but my position is closer to Vidura's than yours. I have been thrown out of the house. I've been fortunate because that so-called household was a wicked place. My father has returned to wicked, sinful life, living with different women, and I don't even know which of them is my mother. He didn't exactly throw me out, but if I went back there, I would be openly exposed to liquor, drugs, sex, and abuse. When they get angry, they would probably try to physically abuse me. So like Vidura, I'm fortunate that my dad left. I would have been more fortunate if he stayed here with us in this recovery program to return to Kṛṣṇa consciousness. But I apply the Vidura story to myself, that I am fortunate to now go out on my own and be with the saints and sages—I'm talking about the devotees in this place—and to hear from them. The relief that Vidura found in freedom from entanglement with sinful persons is a relief that I found. And I'm not going to walk back into it. I say this with no idea of comparing it to your situation. I agree that you have a very happy life ahead of you."

Sandy began to cry.

"You'll heal," Junior continued, "and it's right for you to return to your home, because you'll be straightened out and you'll have a husband who loves you, and that's a normal way for a woman to live, not to walk around begging and being without any shelter. I was just telling you my view. They're different, that's all. You inspire me by your courage. We're both in difficult situations right now. But I think we'll both pull out of it. I'll pull out of my loneliness at not having parents at an age when one usually has parents, and you'll pull out of your feelings of separation from your fiancé and your fear of when you'll recover. You'll recover from your lack of patience, and I will also have to be patient. Anyway, thank you for tipping me onto a good section of *Bhāgavatam*. I think you're a wise girl." Junior made obeisances to her and she returned them while sitting in her chair.

"I'm going to tell Swami Swims that I'm staying," said Junior. "Who'd but a fool would return to that hell?"

My Dear Love,

Please accept my humble obeisances. All glories to Śrīla Prabhupāda.

I was extremely joyful to finally receive a letter from you. I was very relieved that you will be patient with me, and I look forward to the time when things will return to normal and we can go forward with our marriage plans.

Today I finished my first week of therapy in the rehab center. I can tell you a little bit more about my medical condition, as they shared it with me. I hope it won't bore you. It was extremely educational for me, and I think it will help you to know more about what we are dealing with. I know you learned some of it through your own research there. Apparently the emergency room hospitalization focuses on the physical maintenance and stabilization for release to outpatient clinics or long-term facilities; the goal of the rehab center is to maximize the patient's long-term recovery and integration into the community.

I now have for my file a written description of what actually happened. Under "Condition," they have written, "incomplete compression of the spinal cord at C5/6, resulting in motor and sensory loss, possibly reversible.

"Cause of injury: Blow to forehead sustained in car accident.

"State when admitted to ER: Unconscious (Glasgow Coma Scale, 5), hypertension, intracranial hypertension."

Some of these words, of course, are technical, and I don't know what they mean. I remember a tube being inserted in my mouth and my spine being immobilized, the bladder being drained, and some medicine being given—which they called ranitidine—to prevent stress ulcer. For pain relief they gave me opiates. The report said that opiates should be used with caution in my case, because there is a risk of respiratory depression. And then they arranged to transfer me to a comprehensive spinal cord injury center as soon as I was medically stable. And that is where I am now.

In this place, there is a daily management, and they check on all the sensitive conditions that resulted from the accident. I will certainly have to stay here for many weeks. There is a primary nurse who is taking care of me and seeing that bedsores don't develop, and she is coordinating my care and training. There is a psychologist, who is evaluating my emotional adjustment and introducing me to family support groups and services. Of course, this has been wonderfully done in a natural way by my getting to know the other inmates in this sanatorium, who are all devotees.

But I leave the sanatorium daily and go to the physical therapy unit. I've been given a physical exercise program to increase the range of motion, muscle strength, cardiopulmonary function, and balance and coordination. I get training in bed mobility, ambulation, and wheelchair mobility, and in how to transfer myself into and out of my wheelchair. Therapy techniques include electrical stimulation, ultrasound, and use of heat and cold, and they have state-of-the-art equipment for strength building. There's also an occupational therapist who trains and educates me in various activities geared to maximize functional independence and prepare me for reentry into the community. Of course, all I really need to do is read Śrīmad-Bhāgavatam *and chant on my beads. But I appreciate their showing me different things to do with my hands and getting me more and more set. They're even planning to teach me how to use the computer, something I had never planned to do. Maybe they'll teach me how to drive a car!*

I still haven't been here so long, so I can't tell you whether I'm feeling straighter in my spine or better or healthier, but I feel a lot of confidence in the treatment that I'm being given. I feel I'm being given the optimum medical treatment. The physiatrist, for example, is a devotee like everyone else here, and he specializes in physical medicine and rehabilitation. He's responsible for medical issues and overall rehabilitation. So I know he's not going to overdo the medication. The rehabilitation nurse is responsible for daily care and the coordination of treatment and training. I think it's very important that I work with the physical therapist to improve my strength, flexibility and endurance, and my coordination and balance with activities such as moving in bed, using the wheelchair, and walking.

The psychologist usually assists people and their families to understand the changes that can accompany disability or illness. It would be nice if you were here for these sessions so that you could also understand what I'm going through and how it will affect us both. But maybe through my explanations and letters and through the Supersoul, you will understand that I may not come out 100 percent just like I was, but I will try my best and I will depend on your compassionate understanding.

Here are some of the other things we are doing: aerobics, computer education, community integration, and sports and leisure activities. There is also a community luncheon for the rehab patients, but of course the sanatorium group does things together anyway. There is a psychotherapy group, which is something that happens normally in the sanatorium. It's a forum for individuals to express their feelings regarding the impact of their diseases on their life. We can talk about our problem-solving and get support and share information. We learn how to decrease mental and physical reactions to everyday stressors. We learn how to control our body's reaction to annoying or terrifying events and improve our health while conserving mental and physical energy. Some of this may sound a little abstract to you, but I'm telling it from my daily experience.

I'm certainly still confined to a wheelchair, but I can get in and out of it and move around in it, going over curbs and even negotiating stairs with increasing ability.

So much for my impressions after a few workouts in the rehabilitation clinic. I want to be realistic and let you know that I don't know when I'll be able to return to Sydney, but that really depends on too many factors. I'm certainly trying my best to make a speedy recovery and be the best patient they ever had here. And I'm praying to Kṛṣṇa to be in your arms again as soon as possible. If it takes too long, maybe you could come visit me here, although I know it's very expensive.

At any rate, please know that I always think of you with love and that I will cherish our promise for marriage as sacred, but want you to marry a girl who is not crippled. I do not want to impose that condition on you. Only if I am straight and whole and can make you truly happy will I be happy in our union. In your letter I sensed your own urgency that I achieve full recovery as soon as possible. Let us pray to Kṛṣṇa that this takes place and at the same time pray for a little patience. Your surrendered soul, Bhaktin Sandy

He's telling her he's true more than she
knows and she trusts him but she just
wants to spell it out. It's going to
take a long time. "I'm growing fonder
of you ... even if you don't succeed . . .
I give you the break. More
than you know, man of my heart,
I love you so, lately I find you
on my mind more than you know."[1]

But will he accept this little bend
of a girl? "You need me more
than you know," she says, but does
he? "Loving you the way I do, there's
nothing I can do about it. I can't live
without it though I cry oh how I would cry
if you got tired and said goodbye.
I wouldn't show but I would feel
more than you know."

She didn't put it that way in her letter,
but did she even feel it?
Was this too premature a love? What
is love? Mostly someone else's
dream?

Chapter Sixteen

The sanatorium rehabilitation center and hospital were admittedly parochial for Hare Kṛṣṇa people. Their worldwide temples were certainly for *everyone*. Preachers who led tours to various cities throughout the country, putting on festivals with music and dance, were certainly doing this for outsiders unfamiliar with Hare Kṛṣṇa. And there were many other outreach programs. One of the most outgoing events of the movement was the Rathā-yātrā, introduced by Prabhupāda in 1967—in a parade of three large carts, Jagannātha, Subhadrā, and Balarāma go down the major streets of many cities all over the world. One of the most popular and best attended was the parade down Fifth Avenue in New York City, which ended at Washington Square Park. There, stages were set up and entertainment performed, and thousands of free plates of Kṛṣṇa *prasādam* were distributed to the people of New York. In the beginning, Swami Swims was a little puzzled about why Prabhupāda would have such hard-to-understand "idols" parade down the public streets. And certainly most people did think of them as idols, not as God. And yet the people were mostly not opposed to it and appreciated the festival spirit. The police soon learned that it was a nonviolent parade, not a protest, and it was an easy one to police. The devotees always cleaned up after themselves, and a good spirit prevailed all day.

The sanatorium was for the members of the religion. Hare Kṛṣṇa was a small group, and the Vaiṣṇava philosophy was "charity begins at home." Many of its members had no means to take care of their own medical calamities, and so charitable places had to be provided to take care of the ill. There were even plans in the works for a hospice, which would take care of those who had terminal diseases and were going to die within a few months. Those people would be ushered through the last stage of life, up to the moment of death, where they would be given *tulasī* leaves, Yamunā water, and surrounded by caring persons who would chant Hare Kṛṣṇa to them as they took their last breaths. The sanatorium, however, was not for the dying but was for saving people, who could then return to active service. A person like Swami Swims had a chronic illness, but for many years he had struggled outside the sanatorium. He had only been there now for a few years, and he was again planning to leave; he had accepted the offer of a patron to live reclusively and take medicine in a house in California. Others were also going to try to live outside the sanatorium. They only had limited rooms or beds, and persons like Sandy, considered "basket cases," had highest priority. Some did stay on for years because they remained in a critical condition. There was always a question of how long someone should stay or when they might be released. This was always reviewed. Then there were exceptional cases, like Junior. There was really nothing wrong with him physically, but he had somehow been adopted by the sanatorium because he had no father and mother. And then there was the *Sanatorium* staff, which had created a productive literary office within the sanatorium. Swami Swims was using his influence to keep this alive. Jane had diabetes, but in one sense, it could be argued that she could go out into the material world and get a job and take insulin. But she was such a fabulous typist that Swims argued for her working for Kṛṣṇa in the sanatorium and producing Kṛṣṇa conscious books. Some of the older people hovered between staying in the hospital and going on to the hospice stage. Some got better and went out again into the active world. There was always an attempt at fairness and individual treatment.

Swami got ready for his trip to the dentist. He was wearing his white Jagannātha T-shirt. Śacī said the temperature would go up to ninety degrees, but Swami didn't trust that, and so he wore his short-sleeve *kurtā* underneath the T-shirt. But he figured he'd have to wear the T-shirt outside the pants, because otherwise, Jagannātha's teeth and smile would be covered. But when he tucked in the T-shirt, revealing the nice new nonleather belt he'd been given, he discovered that Jagannātha's face was completely revealed! He didn't expect a kiss today and was going to remain aloof about the gifts that he had given last time. Rather, he had complaints to make. The few days since he had been there last had been painful. The bottom denture, pressing against his lower gums, had produced pain. By Saturday it was so painful that he had a choice between either starving, eating baby food, or putting in adhesive (Fixodent). Swami prepared himself to say to the doctor, "I'm going to play the devil's advocate and ask, What's wrong with wearing dental adhesive? It removes the pain. And also, the upper dentures are quite loose. Sometimes they just fall out. I don't see why one shouldn't wear adhesive."

Then he'd hear Danz's preaching about why one shouldn't wear adhesive. It just didn't seem to make sense. As for Karen, surely Swims would be a little bashful about the exchange they had. Maybe they'd say something about how nice the gifts were, but he didn't want to say much back about it, just that he was glad they liked it. Let's get on with business. Let's get these teeth fixed once and for all. Maybe they'd ask him about the T-shirt. He wore a Jagannātha T-shirt last time he was there and they didn't ask anything. That was his black one. Now he had his white one. He'd say, "This is a Hindu symbol for the face of God." But when were they finally going to make those last adjustments so he could eat in peace? Twenty-minute drives to the dentist, even if they are accompanied by pleasant exchanges, are a little too much to take. "And Technicolor pachyderms are really too much for me!"

It may have been ninety degrees out but the air conditioner was turned on in the dentist's office and it was more like fifty degrees there. Swami Swims had worn his white Jagannātha T-shirt to impress the dentist and Karen. But it was too much waiting, too cold, so he asked Śacī if he had something warmer in the car. Śacī came back with a throw-over jacket, and Swims succumbed to it. He walked in and told the doctor it had been a painful few days because of a few sore spots on the bottom gums. The doctor was cheerful and found the spots immediately and put something on there and said now they wouldn't hurt anymore permanently. Swims said also that the top denture kept falling out. The dentist then put something in to make them stay in. Swims said, "I'm going to play the devil's advocate and ask you, What's wrong with wearing dental adhesive?"

"It makes the gums shrink," said the doctor. And that seemed to end that argument.

It seemed that Karen was not present at all. Maybe she took the day off. The dentist said that he should return the day after tomorrow and see if any new sore spots appeared.

"This thing you put at the top, is that going to stay in permanently?"

"No," the doctor said, "we have to wait three months for that hole to heal, where I pulled out the tooth. Then we'll make it permanent. And we'll have to see if any new sores appear on the bottom."

Finally, while the doctor was looking in his mouth, Karen passed by and said hi and touched Swims' arm. It was hardly a personal exchange and he couldn't even look at her, but he said hi. He got another chance to look at her as he was getting up and leaving, but she was quite professional and didn't smile. Neither of them said anything about John Coltrane or Emily Dickinson.

In the car, Swims said to Śacī, "They may be only ten-minute visits, but they're twenty-five-minute car trips each way. They may think that I live next door, but it's really a hassle to keep coming back here." No, it was not true that Karen had "made his day." She was just a plain, straight-haired dental assistant and had no warmth in her heart for him—too busy and too occupied, not only with dental work but probably with another man in her heart, her husband no doubt. And anyway, what did Swims want to have to do with women?

He arrived back at the sanatorium and said he didn't want to talk about the dentist and that he had to go back again Wednesday. His friends groaned. Junior, who was something of a snitcher, came up to him and told him something about Jojo, the old black man who had recently been admitted to the sanatorium for broken arms and broken legs. He had been beaten up by a gang of Hell's Angels who had attacked a *harināma* group that had been dancing on the streets of San Francisco. He was in his 60s but had fought valiantly and knocked a few of them out. He had been an ex-Hell's Angel himself. He had been hospitalized and had now been given shelter to repair at the New York sanatorium. He was quiet and mostly sat on the back porch and listened privately to CDs with his earphones.

"Jojo went to the movies last night," said Junior. "He went and saw *The Incredible Hulk*."

"How do you know?"

"I saw him come back and there was a theater brochure sticking out of his pocket."

"That's not good. Devotees should only watch movies that we show here, that are authorized. I'll talk to him about it."

Swims went out to the back porch. "Jojo?" he asked.

Jojo took off his earphones. "Yeah?"

"I've always wondered about the Incredible Green Hulk. When I used to read about him in the comics, I thought he was a hero on the side of good. But then I saw that the military was always trying to shoot him down, so I couldn't understand whether he was good or bad. Do you know anything about that?"

"Why ask me?" Jojo tucked his head down sullenly. "I don't read comic books."

"Well, a new movie just came out about it, and I thought you might know."

"I think he was just misunderstood," said Jojo. "But I won't go checking out no movies anymore. I got your word."

"Also," said Swims, "it's very dangerous for you to go out in your chair. You need protection."

"I didn't go alone," said Jojo, "arthritic mom took me. She pushed my chair."

Swims shook his head back and forth and went back to his room to take a short post-dentist nap. After about a half-hour nap, Swims got up and brought a chair next to arthritic mom's bed.

"Mom," Swims asked, "I was talking to Jojo about the Incredible Hulk, and I couldn't understand his character or the plot."

Mom was a little taken aback but remained cool.

"What couldn't you understand," she said.

"Well, is he a good guy or a bad guy? If he's good, why is the military always after him?"

"It was all rather confusing to me, and I fell asleep during most of it. I think Jojo did too. One thing was that the more he's hurt with bullets, the stronger he gets. He was created by a scientist who killed his mother, and he saw that and came out born with that trauma. I really didn't understand it except that he's an antihero—very simple but in a mighty form. He smashes everything with his fists. He wasn't attractive at all. I don't know why Jojo convinced me to go. I'm sorry that we went. Please forgive us." She went back to her knitting.

Swami Swims said, "Hare Kṛṣṇa," and walked away. He had his own problems. "Hare Kṛṣṇa, Hare Kṛṣṇa, Kṛṣṇa Kṛṣṇa, Hare Hare/ Hare Rāma, Hare Rāma, Rāma Rāma, Hare Hare," he repeated to himself. Next to mom's bed was Sandy. He turned to her and smiled. "How are you doing," he asked.

She smiled. "All right, I guess. I should not complain. As long as I have the Lord's holy names, everything else is secondary. But I'm a conditioned soul, and I think of things like marriage and having a fit body. I'm trying to think of what you said about patience, and that page you showed me by the poet—how the easily attained gold turns into the lead of patience. I think that the lead can be converted again if we just remember our priorities in this world. I'm struggling, but I feel calm and protected here. And I think of so many people, like people in India who are just dying on the roads and have no one to care for them. Then I feel like an ingrate. Kṛṣṇa's very kind to all of us to give us protection here. I want to improve my chanting. Are you chanting nicely, Swamiji?"

It was an unusual question for a young girl to ask a *sannyāsī*. But she was not a usual girl.

"I could certainly chant much better," he said. "It is a big struggle in my life. I am praying to the Lord to help me, and ask you to pray for me too." He walked away a little shakily—it was as if she had read his mind or something like that. Maybe others were noticing. Noticing that he sometimes fell asleep during *japa* or that his quota wasn't tallying up. But the important thing was quality, not quantity. He wanted to be able to chant with emotion more than with concentration on how many were being chanted. He was still suffering from the Klonopin, he thought, because only since then had he stopped chanting his quota and that his chanting had lapsed as a priority. But he had been so depressed that he needed to do other things to keep a quality of life, and so the writing, the painting. But now the most important thing of all had somehow slipped away. He prayed for it to return.

There will be poems for people
charming. Why don't you get
the nine-volume set he made
two weeks before he died?
But nine versions of "My
Romance" is a little to much.

Not really when you think
what's happening, how unique
and charming. I must say to you
there's a limit on your spending.
Things have to
be curtailed. Send a bill
to the treasurer. They'll tell you
if it's over. Who can afford
such things? One *japa-mālā*
is very inexpensive.
Sit down and try them. Your book
will get written by itself.
The seasons will change

and you will be very happy
to avoid all saloons
and bad accidents. Still can't chew,
still sore gums, still new characters.
Pack them into the sanatorium.

Let's make an altar says Sandy
and they do it and get Gaura-Nitāi
and singing in the morning and
chant together or go back to
bed if they need, and hear the
song divine in their sleep.

He wrote me from Sweden
and said his favorite drummer
is Paul Motian. I never met
him. He's a Hare Kṛṣṇa. A
few of us. Dr. Danz. You're getting
low marks in my book
for not halting the pain.

And I get low marks
for my exposing it and telling
the truth, but now you've
got to improve. Let's work
and say *hari-nāma* even without
the beads. *Haribol, haribol.*
Just say the names and don't
worry about counting.

He will hear your call.
Hare he taught and soon
you'll learn to do it as much
as you can no matter
what someone says who
is hung up on numbers.

I've got my way of loving and
saying and a friend to walk
with and confess to.

Sandy worked out in the therapy room as if she was trying out for the Olympics. She used the leg weights and the arm weights with all her youthful strength. Her therapists pushed her on and said, "Good, good."

She asked them, "What's the earliest someone has walked out of here completely whole?"

They laughed. "It depends. The standard is two years. Sometimes one year."

"Are there some extraordinary individual cases where someone went out real early?"

"Oh yes! There are cases of a person transferring from the wheelchair to crutches quickly."

"Oh! I want to do that." Sandy had already become expert at using the wheelchair. She preferred to use it manually rather than with the battery. She could wheel around and go up ramps and cross distances, and even spin around corners with a flair. Luckily she was so young and in good shape. She used to play basketball and soccer and cricket before she had her accident, and so she was in very good shape.

"I think you may break some records for recovery," said one of the nurses. "But remember, part of it is resting the muscles, not just pushing them. That's true even in ordinary sports. There was one great racehorse whose trainer raced him very fast the day before a championship race, and he was later blamed for losing the race because of that. There must be periods of rest. I know you want to get out and be normal and pretty and married. But you and your fiancé will have to be patient. He may even have to wheel you on your wheelchair down the aisle. How willing is he to accept you, and in what condition?"

"Hmm." Sandy frowned. "I often think of that myself. Does he love me just because I have pretty legs and can dance and walk? Would he be repelled if I had to walk on crutches or use a wheelchair?"

"That will be a test for both of you. But your business here is not to speculate about those things but to just do the regular work, not more or less. You're an excellent patient, so be patient."

Sandy smiled peacefully and continued with hard pulls on the weights until her time was up. She also looked forward to the masseurs rubbing her back, and all the words of encouragement that these people give her. They were so kind and expert, and she felt she owed them her life. Therefore, she always thanked them profusely for what they were doing and said she would always pray for them now and when she left here, and that she would dedicate whatever work she could do to them and their continued efforts to help others.

"It's just our service to Kṛṣṇa," they said. "The more people we can help, maybe we can get a little mercy."

Sandy always felt confident after a workout, but her anxiety stared her in the face when she had to write a letter to Braja dāsa, or wait for one that didn't arrive.

Those old days. The pin man wanted to read something the author had written, but all he had was an EJW from 1997. Diary-ish, living in Manu's room. What were they like? As I handed it over, I saw some sastric reflections on the first page and then the words, "Does God exist?" And then lampooning on words and metaphysics. Light reading, a man struggling. They say the struggling eked out. Or he doesn't dare tell of it now, just says, "I went to the dentist." Keli wasn't in, but at 2:30 she asked if I wanted a snack. I said no, but now I'm starving. I should have asked for an Ensure drink. Full protein. No painting. You'll never climb the Pikes Peak of sixteen rounds or even achieve an interested period of attentive prayer. Discursive prayer, "God, can You hear me? I'm doing better with less headaches, and so now the existential despair is free to come in." Why doesn't this guy avail himself of the panacea of the age? He's willing to ask the little deviants why they snuck out and went to the movies to see *The Incredible Hulk*, but he doesn't call God's name. He looks around the sanatorium alertly, sees just a little dirt, but will tend to that, and again feels the hope of lessening headaches ... Why don't you paint? Because I should be doing something else instead and I can't bring myself to do it. I've lost the drive of duty and the taste and drive of obedience. I'm taking a vacation and who knows how long that could last?

Like Sid Caesar last night. He never drank liquor, and when his friend offered him a cup of it, he at first refused. Then, hesitatingly, he smelled it, then drank it. At once he became a raving alcoholic and it ruined his life and home. W. C. Fields' film *The Fatal Glass of Beer*. Once you're hooked. Heroine: "Take one sniff of this and you'll be hooked for life."

A *sannyāsī* too. Everyone does their sixteen rounds. Or some don't. But all gurus do. Or they should be hanged.

Don't tell this or the people will
quote them in a tribunal.
Say they were fiction.
There was no girl named
Sandy or Jane or a
Swami Swims. It's all made up
to teach us lessons.

Then why do you keep harping
on it? I don't, you do. We
need romantic interest and
so do we need a guy having

trouble with his rounds and
a guy with broken legs.
Will Jane get that biker
to return?

Junior okay? I don't
know the answers to these
imaginings but don't blame
me because they never happened.
I saw them all on the silent
movie stories, Harry Langdon,
Harold Lloyd and Pinky Lee.

You stick to your prayers and
I'll stick to mine. I'll commune
with you if you love me
and give me a break as I'll
give you. Be liberal and don't
find fault. We all trip and
fall. That's what the
sanatorium is for. To pick us
up again spiritually and physically
and prayerfully. When I
fall in love, it will be
forever and I'll let you
know indirectly. You'll see
it on my face.

My Dear Braja,

Please accept my humble obeisances. All glories to Śrīla Prabhupāda.

I haven't received a letter from you, but I'm following up with another one from me. I'm always thinking of you, but another thing that's always on my mind is my therapy work. I'm concentrating on it very much and always thinking how to improve my prac-

tices here. I go every day and do weight-lifting exercises and various things to make my body strong. They tell me that my body is already strong because I'm so young and I've practiced athletics, so this is in my favor. The only thing is that the injury to my spine has paralysed me from the waist down, so they want to keep my muscles strong so that when the paralysis heals, my muscles won't be all shriveled up. They prop me up and make me lean on parallel bars, and I struggle forward, being guided by the therapists. They also put me in a pool that comes up to my waist, and they help me to move around. So they're keeping them in good shape. I'm very attentive to all these things. I do it, however, in dedication to you and Kṛṣṇa. The people are very, very helpful and encourage me.

When I press them for when I will be able to use crutches and when I'll be able to leave here, they laugh and say that they cannot give an exact time. They say the standard time is two years, but people have been known to do it in one year. I asked if there are any record-breakers who did it in less. I think I could be a record-breaker and come to you in good shape sooner than that. Let's see.

It would be nice if you could come here in the meantime and see how I'm doing. Please send me some recent photos of you. I'd be embarrassed to send you photos of me in my wheelchair. But if you insist, ask me. My face is still the same, so there's nothing wrong with that. I could dress up in a sari and make it flow over the wheelchair and you wouldn't even know the difference!

This is a place of patience and waiting, and so I'm more used to it than perhaps you are. I can wait, and I have patience. In other words, even if it did take two years, I could wait that long. But I have to ask you frankly if you could wait that long. And that's why I say I'd like to see you in the meantime. We could at least spend a week or two, in which we could go for walks—that is, you pushing me in my wheelchair—and talks about our present and future. It would revive our attraction and remembrance of our desire to be with one another for the rest of our lives. I now regard two years or one year as a short amount of time. We are both quite young, and when this is over, we'll have a lot of life to live, to raise children and to plan out our life.

Now I'm going to write something silly for you. After I write it, I'm going to write my own interpretation of it, so don't take it literally the first time you read it. People are often playing music around here. Although the orders are that they should only play it with their headphones, they sometimes play it out loud. There's one song I've heard sung by Frank Sinatra called, "My Funny Valentine." As best as I can remember, the words go like this: My funny valentine/ Sweet, comic valentine/ You make me smile with my heart/ Your looks are laughable,/ unphotographable/ Yet you're my favorite work of art/ Is your figure less than Greek?/ Is your mouth a little weak?/ When you open it to speak/ are you smart?/ Don't change a hair for me/ Not if you care for me/ Stay little valentine stay/ Each day is Valentine's Day.

Now I don't think that I am unphotograhable or that I have a weak chin, or that when I speak I'm not smart. I'm smart because I read Prabhupāda's books an I have learned what's in them. I may be puffed up to say that I don't think I have a weak chin or unphotographable looks, but to tell you the truth, I think I'm a pretty girl, and I even won a beauty contest. So there! As for my figure being less than Greek, well, you'll have to decide for yourself whether you think

I'm shapely. But my guess is that you think I am. Excuse me for being so brash.

I say all this stuff, however, to emphasize that at present I am a funny Valentine. I cannot walk. But this song by Frank Sinatra is sung very beautifully by him, full of love. He says, "Don't change a hair for me, stay, little Valentine, stay." Although she is less than perfect, he does not want her to leave. He says, "Each day is Valentine's Day." He loves her somehow, despite all her imperfections. The lyrics may sound odd, but when you hear the quality of his romantic voice, it's a man who really loves a woman as she is. So I want you to love me as I am. I'm speaking very openly. Would you be able to wheel me down the marriage aisle? Or would you want to wait until I would be able to walk gracefully in a wedding gown? Would you want there to be no stumbling or no dis-coordination and without full movements of my hands and wrists? Is your love unconditional? Can you sing, "Stay, funny Valentine, stay," or do you sing, "Wait till you get better and return to just the way you were before the car accident"?

These are some of my inner thoughts, and I must share them with you rather than write superficial letters.

I love you and think of you always and want to know your inner heart. Your loving servant, Sandy

Chapter Seventeen

Free-for-all days. Listen to a hammer and write it down. "Oh, you've shaved up." Lakṣmaṇa cried as soon as she placed him in his arms. Jane suggested to Swami Swims that they go visit Barks' house. He wasn't keen on it. A plane passes overhead. Let me think about it. There could be trouble.

I have to write and chant. That old man was Sid Caesar? I'd never have recognized him with the shrunken neck and face and goatee. That's what old age does to you.

But not to Kṛṣṇa, He remains always a sixteen-year-old boy, with his young *gopī* friends and boyfriends. The father of a man who was initiated by a *rasikā* guru said, "My son returned from India and he has learned so much. But he criticizes ISKCON." Coo coo of doves heard by the resident. She's trying to get well for herself, that's tough. But trying to get well for him makes it easier. I'm not sure I agree. She seems quite into self-recovery for her own sake, whether he waits or not. We've got a life to live. His books won't sell widely, but if it's good, that's good enough.

You're on thin ice. One dollar meal at McDonald's. But the burger at Burger King is advertised for $4.00. Hard to believe. The dentist assures they'll be no more sores, but his words prove false. Less headaches. There's one message on the machine. Why should I bother to press it? I'd rather stay alone. Please do the following: Jump off the bridge; report the yearly revenues received from all your donors; cut off your pinky; follow the four rules; go serve a *mahat;* eat food that's good for you. Now wipe your ass once a day after the bowel movement. You're doing much better except for the Mahā Guṇa.

"What do you say, Swami, shall we go to Barks' place?"

"I'm not afraid as long as you're there," said Swami Swims, thinking of Jane's skills in karate. "My steel cane can also be used as a weapon. Let's make it a date for tomorrow." Swami Swims was actually worried about going, and he didn't see much use in going, but he didn't want to appear timid to Jane.

Not much time for the ghosts
but I do think I'll make it through
another peaceful night
thanks to Albert Ayler[1] discovered
in my drawer. All the devotees
didn't expect other than
harmonium.

I told them there's quite
a world out there. Chaotic.
He was religious. Found
drowned in the East River.

So many misguided. We could save
them if we could reach them. That's
why Jane wants to go into the
tattooed lion's den,

before they kill themselves.
He's not opposed but it's
bedtime. We have to take
our Ambien and wish to
sail through. No didn't
make more than ten.

Don't confess all these
faults. Warm weather.
Rainy. Kids still recovering
from illness. Who prays
best? Don't compare yourself
and be envious.

No ghosts, just angel
Prabhupāda who changed them and you owe
it back to him as *dakṣiṇā*,
the simple *anartha* cast away.
I'll promise I'll make it
within two years, like Sandy. Will
he wait?

It was a pleasant, sunny summer morning. Swami Swims took a seat on the back porch at a distance from Jojo, who was usually quiet. But after chanting to himself for only a few minutes, Swami was interrupted by Jojo, who said, "Swamiji, I'd like to tell you more about *The Incredible Hulk.*"

"Why?"

"Well, you guys talk sometimes after you watch those comedy films."

"Well, that wasn't a comedy film, and you went outside the rules when you left the sanatorium to watch it."

"Hee hee, it was kind of a comedy film. These two scientists were working on birth experiments. The man saw that his wife was going to give birth to a very strange, deformed baby. So in fear of what that baby might be, he decided to kill it. But when he took a knife to kill it, by mistake he killed his wife instead. So this was the first traumatic experience the baby—who was the Hulk—saw when he came out of the womb. He was born with a tremendous traumatic anger. And because of their experimentation, he turned into a tremendous monster of great strength and great anger."

"Jojo, I really don't want to hear this. I came out here to take advantage of this perfect setting for chanting."

"Just let me finish," Jojo said. "It's a kind of moral story. The Hulk was impenetrable to any kind of bullets or machine gun that the army tried to throw at him. When they hit him, he just became bigger and angrier. He was kind of immortal. Uh ... he went around smashing everyone, and his only weapons were his tremendous fists. He was an ugly green monster. All he did was smash, smash, destroy. But there was one person he loved—the general's wife. She tried to work on his original trauma that he had coming out of the womb. I forget whether she succeeded. I think I fell asleep somewhere around that point. But they did a terrific job making this monster out of digital computers . . . "

"Is that all?" asked the Swami.

"Yes, I guess so. It's just been on my mind ever since I saw it, and I wanted to tell you, just like you guys talk about Charlie Chaplin."

"Okay, so it's off your mind now. Let's both chant."

Hare Kṛṣṇa, Hare Kṛṣṇa, Kṛṣṇa Kṛṣṇa, Hare Hare/ Hare Rāma, Hare Rāma, Rāma Rāma, Hare Hare. Their mantras blended, and the Incredible Hulk disappeared in the morning air once again, although Swamiji suspected he might return. Kṛṣṇa! Please save me.

Swims decided that if Jojo spoke again, he would get up and walk and chant. But he had to use his cane in the right hand. His left side was the injured side, the arthritic ankle and the broken heel. It was very hard to chant with your bead bag in your left hand, or even a clicker in the left hand. Śacī said they could walk together, and as Śacī counted, the Swami could count that number as his own. But that could only be for a half-hour a day. Swami's counsellor said that you could forget counting and just chant as much as you could and take it that Kṛṣṇa was not so much interested in quantity but quality. But Prabhupāda and the devotees had always talked about "chanting your rounds," meaning the numerical strength, the sixteen rounds. They meant sixteen, not just chanting without it. But he was in a predicament. He'd have to do the best he could. Perhaps it was the Klonopin, and if he could remove it he would get back to normal. But he headaches were significantly reducing, and wasn't the Klonapin an important factor? Give up writing, painting, watching comedies with the inmates, seeing to their needs, phone calls with the counsellor and the contacts? Quality of life? Chant chant chant, can't can't can't.

Swami Swims didn't know why he allowed Jane to talk him into visiting Barks' house that night. It was too dangerous a mission in the name of preaching. But he didn't want to back out now and seem like a coward. That morning he asked Śacī if he could work out on the heavy punching bag. Śacī was always eager to coach in the gymnasium. He tucked Swims into the big black gloves and then held the bag and said, "Go!" Swami swung hard with a combination of left and right punches into the bag. "Good, good," Śacī said, "punch lower, punch lower, not just at the face." Swamiji started moving around and continued his flurry of punches, concentrating on throwing hard rights to the face. "Ten seconds left," said Śacī, and Swami finished up as best he could, although he was flagging.

"How long did we go?" Swami asked.

"We went one minute. Now we'll go another minute."

"It would make a big difference, wouldn't it, if I didn't have these gloves on?" asked Swims Swami.

"Oh yeah, you could break your knuckles. At any rate, with the gloves or without, you concentrate on punching on the first two knuckles next to the thumb, and you move your punches down as well as up. When some people get into a fight, they just start with these big haymakers, swinging as hard as they can. But if you know how to fight, you guard yourself and you jab as well as punch. Some of those punches in the beginning were hard. I was holding the bag and thinking, 'Boy, I wouldn't want to be hit with one of those.' Okay, get ready again. Start!"

This time Swami wasn't as strong. He started out with a few good hard right punches and left jabs, and down to the stomach too, but halfway through he felt his strength ebbing. He kept on going though, but with less and less energy.

"Ten seconds left."

He rallied up his last energy and hit as hard as he could.

"Good. What are you training for?" asked Śacī.

"I'm not training for anything," said Swami. "But Jane has talked me into going to visit Barks' house tonight, and he'll probably have some friends over, and so I'm a little afraid of what might happen."

"Would you like me to come along?" asked Śacī.

"Sure, if you can manage it."

"Yeah, I'd like to," Śacī answered.

Swami felt greatly relieved. With Jane and Śacī, it'd be like he'd be with Superman and Batman.

Jane prepared a big pot of *kicchari*, and they filled up a cardboard box of books—some of Prabhupāda's books, some copies of *The Higher Taste* cookbook, and some of Swami Swims'.

"Do you know what Barks' attitude is?" Śacī asked.

"No, I haven't had any contact with him since he left on his motorcycle that night."

"Okay, we'll just go prepared for anything," said Śacī.

Śacī wore a T-shirt and shorts, revealing all his tattoos. Of course, there was nothing that Swamiji could reveal that looked menacing, but he carried his stainless steel cane, which he was prepared to use as a weapon..

They arrived around 8:00 at Barks' house and knocked on the door. "Come in," Barks shouted. They opened the door and found Barks sitting in a comfortable chair. He now had a big beard and long hair. The room stank of a combination of liquor, marijuana, and maybe some other drug. In the room with Barks were three bimbos with big breasts and big bellies and two men who were similar to Barks. They had similar hairstyles, and they wore ripped dungarees. The men had surly looks on their faces, and a few scars. They were toughs, but they were not as muscular or tattooed as Śacī. The devotees entered the room and shut the door behind them.

Barks burst into a big smile. "Janey! Have you come to bring me back to the sanatorium?" he laughed.

His "wife" Alice said, "Are these the Hare Kṛṣṇa twerps?"

"Watch your mouth, Alice," said Jane. "We're not twerps. We're just on a peace mission. We were delivering some spiritual food at an orphanage down the block and we have a pot of *kicchari* left over. Remember, Barks, how you liked to eat *kicchari* at the sanatorium? So we brought it to distribute it to all of you."

"Wow, thank you!" said Barks. "Yeah, Alice, you'd better watch your mouth around Janey. She once busted me up. She's a black belt karate expert. She hit me with the heel of the hand under the nose. She *could have killed me* but restrained herself. Then with the same punch she hit me in the groin. I bent over and ran away like a five-year-old kid. She used the same combination of punches on some skinheads who attacked us in the park. She did it on a guy who was about six-foot-six and weighed about 250 pounds. He crumpled up just in time for the police, who cruised by in a car and handcuffed him and threw him in the back of their car. I also decked one of the skinheads with a right to the jaw, and the third one just surrendered. So don't mess around with Janey." At these words the other men shrivelled back. "And look at this man—Śacī's your name?"

"Yeah," Śacī replied tight-lipped.

"Look at his chest and muscles. I'd bet he could take on at least one or two of you guys. Well, Swami doesn't look like much, but that steel cane he's carrying looks like it could be used as a weapon, so I wouldn't trust him either in a fight. Anyway, they're on a peace mission. Let's have the *prasādam*. Get some bowls and spoons, Alice." Reluctantly, Alice got the bowls and spoons, and Jane dished out nice portions of the *kicchari*.

Swamiji said, "I brought some books along, in case you're interested. They're all free. Some of them tell how to cook this kind of food. They're called *A Higher Taste*. And some are about philosophical wisdom of India—books by our spiritual master and a few by me. If any of you are interested, you can take them. And if you'd like to give a donation for either the food or the books, you can." Some of the men reached into their jeans and came up with some change or a few bucks and gave it to the Swami.

One of the women said, "Hey, this stuff isn't half-bad."

"Half bad?" said Barks. "It's great! I ate this stuff for months. It's kind of like peasant's food, but it really grows on you. In India, some of the people eat this every day as their only diet. A person in America would look down on it, but I got hooked on it and thought it was delicious. It's really nice. Vegetarian." He ate his bowl quickly and asked for another one. "Yeah, it's really nice to see you, Janey," Barks continued. "You know, I was falling in love with you." Jane made a real scowl. "But then when I whacked my head that day in the park, my 'real' memory returned and I realized I couldn't live in the sanatorium. I had to come back to this kind of life of 'high living.' Maybe if I get another good whack I'll be back with you people." He laughed. Some of the men didn't like the *prasādam* and left half of it, and Alice scooped it into the garbage. But everyone was polite and seemed to want to end the meeting on a light note, before it got into anything like philosophy or Hare Kṛṣṇa twerps or motorcycle dopes or "Why are you drinking liquor?" So they wound it up after about fifteen minutes. The men certainly heeded Barks' warning, and every once in a while looked at Śacī's massive chest and muscular legs and arms and took note of Jane's tall stature and fully believed in her black belt abilities. So with smiles all round and diplomatic words, the devotees shook hands and backed out of the room with a decent collection. Swami Swims took the box containing the remaining books with him. "Hare Kṛṣṇa."

"If you'd like to drop around again sometime, it's all right with me," said Barks. "Sometimes, though, I'm just so stoned I might not recognize you, or I might be fucking one of these dames, and that would be the wrong time. So you can just back out then and come back at the right time."

"And maybe sometime you can visit us at our place for a pleasant atmosphere," said Swami Swims.

"I'll think about that," said Barks. "*Haribol.*"

The devotees tramped down the stairs of the dilapidated porch. Swamiji said, "You were right, Jane. I was a coward not to want to come. You have a good preaching instinct. Besides, you're a black belt and so you're fearless."

"I was fearless for a different reason," said Jane.

"Well, it helps if you're trained like you and Śacī. Anyway, I was ready to swing this steel thing too and see whether it would break on somebody's head or not. But Kṛṣṇa didn't want us to fight. He wanted us to give out *kicchari* and sell books. Lord Caitanya said fighting was for another age. In this age, you fight with chanting and *prasādam*."

They were all in a jolly mood as they drove back to the sanatorium. When they got back, they told the other inmates the good news. Junior was especially happy to hear that his dad took the *prasādam* and was not inimical to seeing the devotees.

Dear Sandy,

Please accept my humble obeisances.

I will push your wheelchair down the marriage aisle to marry you. Or we'll have a fire sacrifice and sit side by side so you can sit in your chair, and I'll sit beside you. We don't have to wait for you to be all "straightened out." I didn't propose to a body but a soul. You're still there completely whole, as I feel so strongly in your letters.

You are certainly putting me to a test in your letters, I must admit. I have to think deeply. Can I wait two years? What if, after two years, she's still not as perfect as she was? What if she limps? Should I look for another girl who can dance like a ballerina? (But who might also get in a car accident and might wind up in a wheelchair? And what about me? I might get cancer next week.) What's the use of marriage if everything in this world is so dangerous at every step?

I consulted with some senior friends and finally with my spiritual master. He advised me to go ahead with the marriage. He knows you well from his visits to Sydney and says you have rare qualities as a devotee, which are not affected by the spinal injury. He said the vows for marriage that we made, although informal, are binding, made in all sincerity before the Lord, and that we have even exchanged engagement rings. I had spoken about all this to him before and had asked him if I could marry you, and he gave his permission, his blessings, and his order that it be a proper Vaiṣṇava marriage. He doesn't see anything in the spinal injury that would cancel the vows or that should cancel our love and plans for the gṛhastha āśrama. *We have already taken a crucial step and to back out now would be extreme fickleness and disloyalty on my part. The fact that it turned out that I didn't get exactly what I wanted may be a burden for me, but these things are in Kṛṣṇa's hands.*

He was asking if there was a way we could get married as soon as possible without waiting for your physical condition to improve. This would show loyalty and obedience to the Lord. I am willing and have begun to look into the possibility of traveling to the U.S. Too many Australian devotees recently have been denied entry into the U.S.A. due to new security rules, and notes have been entered into their passports. So I have to consult with a lawyer and make sure I go about it in the right way. Maybe even the sanatorium could write a letter saying they needed my services there. Let us see, so that we don't make a mistake.

I want to be with you, and when I cannot I suffer the pain of separation.

Your loving servant, Braja dāsa

Evidence left behind, how many beads
counted, Gandhi left three
monkeys, see no evil, hear no
evil, speak no evil.
In the cash register till,
fingerprints, we've got the evidence
to send this man to Pātālaloka.
Is there anyone present who wants to pardon him
despite the preponderance
of evidence? "Yes, I will."
"Who are you?" "I am
his spiritual master."
"Well what do you want us
to do with him?"

"Send him back to earth under
my care. I'll give him
remedial teachings." "Should
he have done better? Why
such poor evidence if I
may ask?"

"I gave out mercy freely
under the order of Mahāprabhu.
This boy came early and did
good work. But
petered out. Devotional service is eternal
so I cannot forget all he has done for me."

"All right, back to earth."

"Earth? Prabhupāda. Can't I have
a little life extension and try to
make a better last effort in *this* life?
Surely I can."

"It doesn't look like it. The
more time you are given, you're
batting average goes down. It
used to be .300. Now below."

"Okay, no pleas. I do as you say.
Just keep me in your line
representing you true and
loyal. You say remedial,
so teach me those original
books and beads from a junior
position humble to one of your
teachers and no climbing
the hierarchical ladder.
Let it start when you say.
In these last days I'll
do the inevitable."

Sandy asked Swami Swims, "Could we have an altar in the sanatorium?"

"I've thought of that," he said, "but where would we fit it?"

"If we had a small enough altar, it could go right in the middle of the rows between all the beds and everyone could get to see it."

"Yeah, I think it's a great idea. No one here is well enough to be a carpenter, but I know of a real nice secretary table that's not too large and could fit there, and at the same time nurses and helpers could pass on either side of it. I'll get a place there immediately. And there are lots of devotees who have Gaura-Nitāi Deities, so some of them could donate their own and place them there. And I think it will just snowball into a whole thing where maybe Nṛsiṁha Deities, and daily care and flowers will come about." Swami Swims then turned around and made a loud announcement to all the devotees about Sandy's idea and how they should all get together and help create the altar.

"Jaya!" they said. Devotees started talking of what they could donate and how it could be brought together.

Swami Swims then left the sanatorium wearing his *sannyāsa* uniform, which Tim had ironed for him, and he was carrying his *daṇḍa*. He had an appointment with the head official of the rehabilitation center. He knocked on the man's door and was asked to enter. He sat down facing the man, who was a Hare Kṛṣṇa devotee but dressed in suit and tie. "What can I do for you?" the man asked. On his desk it said, "Dr. Bush, M.D."

Swami Swims said, "Do you know of our patient in the sanatorium, Miss Sandy King?"

"Yes, I do," said Dr. Bush. "I know of her father too. He was influential in having her placed here. She has a serious paralysis, but she's a wonderful patient and is trying to recover. Why do you ask about her?"

Dr. Bush impressed Swami Swims as a real stuffed shirt. You could hardly tell he was a devotee. He was bald, and that was okay, but he was so official and there was nothing relaxed about him. You could hardly expect him to say, "Haribol" or "Hare Kṛṣṇa," and there were no Kṛṣṇa pictures in the room. I guess that was because he often received nondevotee officials from the medical world and didn't want to turn them off. But it did create a dry atmosphere. And it made Swami Swims start to feel nervous.

"Sandy King was betrothed for marriage with a devotee named Braja dāsa in Sydney, Australia, shortly before her accident. So by her father's arrangement she was sent to the New York sanatorium. They've been exchanging letters and feel the pain of their separation. Lately they've come to the conclusion that they'd like to get married, even though she's in a crippled condition. They have such a strong love for each other, and he wants to demonstrate that his love is not dependent on her recovery."

The doctor said, "Well, he'd better think about that carefully. It should not be just an infatuation. It's very difficult to marry a crippled person and to take care of her, and it could be many many years before she recovers. He may start hankering after the usual pretty girl."

"They've thought all these things out, and he even consulted his spiritual master, who said that the betrothal and exchange of vows to be married and the exchange of rings for engagement were binding, and so he should definitely marry her and not consider it to be just a boyfriend-girlfriend infatuation."

"So what does this have to do with me?" said Dr. Bush rather shortly.

Swami Swims' palms were sweating and he started speaking quickly. "Well, devotees have sometimes had trouble getting over here from Australia. I thought if you or the rehab center could send him a letter saying that he was needed here to work as some kind of junior therapist, that would help him get his visa."

"Preposterous!" said Dr. Bush. "Don't you know that this rehabilitation center is famous all over the world for the training and expertise of its workers? It would be a scandal if we brought someone in here who had no training at all. You should get this idea out of your head immediately. I sympathize with the two young lovers wanting to get together, but please put this idea out of your mind at once. And forget that you ever came in here and asked me this. Hmph."

"I'm sorry, Dr. Bush. I didn't mean to upset you. I was just trying to help, but I see my idea was very immature. Please accept . . . please excuse me." Swims Swami pushed back his chair, stumbled a little, and started for the door.

"Hare Kṛṣṇa," said the doctor, almost as an admonishment. Swami Swims turned to him with folded palms, taking the inferior position.

"Hare Kṛṣṇa, Doctor," and he went out the door, closing it softly.

What a stuffed shirt, he thought to himself. Of course he's right. It was foolish of me to ask. But he could have offered some solace and maybe another suggestion of what I might do. I'll have to think of something myself.

Swami Swims' brain started to rattle on. Maybe I can get a recommendation from someone else in the sanatorium. I know the old thing is that there's a passage written into the embassy laws that a Hare Kṛṣṇa temple can request a foreigner to come into the country to come into the country on some religious grounds claiming that he can do something in our church, like be a priest or a cook or a *pūjārī*, and for those religious reasons he's let in. Indians are usually allowed in easily on those grounds. But our sanatorium is not religious, it's just beds. Hmm. Maybe we could claim something now that Sandy has started an altar.

Swami entered the sanatorium and was surprised to see that the altar was already fully decorated. Instead of what he had expected—small brass Deities—they had large, beautiful neem wood Gaura-Nitāi Deities, which had been donated by a neighbor a few miles away. Out of respect for the one who first thought of the idea, Gaura-Nitāi were placed facing Sandy. Yet everyone else could catch a glimpse of Them and could go beside Sandy to see Their lotus faces and Their lotus feet. A few chairs were placed there too beside her.

"Oh, Gaura-Nitāi!" said Swami Swims, "how wonderful. Now we'll have to make Them daily offerings and bring them flowers. The sanatorium has become a temple."

Later that afternoon, Swims went to the head of the staff of the sanatorium and asked him if he could apply through the embassy for a special exemption for Braja dāsa to enter the United States to be a *pūjārī* for the Gaura-Nitāi Deities in the "temple" of Gaura-Nitāi, the sanatorium.

The staff boss was congenial but said the idea wouldn't fly. The sanatorium was clearly a place for people to recover their health. It was a medical place, not a temple. Even if they had placed an altar there, that was just for private worship, and it would be scandalous to try to get someone in on the grounds of being a *pūjārī* in a temple.

That night Swami Swims told Sandy the attempts he had made to get a visa for Braja dāsa. She listened thoughtfully and said, "Maybe it isn't as difficult as all that."

"It used to be very easy, in the days before the attack on the Twin Towers. But I have another idea, which is a little sneaky, and I won't tell you yet. I have to get in touch with a devotee who's done it. If it doesn't work, then you'll have to live and love in separation. I'm very glad that Braja dāsa wrote you that he has passed your test and does want to marry you as soon as possible. Keep up that love and that pressure, and even that sadness. And even if you cannot officially marry, you'll be married in your hearts."

Scheming his plot. This is something new.
How about research into the
scriptures for self-help?
Have you become more of a writer than
a spiritual aspirant? I don't want
to get on your back, but plain
facts. Keep a notebook and see
how many you do each night.
Show it privately to your
counsellor

and figure a way to increase.
You've got your embassy plot
all figured out. Why can't you
spare time for the simple syllables
you learned so long ago and proficiently
applied as your guru unto old
age? I'll give you my answer
next week, or next month.

Swami Swims went diligently into his next plan of action. Most temples imported help from foreign countries through a law which had been instituted perhaps around the time of President Reagan that allowed religious workers to come into America by special visas. The foreigner just had to get a sponsorship letter from the temple in America saying that that temple needed help from specially trained priests or cooks or *pūjārīs* or lecturers, which they did not have because of understaffing or some other reason. It worked again and again, and many temples had more central European devotees living there than the devotees of their own country. It seemed a flawless thing.

So Swamiji went about it. He called some temples where this had been done and learned the process. He then went down to the embassy and asked for information on how to get a certain person in another country to come to your country to work in your temple with a bona fide visa. Swami Swims then wrote a letter to the U.S. Consular Services office in Sydney, Australia, describing Brian Dean as a qualified Australian *pūjārī* who was needed for a very special temple within the sanatorium of the Kṛṣṇa rehabilitation center in upstate New York. He said although it was a medical facility, they had recently installed statues or Deities, which were worshiped as God, and these Deities were worshiped just as

Deities in a temple, with daily offerings of food and flowers, and the man they wanted, Brian (a.k.a. Braja dāsa) was perfectly trained for this. All of the other inmates in the sanatorium are in an incapacitated condition and cannot do this work.

Swami also stated that there was a very human element involved in this. He mentioned Judge King, of the Eighth District in Sydney, Australia, who is probably known to the Consular Office, is the father of Sandra King, who had a tragic accident that had left her paralysed from the waist down while visiting America. She was now rehabilitating in their center. She might have to stay there two years or more. She was engaged to marry Brian Dean, and they were both feeling separation from each other. They wanted to marry, even though she had not recovered and still needed a wheelchair. They did not want to delay their marriage, so for these two reasons—that Brian could come and marry the girl he was engaged to, and that he could perform the temple functions in the sanatorium—they requested a special visa—a religious workers' visa, or R-visa—which America granted for priestly duties. Swims showed the letter to Jane for punctuation and editing corrections, and she typed it up in best form on their stationery. They then sent it off.

About two weeks later, they got a letter from the U.S. Consular Services office in Sydney. The letter read as follows:

"Dear Swami Swims, I received your letter and discussed it with my authorities in the Consulate as well as with the Honorable Judge King in Sydney, who is the father of Sandy King.

"Of course, we were pleased to grant Judge King's request that Sandy be allowed to remain in the United States for treatment at the rehabilitation center, where she is now. But although it is a Hare Kṛṣṇa–staffed institute, it does not function as a religious temple in any way. It is strictly a medical facility. Judge King is well aware of the facilities there, as he visited shortly after his daughter was admitted. He admitted to me that it was not a temple in any way but rather a medical center. When he heard that his daughter had erected a small secretarial desk and put Deities there, he smiled at her devotion, but agreed with me that this did not turn the sanatorium into a temple. It is still lined with over 100 beds, and the main business that goes on there is recuperation and therapy. So our embassy cannot accept your interpretation of the sanatorium as a temple, and we cannot issue Brian an R-visa to come there as a religious worker.

"If you have any other questions, you can ask me. Yours sincerely . . . "

Swami Swims brought the bad news to Sandy, and she just sighed and shrugged her shoulders. "I guess Kṛṣṇa doesn't want us to live together for now. He's increasing the pressure of service in separation."

"This issue isn't over yet," said Swami. He went back to his office, stopping to first bow at the lotus feet of Gaura-Nitāi. He sat on his bed and remembered again Rilke's *Notebooks of Malte Laurids Brigge*, which he had passed around to many devotees and gotten their responses. The struggling devotee said that he had been so involved in searching for God that he had himself forgotten God. An intellectual Godbrother wrote back and said, "This reminds me of something Bhaktivinoda Ṭhākura said in one of his books. He said that the *kaniṣṭha-adhikārī* and *uttama-adhikārī* can see God. Only the *madhyama-adhikārī* cannot see God because he has doubts." What did he mean by that? Because he's a manager? Because he has to fend off so many doubts and challenging questions in his preaching? Why should he be in doubt? The *kaniṣṭha* sees God in the Deity and takes it as simple as that. The *uttama-adhikārī* has passed all tests, passed all doubts, and he's simply elevated and qualified to see the Lord face to face. Maybe I'm a *madhyama-adhikārī* with my doubts, thought Swims. But I don't really have doubts. I have lack of taste. I have struggle. And I do have a burden, looking after the devotees. And a yearning to spend more time doing the things I like—writing, painting, and watching funny movies. No time for movies tonight. And a package arrived for me to edit. No time for that either. No time to finish my sixteen. "No time," a disease of the modern man.

After Braja dāsa absorbed the bad news, he sat on his bunk and tried to think of what to make of it all. He'd be true to his Sandy, but when would they ever get together? It seemed best that she should join him in Australia, but she'd have to get well enough to come. And how long would that take? He felt lonely. While he sat there, a girl named Tulasī dāsī came up and sat next to him. She said, "It must be hard for you, waiting for your fiancée to join you."

Braja dāsa's eyes filled with tears. "Yes, it's hard." He looked at her and her astounding prettiness. Her hair was dark, unlike Sandy's. She wasn't flirtatious but was just offering some compassion. He thanked her but felt a little uneasy and a little stirred in a man/woman way.

"If there's anything I can do, let me know," she said. "Sandy and I are good friends. Maybe I can send her letters too." She smiled, perhaps a little more charmingly than necessary. She got up in her lovely *sari* and walked away.

She left him with impressions, and Braja dāsa knew there were going to be many tests he would have to endure. These girls in Sydney were right here before him in the flesh, and they were straight and sturdy and offering themselves to him as a good-looking guy, a potential husband, a leader. And he was a man waiting for a crippled girl who might not come back for years.

Only the lonely could share with him. If he was a drinker, he'd go down to the local tavern and invite everyone to have a drink on him. "Try to think that love's not around/ still it's uncomfortably near/ my poor old heart ain't gaining any ground/ because my angel eyes aint here./Angel eyes, that old devil sent/ They glow unbearably bright/ need I say that my love's misspent/ misspent with angel eyes tonight./ So drink up all of you people/ Order anything you see/ and have fun, you happy people/ the drink and the laughs on me./ Pardon me but I got to run,/ the fact's uncommonly clear/ I got to find who's now the number one/ and why my Angel Eyes ain't here./ Excuse me while I disappear."[2]

Braja dāsa remembered the way Frank Sinatra sang that song, and his own "Angel Eyes" was Sandy. He didn't want a new girl. But they were tempting him like devils. If he could only go to her across the ocean. And if the others would stop tempting him. Oh Angel Eyes, there's nothing wrong with your eyes, and who cares that from your waist below you can't move? I can kiss your eyes and your lips and fondle your breasts, I can embrace your arms and kiss your hands. That's enough for me. Angel Eyes, Kṛṣṇa, protect me from the rest.

He sat down and expressed his heart in a letter to Sandy, then cried himself to sleep.

We looked at each other in the same
way then but I can't remember
in the same way, I can't remember where
or when.

It's been too long, too long since we
parted. Some things that happened

happened for the first time for
the first time seemed to be happening before.

We've met before, laughed and loved before
but where or when? I'm in Australia
of course, you're going away, the accident,
She was carried away, my dear, little
did I know for how long she would
be taken from me.

They said she was crippled. She had gone
to the hospital ER, now she has gone and
you can't see her. She's in a wheelchair,
she can't move. You can't marry her
yet.

Then we realized we can
marry if we want to. We could even get married
by mail
or if she could get on a plane and come back to
Australia.
Don't they have good enough rehab centers here?

Why can't I go there? I placed a ring on her.
Why are these harpies putting my hands on
their breasts?
I belong in some lonely place.
I need some shelter. I need
to pray to God and give Sandy
hope and patience. I'll write
her a letter tomorrow full
of encouragement. Writing has
power. Promise something.
Think of something wonderful.
Discover some true love in
your heart for the lovely
bride that you love.

Braja dāsa was sitting on his bed in his room in the private, sullen mood that had come upon him since it seemed so difficult to join with Sandy. He was also developing more love for Sandy, his Angel Eyes. He was loving her more and more. There was a knock on his door and in came a girl named Andrea. She was a kind of outsider who attended a lot of Hare Kṛṣṇa functions. She was somewhat bold. She wasn't wearing devotee clothes but rather a T-shirt that revealed her firm, ample breasts, and she wore tight dungarees. She was about eighteen years old and had stylish black hair. She sat right down next to Braja dāsa and took his hand. "I can see you're feeling very sad lately with your attempts to go and be with Sandy dashed. I wish there was something I could do for you." Braja dāsa stiffened, as he could see that this was a full-on attack.

"I was thinking," Andrea said, "that maybe you should put thoughts of Sandy out of your mind, because it's just a hopeless case. It'll take her years to recover, and she may never recover. You may never be able to have a normal man/woman relationship with her, and she may never return to Australia. I confess, Braja, that I have a real crush on you. Do you find me an attractive woman?"

"Astounding," he confessed. Bold as she was, she placed his hands on her breasts. She then kissed him and placed her tongue in his mouth. His tongue also entered hers. She embraced him, and by now he had a half erection. But he stopped and pushed her away.

"Andrea, I can't do this. I'm engaged to Sandy. She's my Angel Eyes. I couldn't do this. Even if she's crippled, she's *my woman.*"

"I can't believe that," said Andrea. "Anyway, whatever happens in the future, why don't we just make love right now? It'll take your mind off all these pains. Just lie down here while I take off my clothes."

Braja dāsa was resolute now. He stood up and took Andrea by the hands. "You're a sweetheart, and amazingly alluring. But I just can't do it. Please don't be insulted because of my rejecting you." She looked down, dejected. He saw her to the door.

At the door, Andrea looked up at him with puppy dog eyes. "I don't feel insulted," she said, "and I still have a crush on you. I have my eyes on you, and I'll be back. Sooner or later, I think you'll succumb. I want you too much, and you've already tasted my charms." With a seductive turn of her butt in the tight jeans, she exited out the door.

Braja dāsa sat down and calmed his genitals and his overall being. What the hell was this? he thought. Are they going to come from all sides? Was he really such a good-looking guy? Why were they preying on him like this? He couldn't write *this* in a letter to Sandy. She'd be too alarmed. He needed some protection. If only they could live together. It confirmed in his mind, however, that he wanted Sandy however she was, crippled or not. He didn't want to stick his genital into some well-formed beauty star. He wanted Sandy. And he had heard from a Godbrother who worked as a physical therapist that a man could even have sexual intercourse with a paraplegic, and that they could have a baby. No, he would stay loyal to her and keep the torch burning. But he couldn't take too many close calls like this. Maybe he'd write to Swami Swims about it.

Braja dāsa travelled by train to South Australia, to a farm region. His good friend Rūpa had settled there years ago and lived in a simple house with his family. In a nearby house lived some male devotee workers, who helped him cultivate about fifty acres of farmland. They sold produce and were self-sufficient.

It was a beautiful region with some distant mountains. It was rural, always peaceful. Braja and Rūpa were glad to see each other and hugged on meeting. Rūpa knew about Sandy's accident in America.

Braja: "Rūpa Prabhu, I can't live in Sydney anymore. The girls are so flirtatious. You can't imagine. You know this girl Andrea? She actually attacked me last night for sex. I want to be true to Sandy. We want to marry. I don't care what shape she's in, even if she's in a wheelchair for the rest of her life. She's my girl, and I'm her man. But I can't be bombarded by these good-looking city chicks who somehow think I'm a catch." Rūpa shook his head consolingly. "So I thought of your place," Braja continued. "Could I stay with you, or rather, with your men? I'd work hard in the fields every day. I'm not a slouch."

Rūpa smiled. "Sure. Can you milk a cow?"

"I've never done it but I can learn."

"Can you plow with an oxen?"

"I can learn. I could pull weeds. I can plant tomatoes. The men can teach me anything. I'm a good learner, and I'm physically strong. I can stay out in the sun, at least with a hat. I won't eat much, I won't take up much space. But I just need a little time each day to read Prabhupāda's books, chant my sixteen rounds and write a letter to Sandy."

"I'll take you on on those terms. Besides, you're a good friend, and you've come to me in a time of need. I can't refuse you."

Rūpa's wife, Priya dāsī, who had been standing by listening, wiped some tears from her eyes. "You're certainly welcome here, Braja. We pray that everything will come out somehow and that Sandy, who is also a very good friend of mine, will get out of the rehab center sooner than you think and come back to Australia. I think I'll start writing to her too."

And so it was decided, and Braja had a safe new home. He would be lonely and live a life of love in separation. But his love would be protected, and the key themes of waiting and being patient could be nourished in the best atmosphere possible. He would take Sandy's advice and always chant his 16 rounds and pray for Prabhupāda's protection.

At the Feet of Gaura-Nitāi

Dear Sandy, it's solidified,
I'm your man, no one's
gonna get me. I'm safe
now. I'm with the lonely
farmers. In the cabbage rows.
At least my mind is on you,
Sandy dear.

I dream of you and your lips as
warm as May, no hopeless
schemes. It's not hopeless
that we'll be
back together

because I see you everywhere
in memories and in the present too—
your reminder to me,
"chant your rounds, Braja,
think of Kṛṣṇa, Braja,
I am not Kṛṣṇa, Braja,"
but I hang onto each caress
with you, Sandy.

It's not gone. The loneliness
and heartbreak

I defy! Because I've
got a fortress now, a place to
think of you and cry and hope for you.

I'm solid now. No tigress will
catch me, not even a bad thought.
I want to marry a girl named
Sandy King, even if in her
wheelchair, and hold her hands
and be with her
and bow our heads closely before Gaura-
Nitāi. Let's do it now.

Chapter Eighteen

The headmaster of the rehab center asked to see Sandy King. Swami Swims rolled her in her wheelchair to his office.

The headmaster said, "Sandy, the staff and I have been talking about your case, and we have a proposal that we would like you to consider. It concerns a change in the objectives of your treatment regimen. We're not going to change any of the basics of your daily routine and exercise. But we have a different goal in mind. Our original plan was to keep you here for perhaps two years or more, until you could give up the wheelchair and walk normally. But realizing your anxiety to return to Australia and your fiancé, and realizing some of the up-to-date methods used for paraplegics, we're thinking of a different strategy."

"What's that?" Sandy asked with wide-eyed curiosity.

"We're thinking of making an adjustment in your therapy, so as to enable you to make the return flight to Australia before you are fully recovered—that is, while you are still restricted to the wheelchair. It certainly wouldn't be the first time such a thing has been done. Paraplegics and people in wheelchairs have been flying for many years. But for patients with your type of injury, there are certain risks that we need to address and that you should be aware of. Sandy, as we've explained, complications sometimes develop in patients with spinal injuries such as yours. Now Sandy, for your flight back to

Australia, there are two complications that we are particularly concerned about.

"The first is autonomic dysreflexia. Patients with spinal cord injuries sometimes experience excessively high blood pressure. This is caused by uncontrolled activity of the sympathetic nervous system. If this were to happen, Sandy, it would be a medical emergency and would require immediate treatment. Dysreflexia can even be life-threatening.

"The other potential complication that we are concerned about is deep vein thrombosis. In patients with spinal cord injuries, normal neurological control of the blood vessels can be impaired. This can result in stasis, or sludging of the blood. This in turn can lead to the formation of a thrombus, which is something like a blood clot. The danger is that while you're sitting in the airplane, a thrombus will develop in one of your legs and then break free and become lodged elsewhere, obstructing blood flow. If the thrombus were to occlude a crucial vessel, such as one of the arteries leading to the lung, that would also be very serious.

"So that's the scary part. But there are things we can do to minimize the likelihood of these bad things happening. You will of course need to continue to develop your muscles. We will also want you to increase your cardiovascular reserve, and we have a special regimen that we can start you on to do that. We will also be giving you a special diet, designed to further reduce the chances of vascular complications.

"And Sandy, there's something else that we would like to try. Something new. It's a form a therapy that's a bit on the experimental side. But I assure you, Sandy, it's quite safe. It involves the inducement of deep, relaxatory states in your vascular and musculoskeletal systems that would otherwise be impossible to achieve. We believe that these relaxatory states would optimize the healing benefits of our other therapeutic regimens.

"Now Sandy, in this special therapy, you would lie suspended in a tank that is filled with a special ionic solution. It will feel like you are experiencing a kind of weightlessness. We will then induce a series of very-low-frequency sound vibrations within the solution. Initially, this may feel as if the marrow of the bones throughout your body are being gently vibrated. The vibrations will be regulated through a computer system. As the algorithm progresses, this vibratory sensation will expand. In this way we hope to achieve a state of very deep relaxation in your musculoskeletal and autonomic nervous systems. Once this state is achieved, while you are still lying in the therapy tank, our physiotherapists will then begin gentle range-of-motion exercises. We're even hoping to be able to have you engage in some cardiovascular exercises in the hyperrelaxed state. We believe that this would be of great benefit for your nervous system. So this is another option for your therapy.

"As for your return flight to Australia, you will want to have plenty of room on the airplane so that you can do your exercises while in flight. I would advise that for your flight, you reserve at least a couple first-class seats for yourself, and that you also book a flight for one of our therapists to accompany you. With two seats all to yourself, you will be able to do your stretching exercises, as well as some of those the isotonic and isometric workouts that you have taken such a liking to. You will have one of our therapists there to assist you at all times, and more importantly, if a complication were to occur, the therapist will be able to recognize the symptoms early on and initiate emergency treatment.

"So, Sandy, all things considered, we believe we can help you to prepare to return to Australia within a year's time. Once there, you would continue to live as a paraplegic in a wheelchair. You could visit an outclinic, where you could continue your exercise regimen. You could be married and be with your husband, which I think would be very good for your spirits. So how do you feel about this plan, Sandy?"

Sandy smiled broadly and said, "Oh, what a wonderful idea! What a great goal to shoot for! I'm sure that would inspire me to work harder and harder while I'm here."

"Yes, we hope it will. But don't overdo it. You still have to rest in between workouts, and it's impossible to set the exact time as to when you will be able to return. But it can definitely cut down your time here, and you will be able to return home to your fiancé sooner than you otherwise would. So that's the plan. You like it?"

"Oh, I just love it, Saṅkarṣaṇa Prabhu. I'm so glad you and the staff thought of such an idea out of your kindness and medical expertise."

Swami Swims was smiling behind her. He said, "Oh, such an excellent plan. It must have come from Kṛṣṇa."

"All right, go back to your sanatorium, but don't be overoptimistic about this. I don't want any strained limbs that would set you back even further. Just continue the exercise program that you have been following, and we will add to that a cardiovascular regimen, and we'll set you up for your first session of infrasound therapy. Finally Sandy, we would like to have you meet with one of our nutritionists. Now Sandy, please try not to be overoptimistic. Just pray to Kṛṣṇa to help you. He's always the deciding factor." Swami Swims and Sandy bowed their heads with many thanks, and Swami wheeled her out the door.

On the way back to the sanatorium, Sandy said, "Swamiji, please don't tell anybody about this. I want to immediately write a letter to Braja dāsa, and so I'd like a little privacy."

My Dear Braja,

I just heard some wonderful news from the doctor. He has a new strategy. He says he now wants to prepare me to return to Australia, rather than wait for me to be completely recovered and give up the wheelchair before I return. In other words, he feels that when I'm strong enough, I can get on the plane with the wheelchair and come back to you. Then I'll live with you while still in a wheelchair. Will you have me that way?

I'm very thankful that in your last letter you confessed how that witch Andrea attacked you sexually, and you maintained your chastity. I'm glad that you took action and that you're now safe on the farm with Rūpa in good association. I'm so proud of you. I may also say in my defense that my breasts are as good as hers, and even better. When I see you, you may snuggle against my breasts and hold my breasts as much as you like. And when we kiss, it will be much better, because our kiss is truly a kiss of the soul and the heart. It is not some lust-enforced thing that just happens out of lust only. That was all she did to you, stir your lower modes, and you were smart enough to catch yourself and push her away. When I come back, we can lie together naked in bed, just like normal men and women, and do anything we want. There is nothing missing in that way. And you will see that I am more shapely than ever. I have exercised so much that my female form is now without an inch of fat, and almost to perfection for a person my age. I mention this, but I don't think we want to lie around naked in bed together. Just in case, however, you were thinking that the girls in Sydney could give you something that I can't, put that out of your mind.

The real thing is that we want to live together in love from the heart and soul, uplifting our spiritual life. Spiritual life is the real thing, not bodily sexual closeness. It does not really satisfy the self.

I will give you more news as soon as I learn more of persons in wheelchairs who flew in planes, and when I have a timetable as to how long it will take me to actually do it. The headmaster said it wouldn't be real, real, real soon, but that is their goal now for me—to fly to Australia in a wheelchair. Doesn't it make you happy?

Will you please not be disappointed when you see me come off the plane in a wheelchair? You can just know that even though you see me that way, you will soon see me walking normally. And even in that wheelchair, when we are in private, I can come off the wheelchair and we can hug and cuddle to our hearts' content. You will be surprised, "How did my Sandy develop such a beautiful female shape!'"

Your ever chaste lover, Sandy

Swimmer, where are you going? Do you even know? I hear Mom Arthritis is getting discharged to the care of her son in Puerto Rico, and another man is going to his parents because he is too much a mental case. They may have to put him in an asylum. The sanatorium is for "middle-type" cases, ones who maybe can't walk or talk but who can function mannerly in their beds and obey orders. Swims could even leave here and go somewhere on his own, like California. They're building him a place, and it won't be ready for three months. But a big house will be vacant up there in seven weeks. He seems to have assumed some leadership, some personal, managerial duty here in New York, which he doesn't like. But he loves the Vaiṣṇavas. He'll have to put his foot down when it's time to go according to his own desire. Hide books they shouldn't see, hope they'll let him return. If not, keep moving on. There's always another cow to milk. More paint, canvas, donation, brushes, feeble prayer, my how the days go by. Don't have to see anyone today. Do you want more Sarah Vaughan? A trading library. You should be trading esoteric books by Kavi-karṇapūra.

Yes, he took up space, and his second painting defied the laws of anatomy, as two *sādhus* stuck their arms out at impossible angles, and the *japa* beads jutted upward. But Swims is sleepy, one Klonopin, bad habit. Put it at the top of the list of problems to discuss, but his counselor has bronchitis.

They had no quarrels. They stayed
cool. "This T-shirt is a Hindu
symbol of the face of God.
I thought you wanted me to
stay here in the waiting room
for three weeks."

"You'd get a little moldy,"
said the secretary.
Out into the heat.
Divine through the heat
of the state of New York.

They don't like the
music I do. They haven't
visited the sanatorium
but I know it well.

I think they should have a literary quote
at the beginning
of each batch for the
compendium book.

Why not something straight from
Śrīmad-Bhāgavatam? But
I thought we wanted to go

to a wider audience? You'd
never reach it because you use
words like "Prabhupāda" and
it turns them off.

A new book deserves a plot,
a hunt in the woods.
Emily in a new white gown.
No war necessary. No repeating too much
the old things
like Bill Evans and Picasso did.
Just write and we'll see where
it comes. Zachary Scott[1]
in brown film and wasting
your life in Great Kills gutter.
No prayers, no gutter
until so late.

Braja dāsa was really turned on by the prospect of spending all night every night in bed with his wife, Bhaktin Sandy. He'd have to find out more about her condition. Perhaps she couldn't have any feelings from the waist below. But she could have feelings from the waist up. That would be nice. And anyway, just to be together and kiss and talk was true intimacy. Just to be able to take her in her wheelchair and walk to some secluded place and talk. She was a wonderful speaker about Kṛṣṇa conscious subjects. She was like a *śikṣā-guru*, she knew so much about Kṛṣṇa. And he wasn't so proud not to ask her questions about the scriptures. She was so humble that she freely gave answers that helped him in his spiritual life. He knew some things that helped her in her practical life, and she knew more things that Prabhupāda said than he did because she listened to the tapes more and read the books more. But it was a perfect match because there was no envy. Oh how wonderful it would be to be back with her.

Now it made the waiting harder, in one sense, but much easier in another sense, because it wouldn't have to be so long. He wrote her some of these thoughts and told her again and again how much he loved her and how much he wanted to be with his beautiful bride and to learn to help her in all the different physical therapies that she needed. He wanted to be really accomplished in that so that he could replace whoever it was who had to bathe her, exercise her, and do all the necessary things. He didn't want her to get slack when she came here, but she had to continue to work out at some local clinic. She had to work as hard as ever so that she could return to normalcy and walk straight and dance like a ballerina and jump like a tennis player and feel everything from the waist down.

Swami Swims walked up to where Sandy was sitting in her wheelchair in the sanatorium and asked her if she'd like to go for a walk.

"Sure," she said.

He pushed her outside onto a nice walkway. "I'd like to ask you a philosophical question," he said.

She laughed. "You, a swami, asking me a question? I think you're teasing me."

"No, I'm not. There are some devotees who are disciples of Prabhupāda, but they say they have to read books by other gurus because Prabhupāda hasn't written enough in his books. They especially say he hasn't written enough on *rāgānugā* and the intimate pastimes of Rādhā and Kṛṣṇa. So they go see gurus in Vṛndāvana and read their books. There are even some who say that Prabhupāda recommended this, or that it's just necessary to get this information. But out of loyalty and conviction, other devotees feel that Prabhupāda has given us everything in his books and that we can reach *rāgānugā* through them. What do you think of this?"

"I think that everything is there in Prabhupāda's books," said Sandy. "I once heard Rādhānātha Swami say that Prabhupāda's books are full of humility, and humility is everything; therefore, you can find everything in Prabhupāda's books. I also heard one of Prabhupāda's Godbrothers say that it's true that there are gurus in Vṛndāvana who teach more about the intimate pastimes of Rādhā and Kṛṣṇa and that we could get it more quickly if we went to them. But we might also get something from them that might not be good for us. I might give an example. In the *Śrīmad-Bhāgavatam* and Kṛṣṇa book, whenever *gopīs* are mentioned, their names are not given. For example, it will say one *gopī* fanned Kṛṣṇa with a peacock feather. Another used a *cāmara* fan, another *gopī* spread a shawl for Him to sit on, another *gopī* brought fruits for Him. And then later in the *Bhāgavatam*, when Kṛṣṇa disappeared and came back to the *gopīs*, it says one *gopī* looked at him with an angry frown, another *gopī* put her hand on her lips, another *gopī* stood at a distance from him, and so on. In the *Bṛhad-bhāgavatāmṛta*, in the purports by Rūpa Gosvāmī, as translated by Prabhupāda's disciple Gopīparāṇadhana Prabhu, he says that the reason Śukadeva doesn't give these names is that he would go into complete ecstasy if he mentioned the *gopīs* names, and that he would not be able to speak further. This is true also in the *Śrīmad-Bhāgavatam*, where Śukadeva Gosvāmī doesn't mention the name of Śrīmatī Rādhārāṇī except once, and indirectly, when he uses the word *ārādhita*. So these things are very confidential and not to be cheaply thrown around. Those disciples of gurus who quickly give the names of *gopīs* and *gopī-mañjarīs* may really be doing a disservice to their disciples, giving them more than they're really capable of getting. So

I say they're getting stuff quickly, which they may not be ready to receive.

"And Prabhupāda is gradually giving *rāgānugā* in his books. You'll find many sections. There's one section where he compares *rāgānugā* to the gradual learning of how to type with a typewriter. He says at first you're given lessons and you go slowly, but gradually you learn to type without even looking at the keys. So he uses that famous word of his, 'automatically' you come to your position, and even to your *siddha-deha*, your eternal relationship with Kṛṣṇa. And in the *Bṛhad-bhāgavatāmṛta* it says that the highest position is to be a devotee of Rādhārāṇī, and that this is accomplished by chanting Hare Kṛṣṇa. So what more esoteric information would you want than that? And it's given right in the BBT book, translated by Prabhupāda's disciple. Just before Prabhupāda passed away, they asked him if any more books could be translated, and he said yes, they can be, but it has to be by expert Sanskrit scholars. Gopīparāṇadhana is doing that expertly, and just in Prabhupāda's mood. So we'll get everything, either from Prabhupāda's books or from his devotees who translate books but without any mixture of anything *sahajiyā* or from another line, and we'll get it by chanting Hare Kṛṣṇa and working for Prabhupāda's movement."

"Wonderful, Sandy!"

"Sure," said Sandy, "at any bookstore in Vṛndāvana you can get plenty of those books about Kṛṣṇa's intimate pastimes, about Rādhā and Kṛṣṇa naked, and who knows what thoughts these may cause to arise in you. What I mean to say is you'll get bad things along with good things. But in Prabhupāda, you get all pure, and he was very, very grave in what he wanted to tell us. If someone asked him something improper he would say, 'Why are you asking this?,' and tell them that they were not qualified to hear it."

Just at this point, they saw two VIP swamis, one tall and one short, approaching them with about fifteen followers surrounding them. Swami Swims was astonished, because he hadn't heard anything about it beforehand. The short swami called out, "Swami Swims, we're going to have a *kīrtana* in the temple room above the sanatorium. Do you want to join us?"

"Sure," he said, almost gulping.

"Can you take your patient upstairs too?" asked the short swami.

"No," said Swami Swims, "she's unable to go up the stairs. But I'll take her back to the sanatorium and then I'll join you."

As Swami Swims rolled Sandy back to the sanatorium, she said to him, "Why did you say that I couldn't go upstairs? I've been carried up there before."

"I said it because I was almost sure you wouldn't want to go among so many crowded people for a long *kīrtana*. Did I read your mind right?"

She smiled shyly. "Yes, you did."

"I don't want to go either but it's my duty."

"Thank you, Swamiji," she said.

"And thank you for your wonderful insights into the philosophy." He asked her if she wanted to lie down in her bed.

"No, I'd like to sit and read for awhile," she replied.

Swami left her and dutifully headed upstairs for the *kīrtana*, but as he climbed the stairs he thought of a way to get out of the lecture that might follow.

Hare Kṛṣṇa, Hare Kṛṣṇa, Kṛṣṇa Kṛṣṇa, Hare Hare/ Hare Rāma, Hare Rāma, Rāma Rāma, Hare Hare. Hare Kṛṣṇa, Hare Kṛṣṇa, Kṛṣṇa Kṛṣṇa, Hare Hare/ Hare Rāma, Hare Rāma, Rāma Rāma, Hare Hare.

Everyone in their own head. Some of the babies screaming. The two bearded swamis are leading the singing, and Swami Swims is gently rocking in the rocking chair and joining the singing in a semimesmerized state. He's not thinking of much, except wondering if one of them is curious as to why he has shoes on in the temple room. He's floating, sort of semi-conscious with the chant, which is a good sign. But he does glance at his watch now and then. Doesn't want it to go over half an hour. He's glad it's a Hare Kṛṣṇa *kīrtana*, not a mixture of *bhajanas*.

Hare Kṛṣṇa, Hare Kṛṣṇa, Kṛṣṇa Kṛṣṇa, Hare Hare/ Hare Rāma, Hare Rāma, Rāma Rāma, Hare Hare.

It's more relaxing than *japa*. Singing with some friends. He glances around the room, and some of the women glance back at him—not very good to do. Glances at some of the children. Then keeps to himself and hardly looks at "his" Deities on the altar. What do you do when your mind is wandering and you don't see Kṛṣṇa and Rādhā in Their *mūrtis*?

Hare Kṛṣṇa, Hare Kṛṣṇa, Kṛṣṇa Kṛṣṇa, Hare Hare/ Hare Rāma, Hare Rāma, Rāma Rāma, Hare Hare.

It's nice to sing with limited time. This segment of the afternoon goes by in chanting the holy names in good company. They say there's going to be a question-and-answer period later, but he'll definitely walk out. And then it happens, the singing comes to an end. No one does anything. Then the tall bearded swami starts the "Jaya Oṁ" prayers and does them perfectly. Then again nobody does anything, nobody moves. Swami Swims is the first to move. He grabs his cane and gets up and moves slowly in front of the altar and the others, to the stairs. He pats two-year-old Bhaktivinoda on the head, feels it's sweaty and says, "Are you hot?" But the child never answers back. Swims walks down the stairs into his own room. Changes out of his devotee uniform and into his shorts and Prabhupāda T-shirt. He turns on Sid Caesar. He'd been told that the swamis were moving to another building to have their question-and-answer session, but little did he know they were doing it right over his head. Carl Reiner says Sid Caesar was a master at the sketch act. They do a hilarious one called "Small Apartment," satirizing people like New York City dwellers who live in very tiny apartments. Superb acting by Sid Caesar and Nanette Fabray. Then Swami Swims is about to go up and change the Deities into their evening clothing, but he stops at the bottom of the stairs because he notices a few extra shoes, and he hears somebody orating upstairs. It seems that the swamis are still there. He phones Śacīsuta and learns yes, they're still there holding a question-and-answer session right in the temple. Swims then says he's not going to go up because he's changed back into his leisure clothes. Cat-and-mouse game he plays. He could again change back into his uniform, but it's just too much, too much playing an act, too much hiding. So he'll stay downstairs and spend the last minutes being a real person.

Go to bed with no witchcraft,
simple person drifting to his
poetic self. You must be
the one Kṛṣṇa wants.

The one He ordered to fight.
Footsteps overhead. Now you'll
be told to change the Deities
into night clothes. You're not
on your own here. You
receive orders. Like
when to go to the dentist,

when to get up from bed,
when to take the pill.
Well of course he must be
like that,

tiny *jīvas* under supreme
control. Try to help others.
Give them *prasādam* and
knowledge. Give them
a massage, help his bed sores,
a joke sometimes, or a solemn word
about our serious business in
this material world.
Gosh I didn't know it was so
bad—"a worm with no
direction or exit." I had
it so good and lost everything.
You can gain it back they
say if you work better.

Swami Swims' counselor is sick with bronchitis so they haven't been able to talk for a week. All the counselor does is cough. Swims has a pressing question about subpar *japa*. They avoided it because of so many crises, but now most of those crises have become more manageable, and *japa*, which is spiritually a huge problem that has been held in abeyance, can be discussed.

The pin man comes today and likes to sit and play psychologist for the first ten minutes. But Swims does not trust him enough to speak openly to him. He's willing to take a chance and let him put in pins, because by coincidence his headaches seem to have been lessening since he started the acupuncture. But not *japa*. And a headache seems to be building today, the second day in a row—so much for the marvelous streak of days with no headache.

The pin man asked if Swims got migraines in the right eye.

"Yes," Swims answered.

He said, "Sometimes in acupuncture the patient's pain is transferred into the acupuncturist. Last week I got an excruciating pain in my left testicle."

"Oh, I'm terribly sorry!"

"It only lasted two hours. These things happen."

For thirty minutes the pins remain. He's a kind of nosy man and walks around the room, looks at books, pours himself a drink of water. He said he looked here and there at the EJW and liked the diary style. Swims said it's a mixture of straight spiritual truth, as given in the scriptures, and sensory impressions from the material world.

"Yes," said Chris, "we receive the spiritual world through our material senses."

Swims admitted he was getting less headaches since the pin treatments. But Chris admitted it didn't work for everyone.

Heat, a fan, do you stay indoors? Oh, two of Swims' paintings were indoors. The acupuncturist must have checked them out but made no comment. Send the bills. Find time for *japa*, you scoundrel. A series of paintings of people with *japa*. Blondie is asked how many she's done. She says, "I forget." Bojo says, "Sixteen, man, and one extra for my deceased mudder." A person on another canvas says, "Thirty-two," and the graffiti artist adds, "B.S." Another says, "64," and the graffiti man adds, "B.S." The VIP swamis saw them and liked them—at least they were on Vaiṣṇava topics.

The B.S. is on you. A stick figure in the corner of the canvas with his hands over his mouth: "I ain't tellin'." If they send me those videos and paints, then how will I practice the austerity of chanting sixteen rounds and an extra for my deceased father?

No wood, no canvas, better reason
to chant on beads. No excuse how

slowly the inch worm with his
inspiration to make fun of people
professional style on a hot late
June day. I'm sorry my right
eye hurts. Your right testicle.

I'm sorry my blues causes doubts
in my disciples, can't get around
to see them and don't even have the
inclination to speak the Vedic
score.

Do you know what this means?
She had a dream she
was on the wooded hill
at Gītā-nāgari and it was all
ablaze. I left my *japa* beads down
at the picnic table!
"But if you run down to get them you'll
die in the fire."
"But without them I'll die spiritually."
My friend said this dream inspired
her to be dutiful. But I find
my right eye sting cutting its plow.
Say he forgives
you on those days. But not on
others. On clear days go to sixteen.

Chapter Nineteen

The sanatorium received two Harry Langdon films in the mail today. Langdon is considered the fourth greatest silent film comedian. One film is called *The Strong Man*, and the other, *Tramp*. I saw one of them before.

Swims Swami sat on the couch and started to chant *japa*. Suddenly, he had a vision (or a craziness overcame him) of an orange ball. He jumped up and ran into the art room. He shouldn't have done it, because as soon as he got there, even though he was wearing the orthopedic pad, he felt an excruciating pain in his left ankle. But he couldn't stop himself. He drew an orange ball. He told himself, "Just draw the ball and stop there and come back later." But he couldn't do that either. He got spray bottles and sprayed paint around the ball. He said, "Okay, that's enough, you can stop now and come back later," but he kept going. He drew a female body, naked with red nipples. Got spray bottles. Ouch, ouch, ouch, ouch, ouch—I'm still feeling the pain. Why are you such a maniac? He drew the Irish triskelion sign. A star. No sense. And he wrote something like, "You shouldn't have done it. You shouldn't have done this. You shouldn't have done this," and signed his name. It wasn't even good art. Or maybe it was. Then he went over to the other full canvas and did more orange, orange, orange. Spray, a lot of spray. And what was the orange? Two different on different sides chanting. They weren't all orange. There were different colors. Their beads were black, black with black string. A lot of orange too. They were chanting as if in competition. This guy was yellow spray, the bottom was blue spray. Was it a lot of orange or not? Now it's just painting. White eyes, black eyes. Did they have any clothes? It didn't matter. You had to get the painting done and get back inside before you fell apart with excruciating pain. What nonsense. You were overcome by a mania for painting. The doctor told me to take *two* oxycodones after the snack. But now I don't feel any headaches, so I won't take the pills. Why don't you take two pills for some kind of sanity?

You like big daddies? You like little moms? Once your father said about your mom, "She's too good to be true." I think he meant that she never had sex with him. And of course that one time I left for school, walked halfway up the slope of Samson Avenue and discovered I'd left my wallet behind. I ran back down as fast as I could in my Italian shoes and as fast as I could I unlocked the front door and as fast as I could I ran up the front stairs into my bedroom. I caught father in the "doghouse," which was a little construction where odds and ends were stacked. He was looking into my stack of *Playboy* magazines. I just said, "I left my wallet behind," and raced out of the room, down the stairs, and up Samson Avenue just in time for the Staten Island Rapid Transit Express train. But I was too late when my sister Madeline pushed my door open while I was masturbating. I screamed at her, "Get out!" She continued to open the door. With great anger, and my penis in my hand, I shouted, "Get out!" With great fear and not really seeing what I was doing, she backed out of the room. Crying, she went down to our mother and said that I had been very, very angry with her. My mother then asked me why I was so angry with Madeline. By the time I saw Madeline, she had somehow figured it out. She gave me a saucy smile while I explained that I was sorry that I was angry at her. I was truly humiliated. I had no lock on my door, so I couldn't masturbate in private.

There were very few locks on the doors, but Dad had plenty of time to be alone when we were all out of the house and he had time off from his long firefighting shifts.

Hey, it's time to chant your rounds.

Oh I am surprised, an old man my age.
A white beard and a Western vest
leans into the tavern. Can dance so fine.
Every year he prays to fire off guns
at New Year's Eve. He doesn't
forget the booze has dazzled
him up and Max Roach boosts
his spirits.

He must be eighty years old, "Bud's
Bounce."[1] He has that much energy
but he's kicked out and hopes to live
two more years. That's proper.
He's figured it out. Walks out
into the mud then. Deletes terms.
After the last year he runs
to the minister's house.

Religion. Oh yes. He knows a parson
and rushes to his house. He gets a
gentle person, "Bud's Bounce,"
"give me last rites." Lie down
but I'll give you what I give.
Pray to your 1915 game. Nice birth
if you can get it. Pray for your best acts.
Remember the good you've done. Ask
to be forgiven for all your venial and even

mortal sins, ask the Virgin Mary
to pray for you at the hour of your death.
I am praying here in Christ also
at the last night and the Hare Kṛṣṇas too.

The rivers of the West are sometimes clearly seen in broad country, sometimes unseen deep in the woods, sometimes they run through towns, sparkling in the sunshine. Or on a rainy day. There are many different rivers. Let the writing be like that. It doesn't have to be one river seen only one way. Characters, subcharacters, novel, I person, he person, she person. How to answer technical questions? If a girl was so injured that she couldn't move, and yet she was flown to New York, then why is it a big problem how she can be flown back to Australia? You have not faced all these technical difficulties. But you don't have to face them when you suspend your disbelief. When you hold my hand. When you walk into the church and you have to believe everything in a factual way according to the code, but it may be very difficult, and you may refuse, you may reject the canon.

Such a slow-moving day. Like a slow-moving river. Some people were moving very quickly all day at work, on the telephone. Others were pushing hard in wheelchairs, on subways, pushing big carts filled with coal. Pushing a pen, a computer. Pushing according to the code of a novel, and then rewriting it. Or just once with the pen according to his free-writing inclination.

Oh he's the only one who can do it right the first time, lover, when you're near me … and I hear you say my name … Trane and Curtis. Joshua hit the river at Jericho and the rain came tumbling down.

Swami Swims medicates, I mean meditates, and all the subpersons slowly move on a muddy river. They come from his heart. They are different parts of himself. A pretty girl, an old man. He met one once in a café when he was a very small boy with his mother and father. He met one once when he ate his first radish.

We wailed because we were short
on bread. We did not have the word yet
for bread. They did not invent it—
bread means money ala
Lester. But he also invented Lady
and Sweets and many other words.
We met under the El and said, "Are you
my best wordsmith from friendship and
not one of those enemies?"
"Don't worry," he said, "I'm not out to hurt you
like authorities beleaguer you
for terminology."

Sit back, relax, for life is better,
not hard, wail. I heard something,

a mouse upstairs, I just
wanted to fall asleep
because this seems
like the longest day
in the week.

In a dream they terrorize the devotees, but they never gave them the food. The trip was supposed to take an hour and a half, so there would be time, but they didn't produce it. It was some kind of celebration for the Jehovah's Witnesses. Swami Swims thought they were increasing in number. They had banners, but they were blank. Narahari decided he wanted a *pana*, which was another way of saying pizza. Swami Swims used the Italian word pizza. Somebody else wanted something else. All simple preps. They waited and waited but the food didn't come. Swims got up into a kind of pixie dust at the man and said, "Cancel my order, cancel my order." "No, please take it," they said. They were very poor, so we empathized with them. The boat was just coming into the pier.

"Just give us the food."

He looked again into the oven. It wasn't ready.

"If this boy just wasn't disturbing us, they'd get it ready." The girls were laughing. They seemed to think it was delightful that the whole trip was being delayed.

I wasn't one of the Jehovah's Witnesses. From my birth I was raised as a Catholic.

"That doesn't mean you couldn't become one," said the restaurant man.

"Suppose they'll be any chance for the food?"

"No, no, it doesn't look so likely."

A few Hare Kṛṣṇas walked down the ramp. "The worst thing would have been to have to pay for the food and then find it detestable."

That's not clear even for a dream! Are dreams supposed to be clear? Dr. Krohe said they were just expenditures of energy and that it was good you were having them because it showed that the "good action" was taking place in the head. Imagine, a neurologist having such a simplistic idea with no reference to the unconscious. When I had a dream of my counselor and his family life, I jumped up like a jack out of the box and phoned him at once to tell him what it was. As I was telling him about it, I felt a little ashamed. But he said no, no, no, don't be. I was reminded of one of the many layman dream books, how a man dreamed that his friend's car was being stolen in a big parking lot somewhere in a huge city. He called up his friend and told him exactly where the parking lot was, and his friend rushed to the lot, and sure enough, the car was in the process of being stolen, but he got there just in time with the police and saved his car from being stolen. So it was good that he acted and didn't just turn over in bed.

Then there was a poem I read about two professors in a lounge, and one of them suddenly had a fear that some damage had occurred to one of his family members. The professor asked his friend, "Do you believe in ESP?"

"I think it's rubbish. Why?"

"I just dreamed that something terrible happened to one of my family members."

"I think you should rush home and see what happened."

So the professor rushed home in his car, ran into his house, and saw one of his sons lounging, watching TV. The son ignored him. The professor then turned to his wife, who was looking at him with great concern. She walked toward him. "What's the matter, dear?"

"I just had an intuition that something terrible had happened here at home." They both embraced and kissed.

I recall another story that was very similar. A professor was teaching a class, and a student or another teacher ran in and said, "One of your sons has been hurt in a car accident." The professor immediately ran out of the classroom and went to the scene of the accident. When he got there, his son had already been taken away in an ambulance, but another teacher who was there assured him, "Don't worry, don't worry, everything is all right. It was just a small injury to his ankle. I don't even think it's broken, just strained, but they took him to the hospital. They said he'll be out in a few hours. Don't worry, John, there's nothing to worry about. Come on, I'll take you to the hospital, and we can see what happened."

The professor, who was a father of two sons, said, "The first thing I thought of when I heard of the accident was that even if one of my sons has died, I still have one left."

Oh come on, let's have some spiritual ESP stories! There's the story of my disciple Sāmbha, whose Jeep went off the edge of a cliff, completely flipped over, and went smashing down fifty feet. He said, "Hare Kṛṣṇa" all the way down. The Jeep was a complete wreck, but he climbed out of it without the slightest injury.

There's my story, how I jumped out the window of a four-story building. I broke both my heels. The left ankle is still a cause of great dismay. Unfortunately, that's not a spiritual story, because all I had done before jumping out the window was read a *karmī* edition of the *Īśopaniṣad.* It did give me the impression that there was no difference between matter and space, and so I could jump out the window and not be hurt. I also thought that afterlife was blue.

Here's another miraculous story that happened in eastern Europe during violent times. A devotee who was selling books on the street met a man who seemed to be nice. The man said he wanted to buy all the books, including a book on Nṛsiṁhadeva. But the man had no money, which should have caused a clever book distributor to be suspicious. The man said, "My house is right around the corner. Why don't you come with me and I'll give you the money?" The innocent devotee followed the man around the corner, and they proceeded to a place that was far removed from any houses. The devotee suddenly realized that they were in a desolate area. Then the man turned on him with a knife and was about to kill him. The devotee then screamed out, "Nṛsiṁhadeva!" and out of nowhere a big dog came and jumped on the man. The devotee then ran for his life. His life was saved by the grace of Nṛsiṁhadeva.

There is a story about a woman in Belfast who met the devotees but never paid much attention to their practices. She knew only that they chanted Hare Kṛṣṇa. This woman had a severe case of the skin disease psoriasis on her hands and feet. She went on ignoring the practice of the chanting, and her hands and feet got worse and worse. She knew she would have to enter the hospital. But when the condition became terrible, she began to chant, and her skin condition immediately cleared up and disappeared for good—a miracle.

When the Catholic saint Thérèse of Lisieux was a very, very young child, she was ill to the point of death with fever. In her sickroom, there was a statue of the Holy Virgin Mary. She had an apparition or an appearance in which the face of Mary smiled at her, and immediately her illness was cured.

One of the most famous miracles, which appears in a book of many miracles, is the saving of Draupadī from great embarrassment in the assembly of the Kurus. The sons of Dhṛtarāṣṭra were attempting to strip her naked after they had won the gambling match. There was no one to help her because all of the powerful Pāṇḍava heroes had lost due to cheating in the gambling match. So when Duḥśāsana and Duryodhana stepped forward to pull off her sari, it unwound and unwound and unwound, but she remained clothed! They could not make her naked. Duḥśāsana fell down onto the floor like a clown, unable to make her bare. They had to give up in despair, unable to fulfill their lust and their desire to degrade her and the Pāṇḍavas. Of course, the miracle was achieved by Śrī Kṛṣṇa, the Supreme Personality of Godhead, upon His dear, pure devotee Draupadī.

In the *Rāmāyaṇa*, Rāma and His forces received information that the demon Rāvaṇa had kidnapped Sītā and had taken Her to his island of Śrī Laṅkā. Rāma received this word from the faithful bird Jaṭāyu just before his death in battle with Rāvaṇa. Finally, Rāma assembled a great army of intelligent monkeys, headed by Sugrīva and Hanumān. He determined to cross the ocean. Hanumān said that he would first cross the ocean in one gigantic leap and examine the island, locate Sītā, and examine the key positions for fighting. He did so in a miraculous act. Not only did he jump the ocean in a single leap, but he encountered different demons along the way. When he reached Śrī Lanka, he reduced himself to the size of a small cat and went into the *aśoka* garden, where Sītā was lamenting in separation from her beloved, Śrī Rāmacandra. Hanumān approached her in a friendly manner and sat in one of the trees in his expanded form. He spoke to her and told her not to be afraid of him and that he was a messenger from Rāma, then he gave her a ring he had brought from Rāma. When he gave her the ring, she trusted him. He then told her that Rāma was nearby with an army and that He would soon be there to save her. She became very elated and gained courage to survive while waiting for the attack of Rāma. Hanumān then assumed a huge monkey form and destroyed most of the city. His enemies set his tail on fire, but with that, he burned down most of their city. They captured him, but he escaped and jumped back over the ocean safely to his comrades and Rāma. As if one miracle after another wasn't enough, the monkeys then built a huge bridge made of stones, which floated on the water. They then crossed that bridge with all their fighting paraphernalia and met the gigantic army of Rāvaṇa. They defeated Rāvaṇa's army and carried back Sītā in victory.

Of course, the miracle of the bridge is that stones do not float on water, and so Rāma created a state of weightlessness so that the stones would float. He can create the law of nature, and then He can change the law of nature. Any law created by nature or man can be unchanged by God.

What does the word "miracle" mean? It means the defying or the breaking of the ordinary course or law of nature. The girl's hands had been stricken with a disease, and she was not supposed to recover, but suddenly she was cured in one day. That was a miracle. So when God intervenes, or some inexplicable act happens against all force of nature, then that is a miracle.

Scientists don't like to believe in the unbelievable. Recently, however, even scientists had had to admit they have found proof of some of the very miracles I have spoken of, such as the one of the building of the bridge to Lanka. The *New York Times* recently published satellite photos of a bridge probably made out of coral and probably made during the time of Tretā-yuga. The bridge goes from India to Śrī Laṅkā. They said this bridge may not be of much interest to today's scientists, but it is of high interest to those who believe in the epic of the *Rāmāyaṇa*, because it gives proof of the bridge that was built by Rāma's army.

While writing these miracle stories, Gopī-mañjarī dāsī came in with a constipation drink for me. I told her what I was doing and asked if she knew some miracle stories. At first it was slow, like constipation, but then she remembered a few. Just when I thought I had enough—the climax of the Rāmacandra story—she started coming out with all these mantra miracles. When she was eight years old and living in Bangladesh, her father lost his watch. They went to a priest, who chanted mantras over a stick. The stick started moving. It moved more and more as he chanted, and they started following it. The two sisters and the man began running and running as the stick moved through the village to a lady's house, and then, when it found a certain lady, the mantra began beating her on the head. Yes, she had the watch! And she gave it back. Then Gopī-mañjarī told how even today in Māyāpur, during the flooding season, there are many deaths by cobra bites. The *only* cure for this bite is to go to priests who can withdraw the poison by the chanting of mantras. They say there is no other way to cure it. People quickly seek out the mantra chanters, and when they find them, they are cured. Gopī herself teaches *haṭha-yoga* and Hare Kṛṣṇa at a yoga studio (even now, with her three-month pregnancy). She starts her mantra course with these stories, which are well-known to her and are a sort of proof positive, before going to the more elevated mantra miracles, like Hare Kṛṣṇa, Hare Kṛṣṇa, Kṛṣṇa Kṛṣṇa, Hare Hare/ Hare Rāma, Hare Rāma, Rāma Rāma, Hare Hare.

It has to go somewhere, I
think—to Australia and north.
I think people will go with him,

some of us to help him when our
legs start to twitch
but when we are alone
we are alone
and there is no one else like it.

I said God said (Kṛṣṇa) and they
demanded to say *Kṛṣṇa*
is the clearer name, better defined,
and the International Society
for Krishna Consciousness
shall teach them what God is.
He said that in
1966. We better get a little in
your soul. This soul is the perfective
is all I know.

You mean it's not sectarian. Is that
what you mean? It can be
one fruit or race or religion or another?

Don't know exactly what,
but soul,
    God Supreme Soul
    Superlative, Superlative
    Who applies the screws
    and releases us—
    gives us the light torch
    through the
    dark bogs
    into the playground known
    as Goloka, Rādhā-kuṇḍa.
    What!
Kṛṣṇa lives, the monkeys. A miracle.
A monkey made obeisances besides me
and he smiled—
it's not easy for the
monkey to do that,
the way he is physically formed,
but it confirmed my promise
to be an authentic preacher
and love all people.

He was telling me he would help
you to do it.
Just be eager
and spiritual, not mundane.
As you seem to be growing weaker,
asking you now to take in
whatever you can.

Chapter Twenty

Dreams, dreams. Swami Swims dreams of a new medical therapy that has been invented for paraplegics. Sandy is immersed in ten feet of water with an oxygen tube. He is also immersed alongside of her. The water is then injected with waves of sound, which have a strengthening effect on the body. In the water they are weightless, and so they begin to jump up and down three or four feet at a time. They touch hands and do a ring-around-the-rosy dance, and start to feel wonderful vibrations in their bodies. This is especially surprising in Sandy, who normally cannot stand. They are both delighted to see that she is able to do this. This is a state-of-the-art invention that has been tested only a few times. The New York rehab center is one of the first places to try it. They're all eager to see the results, and they're a little apprehensive. The therapists and high-ranking doctors are looking down into the water and are very pleased to see that Sandy is actually standing upright and is breathing and moving her body properly. Swami Swims moves her arms up and down and engages her in a playful dance that makes her knees bend, and she dances like a child.

Swami Swims sees Sandy as an angel with wings flying away from the sanatorium. He is happy to see her go free and so quickly across the oceans and lands to Australia. They wave goodbye as she sets out on on her miraculous journey. He realizes he is emotionally attached to her, and so in one sense it is good that she leaves. But he would always remember and correspond with her. He hopes his own life would make some miraculous turn so he could too go out and do good for the people of the world.

They go back and forth in a slow-running way. He then asks her to just walk straight, and she does so. He then walks her backward, which she does without collapsing. She can do everything he asks her. They were told that the body could only stand the health-giving waves for fifteen minutes, and soon they are helped out of the tank. The therapists immediately place Sandy on a gurney and take her to the rehabilitation examination room to measure changes. Swami Swims puts on his normal clothes and goes back to the sanatorium. He lies down in bed, and one of the therapists questions him about how he feels. He says that he feels great—much lighter, and that he has no headache. He does feel a little tired, but he feels otherwise normal, and a little extra strong. He's very anxious to hear of the improvement of Sandy. They leave him alone.

Swims dreams how his feelings toward her have changed. He's growing more attached to this girl, although he knows it's not anything that he can follow through on. She's just a very nice Vaiṣṇava.

Dreams, dreams. The old black man Jojo with the broken legs dreams that after a long wait his legs heal enough that he can walk on crutches. He's not been allowed any drink or smokes in the sanatorium, so he heads for those sources as soon as possible. He doesn't have a record of being a terrible addict, but he just wants to get back into it on a "decent" level. He wants to see some of his old friends again. They aren't such strict

Hare Kṛṣṇas. He wants to live with his mom, watch "unregulated TV," and eat food the way she cooks it. He especially wants to watch a lot of sports and hopefully get out on his crutches and see his old friends. He used to go to the tavern sometimes, and maybe he could do that or bring a bottle of beer home once in a while. The quiet life of the sanatorium has been getting to him. No old-timers to talk to, no old devotees that he used to know. He likes to chant on his beads, but somehow he hasn't been doing it so well since he's been here. He thinks that he'll do better following his own pace outside. He's not a racist, but there are only two or three black people in the sanatorium, and he thinks it will be helpful for him to live in his neighborhood, which is 90 percent black. But he's got a plucky spirit while he's waiting. He dreams an angel comes to him and tells him it won't be long, it won't be long, we're coming for you, maybe sooner than you think. Just don't give up.

Mom Arthritis dreams that they should just let her go. She's going to put in an application that her son come and take her out of here. She has had her arthritis much of her adult life, and she feels just as bad now as she did before she came in here. Her son used to take such wonderful care of her. Without giving her that loving care, he just feels arid. They don't live far from the temple in Puerto Rico, and she would get news of the temple, and sometimes he would take her there, and the spiritual master would visit there maybe once a year, and she'd go to the festivals. She wants to go home. She dreams she's actually back in Puerto Rico. It's so beautiful there—no snow in winter, the wonders of the tropics, the banana trees, the folks who love her. In this dream she suddenly completely recovers from the arthritis and goes back to her old job in ISKCON, doing the cash register at the Hare Kṛṣṇa restaurant in San Juan. Everyone comes in and knows her and says hi mom. It was the best year she ever had. She wakes up crying that it hasn't happened yet.

After his dream, Swami Swims wakes up with a headache. "Ah, reality is back again," he said. This time he takes an oxycodone just to get blessed, pain-free sleep. Dreams are dreams, but I can't do anything without being pain free.

In the rehab center, some of the doctors and therapists are very happy with the program they have devised for Sandy, and they think of science and Kṛṣṇa and how improvements can be made to save devotees. This was a reality. Maybe more and more in the future they can patch up devotees and send them out without the lead of patience being such a burden on the devotees. They thank Kṛṣṇa in their prayers that their own work is being rewarded.

Bhaktin Jane wakes up and worries about *Sanatorium.* She worries about Swami Swims. She realizes he's been very lucky. She wonders if he's aware how much mercy Kṛṣṇa has given him within a short period. Will he be able to keep it up? He's been relatively headache-free, and inspirations, plots and characters have come freely. He's been working very fast, maybe too fast for his body. There's no harm if he calms down and waits to get the best inspirations possible. But he'd love to keep going forever at the rate he has been going. But now there's a little hesitation. Jane notice it in his opening words. Where are they going? She's right behind him, wanting to support him. But she knows he's all alone. There's nobody who can help him. A writer is alone. She prays to Kṛṣṇa to keep him going, because his books are valuable to the world, and she is very attached to him in a platonic way as his typist. She's his left and right arm, typist and protector. May Kṛṣṇa let this slim swami go on with the work, which is not yet appreciated, not even in ISKCON.

Somehow let those books continue from the mind of this sometimes fragile man.

Junior wakes up. Was he dreaming? He just feels satisfied and protected. He realizes his case is very unusual. People would say that he came from a very bad home, that he might have bad impressions and should go to a psychiatrist. Imagine not even knowing who your mother was and walking in and seeing your father having sex with all different kinds of low women. He's truly been saved. He likes his little bed, catty-cornered in the room with good friends. He likes Kṛṣṇa consciousness. A feeling of contentment comes over him and he again falls asleep.

Tim sleeps soundly. He'd been mowing the lawn all day. Every once in a while the rehabilitation men call him in to examine him. He's twenty-one years old and he has colon cancer. They caught it at an early stage, and at his request he's opted for alternative treatments—herbs, acupuncture, etc. But if it doesn't clear up, they'll do surgery. So it's certainly not a lightweight thing. His sister is concerned and thinks he should get an operation. But he mostly feels it's in Kṛṣṇa's hands, and he goes about his duties with an even mind. He's certainly not on the lightweight list in terms of illness.

Dreams, dreams, what are they? One allopathic doctor told Swami Swims that dreams were just proof that energy was discharging itself. A real reductionistic explanation. Nothing Freudian or Jungian, just that thoughts were being processed, and so it was quite normal they were coming out in the form of these symbolic signs which had no deeper meaning. It seemed like a ridiculous "explanation."

But as to what they actually are, what the symbols mean and how to read them, who knows? For purposes of his writing in EJW, Swami Swims read about a dozen popular books on dreams, some of them theistic, to understand how God might be speaking to us in dreams. He read other books about how to know what dreams may be revealing to us. He read one which said that the way of knowing a dream was to hit upon the "a-ha" realization, or suddenly realizing what it meant. Others said this was too simplistic a way of discovering a dream's meaning and one had to go to a psychiatrist and go over childhood needs and so many things.

They really did seem ultimately enigmatic, except for the big dreams—the ones that really knock you over with their vividness and leave you in a deeply emotional state afterwards, or that were somehow very clear in their direction, pointing you to something you ought to do or not do. Dreams like that couldn't be ignored. It was good to talk to a counselor about those.

Dreams, dreams, floating through the sanatorium like a vapor or chloroform, every night dozens and dozens of dreams. Whenever the patients reached a level of rapid eye movement, they began, those cinematic stories, sometimes expertly constructed as if by short-story writers or movie makers. And sometimes totally chaotic. When Hamlet was thinking of killing himself, he said why not do it? "To sleep, perchance to dream; aye, there's the rub,/ For in that sleep of death, what dreams may come,/ When we have shuffled off this mortal coil."

The dreams continued until the first rays of dawn, or the first restlessness of the dreamers stirred them into the waking of the day. Another day of waiting and patience and prayer.

In the middle of the night, Sandy turned on her bed light. She wrote a matter-of-fact letter to Braja dāsa, telling him of her first infrasound treatment.

Oh darling, I may be seeing you sooner than I thought. Even the therapists and doctors are abuzz here about my new program. Everyone is so excited—they're looking forward to making some real break-

throughs. Now I think we just have to contain ourselves and be patient. We were asking for a different kind of patience before, thinking that it would be "forever." Now we have to be patient to think that it won't be next week or next month. It will take some time, but it looks like the time will be greatly reduced. Oh Kṛṣṇa! Thank you for shortening the time for bringing me back to my beloved husband and the wonderful country, which is our prabhu-datta-deśa. *Aren't you happy, dear? Write to me as soon as possible.*

I've got nothing to worry
about because you're my thrill.
Those content sixteen rounds.
He writes about himself.

Sultry day, turned the fans
off.

Are you playing with dolls?
Angels flying to Australia?

Paraplegics who everyone
falls in love with
from the waist up? What

happened to the wandering "I"?
Even Jane worries. I say
don't worry, it's going
well.

Who can stop us? We can do whatever we want.
"Did you read the Coltrane
book?" Only the inner covers.
I can do whatever I want.
Threw my golf clubs into the river

like W.C. Fields.
The Reddy's will be gone tomorrow
for a week but I have no
surface to paint on!

Sixteen rounds today.
Comes love there's nothing you
can do.[1] You have to do. Do
the mechanical clicker and
that's the rest. Comes love—
nothing can be done
until He wishes. Comes the counting,
that's a good thing.
Your quotas, canvas and paint?
Very good. Comes a toothache, see your
dentist right away.
See a mouse, you can chase him with
a broom—comes love, nothing you
can do. If you've been in love you know
what I mean, comes love,
nothing can be done,
but wait in lead and patience.

Rank and file. Looks like we'll have a lovely week coming. A week of solitude. The Reddy family are taking a week's vacation at Lake George. A few helpers will be around to cook for us. Would you get your rounds done, mates, or sleep too much? Get out for walks. We are really getting warmer summer days. But Swims' ankle is getting worse, and mom (who wants to go home to Puerto Rico) really can't walk much anywhere. You can sit at the beach, feet in the waves. Who are the lucky ones, who look to God in the sky under sun hats or rain hats and utter his names, sincerely feeling, "I want to go home"?

This miserable body, this life, the *Vedas* say. But if you are living with the eyes of the *śāstras*, then it can be very nice.

One of the first great twelve-inch LP records was Sinatra's *Only the Lonely*. And then, *The Wee Small Hours*, all sad ballads. We are consistently sad too, but jolly at moments when an irrepressible swinger comes on. You can't deny them. I like the idea. You read poetry live in hip café, and there are images playing behind in your studio, weird pictures like the violinist playing to Frankenstein's monster, who is smiling and smoking a cigar, and anything you could imagine—a woman running behind a dog and falling down in slow motion. He or she is reading the poem live onstage and the images are jumping, music spoken, silent but spooky, goofy, beautiful slow-motion of Chaplin, anything. Yes, we approve, read from any of our books.

And that ten-foot medical tank was not a miracle. Two days after her first infrasound session, Sandy developed rashes on her legs as well as indigestion. It wasn't such a miracle. They examined what could have gone wrong. Sandy wrote another letter to Braja and told him the unhappy news. They were back at the drawing board, the lead of waiting and patience. But let's not be depressed. Kṛṣṇa is testing us. He doesn't want us to become overdependent on modern medical machines. I am chanting on my beads, and I think of you, my dear lover, I answer you in spirit and from my heart to your heart. Kṛṣṇa may still have a different miracle in store.

Swims was musing. It's funny. I think I'm getting a transference from some of the other patients here. Most of us can't leave the sanatorium. Sandy is the prime example because she's in a wheelchair. I can't leave here either, because of my headaches. I just spoke to my doctor, our 11:00 A.M. once-a-week phone call. I told him our plan in the making, that I go to California, where they're renovating a house for me, where I'll get more seclusion. It's our medical leave of absence, as we call it. But today he surprised me and said, "Yes, you could go there, and how long would you stay? Two months?" Doesn't he know I intend to stay there longer for seclusion? He said you could stay there for a little while and take a "short trip" to Europe and visit places.

"From California to Europe, a short trip?" Swims asked.

"Didn't you once say you were going to take a short trip to Europe?"

Yes, but that was when I was in Ireland, Swims said to himself. The doctor seems confused.

"What I was thinking of doing was visiting New Jersey, Śamīka Ṛṣi's house, and having a disciples' meeting before I go to California."

"Oh yes, that would be very, very nice."

But the main thing is we're going to California, and how soon. I really am looking forward to that seclusion. More quiet than here. Fewer little children. There'll be disadvantages, but big advantages too.

In a dream, all the GBCs were gathering—I mean people who were GBCs from many, many years ago. Harikeśa was one of the main people, and TKG. I mostly saw them from the back. I vaguely recall that they were dressed in black. And I was supposed to attend too. It was going to be some complete restructuring and reorganization of the GBC from the ground up. They said I also had to attend. I adamantly said I was not going. They insisted that I had to go. Then I got even more adamant and said *the individual conscience is more important than the group decision.* I made a strong individual decision on this matter, and that will prevail. I was very decisive about it, and at the time I didn't even follow up on the possible consequences of it. What if it meant I got kicked out of ISKCON? What if it meant that I was showing I wasn't faithful to Prabhupāda? At the time, it simply meant that I wasn't going to be bullied by a bunch of men into doing something they thought was best. I was going to do something that I thought was best for my Kṛṣṇa consciousness. No more bullying. Yes, that was an outstanding dream, and I'll tell my counselor. It seems like the direction I'm heading—and it may be dangerous.

Dear Sandy,
Where or when will we be
back together again?
Yes, it's frustrating to hear
you went to a miracle
tank with another man and came out
with rashes.

But I believe in spiritual cures
and your true heart.
I believe in you more
than all the doctors in
the world.

The ward is okay and
the farm is okay for
the time being.
But who knows where
or when we will get
back safe into each others'
arms?

I'm feeling a little sorry for
myself, for you and me, but
sure we have our guardian
angels. Your legs, your beautiful legs
are getting stronger and
more shapely
just by the regular practice

of exercise—as are mine by
farming—by the time we see each
others', we'll be perfect pictures
of health.

Auden wrote a couplet: "If equal
affection cannot be, let the
more loving one be me."
I ask for that. But I know
you're a strong lover and hard
to outdo. Let me at least
match you.

And please take my word
guaranteed. I want you in
a wheelchair just as much
as I would if you were walking.

I am very anxious to receive
the book you have (which
you're still reading) on how
a wheelchair person can fly
on a plane and how
a wheelchair couple—
a girl like you and a man
like me—can even
have sexual love
and babies.

And what I already know—
but must teach my heart
and learn from you—
        I want to know all
love and possibility comes from
Kṛṣṇa and we should stay

focused on Him for His pleasure
not ours. He will make
us happy. Teach me, dear one,
write to me. Be Sandy.

Chapter Twenty-One

Aimless? Who? The army sergeant? The videos, sex is back, Fixodent is back just a little bit? How's that for a title?

Mel Brooks: "After writing for Sid, I never wrote for any other comic. I did a little for Jerry Lewis. He's funny, but he's not profound. Sid was a great actor." So-and-so was good. Self-promote. This sanatorium is full of dust balls. They don't change the sheets. They bring them in clean and expect the patients to change them, but some patients can't move, so their buddies help. Low-paid help, even voluntary. Fans on low, but some argue it's not healthy at night. Flies, flies, gnats, like India. I need mosquito nets. You hear them out there, eager to get in and suck your blood.

Swims went to paint, but he didn't change into his orthopedic inserts. He thought he might get paint on them. The first canvas was humorous—a scene on a subway with four people. On the far left, a well-shaped young woman, breasts, jeans, kitten on her lap, sitting up straight and trying to be indifferent. She and all other figures carry bead bags. The man next to her is standing, hanging on an upper handrail and leaning down, looking at the chick with unabashed, flirtatious eyes, big smile, and hand in bead bag. On the far right, an enormous, ugly woman with huge brown coiffure, a big black handbag (which could also be used as a weapon), and many chins. She's scowling fiercely. Dangling in front of her, left hand inserted in the handrail, is a small boy. He's so small his feet don't touch the ground. He's sticking his tongue out at the ugly woman, and he too has his hand in a bead bag. Okay, Swami thought, good Kṛṣṇa conscious humor. Let's move on to the next one (this is just a warm up). But his left ankle hurt so bad he could hardly move. He had not put in the orthopedic pad. He could barely throw the paint brushes into the bucket of water, even while using the cane, and he limped up to his room to sit and recover. "Damn! I'm not even sure the pad would have helped. I think it's getting worse again. I'll have to wear that pad always."

Other inmates were returning from their attempts at afternoon sports. Some had ventured at rowing, tennis, or golf, and almost every one of them was complaining, if not outright, then by groaning or placing their hand on a sore spot. Each one of them, it seems, had overdone it. A monitor at the front door saw them coming in and said, "You people are overdoing it on a nice day. You're setting yourself back weeks with this overexertion. This is really a rest home. Just do little adventures and you'll get better in the long run." His admonishing words were cause for more groans.

"What's for supper?" asked Jojo. "I could use some good vittles instead of pains and reprimands."

Two Poems With Allusions to Bud[1]
1

Somebody loves us all but
each one is special.
She said that. I want someone
special to care for me. Well,
I couldn't consider it.

Now I do when Bud plays it.
He means each of us and some
make it true for all the lovers in
their way.

I'd like to serve in that way
but it's hard to avoid the ego.
Somebody loves you, I wonder
who? Kṛṣṇa of course. And
very personally. You don't
need another. But His
pāriṣads are included and
His piano players.

Don't envy anyone. Be
part of the show.

2

I should care. So what?
I'm left out. Ah, come on,
you don't mean that. You *do*
care. You're not just covered in
layers (as they said) and can't come
out with all your potential.

I shouldn't care what they
say. Blossom your own way
like in that nightmare, "Give
me liberty or give me death!" *The*
individual conscience knows better
than the force of majority.
Peacock feathers,
white fluffy ones.
That was at the peak of the
dream. When I woke it
faded, I should care.

This part of the day you have to decide whether you're going to continue to go on chanting *japa* on the "machine of offense," but it broke again. What's the chance? Got no malted. Didn't know what to drink. Don't phone. Don't talk. Recover, but don't paint. Don't analyze if you do. Twenty years and no one knows what's wrong. Frova, the big bomb. The secret policies by men who are on the enemy's side. Get a sultry size and listen. No, the Frova immediately, then lie down and talk with your counselor. There's no solution. No solution, play catch with your Spalding ball until it splits in half.

Sports mania. Sex mania. Mango mania. Work mania. Educator. Frova. Down the hatch at 3:40 P.M. Canal Gaṇeśa call. Wearing khakis and a Hare Kṛṣṇa sunset blue T-shirt.

You're on the pot pulling out some good stool and the phone rings. I can't stop. They'll have to call back. And they do. They have some ideas, but I've hit a terrible letter-answering block. I need a person to listen to me. Can you think of someone? They're piling up. "I know you like to be done when you are not sick." But maybe I'm not too sick to answer letters to him. Yes, I am. Could you pack audiences and read my poems while we showed animated creations on video?

"Yes, she could pack a stadium!"

"What clothes would she wear?"

Anyway, I can't answer letters now. Just lie back and decide whether to take another oxy. You took one seven hours ago.

"Who would make the images, make the data? How about going to California earlier? Young man, go West."

"Hey, this is neat (the CA scheme)."

Yes, now fill it up.

Rain boots. Rattlesnakes. But today I have to recover from the ravages of an ankle and headache. These dolors, they come and go. In “Small Apartment,” Sid Caesar burned his body against the hot stove with the turkey inside, and then he smacked his finger with a hammer against the ice container. Two minutes later he swung the door hard into his wife’s face. At the end, the closet rack collapses and the Murphy bed springs up, leaving him pinned against the wall with only his fingers and the top of his head showing. He crawls upward and says, “Dear, please phone the realtor at once and buy us a house in the country.” She grabs the phone and says, “It’s an emergency! It’s an emergency!”

You still have to ask someone if they think you should take more painkiller. Four hours ago I took an oxy, four hours ago, a Frova. Don’t stand around, right? Get it out. Try some more Radox. What good is Radox when all you have is pain? You can write about pain. Aquinas was in pain of migraine and wrote a treatise of God. A better man than I.

Oh those lovers with no chance of
ten-foot miracle tanks to fly
them to Australia in two weeks.
At least the last rashes have gone away.
“My love has gone away?”
He said, “No, it hasn’t!
I don’t need my darling
to be described in a
dream or by some
big-shot lyric writer.”
But I dream that
I set my cheek against your cheek,
I find my love, I found
that I could
do that too.

They smile. Something's coming soon.
Without a ten-foot tank they found they love,
they together pledged,
I'll be home sooner than you
think. Please embrace me
in the wheelchair and I'll teach
you how to love me
in this way.

We both like Bud Powell and
lovely Australian weather and
sensual things.
I am eager to return

and it *will* be *sooner* than you
think and I won't have changed
and you *won't be changed*
and the love in your eyes
will still be there.

Somebody loves you, I wonder who.
Maybe, darling, it's me.
Waiting early. Sorry I can't write excellent
lyrics, but true love.
Yours, Sandy.

Dear Sandy,

Okay, no miracle. They come from God, and maybe one will come. And now your rashes are gone. Somehow this fanatic attempt in the anticipation that I sense in you this week has made me become even more eager to be with you. It makes me particularly *more in love with that girl Sandy King in the wheelchair. I don't care if you ever get out of the chair, but I am very eager to hear the very exciting plans about how a wheelchair person can travel in an airplane, provided proper care is taken and she is well-exercised. That fits you to a tee. Śrīla Prabhupāda flew from Delhi to England and back to Bombay in terrible shape, but got determination from Kṛṣṇa. I think the plane authorities were even debating letting him get on. But when you get a beaming smile, with your shapely legs, strong arms, attractive bosom, they fall in love with you and don't want to let you get off the plane. They want to know who is this twenty-year-old girl. Tell them, "I'm sorry, but I have to rest for a ride to a farm to meet my husband, Braja dāsa." It really all seems quite possible, but I just want to save up my hope. I have to swallow, as I may have to if the news changes and you have to stay a little longer before you come. Please send me recent information and pictures of you. Send me a picture of the family there at the sanatorium, so I can know more about your friends Swami Swims, Bhaktin Jane, Tim, even your father and others.*

I'd better get back to the cabbage field and harvest it before the rabbits do. Your surrendered soul in Kṛṣṇa consciousness, Braja dāsa

I think if a man recovered from headache, his eyes no longer burning, he could concentrate and say *japa* instead of writing about his sister. Wouldn't that be better? Wouldn't that be placing the priority where it belongs?

Śacī said the day before he left for his vacation, he gave a rip-roaring talk to his men. A few days before they had lost $70,000, so he read the riot act to them. He was about to go on a seven-day vacation and he didn't want anything disastrous to happen while he was away. He deserves a vacation. But I need to keep going because I have to finish before I go to California. Shut the door. It's got nothing to do with Elvis Sinatra.

It has everything to do with *hari-nāma* being the top priority. It's only twenty minutes to 10:00. I'll let you do this loose prose, but then no poem. Who's "I"? "I" is Swims. It doesn't matter if you sometimes change them. We want it to be a seminovel, and it's going okay, especially if we wind up with plenty of plot, with Sandy going to Australia and Swims going to California. And in between that, some juicy stuff. We don't need a tight plot, but just something to keep us rolling along. There was nothing wrong with the old free plots. It will give us a lift when Śacī comes back. We can hear about what happened during his vacation. Play with Lakṣmaṇa. And now this rash of headaches. That's not repetitious.

New man waiting in line. Just take whatever you need to relieve the pain. Good old Nitāi-Gaurasundara with the same line. He hardly ever gets to the point of saying, "No, that's too much medicine." He just says to keep stoking it in there so you feel no pain. I know he disagrees with the others, and I like it. Keep the new batteries in, and keep the meds in. But where's that Paxil? We've almost run out. This morning I thought it was afternoon. I'm zonking again. I need my old guardian Śacī and getting in there in the gym and doing the exercises.

What's the most important of all the spiritual master's instructions? To chant sixteen rounds daily. Out of three batteries lying on the bed, any one of them could still be alive, so I'll have to count that they're all dead. Even though Śacī's away, I can still do exercises, right? But *with* the changed pad. And the same with painting. Don't become an eighty-eight-pound weakling. But I don't like the cooking. If only Mother Kaulini could come here and rescue the day.

That Godbrother is really going to write a book like Henry James or a Victorian novel? More power to him. My niche has been picked out for decades, since I was seventeen years old. More power to me. And I don't need marijuana to do it.

I hope these letters are authentic. I hope they do love each other.

Śacī's three-year-old daughter stayed out on the lake until midnight in a kayak, even though she doesn't know how to swim. Sign up for fun in New York, U.S.A., Lake George. They finally coaxed her to come in. Kṛṣṇa-kīrtana is learning how to set up canvases for me every day, if I can only get out there and do it. The eye, the ankle, the distraction, the head, the energy. The *japa.* How much do you want to paint? How important is it? The swamis liked the one I did of people on the subway chanting *japa.* At least it was a "spiritual" topic. That's sometimes rare for me, so I'm glad they caught me on a day like that.

Just as dinner came out, Swami Swims got to talk on the phone with Dr. Nitāi-Gaurasundara. As expected, he said we must keep the pain under control. So he recommended another oxy and then during the night, another oxy if required, along with Ambien. "We must keep the pain down." Swami went back to dinner, but it was extremely spicy for the two Vṛndāvana-dwelling swamis and their congregation. He could hardly swallow a mouthful. But he played a Prabhupāda lecture. At first it was one he had just heard, so he flipped it ahead to number two. Prabhupāda was saying, *man-manā bhava mad-bhakto*, if one always thinks of the lotus feet of Kṛṣṇa, then he will immediately be thinking of Kṛṣṇa and never be away from the thought of Kṛṣṇa. It sounded wonderful. It struck home. You will see Kṛṣṇa. He didn't understand exactly what it meant, but that Kṛṣṇa is a person, and you would see Him and you would love Him. It would all become understood very simply. It didn't matter what kind of food you liked, whether spicy or the way Mother Kaulini made it. Just think of Kṛṣṇa always and you will see Him. His attention reverted back to his head pain, but he didn't forget the message. Devotees of Prabhupāda have heard a lot about Kṛṣṇa and seen His pictures and *mūrtis* and understood to some degree the relationship of His name to His *mūrti*. We have a big head start over the Māyāvādīs. So just see that form and say that form and pray to that form. Believe in Him. Even through your pains. It's all for some reason, it's like innerness, a kiss or a hug. It's purifying you of the things that keep you away from Him. Believe in it. The inmates have got a reason to be here, and our little artistic projects are also part of it, and our pinches and embarrassments, and our loves for one another. "It all belongs."

Swims is dropping through a real bad day. Maybe he's caught the disease that everyone around here has been having. A little nausea, burning eyes, indigestion, headaches moving all over the cranium. Lying in bed almost twenty-four hours, all different kinds of pills don't work. Pain, pain. And yet the doctor wants the pain to go away. You think of the Charlie Chaplin "Wanted" ad, where he's wearing the black-and-white hat and striped shirt, escaped convict. That's you. Wanted by some disease. Escaped convict. You think of wanted convicts and how they used to put up posters about them in the post office. The guy would see it and urgently change his coiffure, his black glasses, and whatever else he could. Put on 200 pounds and flee to Trinidad. Is that a version of what you're planning? Get away from VIPs, families, noises? But you won't be able to get away from pain, will you? And e-mails, snail mail. Confidential mail response. I think we'll do better.

Chapter Twenty-Two

Dear Braja,

I received in the mail the book Spinal Cord Injury: A Guide for Living. *It's described as a "comprehensive resource for coping with medical, emotional, and practical challenges." Strangely, I wasn't in a hurry to read it. It's too big for me—288 pages. I was more eager to get into the therapy room and to work out in all the routines there—exercising underwater, "walking" on the parallel bars, exercising my arms and shin muscles by lifting weights. The therapists say all those muscles are developing very well and that I'm making better-than-usual progress. So our strategy is that I should continue motivating myself for getting well enough to fly on an airplane before I've fully recovered.*

When my muscles are strong enough for that, there will be a lot to learn about getting in and out of the wheelchair. As the book says, "For most people with a spinal cord injury, the need for assisted mobility is the most obvious change from their previous status. To participate in almost any activity, you must be able to get out of bed and either walk, perhaps with a walker or crutches and braces, or use a wheelchair to move around your room, around the hospital, and, ultimately, around your home and community."

That's what I've been doing here, gradually learning self-sufficiency with wheelchair skills. I'm trying to become a candidate for leg braces, crutches and canes, and combinations of these. I may have the option of walking for short distances and up steps, while still using the wheelchair for longer distances.

Since I am so young, I don't want to look like a hopeless case. Therefore I like to talk about these feelings with my therapists, and with you also. I don't want it to press me or our marriage. I don't want to be pushed everywhere, and I want to continue all my recreational therapy to help me eventually participate in recreational leisure activities and daily living skills, including going to sports events, learning to paint and do crafts, shopping, and going to a restaurant or other public places.

It can be a big stigma to be seen by others as a cripple, a "disabled person, one of them." This is certainly manifest in discrimination in jobs, education and in the general society. So I have to be ready for this. Even if I feel good, many people may reject me.

The first thing will be the airplane trip. I'll have to learn how to be able to use the toilet on the plane. I'll have to get a seat near the bulkhead and learn how to maneuver myself in the toilet room. The fact that I'll be flying first-class and that a therapist will be there to help me should make that easier. We're actually practicing for this exact thing here, and so it won't be like I'll freak out, having never practiced it before.

I would rather you read the part of the book about practical preparations for sexual intercourse, and we can discuss it together when I return. It's not that I'm embarrassed, but there are things about emptying the bladder and bowels and so on, so that accidents don't happen in the middle of sexual intercourse.

I think we've already established the basics—that we so much enjoy sex pleasure for the emotional satisfaction of our own physical closeness. It's not just a sticking in of a penis into a vagina. It's the being together in the touching and the embracing that lead up to the mechanics and the orgasm. In other words, "making love" requires much more than just the right mechanics. The book says, "As in other areas of life, you'll find it hard to have a good attitude if you're focusing on losses." I remember when you and I made love. It was really like that. We would rub our bodies against each other and take pleasure feeling each other's hair and smelling each other's bodies. And all this we would discuss later as lovemaking. They call it foreplay, but for us it was love, and would eventually climax in intercourse. But it was important that we actually loved each other and loved to stroke each other. So I think we have a great advantage.

They have discovered that all kinds of erogenous zones in the body become even more erogenous *after an injury to the spinal cord. We have to explore these very gently—make a kind of inventory—and that can increase sexually exciting exchanges. We should try to* give *each other love, and that's part of the new excitement. So there is more adventure for us, and new techniques to look forward to.*

There are a lot more ideas that I don't want to discuss in this letter but that are spelled out explicitly in the book. I'd rather you read it and that we discuss them face to face, and that we actually try them when we are together. I want us to have a full sex life, and I say that without blushing. Sex life is a large part of human life, and so is fertility. The main sentence in the book here says, "Female fertility is not affected by spinal cord injury: for a woman of childbearing age, the ability to become pregnant persists unless she has some unrelated fertility problem." So *all this planning can take place when we are actually together, and I hope this is soon.*

Living here in the sanatorium, my dear Braja, I see so many people with injuries much worse than mine who have no hope of returning to real life as you and I do. So I'm very grateful to Kṛṣṇa. Even those who have no physical or psychological chance of revival, because they are Hare Kṛṣṇa chanters, they are fortunate, and we should always thank the Lord and the spiritual masters that we're on the right track, no matter what difficulties we go through. You know all this, and I should not be preaching gratitude to you. But I can't help but express it as a kind of prayer.

I wanted to write you a little summary of some of the parts of this book, but I've saved most of it, rather than mail it to you, because I think it's something that we should share when I come back, and we should read it together. Don't be angry at me for that. I think it's something to go through slowly. The main points, however, are that we can have sex, we can have children, and certainly I can fly on the plane and be with you before very long.

Please try to save some money, and I will too, so that we can make our plane trip a reality. I'm sure my father will chip in.

Praying for you every day, your dearest lover,
Sandy

You can, you can, don't say you cannot. Be a hoper, not a hopeless. Yeah, but there are some things, some people ... really get you down. That can be because they can't see the silver lining. Black act of the twentieth-century holocaust. Previous centuries too—plagues, massacres, times in which there seems to be no good in the hearts of men or gods. Individuals become cutthroats and drink or sniff, torturous abuse of animals and lands and nations by "decent" voters and elected populations with high-tech smart missiles. Priests who fondle tots' genitals. Why should I list it? Hare Kṛṣṇa *gurukula* abuses. The lawyers want the money, the children want everyone blamed, they want the pure *ācārya* accused of a conspiracy plot. I should stop this writing. Fight away. Don't push me into pro-money collecting, sitting around tables fundraising. I paid enough. My body and mind have broken into anxiety disorder migraine syndrome, no shit. Phone Bugs Bunny Studios and ask permission from Looney Tunes and Merrie Melodies. Ask if we can use a reproduction of Bugs sitting in a beach chair with black sunglasses while the nuclear mushroom is going off nearby. "Yeah, I know. We asked that two years ago, and they refused."

Well, try again. Ask the Looney Tunes people. Or ask Walt Disney. Pray to his frozen body. Ask for a copyright for the use of Goofey in a Hare Kṛṣṇa *dhotī*.

It's not *that* early,
Edna, but I can ask a girl to sit
beside me and listen to Mingus
or watch Edna Purviance on *Sunnyside*
without Chaplin on the screen.
Chaplin directs the film.

I should really chant my *japa* or
I won't reach sixteen, but I get to see
the set, and after that
it will make me want
to preach to you, "why
don't you think of *japa*?
Don't you know it's at
the top of the list!"
Oh Edna, I sit and invite

you to sit beside me and watch
the one film in which Charlie
didn't appear but directed,
so I could see you.
I wouldn't want to do that
with an audience.
It introduced Adolphe Menjou.
But who cares about him?

Can I have a little solitude and still
make it to sixteen? No, I
don't think you can make it.

Then split it up in half.
Stay ten minutes with Edna and fifteen minutes
of *japa* (short of sixteen), and go to bed not guilty
and talk to your counselor
tomorrow how to
settle it up. There's just too much
to do in a day.

Color of garden's fading. Lake George
vacation.
This body's
made another day.

I hear each day how beautiful it is at Lake George, thought Swims Swami. They're motorboating all around, and sometimes they put the little children in a big inner tube and trail them at high speeds behind. But while they enjoy, they've allowed workmen to come to the grounds right near the sanatorium and do a lot of carpentry and hammering in the barn next door. So there's no silence here, even though it's sunshiny. There's one part of the grounds where we could sit with our many different baseball caps, and some of us flop there and read different books. But it's still too noisy. The best place for the *Sanatorium* writing folks is their own little room, but it's rather tight in there. Still, it's quiet, and silence is golden. They have a fan in there to make it cooler.

All right, all right. Let's hear something angelic, you complainer. I'm planning a crucial talk with my counselor today about how to make it a priority and get the rounds up to sixteen. One thing I'll have to do is stop talking every day to one of my editors. He's a jazz fan, and I've started lending him my albums, and then he sends them back, and we talk about them. We also do some very important work on the book. His suggestions are magic. So they're not slight things, they're important. But what could be more important than chanting? But when I talk to these two editors in New York—they work two cubicles apart in the same professional publishing company—it could wind up being an hour each day. Take an hour from one of my days, and take thirty minutes for comedy movies at night, and you've got a big chance that you're not going to get in your sixteen rounds. Plus the fact that you take a nap because of your medicine. Plus the fact that you're kind of indifferent to the whole endeavor. I just read something in a previous manuscript of mine. It said, "I'm not complaining, I am admitting I don't 'go out' to preach. I go in to preach—letters and books—and lately I've been talking as if I don't even want to try in my *japa*, *japa* reform is over—ah—oh—and I am wanting to admit where I am and then proceed to the best of ability." By that quote I mean to draw your attention to "*japa* reform is over." So that's what I want to get straightened out and start a new *japa* reform. Placed a call to my editor, who was away from his desk. The message said he'd call when he comes back. When he calls, I'll tell him there's going to be an editor's reform, starting today. It's become "too much" of a luxury.

Here's a good example of settling something up. My ankle is too painful to stand on, but I want to paint. I phoned up Kṛṣṇa-kīrtana, who is in charge of just about everything connected to painting these days. We have the big roll of canvas, we've got enough paint to go for awhile (I've got to phone and *reach* our paint source, Trivikrama, to get some more paint), and we've got our art space in the garage. But I can't stand on my ankle to paint. So I phoned Kṛṣṇa-kīrtana and asked him what to do. He said, "No problem. We'll just hang the canvas at an angle, and you can sit and paint." I didn't even know what he meant. But he said it so authoritatively that I took it for granted—he can put it at an angle, and I can reach all my materials, and yet sit in a chair. Now that I'm writing it down, I haven't a clue as to what he meant. Where will the canvas hang from? He said he'd set the screws at an angle. Sounds like a skyhook from Boy Scout days. Does he mean the angle would be all the way to the floor, and that my legs would go up against it and get paint on them? Anyway, he's a sensible man, so I guess he knows what he's talking about, and when he comes over, we'll just do it right. Yeah, we'll do it right. When you talk to a sensible man and he tells you that he knows what to do, he does. I'm a karma dummy. I mean to say, as somebody put it, "You have bad karma for machines." I don't know how to run machines. I even asked the ladies how to run different VCR machines, and I don't even bother to ask the ladies how to run a computer because I wouldn't know the first thing about it.

So I feel really good that I'm fixed up tonight for 7:00 o'clock (rather late, but that's the earliest he can come).

Now, at 3:00 I talk to my counselor. I've got a bigger question for him, and I don't think it's going to be so easy to set up. It's the biggest question that I've asked him since we started working together about a year ago. It's, "How can I chant my quota of *japa* every day?" We've gone through many crises together, and he's given good advice, and we've sweated through them with blood, sweat, and tears. One time I hung up the phone in tears, saying, almost incoherently, "I'm in the worst period of my life." But now I don't feel like that. I am sort of lighthearted in voice and attitude. But I know that objectively, I'm talking about the worst crisis in my life. And that is that I'm not chanting my quota of sixteen rounds. There, I can say it quite calmly. I can say it quite openly, even though it's the biggest scandal. Other scandals I would hide under the table and not let anyone see. I would lock them in a lead box and drop them in the ocean. I would swallow them. But somehow, for this scandal, I'm writing it out on the page. Of course, I'll say it's just temporary. For over thirty years I chanted wonderfully. I was very exemplary. They told funny stories how I used to hold a mirror in front of my mouth to try to improve my pronunciation while chanting. Once I did it in a temple room, and one young fellow was laughing at me. Ādi-keśava went over to him and said, "If you're laughing at Swims Mahārāja, I'm going to punch you in the face." So I was such a good chanter. Yeah, man. But it's been about six months, let's say, since I started taking the medication Klonopin. It has other names, like clonazepam, and it belongs to the family of medications known as benzodiazepines. It's a tranquilizer. As soon as I started taking that, my headaches went away and a sleepiness came upon me, which makes me unable to regularly chant. This is the core of the predicament, and it remains to this day.

I talk about it every Saturday in brief conversations with my medications doctor. It's ironic that this week I had two terrible nights of headaches. I had one headache that lasted over twenty-four hours. In that time, I took oxycodone twice and Frova (we're talking about big medicines—oxycodone is a powerful drug used to treat severe pain, and Frova is for migraines), but the headaches continued. Then they finally went down, and the next night again—two oxycodones and Frova. So it's not a good time to argue in favor of getting off medications. I'm completely off the medications that cause rebound headache. Rebound was brought on by Advils, and I stopped the Advils over three weeks ago. I'm not ever taking them again, or any kind of rebound-producing headache makers. I know a few antimedicine people who will say that even oxy and Frova will cause rebound headaches. You can't argue with them all. But right now I really shouldn't be getting rebound so quickly from the medicines I am taking.

So therefore I'm not talking about adjusting my medicines! I'm talking about this inability of mine to fit my rounds in during the course of my day, from when I get up, at about 4:00, to when I take rest, at about 9:00. It's not a problem of being incapacitated because of pain, but a problem of being able to do things, but doing things other than chanting. I write like anything! I've been writing faster than ever before. (One reason for that is that I've been talking directly into the microphone, rather than always taking my time with the pen.) Another reason is I've been making phone calls to my editors, as I told you a few pages ago. Another reason is that until my ankle accident, I was painting. Another reason is the movies at night. And that's about it. I wish there was time for everything. We all say that. But if there should be time for *anything*, it should be *japa*. One should chant his *japa* first, and then consider—"Is there any time for writing? Is there any time for painting? Is there any time for movies? Is there any time for talking to editors?"—but you can't pull that on me. I'm just too addicted to all these quality-of-life, life-giving, happiness-giving things. I can't give them up.

harer nāma harer nāma
harer nāmaiva kevalam
kalau nāsty eva nāsty eva
nāsty eva gatir anyathā

But there is no way of saving yourself from all the bad things of Kali except the chanting of the holy name, the chanting of the holy name, the chanting of the holy name. That's it, folks. Only the Lord's holy name.

So what you're really saying is you don't have a taste for the holy name—you've lost it along the way, after all this period of not practicing. Whether it's due to medicine or whatever it's due to, now you can't pick it up again, and the Lord is not giving you the taste to even do your routine, mechanical chanting. You don't know how blessed a state it was to be able to do the routine, because now you can't do it, and you can't call on any power to enable you to do it. It's dropped to such a low priority that you do the things you *like* to do, rather than what you should do. It's the *preyas*, *śreyas* thing. You're like a baby who does what he wants to do, rather than an older, more serious child who has submitted to doing what he knows he should do, such as going to school. You are not chanting your sixteen rounds because you'd rather do things that are vastly inferior, even though they're lots of fun.

But I hope my counselor comes through as usual. He's such a sensible and loving guy. He wants me to be myself. Did I say compassionate? I meant to. He wants me to be myself and to be happy. He'd even go so far as to say, Well, if the real you doesn't want to chant sixteen rounds, then why should you force yourself to do it? Just like that Nobel Prize–winning writer Isaac Singer wrote in the introduction to Satyarāja's book, "I so much believe in not killing animals that even if I believed that God was in favor of it, I would still be against the killing of animals."

But that's dangerous territory and I can't enter it. The doctor might go so far as to say, Oh, you've chanted so much. Let's just take it easy for a while, and you will get back to chanting again. You just have to rest and don't give yourself anxiety, because for you, *the worst thing is to get pain or have anxiety.* And he'd say, Let's gradually work up to the sixteen rounds. Or maybe he'd put his foot down and say, Cut out one of those other goodies. I've already cut out the daily phoning to the editors, so there's a half-hour right there. And I can be real careful of the time, not lounge in bed so much. Just somehow get yourself up. But you have to avoid causing a strain to your body. My counselor might say, You have to decide who you are. Are you Swims Mahārāja, who's not a hypocrite and chants his sixteen rounds, are you a *sannyāsī* or are you not? You have to face yourself—what do you want to be? So this is being true to Prabhupāda, and you have to do it, that's all. So chop off the hour that has to be chopped, and let's do it. But don't look at it so drearily. I'm sure we can get in a lot of good things. The doctor will not drop me real low. He's very wary. He's not going to drop me completely off that medication. And you yourself are just going to refuse to cut off painting, or you may refuse to cut off any of these activities, so you may take time. Twice last week you did sixteen rounds, so you can do it. But one of those days you cut the painting. So a little less of this, a little less of that. I don't know what to say right now. Let's talk to our counselor.

For Nāndīmukhī

You remember Kṛṣṇa
from the earliest paintings
they are restoring at
great expense.
26 Second Ave. we reminisce.

She's in love with the place
and so happy they have it
as their Kṛṣṇa conscious temple
where the boys and girls first went
to see Swami and give their money.
Steve is one of her favorites
and she likes to quote things he
did when she digs them up
from the archives.
I don't mean Steve Kowit.
He was a few blocks away.
Might as well have been a
million miles away and then
ran away to South America
to escape the U.S. Army and Vietnam.

Steve Guarino stories she likes. I
just read one in an essay she wrote
but threw it in the circular file
because it will be published soon in
Among Friends.

Among Friends is still well alive
and 26 Second Ave. is still growing,
a big center in New York City
packed for lectures and feasts.
SDG not often
seen there with his agoraphobia
and headaches, but his heart is growing inclined
to take part in it.

Japa must come first. New York
know-how. Charlie Mingus
flutes. *Hari-nāma* quota.

Chapter Twenty-Three

A child shouting in the street wakes Swami Swims from strange dreams. He is thinking of going to California. All the things that pass, and you forget them. I imagine the plot for a movie in which a man seduced a virgin, and then she said she would never have sex with him again. She would go and look only for other men. She was hardened. She was no longer the sweet Edna Purviance.

Swims Swami reread the previous book in the trilogy. He felt he overdid it a little, being bitter about past GBC days. But he decided to leave it because it was true. He took some of it out and wrote about the inmates being annoyed and inconvenienced by all the visitors coming from the festival. Visitors didn't seem to be aware of how much pain and inconvenience they were giving the patients. Oh God, it's July 2. In two days they'll have their fireworks.

Dear Sandy,

Please forgive me but I didn't like the idea of your telling me that I couldn't buy the book Spinal Cord Injury *and had to wait until you brought your copy home. So I went and purchased a copy of my own. When I brought the book home, I wasn't so much eager to read about love and sex. I turned more to the begin-*

ning for understanding what the spinal cord injury actually is. I'm trying to understand biologically and emotionally what you went through. I looked for a long time at the numbered vertebrae, showing where you had been injured in the car accident.

Fortunately, yours was diagnosed from the beginning as an incomplete spinal cord injury. When you come back, you can tell me exactly what really happened, whether you underwent surgery or had to use a halo brace or whether they had to hold your head in place by "tongs." I read about the neurogenic pain, which is caused by abnormal processes inside the spinal cord, how it's very frustrating because it affects an area of the body that is anesthetic, a region that has no sensation for external stimuli. In other words, the whole gamut of antipain medicine may not have been a relief for you during that time.

I don't feel myself much more educated than I did when I first received cryptic messages from you about how you were recovering. But I'm glad to hear that you have been getting better, that your psychological attitude has always been upbeat and that the professionals around you have always been encouraging you. I have not taken this as something cheap. I know that you took to your wheelchair enthusiastically, not taking it as a curse against you but rather accepting anything they offered you as better for you. No anger, not much anxiety, not much dependence—it brought out all your good qualities. So much so that it even brought out the good qualities of the other members of the sanatorium and the rehabilitation center. In the book, it mentions that social workers can help by talking with the injured person's spouse or family about the person's progress. Too bad I'm cut off from that kind of communication. When we can move you to Australia and you begin going to a clinic here, I'll be sure to be active and keep in touch with the people who are taking care of you.

In the book they talk about the case of Vanessa. She broke her back while riding in a boat. She was doing well in therapy until a friend made a remark that she ought to give up her crutches. She didn't think she could do it. She was afraid because of her self-image. I don't think you ought to worry about that since you've got me, and there's no way *I am not going to accept you wholeheartedly, and I'm going to take you all over. You don't need to worry about getting a job. If you want to get a job, you can do that, but I'll constantly be there to help you keep up your humor, talk about your interests and ideas.*

I'm up to chapter 4 in that book. I'm not in a hurry to read the rest. Maybe you're right, maybe we should read it together gradually. I care more about you than the book. Your letters to me mean more than the book. I want to know how you're doing in your life with the inmates. I want to do more research about when you'll be able to come back. Have you been discussing that with the airline people or with people in your rehab center regarding your specific condition and the facilities of airlines? How do they go about it? Do they have to come and examine you? I'll do whatever is needful here, and you do whatever is needful there. When we get the okay, then I'll immediately be able to purchase the tickets, and if there's any difficulty financially, your father has assured me of his help. It will be a great welcome home trip. In the meantime, I'm dreaming of you and wanting you close to me, so please don't feel lonely. I think you're in good hands now with the Supreme Lord Kṛṣṇa, with all His great pāriṣads *of the spiritual world, and with that likable band of devotees there in New York. But you and I have a special destiny to carry out, and so we are both looking forward to that happening soon. Your beloved, Braja*

There was a girl who grew up in *gurukula*. Because of the abuses she suffered there, she maintained a hatred for chanting the holy name. She would never chant a single Hare Kṛṣṇa. She married a man who did chant Hare Kṛṣṇa, but he could never convince her to take it up. One day they were driving together in Mexico, and although their relationship was a good one, they were having some problems, which they were working on. She asked him if there was anything she could do to improve the relationship. He said there was one thing—that she could chant Hare Kṛṣṇa. She said, "No, that's one thing I can't do." Later that day they sat on the beach, and he took her in his arms and began chanting Hare Kṛṣṇa. They had no beads, but just began to chant together in a loving embrace. She took up the chanting with him. Hare Kṛṣṇa, Hare Kṛṣṇa, Kṛṣṇa Kṛṣṇa, Hare Hare. She thought to herself, "*This* is better." It was chanting with love, not under force. She loved that chanting, although she did not continue it. A few years later, she began to chant now and then, and then a few years after that, she decided, "Now I have to get serious and develop my relationship with my spiritual master. So I'll have to chant Hare Kṛṣṇa." And so she began to chant a steady eight rounds a day.

This girl's mother was a *gurukula* schoolteacher, and according to the one who told me this story, she left Kṛṣṇa consciousness in great bitterness and also vowed never to chant Hare Kṛṣṇa again. She joined the Unitarian Church, which accepts all religions. They knew that she had been a Hare Kṛṣṇa, and they continually pressed her to give a lecture on the *Bhagavad-gītā*. She resisted, but one day she gave in. After her lecture on the

Bhagavad-gītā, the beautiful choir of that church began to sing, accompanied by their organ, the Hare Kṛṣṇa mantra for a sustained period. The *gurukula* mother broke down in tears of spiritual emotion. I did not hear whether she followed up with more chanting, but she was certainly touched by the revival of the holy name at that point in her life.

Oh Holy Name, You touch us once and then again in our lives. You do not let us go. You are very rare to obtain.

I especially want to pray that one *gāyatrī* mantra every day, *aiṁ gurudevāya vidmahe kṛṣṇānandāya dīmahe tan no guroḥ pracodayāt.* "Let us try to understand my spiritual master who is always in blissful Kṛṣṇa consciousness. Let me meditate on him being enthused as he enthuses us." I want to know this spiritual master. I want to know his secret identity. I want to know who he is. I want him to give me the *śakti* to chant Hare Kṛṣṇa. Please, Śrīla Prabhupāda, give it back to me. You gave it once, and now somehow I have lost it. Just that one *gāyatrī* mantra will be sufficient.

So many stories of devotees getting the holy name, losing it, and gaining it back at different points of their life. A precious jewel, tossed aside and gained again. I have been incapacitated, it's true, and I've lost it. My plea is that I lost it because of medical reasons. But I'm going to find a way back, and I pray to the Lord to gradually let me bring back all the aspects of my life which give me quality of life without leaving out the holy name. You are a very wise philosopher and a trickster, and You will give me everything again no doubt. Please trick me into chanting the holy name out of taste, out of pleasure, and without leaving out the fun of the things I've become so passionately attached to as a means of glorifying You and being satisfied in Kṛṣṇa consciousness.

Thoughts while in bed. They're mostly gone now, but let's see if I can get them back ... The tail end was that the ankle is the bone that holds up the whole body. There was a kind of randomness in thinking. Perhaps it was just the day coming, and the dawning of all the disjointed thoughts coming to me. Like last night, watching Sid Caesar, painting with Kṛṣṇa-kīrtana, being with Gopī, and then her going away and thanking her for being with her, and thoughts of going to California, and thoughts of the kind of book this is turning out to be, and how it's already being read in California in a manuscript form by Aghari and his son. His son was in the backseat, and when he heard the first word, he said, "Cool!"

I remember the dream had something about the first paragraph they were reading. I was trying to remember what the first paragraph of the preface said. It said that I am sick of people coming to the book table and saying that this is a diary. So I tell the booksellers not to tell them it's a diary, that there's much more to it. There are poems and essays and lots and lots of different things. I didn't tell the story of Nitāi saying to me that a sophisticated devotee, Satyarāja, came up to me and said, "So this is Swims Swami's diary." Nitāi said, "It's more than a diary," and Satyarāja said, "Can you tell me how it's more than a diary?" Nitāi was overwhelmed and said to him, "Can you come back tomorrow? By then I'll be able to tell you." He then searched his mind and thought of what to do. He thought of Kaiśori, who would certainly have a good answer. Then he thought that wasn't fair, and he searched his own mind to come up with some answer. He wrote a little essay, but Satyarāja didn't come back the next day to ask the question.

This book is a kind of answer, because it's not just a diary, although I have nothing against the diary genre (do I?). This book has no times and dates, and it doesn't use the first-person "I" (later Swims Swami decided that was too confining, and he is using the word "I," as well as the name Swami Swims). So in my thoughts before getting up this morning I was reviewing all of that and thinking how I got over it with Dattātreya. I was satisfied with that new explanation of things in the preface. I don't remember if there was any "tack-on Kṛṣṇa consciousness" in it, but Kṛṣṇa consciousness always comes floating in sooner or later.

Even if He is tack-on, He comes. It's just like a nurse who's going to take your blood. She says, "This won't hurt too much." Then you feel a little liquid on your arm. Then she says, "All right, breathe in," and you breathe in, so so far there's been no pain or penetration (using this as an analogy to Kṛṣṇa), then all of a sudden, Ow, there's Kṛṣṇa. He suddenly appeared. In fact, in Ireland I once received a needle for a blood test, and I was looking out the window at a crucifix on top of a church. I tuned in on it and decided that I would look at that crucifix as they stuck the needle in. Of course, the needle isn't very painful, and yet, in a sense, it was. So as the needle went in and stayed for the long period in which she took out my blood, I thought, "What a tiny pain I'm experiencing compared to the pain of Jesus Christ on the cross."

July 4, get a newspaper. Here's some crap about patriotism and armaments in danger of terrorism while the fireworks go off. I don't know how loud it will be in this neighborhood. They have a sign, "Quiet, Hospital Zone," but it's summer vacation and I don't think the cops care much. In the old days, it was one and a half–inch firecrackers purchased by a boy, Dick Kohn, who would buy for all of us in Chinatown at a profit. Then he bought two-inch firecrackers, tornadoes and cherry bombs. A homosexual barber named Nick tried to bribe me for oral sex with a bag of cherry bombs. I was thirteen years old and very virtuous from my upbringing at home, so I refused him, but I accepted the cherry bombs anyway.

"I pledge allegiance to the flag of the United States of America, and to the Republic for which it stands, one nation under God ... " That was how it began in the 1950s. Have they eliminated words about God and make some allusion to gays? What a nation, always was, gun-totin'! Praying with the Bible and killing, starving out the poor to give to the rich. No tradition but immigration and the melting pot of sin, let freedom ring!

He helped me fix up the paintings
and take them down
but didn't say anything about them.
I should have asked: "Do you
like them?" And he'd have found
something to like.

It wouldn't even have to be
Kṛṣṇa conscious, I don't demand that.
I paint so fast
so fast and primitive. What
can I expect because he's
so expert.

You're a beggar, always a
beggar asking for praise,
encouragement, like a little
child, like a lover.

I think it's my forgetfulness,
I'm broken down.
Do you like me with my fancy steel crutch
and my receding hairline?
Do you like my pleas
for seclusion, outspoken
"loyal" dissension?

I heard the ambience nowadays
is for liberal but someone might
pull on your leash and you'll
have to decide.
Take it easy.

Take it easy. Present your
credentials. You've got to
go slow, poor little rich
guy, the flowers are all
abloom and Kṛṣṇa-kīrtana affords
me a way to *sit* and paint
and Dr. Nitāi-Gaurasundara a way to take
two pills and endure.

They're all so loving.
I'm pushing on agents,
the odds. Those books,
you will like them
if you're cool. Okay.
I'll trade you Cecil Taylor and Anthony Braxton
if you'll just encourage me; I need it.

Tomorrow is the Fourth of July, it is also the day the acupuncurist visits. Swims Swami still had blue and red paint on his legs. He had not painted yet today. There was a great story in world literature, the *Mahābhārata*. He had not found the secular pillow for the pin man yet. Among the priorities it seemed painting was very important right now (what with gel on the ankle) and then *japa*. Dad was dead, maybe mommy. He asked a good painter for suggestions after finishing his own. Why all the noise? "They are building a small Montessori school here." Swims is definitely getting out.

The girl hit a car and her car caught on fire. Many cars passed by but no one stopped. A forty-year-old construction worker said, "Somebody has to stop and get her out." He got out of his car and immediately pulled on the door of the woman's car while smashing on the glass. Another man helped, pulling at the damaged door until it broke off. They pulled her out. Moments later the girl's car burst into flames. The paramedics arrived. They placed her on a stretcher. There's a photo of a firefighter with the fire hose, but water is only dripping out of it. They strapped her into a stretcher. A rescuer went over and she said, "Thanks." "Hey, I was only doing what I had to. I can't believe how many people passed by your car oblivious." Then the car blew up, and the water came out of the hose.

Jojo was reading this out loud from the newspaper.

"Why do you read all that stuff out loud?"

"There's more about making an amendment to the U.S. Constitution against sending some troops to Liberia."

"You're just trying to annoy everyone."

"I'll be in the art room if anyone wants me," said Swims.

He painted. Was it good? Was Kṛṣṇa in it? Well, the first painting showed a figure like Adolphe Menjou, which was influenced by the movie we saw last night. He himself wasn't Kṛṣṇa conscious—he was smoking a cigarette. Beside him was a sexy girl with exposed breasts, like at a nineteenth century ballroom dance, and she was smoking a cigarette too, and they were sharing a big, white cloud of smoke. She was Edna Purviance, but I didn't like her. I guess I'm getting fickle. Was there anything Kṛṣṇa conscious? There was a third person to the far right of that picture. He was more like a monster, not at all one who would be allowed to come into a salon and dance and smoke cigarettes. Adolphe Menjou had a tuxedo on, and the girl was with a very formal man. This man was more like a beast from the jungle, with beast-like teeth. Did I write any words in the paintings? I can't think just now. No, I don't think I did. But it was a pretty decent exercise in painting.

My ankle was holding up. A second painting was a self-portrait, but I didn't have a mirror or anything, so it wasn't much of a likeness. I just painted it the way I used to paint them in the old days in Wicklow. I wrote the word "SERVANT" in big letters at the bottom, so that was a religious or ISKCON context. Big eyeglasses of yellow, to simulate gold, little mouth like mine, big brown eyes, some innocence but some torture. I made him black at first but later came back with some pale pink chalk. The chalk was very hard to get onto the oil-covered canvas, but gradually I was able to get it on so that it looked more like my pale skin. And it made for an interesting combination. Ears sticking out, the servant. Perhaps it wasn't as good a painting as the other one. Now that I think of it, I actually wrote the words "Hare Kṛṣṇa" in the upper left-hand corner of the salon painting, because it was too outrageous without any explicit reference to Kṛṣṇa. So both paintings had Kṛṣṇa content. Servant and Hare Kṛṣṇa, and by Swims Swami on this hot July 3. He wants to do as many as possible to please people, leaving them behind to create some awe and pleasure and have some people keep them in their homes to cheer them up. That's possible because there's a lot of wall space and a lot of drear.

I heard the front door
open and now, "I just
wanted to let you know I'm
home."
Yeah but what about my
inspiration? Tell him
you'll come out in five minutes.
It's an alternate. You chanted
that Hare Kṛṣṇa bland

five beads, you don't
do it "again," you
don't "rewind." You just
go ahead like before.

You do it again means
the same one. No, it's a retake.
We are giving it a new life. We
put ourselves in it again to
total 1,728 beads.

Ohh Lord, yeah,
it's the Thursday afternoon prayer—
hallelujah, wheew.

So blasé. That
may go on in boredom until
it comes from love not
force.

In the meantime do what you can
and the rest by love, by love
edit and read and of course you
chant because part of love
is the effort to serve the
master even if you have to
limp a part of the way
up the hill.

That makes sense. The doctor does not
want me to get
a headache even if it's a choice
between sixteen and a headache.
And when you get down to it,
sometimes there's no choice.
You lie down and wait for a better phoenix

to rise from the
fire stronger and developed.

And he *is* better.
I know, they know,
they see, give him
a chance,
say oh yeah,
oh yeah.

Early morning, July 4. It was peaceful. Not a single fireworks. The inmates slept peacefully. At 5:00 o'clock the newspapers were delivered. Jojo took one, then stood in the middle of the sanatorium and in a very loud voice read aloud, as if he was the town crier. He began shouting verbatim from the newspaper: "'An immense throng of people gathered in front of City Hall on July 9, 1776, to hear the Declaration of Independence read aloud in public for the first time. Colonists no more, they had cast off the yoke of British rule. Freedom from oppression was an intoxicating notion. Excitement built to a fever pitch in the two weeks after the signing of the document in Philadelphia on July 4, 1776. Interest was heightened because native son Phillip Livingston was one of the signers. The crowd jammed Market Street and filled Hudson Street down to the river to hear the reading.'"

"Hey, knock it off, Jojo. It's only 5:00 in the morning. You're being intrusive. Stop this reading out loud," called out Mother Arthritis. But Jojo continued.

"'*When in the course of human events it becomes necessary for one people to dissolve the political bands which have connected them with another*, the reader began, and the crowd responded exuberantly, the applause and sincerity of expression born of resilience and bravery being such as the ancient city had never witnessed,' Collier Reynolds wrote in the *Albany Chronicle*, a book of local history published at the start of the twentieth century.

"'The excitement of Independence Day faded quickly in light of the harsh realities of the revolutionary war.

"'It wasn't until 1895 that Albany began marking Independence Day with large celebrations and parades. The fireworks came in later years.'

"Also in today's front page we see the headline, 'Bush Pressed CIA on Terror: Internal review says President put heat on the agency to prove link between Saddam and al-Qaeda before war.' 'The Bush administration pressed the CIA before the war on Iraq to look for evidence of close cooperation between al-Qaeda and Saddam Hussein, but the agency found no proof, according to a CIA internal intelligence review. The review also reaffirmed that U.S. intelligence agencies had no creditable reports that Saddam knew in advance about the September 11, 2001, terrorist attacks on New York and Washington. Polls have found that a majority of Americans are convinced there was clear evidence of a connection between Iraq and al-Qaeda.'"

Jane came running out of her room. She went to the foot of Jojo's bed and in a commanding voice and with body language said, "Time out, Jojo."

Jojo immediately stopped reading the newspaper.

"Swami Swims told you yesterday not to agitate the devotees by talking so loud in the morning like this. Give us our peaceful mood that we've come here for. Give us our peaceful day."

"All right, Jane," he said obediently. She turned on her heel and walked back to her room.

Swami Swims got on the telephone to reach Jojo's counselor. Even while the connection was being made, he knew that he had failed to be assertive enough yesterday. He was just too hassled with other things he had had to do, and so he hadn't left a definitive enough impression on Jojo that there was to be no more reading aloud of newspapers. He had wimped out and gone off to paint in the art room. There was always a constant challenge between some of the inmates and the older members. The younger or more challenging inmates were like children trying to see how much they could get away with. When they saw that they could get away with a challenge, they just kept going and going. But as soon as their challenge was stopped, as Jojo's was with Jane's strong "Time out!," then the confrontation was over.

Swims reached Gopal Guru Prabhu, Jojo's counselor. "Gopal Guru Prabhu, this is Swami Swims."

"Good morning, Swami Swims. How can I serve you?"

"I hope I'm not disturbing you. Do you have just a few minutes to speak with me?"

"Yes, I do. What is it?"

"Well, Jojo's one of your clients, and the last two days he's been manifesting antisocial behavior. He's usually a quiet fellow, although he seems to be sad. But the last two days he's gotten a copy of the newspaper and read it out loud right in the middle of the hall, disturbing everybody. The first time he did it, I wasn't forceful enough in telling him he shouldn't do it. That was my fault. And now he's done it again this morning. Bhaktin Jane said, 'Time out!,' and really enforced on him that he shouldn't do it again. So he quieted down. But this is a sanatorium and rehabilitation center of love and understanding, not of force.

"I know that you and he have developed a friendship and intimacy, a confidentiality," Swims Swami continued. "We could really use your help soon. Can you give him an appointment?"

"Sure, Swims, he can come and see me right now. I don't have any other appointment. I think someone will have to help him in his wheelchair."

"Oh, great, Prabhu. Thanks very much. I'm sure you'll do him wonders. He has complete confidence in you. I know he had a terrible history before he came here, and maybe he hasn't had such good encounters among the devotees either. He'll be real happy to know he can talk soul to soul, man to man about whatever it is that's bugging him these past few days, whatever it is that's popped up. I'll send him right over."

Sure enough, Jojo was very happy to hear that he could talk with his soul mate, his counselor. With a smile on his face and no embarrassment about it, he was wheeled off to see Counselor Gopal Guru.

What the patient and client said in their meeting was confidential. For all I know, he may have told him to go into the middle of the field when he has these feelings and just shout out to the world that they can just shove it up their ass. Or he may have given him many interesting hints regarding how to be kind to his *prabhus* in the sanatorium and at the same time deal with some of his "deep" stuff. It's essential to have a counselor whom you can be completely open to and Kṛṣṇa conscious with, even in your lack of Kṛṣṇa consciousness.

Yeah, it's a good place where you
can get help like that, loving people
who know how to take care of you.

Rādhā took the thorn out of the
calf's hoof, it was Kṛṣṇa's calf,
He knew how She loves His favorites.

Come down this lane with me.
Why? Are you going to steal
all my books and kill me?

No, *this* lane will be safe,
the footprints of Kṛṣṇa and the melted
eye tears of the *gopīs*.

Come down this dream lane
with me where Chaplin dances with
nymphs (dressed), led by Edna Purviance, and
that we know is a dream.

Come down this dream of your own
life as it is. I know you won't
get out of it. "What is this
thing called love?" you sang from the
shower. A Cole Porter tune to
begin our set. Next set.
Can we get through the day?
Yes, with a well-wisher. We have
supporters.

Down the last to death of cares and
he may not be as strong
as we've been told. You've got to
be ready. The others who have already
passed and taken up new places in
new bodies. You've already been awkward.
What?
This new suit? New name?
New chores?
New hierarchy?
New study and umpires?
Not everyone
is perfect. Please, Lord, let me work
for Your cause in the best way
to make the next life a better place
and see so many people working here
with compassion. Why not
me? Roses!

Chapter Twenty-Four

Everyone tends to take their local pain as the foremost news. If we had a true sanatorium newspaper and you interviewed the inmates, the first concern would be the ailing body, my cancer, my broken ribs, my pulmonary operation, or shall I not take it? How shall I decide to go through life, blind or semiblind—what decisions do I have anyway? But they say if you want to go without an operation, you've got a 50 percent chance. You have to die anyway. But no one is allowed to smoke cigarettes here. It's a free country. You can read the newspapers and vote in the election, but the inmates don't tend to care much.

Raise the reward for killing Saddam Hussein to $25 million. You scramble to throw the newspaper away and chant at least twelve rounds. Argument: Anything you might write in *Sanatorium* on a day in which you chanted under sixteen is bogus. And it should be listed: "This was done by a subpar person." Just as you might put up a sign: "This store is being operated by an ex–child abuser." Or, "This car lot is owned by a man who was convicted of robbery." Yeah, but there's a difference here. On this day I painted two Kṛṣṇa conscious canvases and wrote two poems, and so far I've chanted seven rounds. I'm ending twenty years of migraine and beginning to do things that give me quality of life. I mean I need to love the holy name. But I've done so many things out of force. It's a narrow line, and I barely dare to confess because of those who are likely to condemn me. But being subpar is like walking with a cane and taking oxycodone and taking naps that last two hours and that you wake from with a very deep, conscious feeling—all parts of recovery, healing. Medicinal crutch. I damn *you* who condemn me and look down on my pain or the orthopads in my shoes or the meds I take. I damn you for stigmatizing me or anyone in the sanatorium for doing anything below the religious standard if our doctor says, "You're not strong enough to do that, take the medicine you need." Go slowly. You are doing very well. They don't expect you to recover in two weeks and spring out of here by some miracle. They don't damn you for being subpar in some aspect of your *sādhana*. You talk that over with utter trust and openness with your counselor, and with your interest at heart he'll tell you what to strive for.

Bhakta Junior read to the devotees, who sat around honoring *prasādam* in the writing staff's room.

> Thus the happiness found in devotional service is much greater than the liberation born of *samādhi*. And by the mercy and sweetness of the Lord, so affectionate to His devotees, that devotional happiness expands.
>
> Commentary: The Personality of Godhead is always enjoying His infinitely invaried pastimes, and He likes to share His enjoyment as much as possible. Because the Lord is very kind and so exceedingly attractive, His devotees feel transcendental ecstasy, as the spiritual potency of the soul is unlimited. Although he's *sat-cit-ānanda* (eternal, conscious, and blissful), simply to realize those qualities provides merely a static, monotonous kind of spiritual existence. But when the soul goes beyond mere self-realization to realize his relationship with the all-compassionate Lord, the divine energies bestow upon him incomparable happiness.
>
> —*Bṛhad-bhāgavatāmṛta*, *Jñāna*, Text 216

> The original pure existence is eternally all per–vading, yet that all-pervading existence does not break off even a small piece of one leaf of the tree of material illusion. But if Your name, oh almighty Lord, is seized by one's tongue for even a moment, the tree of material life is destroyed down to its roots. So which deserves our attention—Your all-pervading existence or Your holy name?
>
> —*Bṛhad-bhāgavatāmṛta*, Vol. 2, p. 424

Several devotees uttered, "Wow!" Swami Swims was silent but thought, There it is again, the undeniable glorification of the holy name as the topmost practice of life.

What did he keep in that notebook? What did she write in
those letters home? "I hate this
place." No, not much of that.

More like, "I'm hanging in
there." St. Christopher medal
around jockey Santos at the Belmont
Stakes. At least he didn't
break his leg.

Pray to God for your local good
luck. I take it back—I
don't condemn
anyone
if they think I'm a gimp.
I'm a sinner. I, a Charlie Chaplin.
I'm a thin blade–shouldered
Brooklyn College literateur,
squeezed out those A's
because I knew how to
write a professor-pleasing essay.

Get back a C from geology.
Could he have given me a B?
And B for Shakespeare,
Richard II, what
an insult.

Don't hang out at the
afternoon cafeteria goggling
at the girls or making dates,
head straight for
the two-hour trip to Great Kills,
home and dinner and homework,
a little family TV,
and go to bed.

A little jazz. What did they
write in their notebooks?
Memories like this or
fervent prayers to meet
the Supreme Lord in
His abode? I'd like to take her
but you can't take
a chick on your arm.
Don't look good. Leads
to thoughts of embracing
afterwards.

Just go for the listening,
for the artist and
sublimate me in your
own art up to the
highest, we're going
to Kṛṣṇaloka with
Joe Henderson and Lee
Morgan, no (shot dead by
his mistress)—you really believe you

can learn from them? Believe their
holiness in sinful life?
Bring that up later.
I've got to feel it deeper.

It's a long weekend. You've got no money to print the books. Lining up the manuscripts, edited and all, but you've got no money to print, which I think means you've got no customers flocking to buy a $10 book. "You've got a 4- or 5-hour window at the New York Rathā-yātrā to sell books, and it's intense. No time for chatting. They'll buy anything. A colorful cover of *Every Day, Just Write*, the Govinda Gallery catalog, $10. 'I'll take one.'" Keep selling until the boxes are empty. "You should have brought more." Sold $2,000 worth. He was spaced out. The other man was talking one hour with a woman who had hardly anything on, and another hour with a bearded gent, all within a 4-hour window shrinking to 3, 2, 1, books almost out.

Śacī and family returned from Lake George. Stubble beard, light tans, kids had fun swimming in the water, water chutes, mom and dad tired from carrying them around. Lakṣmaṇa learned to crawl.

We don't have much to report here. A heating alarm went off, so we turned it off. Don't have money to print books. Some of our messages got mixed. No e-mail came in because no one here to receive it. Swims wears his khaki safari shorts when there are no swamis around. Something big and sudden doesn't have to change. The doctor wants me to exercise tomorrow. I often prefer to rest. But talk with inmates. How is Sandy doing? Is she getting ready to fly in the airplane? How did I wind up here? Tell them how it began.

Once I dropped acid in a sugar cube. After hanging around for a long time with dumb immoralists Elliot and

Maria. (Was that her name?) World War II refugee from Italy. I was alone in a St. George, Staten Island, apartment. Reading the Mentor edition of the *Īśopaniṣad* about the nonreality of the apparent reality. Felt the spin of my life with Elliot doomed. I should do the brave thing and jump out a four-story window while wearing only Jockey shorts. Jump into Stygian hell. Besides, there is no difference between matter and nonmatter, it's like poking your finger through a nonexistent wall. How could it get hurt? (*Īśopaniṣad* wisdom.) A voice deep in my sternum uttered, "Do it," and I jumped.

I smashed into the cement and broke both my heels. So much for nonmatter. Tremendous pain. I felt as if I was a cave man trying to walk thousands of years ago. I shouldn't have been walking, probably, should have just lain there. But who would come and help me? I walked around to the front and finally saw someone and asked them to help me. Told him I fell from the window. I remember I was in an ambulance, and then in a room where they were asking me questions. I seem to remember somebody saying, "Pretty bones," and then being asked my religion. I said, "Tao." Name of father and mother, address. And then I passed out. The next thing I knew it was morning. My imagination was working. Just before they took me into the ambulance I thought that all the people were leaving the earth in spaceships and I was being left behind. But now I was in a hospital, and nurses moved about in white nurse clothes. I was aware that I had taken LSD and didn't want to be caught in an illegal act.

Then nurses and a doctor came, and I told them that I was standing near the window and I lost my balance. That was published on the first page of the newspaper. Then came a doctor looking very worried. I think he looked worried because he thought he was looking at a crazy young man. He was more afraid of the craziness than the physical damage. They started wrapping me up in casts. He explained what had happened and said something to the effect that to walk I would have to go up and down like a tractor without side movement. Did he say that I would have to do that, or that there was an alternative? Now, forty years later, I'm not walking like a tractor, but I have side movement.

A few hours later my parents came in looking very worried. They had a look of worry for a crazy son. My father had already cleared everything out of my apartment, including the writing that I did each night when I came home from work. He said, "You really like this guy?" He meant my supervisor Yaśomatī, who was a very likable combination of a Japanese and Negro. He very much encouraged all the workers. Obviously my father, who was a racist, didn't like the combination of a Jap and a black man. I just said that he was a good worker and that this was my writing. My father said that they would close the apartment and that I could live at home with them for six weeks while my heels got well.

My dad scavenged through my apartment to see what he could find. Luckily there was no marijuana there. But he found an envelope to subscribe to a sex magazine. I was terribly embarrassed by that. One day he came up to give me a daily rubdown with witch hazel, which he did to relieve the sores on my back. He mentioned the subscription to the magazine. I was surprised that he didn't reprimand me. Rather, in a roundabout way, he talked about how he was frustrated in his relationship with my mother, because of the strict code of the Catholic Church. He never liked the priests. He always thought all they were interested in was money, and then on the other side, they controlled a man's sex life with his wife. Every year, as a naval officer, my father would go on the annual cruise. They would go for two weeks and stop for a weekend in some exotic port, often in the Caribbean, like Trinidad or Santo Domingo. During the weekend on shore, it was understood that the officers as well as the sailors would get plenty of opportunity to have sex with prostitutes and get as drunk as they pleased. And the officers' brand of sex would be a little more high class, in a hotel with better-looking prostitutes at a higher price.

When my father returned from a cruise, you could always tell that he had had "a good time." He had that look of the cat that swallowed the canary. My mother didn't have to ask anything, nor did she, but it was dad's annual release from the law that you couldn't have sex except for having children. Of course, even Catholics are allowed to have sex under certain loopholes, but I believe my mother was particularly rigid about it. Or one could say frigid about it. I never knew any of these things because they were never discussed with me, but at moments like this, sitting on the bed with my father, he revealed just a little—little loopholes of what he was going through and what he was thinking and what his sex life, or lack of sex life, was. He was very much a he-man type of person, very strong. He worked in a firehouse, where almost every other word was "fuck you" and where every fireman had a locker with a big pinup of a naked woman. And yet he didn't have sexual intercourse regularly with his own wife, nor was he the type to go out, as far as I knew, and pick up whores in bars or brothels. He had too much of a sense of honor to his wife and was kind of under her spell of chastity.

One day, father came up with the witch hazel rub, but in a different, stern mood. He said that they were building a new home in Avalon, a vacation home, and that I would have to pay for part of it. I couldn't just go along for the free ride. I was taken aback but agreed that I would give a percentage of my earnings as he decided. I was kind of shocked, though, at how tough he was, and so accusative toward me as a freeloader. After all, I didn't have to live with him at all. Neither did I have plans of living with them after I recovered from my heel injuries.

Another day he came up and after giving me my massage he tossed a copy of *Playboy* magazine on the bed before he left. What was the meaning of that? I was in the mood to abstain from that sort of thing. I had been reading the Bible and Eastern spiritual literature. And although I had intended to subscribe to that magazine in a kind of contradictory way, I was on the other side now, trying to abstain from looking at lewd pictures or masturbating. But he fed me the bait. I let the magazine go unopened for about a week, and then bit by bit starting looking at various pages until I swallowed the whole thing in a climax.

Dad also made me a desk with wheels, so that I could wheel it into the other room and use it to write on. The other room used to be my sister's bedroom but she was married now and gone. I began to write a journal, which I called "Loose Notes," telling about the adventures I had gone through after jumping out the window. I was doing it in an avant-garde style, and later showed it to Allen Ginsberg and Peter Orlovsky. My friend Murry Mednick went along and showed them some of his writings. Allen wrote a foreword for it but we never raised the money to publish it.

I used to sometimes listen to baseball games at night. One thing my father and I shared was that the great Los Angeles Dodgers baseball pitching star Sandy Koufax regularly lost when he came to New York City and played the New York Mets, who were perpetual losers. We really liked the idea that Sandy couldn't beat the Mets.

One time my father carried me piggyback, taking me downstairs for some reason. At that time, in an offhand way, I mentioned to him what I really would have liked to have been in life. I said I really would have liked to have been a college professor.

He said, "Oh, that's the end of the line." He seemed to think that that was the worst kind of job, like a garbage collector, whereas to me, it was the really desirable vocation. It just showed what a gap there was between us.

Is Swims telling all these things to Śacī and family, who have just returned? No, he's just talking to his mind. For the family, he's just glad to see them in their wonderful pink skins and happy stories. He's glad none of them were hurt or drowned or anything like that. He's glad that they're back around the house. But he's also looking forward to convalescing to a point where he can evolve into new life.

You believe me, maybe I'm
making up lies, starting another
project. Got to wear my
sannyāsa clothes starting soon
because Bhūrijana's coming.

May stay for a week. I'll
talk with him. We both
bow our heads down and
begin talking humbly.
"Very nice." But he's very analytical
and I'm very Sonny Rollins, softly as
in a summer sunrise.

Can't wake at the same time.
Only a trio? Yeah, that's enough
to carry a house if the people
are respectful.

Softly as in a summer
sunrise. Take her carefully to the
airport in a special
paraplegic vehicle, unload
her. But how up the airline's
steps? They know.

Carry her. Bring chair up
first. She's Olympic strong and
limber. Then set her down
again. Short turn to the bulkhead.
Then carry her to her seat.

There will be an urge to pee.
Almost sure. Get up and do it
as you have practiced. This girl
is so well-trained and cool
she'll do it without
even sweating her brow.
She'll be thinking of
Kṛṣṇa
and praying to Him in His personal
form and writing her man along
the way.

Softly, please lord, softly.

Tim had cancer. So the night finally came and he was transferred to the hospital. The disease had quickly come out of remission and had gotten worse. He was a wonderful person, friendly to everyone.

There was always the question, which is especially discussed among the Hare Kṛṣṇa devotees, of whether to take morphine at the end. For most people, it's not a question; the hospital simply does it. Some devotees have what they feel is a martyr complex, or, to put it in honorable terms, they feel that they're suffering because of sins they committed and that they should not take medicine. They feel they will get a better place next life if they simply suffer whatever Kṛṣṇa has given them. Others argue that the state of pain they are put into may cause such lack of clarity that they won't be able to chant the Lord's names or associate with devotees properly at the end. If they had been willing to take some morphine, they would stay clear.

There are good examples to support both views. In Boston's Public Garden, there is a statue depicting the invention of anesthesia. It shows an idealized group of angels surrounding a suffering person. It moves you when you see it, and you do think that it is the power of angels that can remove pain. So why not do it? The counterargument is that it's a greater angel who refuses that help and who simply depends, drop by drop, on the power of the holy name. For myself, I have already shown my tendency to use a drug. For ten years I did not take any medicine and suffered excruciating pain in the head. It did no good for me. I accepted religiously the general writings of the natural path, in which all medical treatment is damned as if from the devil. The body has enough strength to take care of itself. That statement is denied by the *Vedas;* in the Āyur-veda many medicines are described. So our own traditions do not accept the idea that the body can take care of itself without certain medicines. I do believe that there are many natural things, like exercise and good behavior and good thinking and good psychology and being free of anxiety, that will keep you from getting disease. But I also believe that pain is harmful over the long run. I have read that there is a consensus both among the medical section and the psychiatric section that the side effects of medicines are less harmful than the side effects of pain. I have suffered for over twenty years (or is it now twenty-five?) from the side effects of pain. Now I work with a doctor and counselor who say to put your foot down and don't suffer from pain. It is not good for you. It will harm you too much in the end. Also, pain steals my quality of life. I cannot do anything, like chant all the rounds I want to chant, or write and paint. And I'm very unhappy to simply lie down in a dark room feeling excruciating pain behind the right eye all day. I won't have my life stolen away like that anymore.

I've learned a lot about rebound headache and how to stay away from the harmful medicines that cause it. I work with doctors who are also aware of rebound medicine, and I have available now medicines that keep me away from that. I'm also aware that the medicines I'm taking will eventually have to be withdrawn. But I hope to do that in time, over a long period, as I gain strength from a pain-free body.

As for dying, why not die with some clarity? The same thing may be said for not taking drugs—if morphine covers you over completely so that you have no clear consciousness, that's not good either. But if you can have some kind of clarity, so you can think of Kṛṣṇa and be read to and understand, then that is not hurting you. That is helping you on your way to the last moments. It's an individual choice, and one isn't necessarily better than the other. It also depends on individual natures and thresholds of pain. The person who takes some medicine shouldn't be condemned, and neither should the person who goes through it all the way without a drop of medication.

Tim decided to get some medical reinforcement as he went through his last steps. He certainly got much reinforcement from the Vaiṣṇavas, who gathered around him whenever they could, took shifts, and talked with him about Kṛṣṇa and the next life, so that his consciousness would be raised and not depressed or fearful. No regrets, you're serving in Prabhupāda's care. Just try to think of him and your desire to serve him forever.

Mail in until the end,
mail out until the beginning.
Don't lose the beat, conga is
allowed but no smoking.

Sprinkle a lawn, play all
day. Give me a typist.
Subpersons have a right to speak.
They have a tough letter to write
because they received one.
It comes tough from the heart
so I should write one from the heart.

For that I need a typist who
is close to me, doesn't
mind what I say as long as I
mean it.

I don't mean to hurt one.
I mean to preach
Kṛṣṇa consciousness
and to apologize
for my misbehavior.

You don't write to me and I don't
write to you. I'm sick in
the head and you don't get around
much anymore either,
my friend.
Hey boy, when is the
last time you saw Rādhārāṇī?
"You mean in person? In direct
particulars?" A Vraja urchin asked me
after we bathed in Prema-sarovara. I said
we saw Rādhā *and* Kṛṣṇa
this morning in the ISKCON
temple. Is that good enough?

"Oh, I see Her everywhere."
Well good for you. And then
he disappeared barefoot after
begging ten rupees.

When's the last time you wrote a
tough letter? Your writings of
the 90s don't turn her on.
Your painting doesn't turn her on.
She's a Taoist now 70 percent.
Well I is 70 percent Kṛṣṇa conscious
and 30 percent failure. But I'm
not going with the old
Chinese masters.
No, Prabhupāda! Even 10 percent
Śrīla Prabhupāda and 0 none else.

Chapter Twenty-Five

There was a rather solemn gathering around Tim's bed in the hospital. He was holding his own, but his father and mother, two younger brothers, and an older sister had come to see him. They also brought their lawyer with them. The Hare Kṛṣṇa lawyer was present too. They intended to discuss Tim's will and Tim's father's will. There were some legal technicalities regarding a life insurance policy that the lawyers wanted to talk about. Tim's lawyer—a friend named Rasa—told him to be as little a part of this as possible, and coached him how to do that.

Tim said, "I'm now twenty-one years old. I've already made up my own will, and it's been notorized. Therefore there's nothing to discuss about that. I'm also in a painful position and don't want to discuss legal matters. But if dad's lawyer and my lawyer want to discuss issues about life insurance policies and changing my will, I request that that be done separately, just between the two lawyers. I don't want to be present for it. My lawyer can come back to me and discuss what I need to know. So you lawyers can just go and discuss this. I just want to spend a little time with my family members now. Every morning at 8:00 we have a reading from *Kṛṣṇa* book here in the hospital, and we sing, and we give out breakfast. If you'd like to come, you'll get a little more of an idea of how we live here. It's a shame you never came to visit me before. I really wasn't in much shape to come home, but perhaps I should have tried more. Seeing you together really moves me, and I remember all the sweet times we used to have together." Tim ruffled the heads of his brother and sister and stood up to kiss his mother and shake his father's hand. He then indicated that he was tired, and he lay back in his bed. The meeting was over. Led by the lawyers, the little group exited from the bedside.

Oh oh, it's hot up northland and the children are playing in the sprinklers in the greeny backyards. Keli says to me, "I bet you're not glad we returned, with all our yelling." But I don't mind. I get a typist back, and a friend. But there'll be more visitors coming. And the reality of our moving seems to be gathering, too. It has cast a cloud over the sanatorium—that and thinking that Tim likely will die, even though he may linger on for weeks. He dealt so coolly with his relatives. He knew they had no love for him as a Hare Kṛṣṇa.

Swami Swims used to try to phone his mother again and again over a ten-year period, and she would say, "Where have you been?" He'd say, "Oh, I've been traveling around with the Hare Kṛṣṇa people. I'm now in Arizona," and she would say, "As long as you're with those people, we don't want to have anything to do with you."

Other devotees had much more success with their families, although they would sometimes say it was a questionable success. Their families were always around—grandmas and grandpas playing with their children—and they would get quite involved in family life. The devotees who were cast off and disowned have no family except the family of devotees, and so they address themselves to their nondevotee families by trying to give them Kṛṣṇa consciousness, as preachers do. Tim knew that he was in that category. He knew his father's and mother's hearts were like ice, and they were just always afraid that somehow they might lose some money by some trick of the Hare Kṛṣṇa movement, after every penny they could get. They would be very sure in their dealings with Tim's lawyer that he was cut out completely from anything that he might have coming to him as a normal son. Nada. Not a penny. The Hare Kṛṣṇa movement could burn his body when he was dead, but he couldn't even set foot back in his old house to see if there were some photos or roller skates or old jackets that he might want to take. "Don't you dare or you might find a shotgun aimed at your butt." After all, dad was a state trooper. He knew them Hare Kṛṣṇas and their tricks.

But none of that was true. His parents lived in a world of ignorance about Hare Kṛṣṇa. They listened to the anticult propaganda, the right-wingers, those who muckraked about the mistakes that the Hare Kṛṣṇa movement actually made and which were published in newspapers. They never sat down to hear the other side. Too bad Tim couldn't have taken his brothers and sister aside. Maybe he could, or maybe one of the devotees here could. But the parents would be very wary of that and would not let them stray.

"Don't talk to them people."

The sun is going down mourning
grace. We've got eternal souls
so the body gets worse. Hope he
goes without too much pain.

The wonderful, natural seaside
shoals, deep valleys, high
peaks. Give me a place where I can
be alone to come out with
something fresh and new.
I've been doing

that for several months,
since I've been here.

For her? Does it help her? It's
supposed to. But if it fails, that's not
my failure. Any painter does his
best. They may take it or leave it—
"the bastards."

Go on your way. You have no choice.
Don't copy your own way or their way,
do what comes. They say, "But it doesn't
move me." I say it moves me.

You don't like it. But I like
to do it. It has meaning
to me. It's a song of mourning for Tim—
hit the drum. Walk alone,
say some prayers. You'll get
better. I think you are
already getting better. Goodbye tough girl,
I'm in the new writings.
Come look us up.

What happens after you die? On one of his morning walks in Los Angeles, Prabhupāda saw a huge billboard: "Is There Sex After Death?" In his lecture that morning, he said that this was their only concern. If there's sex after death, then they don't mind dying. There are descriptions of many places you can go to and what life is like there. I remember at the very beginning at 26 Second Ave., Rāya Rāma persisted on keeping his beard and wearing pants and shirt. Prabhupāda was very lenient and didn't push him. But some of the initiated devotees used to really bug Rāya Rāma and tell him that he ought to wear his *dhotī* all the time. Rāya Rāma was persistent and said, "I'm sure there's a planet where they wear pants."

A devotee joked back, "Yeah, there's a planet where they wear pants. This planet right here. The miserable material planet."

But I wasn't attracted by higher planets just because the people there wore beads and *dhotīs* and crowns. Planets of "opulence," planets where you could fly. The real thing was the planet where you could play with Kṛṣṇa and live in eternity, knowledge and bliss. And that was very, very rare to attain. You could attain it by chanting Hare Kṛṣṇa, but you had to get rid of all your *anarthas*. It was made easy in this age by following Lord Caitanya and preaching and chanting. But even that easy path was hard for us because we had so many bad habits. And it's still like that.

So what will happen after death? Prabhupāda used to say that in India, in the medical college system, if a student went for four years but failed the final examination, he could not become an M.D., but the government would give him some kind of a license whereby he could practice medicine. So he said practicing devotional service but not becoming a pure devotee would be something like that. You would be given credit for your devotional service but not attain the highest perfection.

Would we come back to this material world and work as a devotee? At least a human being? Would we get to see Prabhupāda? You have to really strive. Talk about it, speculate about it.

Sometimes you don't even want to talk about it. So many books by scholars, so many lectures. So many temptations to do the wrong things. Writing all your own books. Swami Swims mulled about his own headaches, but being in a sanatorium was good for you because it made you see the sufferings of others.

He couldn't help but be grateful seeing Sandy, and he hoped the best for her. They were hoping they could get some money if Tim had to pass away. Tim said he wanted to get money and give it to Sandy for her traveling to Australia and setting up a new home there. But maybe the lawyers wouldn't allow it. Sandy thanked Tim for the offer but said Kṛṣṇa would take care of them one way or another. It's easy to live when all you do is depend on Kṛṣṇa. Somebody comes along and helps you. In the sanatorium you can take your mind off self-pity and write poems while listening to expert musicians and be introverted in a good way. Being quiet, not pressuring people and not letting them pressure you.

All the things You are to me—water—air—
sunshine. Tell him I think I'm going to
stay here a little longer, start
another project

another protest.
I'm sorry I was so blue and
obnoxious from the grave,
spitting at you.
It doesn't matter anymore.
I just want to say

I like the books. They need time to read.
You say there's nothing in them anymore,
no spark, no illuminations?
It's really fizzed out? Well look at
the new stuff. And look at the

karate-girl typist kicking ass
and the lad Junior, who wants
to publish his essays.
His confrontation has merit.
I could answer back

all I know is radishes and
dental appointments and people
supporting me with donations and
the pills seem to be working
without Klonopin for weeks
now. Thought you might
like to know.
All the things you are.

They cheered and gave a choice
to the shaman to nap and *japa*
in that order
but I don't think I can write
poems on a theme.

Boy, we were smacking the tennis ball back and forth without a net. The modern way. She says my paintings don't relate to her. I said that's subjective. Others like it. Slamming the tennis ball back-and-forth to get out of our grief for Tim. Put up the net again, that's right.

Let's go in and be with him. Gather around his bed. Turn on the fan. "What book would you like read to you?"

"There's been a lot of reading today. I'd like to just talk."

"Tell us how you came to Kṛṣṇa consciousness, Tim," said Swims.

"I was part of a youth scene of graffiti artists and straightedge music groups in Baltimore. My graffiti name was Stain. There was a relationship with these folks and some of the Hare Kṛṣṇas. Hare Kṛṣṇas had straightedge bands, too. Sometimes we'd see them with some Hare Kṛṣṇa tattoos, and they invited us to their Rathā-yātrās. They invited one of our groups to perform. Many of our groups already were committed to not eating meat or smoking, so there was some kind of alliance there. One of their old swamis said that they thought we had been born as Hare Kṛṣṇa people in our past lives but had not perfected it."

"Far out!"

"So we had come back this life to become pure devotees. When my father heard this going on, he got extremely angry. I was only sixteen years old. He forbade me from going to the temple. He showed me books and magazines telling of how the Hare Kṛṣṇas were criminals. So anything I did I had to do sneaking. I would chant on small beads in my coat pocket or under blankets at night. I would read the *Bhagavad-gītā* under my blankets with a flashlight. Once when he caught me doing one of those things he beat me with a black belt. He caught me again and beat me even worse. Devotees had a psychologist who was sympathetic with Kṛṣṇa consciousness meet with him, and that cooled him down somewhat. After all, my dad as a high-placed official, so he couldn't go around too much like a Nazi. But I had to tone it down too. I promised not to live in the temple or get tattoos. I would just chant beads softly in the house and not go on *harināma* in the street.

"After talking to the professor, my father gave me the benefit of the doubt and didn't force me to eat meat. In other words, he became a little educated about the Vedic ways. Some of the girls in my sisters' high school were kind to Hare Kṛṣṇas. My sisters became friends with them, and those girls used to come over to our house. That increased the thaw."

Swims stood in the corner. Tim was so young, telling about his early days, but he was probably going to leave soon, too, without much chance to see holy places in India or grow mature. It didn't seem to bother him. He seemed even-minded and enthusiastic. He had plenty of *utsāha*. More than Swims himself. He hadn't deteriorated. He was running on his original charge given him by Kṛṣṇa and the spiritual master—the happiness of beliefs in Prabhupāda, the joy in learning the *Bhagavad-gītā*, faith in *Bhagavad-gītā* and chanting Hare Kṛṣṇa. The excitement of rebellion from the normal way.

Swims began to feel sleepy, probably from his meds, and he wandered out of the stuffy room and went back to the sanatorium and his bed.

"Are you tired?" asked Jane.

"Yes," said Swims, "and feeling grief and wondering when this will end for Tim."

"I think Tim's spirits are more upbeat than that."

"Yes, you're right," said Swims. "I'm just tired. I like Tim very much, but I failed him. I failed Prabhupāda."

"No, you haven't," Jane said. "Prabhupāda loves you very much. All of us love you very much."

Swami Swims began to cry.

She's singing songs to the great
Musician. I don't need any
of this, not even children
playing on the lawn in
the sprinkler.

I don't need an agent to
change my book to sell
it, he'll mess it up.
We'll keep it as it was
and sell 2,000.
You get a man like NK
and he can do that.
I ain't changing, honey, neither
me nor did Cecil Taylor
or Monk or the other

unchangeables who preferred to
starve. Charlie to Phil Woods:
"Did you eat today?"

Keep that book the way it
is. You can't understand it if
it's changed, the sensitivity and chance
is taken out of it.

Did you hear the rumor
that the well-wisher wants to sell
my manuscript to
a top New York City literary agent
and I said "f___ you"?
"Why, don't you want
money?" "Money is fine
but you don't sell your soul."
Keep the book pure
the best you can. It's already not very
authentic. Don't make
it worse. Don't make it worse.

Oh Lord, You have me by the tail. If
You want a sacred book let me know
and I'll run after You with one
lickety split.

Swims massaged Tim all night. He told him how Kṛṣṇa is kind. Wherever he would go in the next life, it would be a wonderful place. Prabhupāda would be there at the end to say Hare Kṛṣṇa. If it gets too painful and you can't even say the words, then think of them. Think of Prabhupāda. Just ask for mercy. Accept whatever is given.

"Thank you, thank you," Tim said.

"You are a perfectly submissive soul, Tim," said Swami Swims. He felt melted in the submissiveness of Tim and kept massaging as best as he could.

"Are you feeling much pain?"

"No," said Tim. "When you talk about Kṛṣṇa, I don't feel any pain. This material world is pain, and I'm finally leaving it. I wish I could have done more here, been a healthy devotee and gone around to tell people more about Kṛṣṇa. Maybe I'll come back and do more of that. Whatever Kṛṣṇa wants me to do, I must be ready. Hare Kṛṣṇa, Hare Kṛṣṇa, Kṛṣṇa Kṛṣṇa, Hare Hare/ Hare Rāma, Hare Rāma, Rāma Rāma, Hare Hare." Their mantras blended together with the massaging.

Swami Swims remembered the witch hazel that his father used to massage on his back when he was in his casts, and he now rubbed it on Tim's back and legs. "That will make you feel cooler. No way out of this material body, but no harm giving it a little relief."

Hare Kṛṣṇa, Hare Kṛṣṇa, Kṛṣṇa Kṛṣṇa, Hare Hare/ Hare Rāma, Hare Rāma, Rāma Rāma, Hare Hare. Hare Kṛṣṇa, Hare Kṛṣṇa, Kṛṣṇa Kṛṣṇa, Hare Hare/ Hare Rāma, Hare Rāma, Rāma Rāma, Hare Hare.

Junior Barks came up behind Swami Swims, who was now only wearing a *gamchā*, and Junior began massaging Swami Swims with the witch hazel. He too started chanting.

Hare Kṛṣṇa, Hare Kṛṣṇa, Kṛṣṇa Kṛṣṇa, Hare Hare/ Hare Rāma, Hare Rāma, Rāma Rāma, Hare Hare. Hare Kṛṣṇa, Hare Kṛṣṇa, Kṛṣṇa Kṛṣṇa, Hare Hare/ Hare Rāma, Hare Rāma, Rāma Rāma, Hare Hare.

Swims appreciated it because his own back was becoming very sore.

Hare Kṛṣṇa, Hare Kṛṣṇa, Kṛṣṇa Kṛṣṇa, Hare Hare/ Hare Rāma, Hare Rāma, Rāma Rāma, Hare Hare. Hare Kṛṣṇa, Hare Kṛṣṇa, Kṛṣṇa Kṛṣṇa, Hare Hare/ Hare Rāma, Hare Rāma, Rāma Rāma, Hare Hare.

The pain relief went through three layers of men as they prayed to the Lord. There was a picture of Gaura-Nitāi above the bed, and a picture of Prabhupāda to the right, and a picture of Rādhā and Kṛṣṇa to the left. They each glanced when they could and took in the mercy.

Hare Kṛṣṇa, Hare Kṛṣṇa, Kṛṣṇa Kṛṣṇa, Hare Hare/ Hare Rāma, Hare Rāma, Rāma Rāma, Hare Hare.

"This may be the last time that we're together in this material world. But then we'll meet again somehow or other in the spiritual world. You never know how God arranges these things. So many souls, but when they're likeminded, he brings them together again. Like with us. We're Prabhupādanugas and we love each other. We love to serve him. So he can bring us together again in that exquisite service."

"Oh Prabhupāda," said Tim, "why couldn't I serve you better? Why couldn't I taste the nectar of your books? Why couldn't I follow your instructions and inspire the devotees? These two *prabhus* are so loyal to you, and loyal to me. Why couldn't I give them more inspiration, so they could serve you without fear?"

Hare Kṛṣṇa, Hare Kṛṣṇa, Kṛṣṇa Kṛṣṇa, Hare Hare/ Hare Rāma, Hare Rāma, Rāma Rāma, Hare Hare.

The time didn't seem to pass very long, but eventually it was 5:00 A.M. and a nurse came in. She asked the men to leave. She wanted to check on some particulars about Bhakta Tim and how he was progressing or decreasing.

Swims Swami and Junior went outside, where the sun was starting to rise. They walked and continued to chant.

Tim and a few suburban neighbors his age had been graffiti artists since their early teens. He told how he and his friends "saw" a man in the wall under a bridge. He was mostly made of cracks in the cement and he had considerable detail. "Do you see him?" "Yeah! Do you?" "Let's paint him." Their prime tool was a tube used to give a new coat of color to worn-out sneakers. They would buy the tube, pour out the contents, and fill it with India ink. They also used a fluorescent gray ink. This "man" they found in the stone was about ten feet tall, so they got on each others' shoulders and painted in the vision. The next day they all caught the flu. At least they hadn't been caught by the police. Graffiti is illegal, and police often give a hard stick-beating to graffiti artists, plus fines or jail. Nevertheless, the subways in Philadelphia and New York are virtually covered on the outside with fat initials, designs, and incomprehensible words and forms.

Tim didn't come to Kṛṣṇa consciousness directly through graffiti. It was more the straightedge music. But some of the straightedge musicians and fans shared a liking for graffiti, and *all* wore tattoos, so there was a kind of camaraderie. None of them painted Hare Kṛṣṇa words as graffiti because it would attract the police to them. But almost all the graffiti tattoos had some direct Hare Kṛṣṇa word or allusion. One man had a huge "*Ahaṁ Brahmāsmi*" across his abdomen. He said in between the tattooing of each letter he had to lie down and take a rest, it was so painful. Many of them had the Sanskrit to the Hare Kṛṣṇa mantra around their wrists. Tim was one of those.

"So it looks like Giovanni knew a thing or two after all," said Swami Swims with a sad, loving smile.

"Yes," Tim said, returning the Swami's smile.

"What's important is how Kṛṣṇa conscious you are," said Sandy. "It's not how long you live or how healthy you are or how rich you are."

"Ah, it's how fortunate you are to have such friends in your last hours," replied Tim. "I was raised a Catholic, and we prayed, 'Holy Mary, Mother of God, pray for us now and at the hour of our death.' There's a prayer that ends that way in the *Īśopaniṣad*, too."

"Tim, why don't you have a spiritual name?" asked Swami Swims.

"I don't know. Is 'Swims' a spiritual name?"

"That's the name you guys tease me with. My initiated name is Śyāma Swami."

"Yes, I'd like one. Can you give me one?"

"Are you following the four rules and are you dedicated to Kṛṣṇa?"

"Yes," answered Tim.

"So your name is Trikāla-jña dāsa."

"What does it mean?"

"One who can see the past, present, and future," said Swims.

"I almost feel I can see that now," said Trikāla-jña dāsa. They began another soft *kīrtana*.

He's going and we are sad.
The hope we had for happiness
is never bright and sweet tonight.
These crowds and children ...

Tim never grew up to make some
Big Contribution.
Even his intimate leader didn't
initiate him until at his death.
Dear to a small number who
knew he's a special person,
known even to Prabhupāda
who passed away even before Tim was born—
that doesn't matter in spiritual connections.

You can now go to your father
and he can embrace you as
you pass away. He kindly says
Dear Trikāla-jña dāsa,
you must serve in
all directions, keep growing
in all dimensions.

You have a lot more to do and
I will give you strength
to do it. Come now, accept
birth in a fine Vaiṣṇava
family who are eager
to conceive you in
pure nonlust. Saintly eagerness
for a boy to learn the holy names
from the beginning and get a
jump start from Lord Caitanya.

Chapter Twenty-Six

The crematorium service at the hospital prepared the urn of ashes, which a reliable devotee was to carry to India to place into the Yamunā. Different devotees spoke about Trikāla-jña's devotional service. When it was over and the devotees started back to their beds at the sanatorium, many of them began to feel their physical ailments. It had been hot in the crematorium hall. Someone stopped Swami Swims and reminded him that he had to speak to a couple of guests. These guests were disciples of his who had come to visit him. He had forgotten about the appointment. It was a man and his wife and their seven-month-old child. The man had written many letters to the Swami saying he was having difficulty in his marriage. They sat down, and the first thing the Swami could think of was to recommend that they get family counseling from a trained psychologist who was himself a Hare Kṛṣṇa person. Swims said it was an archaic idea to think that devotees couldn't receive counseling from trained persons. The husband said they had thought about doing that, but there were practical obstacles, such as not being able to find a person in their area and the lack of confidentiality. Swami Swims then confessed that he had a counselor. He said it can be done by phone. He then realized it might be too expensive for them. They said that they could be more open with one another. The basic difficulty was that the man wanted affection and intimacy, and the wife was more standoffish. But they had to find a way to come closer together. The wife spoke optimistically, saying that the coming of the new child into their lives had improved her life very much and made it happier.

Their visit was a diversion from Swami's grief. That's the way life is, one diversion after another. He couldn't concentrate. He had shown his guests his painting room, showed them his latest painting, "Hare Kṛṣṇa Aborigines," and explained how at first it just looked like a sexy picture, but then he had thought of the aborigines from the Kṛṣṇa book. Then he showed them his rather wimpy-looking picture of Rādhā and Govinda. He was going to show them the workout gym, but there were workers in there drilling and hammering. Distractions. Their baby, Mukunda, was very restless, squirming around from his mother to his father. The husband had a video camera, and he made a video of them up in the temple room.

It was very warm. Some inmates didn't like the air conditioner, and some did. There was never an agreement on this. Trikāla-jña dāsa's bed was empty. The managers would have to decide what to do with it next. Sandy was looking through the book about spinal injury. She was rereading some pages about returning to the real world, rehearsing steps up the airplane, into the seat, into the toilet, out of the toilet, doing her in-flight exercises, and arriving at her destination. How people see you, how you see them. Arriving at your home. Seeing your loved ones. A time for recovering. Talking about training for a job. Time for love. Time for play. Time for work. Time for worship. She hoped she would be able to keep up her *sādhana*, which so far she had kept going strong. She had been a good inspiration for the devotees. Some of them were rather slack. But when she was back home among healthy people, maybe she wouldn't be the "star" *sādhaka* anymore.

How to keep peoples' spirits up? What about keeping in touch with counselors? Finding a new counselor? Is one necessary? She couldn't call from Australia to New York to talk with her old counselor. You can start fresh with a new one in the same way.

Swami Swims was set with his plans, which he wasn't revealing to anyone. His previous confidant was Trikāla-jña dāsa. He would have told him the date of his departure for California and what he expected to do there, but now he was more tight-lipped about it. He was planning to leave the sanatorium on August 15, which was a few weeks away, and his flight was scheduled for August 18.

Start a new life. Leave all his friends behind. But not even tell the authorities here? No, you have to do that to keep a good record. Think of what you would tell them were your reasons for living. Say like Sandy, "I think I've recovered enough so I'm going home." Yes, the equivalent. Two authorized letters. One from the psychiatrist: "I recommend a medical leave of absence from the stressors of duties in the sanatorium. This patient is really not living in a restful condition but is too active and is facing stressors and crises every day. I am not able to adjust his dosages of Klonopin or Paxil or Depakote in a manner necessary to reduce his pain. He needs oxycodone almost every day. He's surely progressing, but would do much better in a secluded environment with no responsibilities." His counselor knows Swims is crying to get out of the sanatorium environment and that he will do better in a secluded medical environment. It does not have to be permanent. But he should be given a chance. He has worked hard to live with stressors *and* the medicine. Now give him a chance to live alone without pressure, as he wants. He deserves it. Let him be himself in a new creative situation without noise and stressors, pressure of schedules. He has desired this for a long time.

But when he goes, who will talk to Jane on those rare occasions when she needs it? Who will Junior look up to as his dad and go swimming and play with, exchange Sanskrit *ślokas* with? Who will protect the inmates when they get abused by the system? Jane can do it when it requires brawn and might, but when it requires the pull of Vaiṣṇava etiquette from a Vaiṣṇava *sannyāsī*, who will go to bat for them? Surely comic movies will eventually be banned without Swims.

But he needs his own time. They've even seen in your books that you don't seem to know where you are going or who you are. What do you want? Are you a sanatorium writer? A left-footed poet?

Jane

She's our girl one-man bouncer
and typist at 123 words a minute.
Protect the sick devotees
from an attack of bikers
or a bear
or cougar or policeman.

Doesn't it seem lonely without her?
Old man just wants the
regular *saṅga*, the *sevā*,
the project bona fide.
If he goes she can still type
from a thousand miles away.
Send it on the desk.

We can all be together.
He needs more solitude.
But does he really or is

he hankering for love? What if
he can't find what he wants
among the empty
acres of redwoods
and high acres and deer?

No, if he's lonely he'll
paint it, write out.

It is better to be lonely.
If it's too much he can return.

Oh Lord, that's the plan
with plenty of paint and
ink and with whatever else
you need. Come on
out and guide me.
Not everyone will
agree. They think
you're nuts.

Jane, mom, Junior, Jojo,
recover your *japa.*
Summer, a snake shot off
under the porch—that's what it's like
in Hudson.

It's not that bad, thought Swims. I could live here for the rest of my life, especially if I knew it's what Prabhupāda wanted me to do. If he revealed it to me in a dream or something like that. It's a humble kind of service. I do have this migraine, and it does prevent me from going around, and it's swell to be able to take care of all these devotees and have them look up to you in a genuine sense. Because they're indebted to you. They can't get around, and you can't get around much either. So it brings out your kindness. But you have this artist sense in you, this sense that wants to find your own being. Sounds like a lot of crap, I suppose, but it isn't. I want to paint and I want to write, and I don't have full facility to do it here. Very little facility. I have so many duties. So if I could be alone for six months I could just think of who I was. It might solve my *japa* problem too.

Just give it a chance. Looks like I'm going through with it. I'm hoping I don't disappoint Kṛṣṇa. The people in the sanatorium will hang on without me, because in one sense I'm not doing so much for them one way or another. They'll depend more on themselves.

My counselor's really yelling at me. He reads what I write about myself and says that you're really screaming to go and be more on your own and to express yourself. Can't you hear yourself? Yes, I'd like to try it. It's a noisy place here, and I want to try some more big doses of being alone in the country and letting myself come out. Letting myself be more Kṛṣṇa conscious, if that's possible.

I've been given the assignment of taking care of devotees, and I'm walking out of it. But I'm walking into territory of taking care of myself so that I can be more fit for taking care of them. That's the idea. And a *sannyāsī* likes adventure. I haven't done anything so adventurous lately here. I go through the same routine. In California things will be completely different. I have no idea what it will be like. Prabhupāda was always ready for a new adventure—in Africa, in Malaysia. Why not try it if you have not been there before? That seemed to be his attitude, to go somewhere you've never been and test your Kṛṣṇa consciousness.

It won't be long before my old friend Bhūrijana comes, and Dhanurdhara Swami. Sit around the table and joke, talk light, and then later talk serious and heavy. But I won't talk about medication or tranquilizers or even about psychology or counselor. What's left to talk about? Won't talk about California. I've got too many secrets. Won't talk about being a poet. Come on, you've got to let on something if you want to be their friend. I can't talk about Vṛndāvana. I've got no Vṛndāvana. What do I have? Sonny Rollins? Poetry, poetry. Harry Langdon. No, there's not so much to talk about unless one knows my inner nature, unless one reads my books. And as one girl recently wrote to me, "When I read your books, I don't get anything anymore. There's nothing there. Nothing. It's finished. When I see your paintings, there's nothing there. Everything's finished." So when a person's like that, I tell them, "Okay, tough girl, just go your own way."

Swami Swims called for a meeting with Jane and Junior, the remaining members of his writing staff. He said, "I suppose you've heard some rumors that I'm going to be leaving the sanatorium in about a month to go live in more seclusion in California. I plan to make a pattern of this—six months there and six months back here. I want a life where I can have more introspection, because the duties here are really sometimes overbearing. For example, today just suddenly blossomed into much more than I expected. A disciple arrived with his wife and said his marriage was on the rocks, then suddenly news that my old Godbrother is coming, along with a swami, and we're going to have dinner, and that's going to be cooked by a visiting Indian family, including the man's wife and son. And they're all going to stay overnight. I thought it was going to be a quiet day. And who knows what's going to happen tomorrow. There'll have to be an intimate meeting with my old friend. So I need to be in a place where I can have really uninterrupted days in which I can get up in the morning and not have to ask myself what's going to happen today. I need to find myself.

"But I don't want to be neglectful of you or the writing. In fact, I think the writing will be enhanced by my moving. I'm nearing the end of *Sanatorium*, and when I go to California I'll start something completely new. But I couldn't think of a better typist than Jane or a better editor than Junior. Jane types at a record high speed. But Jane, you could also learn some other skills that actually Trikāla-jña dāsa had to a higher degree than Junior has, and that is how to incorporate editing while you're typing at the same time. He knew my writing style so well, as well as the art of editing so well, that he was able to do this almost miraculously. Then I would get a manuscript with changes made, and yet options for me to make, which was very high level.

"But the real option is up to you. What do you want to do? I don't think, Jane, that you're in the sanatorium for any illness that's so severe you couldn't go out and get a job as a typist. I know you have no material desires—you don't seem to want to get married, but I really don't know. I haven't sat down and talked to you enough about it. I'm willing to have that talk with you. But you seem to be so content to work here and never thought of doing otherwise. Perhaps you never thought it would be changed and that you had to have another option. So you could leave the sanatorium, I think, and get another job. But I'm offering you a job right here. When I go to California I'm not just sitting on my duff. I'm going to produce tapes at the same rate that I've been producing them here, and give you as much work as I gave you here. I'd like to promise that. What's the sense of going to be alone if you can't write? And it would leave plenty of work for Junior, in addition to his duties of keeping the office clean and being part of the infrastructure of the sanatorium. On the other hand, Junior has no illness and is free to leave. In your case, you're definitely free to go and seek an education and do whatever you want. All I'm saying is I'm willing to work with both of you if you care to stay here. Actually, as I say this, I see I'm making you no offer at all. But Jane, even if you do leave the sanatorium and move somewhere else, and you've got some time to do some typing for me, my offer still stands."

Later that night Jane came back to see Swami Swims privately. She said that she was very attached to typing for him. It was a personal *sādhana* for her, part of her Kṛṣṇa consciousness, and she couldn't see giving it up. So she wanted to do it in any case, no matter where she moved or whatever happened. She would learn whatever skills she lacked. She said as far as her background was concerned, he could probably understand it. She had a lot of drug problems before, a lot of men problems, and really didn't want to have anything to do with either one of those things. She had gone through the Twelve Steps program for drugs, and had even done some time in jail, and was disgusted by it all and was firmly committed to her Hare Kṛṣṇa *sādhana*.

"I am very attached to you personally, Swami Swims," she said, slowing down in her speech. "I don't mean as a boyfriend or someone to go to bed with. But I don't mean exactly as a brother. I look to you as a spiritual master. And as you initiated Bhakta Tim the other night, I was very touched, and I want to ask you to give me spiritual initiation also, before you leave here. I am officially qualified with the four rules, and I read Prabhupāda's books and all that. I would die for Prabhupāda, and although I don't like the bureaucracy of his movement, I certainly feel loyal to him and his mission and want to serve it however I can. And you know physically I would die defending one of his Vaiṣṇavas. I'd even take pleasure in it with my Vaiṣṇava spirit. And I would take pleasure dying in defending your life. I wish I could live with you and be your bodyguard. I don't think you'd allow me to do that, I mean go with you to California and fight off black bears and timber rattlers for you. I'm sure you wouldn't want a woman with you there. It would be looked down upon. So I'll stay away, but could you initiate me?"

Swami Swims said, "Yes, I will. I consider it my duty, and it would be a great pleasure. Would you mind if we do it just now, in a very informal way? Give me your beads."

She handed him her beads, and in the private room he chanted all sixteen rounds while she chanted along with him. Then he said, "I do not have time for an initiation lecture. But please hear tapes of my initiation lectures regularly. Your spiritual name is Janeśvarī devī-dāsī. Do you like that name?"

"I think it's perfect."

"Tell people that's your new spiritual name, and that you're now initiated and have new responsibilities. You can dress the same way you always have, but always behave in an exemplary way with your language and everything. But I won't stop you from fighting if the occasion arises." He chuckled. "Janeśvarī devī-dāsī, my fightingest disciple. My Hanumān. My dearly beloved servant. Did you know that Hanumān was the dearest servant of Lord Rāma?"

Janeśvarī's eyes filled with tears. "That is what I want to be, your most faithful servant. I will not do it with a club but with a typewriter. And I will get the best new computer equipment I can, by begging or borrowing, and learn how to do things in a most modern system so you'll be proud of me. Even if there's only you and I, we'll produce these books faster and faster, to your satisfaction."

She bowed down and said her *praṇāmās* to her spiritual master for the first time and made plans for how she would keep his picture on her altar. While she was bowing down he patted her on her head.

Sweet and tender the sun
goes down the hill.
Fan on in the hall. Guests
ate what they could
of a large meal cooked
by Śamika Ṛṣi's family

while we talked lightly.
He wanted me to stay longer
when I go to his house. I said
"to attend the pleasant meeting
tonight I took two narcotic
pills. That's heavy. When
I go to give the lectures
at your house it will
be much heavier. Can't you
see? See this stainless steel
cane?" You're going to show me
slides of Govardhana. I'd rather
show you twenty minutes of Harry Langdon.

That's the kind of relaxed
guru he is. You might not
like it but most of us
like this kind of guidance here.
Sweet and tender
and jokester and ease.
He is himself.
Goodnight, sanatorium. I can't
even remember Janeśvarī's old name,
And Tim, what's his name now?
Trikāla-jña.

My dear Braja,

Everything is going fine in the area of my steady love for you. There is not an iota of diminishment. I think of you always, and our physical separation is no barrier. I do all my exercises with the thought of bringing us together again, and I look forward to being with you. Even not being with you I cultivate my Kṛṣṇa consciousness so that I will be a qualified wife. I learn all I can for this purpose, so that I'll be a devotee you can be proud of and a mother of children you can be proud of.

My exercises are going steadily, and the therapists continue to tell me that my muscles are developing well and on schedule, and that it should be a matter of months only before I should be fit to travel with my wheelchair on an airplane back home.

A spiritual matter has come up on which I have to consult with you. I have been a devotee now for several years. So often by this time a devotee is initiated. I've seen and heard quite a few ISKCON devotees come and give lectures in the temples, especially in Australia. You know there is an initiating swami here, too, whose actual spiritual name is Swami Śyāma, whom the sanatorium devotees affectionately call Swami Swims. He is like a family member to us, and we're all very close to him. He always sticks up for our rights. Like us, he has a serious malady, and so he's close to us in that way. I wrote you about how he has had a migraine condition for over twenty years. It's something called anticipatory anxiety migraine. So he's able to be empathetic to the pains of other devotees.

Recently he revealed that in about a month he is going to leave the sanatorium for a medical leave of absence and go to California. He intends to live for about six months in a more secluded atmosphere. He actually does a lot of administrative work here and a lot of hands-on work with the individuals, interviewing them, managing them. It's the kind of work which is in one sense against his psychophysical nature.

He is more of an artist and writer, and that's why he has established a writing office, which is producing books. He's also a painter but never gets a chance to do his artwork. His medical doctor told him that it would be very good for him clinically if for half a year he would go to a place where he doesn't have these administrative duties and is able to just do what he wants without being forced and without having to follow a strict schedule. Śyāma Mahārāja thinks it would also help his writing if he was on an open schedule. They want him to give himself that chance to find himself, and they think that it will free him more from pain if he could be free of the force that he has endured for over thirty years—force, force, force, which has covered his real identity. He is seeking permission for it through strong letters of authority and is looking forward to it.

Hearing that he is going to leave, one of our favorite young devotees here, Bhakta Tim, who was about to die of cancer, asked Swami Śyāma on his deathbed if he would give him initiation. It was very touching. Swami gave him the spiritual name Trikāla-jña dāsa shortly before the young man passed away. He also initiated a woman named Jane, giving her the spiritual name Janeśvarī devī-dāsī. Other devotees realized the opportunity but did not want to be initiated by him, having already chosen other ISKCON devotees to be initiated by.

I have given deep thought to this because I have become attracted to Śyāma Mahārāja as my possible spiritual master. He is quite an individual. About fifteen years ago, he introduced a book called Entering the Life of Prayer, *in which he made references to Christians who prayed privately. That raised some eyebrows among some of the members of ISKCON. But it became a kind of bestseller in ISKCON, and many individuals love the book and were refreshed to under-*

stand that there was actually private prayer in ISKCON. He filled the book with quotes from Vedic sources to show that private prayer is also recommended for the devotees. Then about ten years ago he again raised eyebrows when he started painting. His paintings appeared in a one-man gallery showing at Govinda's Gallery, in Washington D.C. He made a catalog and submitted to the prestigious newspaper The Washington Post. *It was reviewed in their art review section and got a very high recommendation as "awfully exuberant." Once that hit the fan, devotees understood that it had great preaching potential and they began to buy his canvases and hang them in their homes. He used to be very quiet, and although he's still quiet, he is becoming self-assertive. He's gone through traumas as a GBC man, as he was always submissive and afraid to express his own feelings, which were sometimes different from the institutional feelings. Now he's retired from the GBC due to the pain of his migraine, and he's been able to express more his strong desires to write poetry and prose and to paint. I am very attracted to his emphasizing individualism in Kṛṣṇa consciousness and saying that Kṛṣṇa wants our individual expression, not just institutional expression. Kṛṣṇa wants us to give from our own heart, and that will please Him.*

What do you think if I accepted Śyāma Mahārāja as my spiritual master, even though you have a different spiritual master? Do you think this would cause any conflict between us? I have asked the devotees here, and for the most part they don't see any conflict. In fact, only one married couple have the same spiritual master. Most husbands and wives have different spiritual masters, and they don't find it a conflict. They say it is an archaic idea that married devotees have to have the same spiritual master. But I want to know your opinion. I don't want to cause any conflict between us. Please consult who you feel is an important influence for you, and let me know. I want to please you and not be an independent wife in this matter.

Depending on you for direction in my life. Your dearest loved one, Sandy

Chapter Twenty-Seven

My dearest Sandy,

Please accept my humble obeisances. All glories to Śrīla Prabhupāda.

My own spiritual master recently passed through here, and I was able to talk to him about your question of disciples being initiated by different spiritual masters. He said he didn't think it was a good idea. He said he thought it would tend to lead to conflicts. One guru might say something about practices and sex life, and another guru might say something else. One guru might favor one kind of liberal attitude, and the other guru may be more conservative. These differences would cause conflicts between the married couple. If they had the same guru, then everything would be lined up the same way. That was his opinion.

I also asked the temple president, and he was of a similar opinion. He said it was better for management if the married couple had the same guru. That way he wouldn't have to gather different opinions on matters but could organize things by just getting the opinion of the one guru.

I realize on the one hand that this could sound very institutional, and devotees are accepting different gurus. We don't want to be too strict about that, for example, saying that a disciple could only accept a guru from the same race. There has to be some individual choice and liberality. I would subscribe to that too. If you really have it in your heart that you want to accept Śyāma Swami as your spiritual master and take direction from him, then I don't want to get in the way of that. I would like to get to know him more. Could you ask him to write me a letter and tell me about how he feels about married life and about your life with me? I think that would help us.

Your loving Braja

Dear Śyāma Mahārāja,

I have written a letter to my husband, asking that you accept me as your spiritual master. He has written back, saying that his spiritual master thinks it's better that married couples have the same spiritual master. My husband wasn't absolutely firm about it, and realized there can be exceptions. So Braja dāsa asked me to ask you if you could get in touch with his Guru Mahārāja and see if something can be worked out.

I just want to let you know formally that I am very much in admiration of you and your style of spiritual mastership, and if I could get permission, I would like to become your disciple.

Your aspiring servant, Bhaktin Sandy

Dear Bhaktin Sandy,

I remember initiating a girl who was the wife of a Prabhupāda disciple. Her husband wanted very much to be involved with my initiating his wife, and so we corresponded and got to know each other. It was helpful. It's not that I initiate his wife and he has nothing to do with the ongoing relationship. Let's not make a rash decision. Please ask Braja dāsa to write me and express any fears and anxieties he has. His spiritual master has already expressed his apprehension. I don't want to cause a conflict. But I do think the decision is ultimately up to you. Finally, he will have to go back to his guru and ask permission. But I hope he will be reasonable if Braja dāsa presents his reasons.

Thank you for the compliment of wanting to accept me as your Guru Mahārāja.

Yours in service to Prabhupāda, Śyāma Swami

Dear Gopīnātha Mahārāja,

Please accept my humble obeisances. All glories to Śrīla Prabhupāda.

Your disciple Braja dāsa has written to me explaining that his wife-to-be, Sandy, who is now a paraplegic at the sanatorium in New York, wishes to accept me as her spiritual master. She said that you feel it is best for a husband and wife to have the same spiritual master. Braja dāsa, however, is willing to accept Sandy's having me as her spiritual master. I also think that exceptions can be made.

I would be willing to consult with you on important matters and not do anything in conflict with you. I feel that if the girl really has in her heart a desire to accept her own spiritual master, she should be allowed to do so. Let us discuss this further. I want to work in cooperation with you, but I want to let the free spirit accept a spiritual master as she desires.

Your servant, Śyāma Swami

I don't see anything wrong with
mixed gurus.
Yeah, but you used to.
You used to be envious.
I remember.
You wanted everyone in New York City

and Boston
and Philly to be yours.

Yeah, you've grown out of your
envy or you'd be dead. You were
dead with green skin. I take
narcotics. Too much is too much.
All are too much.

Pink flowers. "Did you
get the job?" "Yes, I'm a shoo-in.
My mother is the
chief administrator." (But
sometimes that works against you.)

Shelley drowned in the sea but Keats
in the bed from constipation.
The debate goes on. I don't know
what I said. Staying only from
a chair at your house. Then fly out
to California. In California
we'll get out at the racetrack. Don't need
so much luggage, simply
the names of God and 716 narcotics.
I told him the narcotics don't like
my subpersons. I don't like them tough
letters and tough
negotiations to survive
the tough girl's letters, complaining,
nothing stirring, no spiritual spark.
The same for me,
so go your way and I've got to
live.

They said the lady they called Mama was a complainer, but it wasn't really true. She had arthritis and she liked to talk, so she talked about her arthritis. She tended to talk about little things, not philosophy. She talked mostly about Puerto Rico, where she had come from, and her yearning to return there. She talked positively about the *kīrtanas* there and the wonderful *kīrtana* leader, Balarāma Prabhu, who used to lead the devotees around in a dance and who sang wonderful melodies. She would praise the climate in Puerto Rico. She did complain about New York winters, saying they were horrible *compared to Puerto Rico*. So it was mainly a praise of Puerto Rico, not so much a complaining of New York. She praised the fruit, the beaches, the sky and the people whom she knew in her homeland. So she never quite caught on with the people in the sanatorium. She remained an alien from her home place, her *prabhu-datta-deśa.*

She had entered voluntarily, as her arthritis seemed to deteriorate in Puerto Rico, but it didn't get any better in New York. So on her own will she was allowed to be released under her son's care. He was completely devoted to her. He had a little house in the mountains of Puerto Rico about fifteen minutes from the ISKCON temple. About three times a week he would take her and her wheelchair in his car to the temple. They would never miss the Sunday program for the dancing and the feast and the talk among the devotees. She preferred to speak in Spanish, although she could speak equally well in Spanish or English.

Mama's son's hair was graying, but he still had a muscular physique. He taught weightlifting at a gym, which was how he earned his income. So one day he flew to New York and took his mother home. They had baked a cake for her and had a little celebration. She cried, and her loving feelings for the devotees she had lived with for several years came out, and their feelings for her also. They had lost another friend. But they knew it was best for her and hoped that her arthritis did not get worse from being away from the exercising and the therapists. They seemed to think that the high spirits she would gain in Puerto Rico would make up for her "complaining" nature in New York.

Once her son took her on a trip to Vṛndāvana with money that he had saved up. The trip was a great delight for her, and so her son had again saved up to take her there. So now that treat awaited her too.

"Goodbye, Mom, and please don't forget us in Vṛndāvana."

"I will send you things from Vṛndāvana, and Puerto Rico too. Hare Kṛṣṇa. Goodbye, Prabhus."

Lovers, I haven't seen so many—
you fool, they're all over. Lovers,
the groundhogs, the babies,
grass and I see men and women characters
in the old-time movies.

Some of us abstain. A
fast-beat Coltrane and Byrd
run through "lovers" and that is
sheer music, can't say it's
lover, it's music, but that's
the next step,
the love of husband and the
love of guru. There should
be no conflict.

Love of God is the center
and the gurus are the helpers
to bring disciples, so don't be petty
spiritual masters saying "my disciples
have to marry only my disciples
and wear their *tilaka* thick."

Well I think that's silly.
No, live your own life
and let others live theirs.
No conflict because gurus are
not controllers of your life
and the heart is a private place.
That's what one
thinks. The other is an imperialist
so I don't know what to say. I don't
want to hurt a marriage and yet keep
my mouth shut on a spiritual issue
that seems right.

"Lover, when you're near me and I hear
you speak my name" that's what
Kṛṣṇa wants and that guru is he
who gives the name and encourages
you to sing it as much
as you can and realize.
Kīrtana exists also in
writing, children making, running,
learning to make words,
speaking the alphabet, not
going to the atheists or the
Māyāvādīs.

We expect you to do it because
you are a disciple.

Swami Swims used to sometimes take a chair and sit beside Sandy's bed. He was not aware of the flurry of letters between her and her husband-to-be about initiation. She said to him, "May I address you by your spiritual name, Śyāma Mahārāja?"

"Sure," he said. "I don't know how that 'Swims' stuff started. They were teasing me and I just tolerated it."

"Śyāma Mahārāja, I've been a Hare Kṛṣṇa devotee for three years now, since I joined in the Sydney temple. I've heard many ISKCON swamis preach at our temple, and since I've come here, I've heard you give a few lectures. What's more, I've seen how you behave with the devotees, and I've seen your example. When you initiated Tim on his deathbed, I was really touched, and I thought I wanted to be initiated by you."

Śyāma Swami looked very somber. He decided not to let the devotees refer to him as Swims Swami anymore.

Sandy said, "So I wrote to my fiancé, Braja dāsa, who's initiated by Gopīnātha dāsa Goswami. I asked him to ask his spiritual master and his temple president what they thought of a wife being initiated by a guru different from the husband's. Gopīnātha Mahārāja said he did not think this should be done. He thought husband and wife should have the same guru, andthis would make for more harmony in the marriage. There would not be disagreement over what project to work for, what to donate money to, and so on. The temple president had the same opinion. But some devotees didn't agree. They said that they were grownup individuals, most of them married, and that initiation was a private matter of the heart and that they didn't find any conflict. In fact, the majority of the married devotees in the sanatorium have different gurus, and the majority of the devotees in the Sydney temple have different gurus, and it's not a cause for strife. So their consensus was that it was a kind of archaic idea from the old days in ISKCON, in which you had to have the same doctrine and the same guru, you had to have the same opinion, you had to give money in the same way, and so forth and so on. The individuality of expression is healthy and doesn't cause stress. It's the choking off of individuality that causes stress."

Swims Swami said, "I'll write to Gopīnātha Mahārāja and try to develop a relationship with him, and then we'll see what will happen."

My dear Braja,

I have never disobeyed you or tried to second-guess your decisions. But here I am receiving one of your letters and writing back, questioning further, asking you to think deeper about what you have said and to reconsider your decision.

I have not made my decision to be initiated by Śyāma Swami in a frivolous way. I have been meditating on it deeply as I go about my somber daily activities, trying to recover my health. He always has an encouraging word. As you know, he is struggling himself with a very serious disease—anticipatory anxiety migraine syndrome. He's gone through a lot of sheer, simple pain, but he still keeps up his spirit whenever he gets clear of the headaches.

He's a man Prabhupāda entrusted. I still intend to be your wife, without any lack of chastity in our husband and wife relationship. The place of the spiritual master is different, and so I want you to think deeply and reply to me again.

Your most beloved, Sandy

Dear Sandy,

When I got your letter I thought, 'Oh boy, this is going to be trouble.' What if I ask my spiritual master again and he says no? I took a long walk and then I went into the temple at a time when no one was there. I sat before the Prabhupāda mūrti *for a long time in silence, seeking communion. Then I went and sat before the* mūrti *of Balarāma, who is the Lord of the spiritual masters and gives you strength to worship your spiritual master. Of course, right beside Him is Lord Caitanya, and I prayed to all the Deities—to Kṛṣṇa, and to Rādhā, who is so kind—but ultimately I went back to Prabhupāda. All this time I was chanting the Hare Kṛṣṇa mantra.*

Ultimately, I decided it was not a big, big problem. It was a simple thing. It is something between you and me. Therefore, the question is whether I trust you. Do I think that you are a foolish girl who is about to choose the wrong spiritual master? Do I trust that you have considered rightly and that you have the guidance from the Lord within to choose the right spiritual master? Do I believe that there are many qualified spiritual masters in ISKCON? Yes, I do believe that there are many qualified spiritual masters in ISKCON, and that is what the GBC says also.

So ultimately I put my trust in you and in our love for each other. That is the most important thing. I don't want to distrust my guru or your guru or any guru. But if the distrust was ultimately between you and me, that would be the worst thing. Then I would be second-guessing and thinking, 'Oh, Sandy may have made a mistake,' or you may be thinking, 'Why didn't Brajajana let me make the choice that was in my heart?,' and there would be a doubt between us, something that stood between our love. I would be restricting you, not trusting you, and you would see that I did not trust you.

Do you see what I mean, how it became so simple to me? It may not be simple to someone else, but it is to me. I don't think for the time being I need to explain it to my spiritual master. It's something I disagree with him on, but it doesn't lessen my trust in him in all spiritual matters in which he may teach me. It's something in which I don't feel he has the right to overrule me in my dealings with my wife. Neither does my temple president have that right. If I believe this girl whom I am marrying has chosen a guru in her heart, I don't want to tell her, 'No, you take that guru out of your heart and you put this other guru in. That is my order.' I want more love to be between us than that. I want you to trust that I have chosen a bona fide guru, and I want to trust that you have done so also.

In the future, if there is any distrust or disappointment, that can be overcome as our gurus get to know each other and get to see the beautiful children we produce. So that is my simple decision.

Now you go on getting well, wheelchair girl, and get yourself initiated before you come home. We don't want any karmī *girls here. Let me know in your next letter the spiritual name he gives you. I know it will not be a big fire* yajña *affair, and that is good too. Just an intimate affair between you. But I want to send you beautiful beads from Vṛndāvana. I am sending them FedEx right away, so you can have new, first-class paraphernalia. And I am sending* guru-dakṣiṇā *for the affair. In this way I want to show my full support.*

Call it henpecked if you like, but I am your servant, just as you are my servant. In spiritual affairs, I want to show my full support. From what I have been hearing of 'Swami Swims'—also known as Śyāma Swami—I am building trust and affection in him. He has been taking care of you very nicely all these months, so I am indebted to him.

Your loving servant, Braja dāsa

For the initiation of Bhaktin Sandy they set up a tent outside and had a fire *yajña*. She sat in her wheelchair, and Śyāma Mahārāja sat facing her. There was a platform and a fire *yajña* between them. As many inmates as possible came out to see, and others gathered at the door. He gave an initiation speech, which was rare for him. Then he took the *japa* beads, which had been FedExed from Australia, and chanted on them while she also chanted. She looked very lovely in a new *sārī*, and Janeśvarī placed the new neck beads around her neck. In his short speech, Swami Śyāma said he was very honored to serve at the sanatorium, and he considered it the cutting edge of preaching in the Kṛṣṇa consciousness movement. When devotees who were sidelined with injuries proved that they could continue their *sādhana*, or just continue to try, they were setting the best example. He had all respect for them, whatever they could do, and he was sure that Kṛṣṇa and Prabhupāda were willing to take them back to Godhead at the end of such exemplary lives.

A quiet "*Jaya!*" went up from the group, who held that desire deep in their hearts. The administrators and therapists also gathered in a deep mood of gratitude to see their patients in such a mood of worshiping life. They all had also gathered in especial affection for Sandy and were glad that she was not far from getting well and going back to her home and that she had chosen her spiritual master.

Sandy could not bow down before her spiritual master, but he touched her on the head. He felt very, very lucky. Who else could expect to get such an outstanding disciple as Bhaktin Sandy? He told her, "Your spiritual name is now Subhadrā dāsī. She is the sister of Kṛṣṇa. Is that all right?"

"Yes, thank you. It's a beautiful name," said Subhadrā. "Now no more sand in my sweet rice," she laughed.

The inmates all had various little gifts for her, and she accepted them with grace and humility. Then everyone had a *kīrtana* for about fifteen minutes. When the *kīrtana* died down, the head nurse rose and said, "I would like to add some auspicious words to this ceremony, on behalf of Dr. Jamieson, the head physician who is in charge of Subhadrā's care. Dr. Jamieson feels that Subhadrā is now well enough and strong enough to make the flight back to Australia."

All the inmates shouted, "*Jaya!*"

The head nurse continued, "We at the clinic are so proud of her ideal behavior that we have taken up a collection to help with the expenses of her flight, and we would like to present it to the bride-to-be at this time."

Subhadrā exclaimed, "Oh Prabhus! Oh Gaura-Nitāi! Thank you very much."

Subhadrā was full of smiles as her friends accompanied her back to the sanatorium building. She was too happy to do anything and just sat beaming, a little embarrassed to be the center of so much attention. Then she said, "I don't want to feel puffed up, so I think I'll read one of Prabhupāda's books for awhile." The inmates left her alone.

Śyāma Mahārāja then made an announcement: "Subhadrā has reminded me that everybody calls me Swami Swims, although that's actually not my name. So from now on, I request you all to please call me by my actual spiritual name. It is Śyāma Mahārāja. Do you get it? Śyāma Mahārāja. The other is just a bad joke, and I don't like it."

"All right, Śyāma Mahārāja, all glories to you."

He held up his hands and said, "Inmates of New York sanatorium, all glories to you. Śrīla Prabhupāda, all glories to you. Gaura-Nitāi, all glories to You. Rādhā and Kṛṣṇa, all glories to You."

Somewhere

Somewhere in upstate New York
there's a Hare Kṛṣṇa sanatorium and I've
just told you a little bit
about it from the viewpoint
mostly of Śyāma Mahārāja.

He's leaving now but says he
might go back in half a
year
if that's his calling.
If he does I'm not sure any
of the same people would
be there. But the pain
would be there, and the attempt
to become Kṛṣṇa conscious.

Would you like to hear
more about this sanatorium
or are you sick and
tired of its tortures
and you've heard quite enough
for a lifetime?

Let Śyāma Mahārāja know
if you think it's a good service for him and
something you'd like to hear more of.

Whether you go back to that sanatorium
or not, the suffering
will go on. So let's bless
those brave
souls who endure it and those
who serve them,
directing them towards
Kṛṣṇa's will.

Notes

Chapter One

1. Rudolf Steiner (1861–1925). German philosopher and clairvoyant who endorsed a mystical philosophy involving imagination, defined as a higher seeing of the spiritual world in revealing images; inspiration, defined as a higher hearing of the spiritual world through which the creative forces and creative order of the spiritual world are revealed; and intuition, by which penetration into the sphere of spiritual beings becomes possible. Steiner's books include *Truth and Knowledge*, *The Philosophy of Freedom*, and *Mysticism and Modern Thought*. He was one of the editors of the Standard Edition (Sophien Ausgabe) of Goethe's Complete Works.

2. Booker Little (1938–1961). Memphis-born trumpet player and composer Booker Little had become a well-established jazz trumpet virtuoso before his untimely death from kidney failure at the age of 23. Booker's virtuosity complimented that of Eric Dolphy, and their collaborations constitute Booker Little's best-known work. His sister, Vera, is an accomplished opera singer who has recorded with the London Opera.

3. Eric Dolphy (1928–1964). Jazz virtuoso on saxophone, bass clarinet, and flute and brilliant composer who died at the age of thirty-six from complications of undiagnosed diabetes. His album *Out to Lunch!*, recorded in February 1964, is one of the most important jazz albums of the 1960s.

4. "Coming on the Hudson," a jazz composition by Thelonious Monk recorded live at the Five Spot Café in August, 1958, and released on the album *Thelonious in Action*. Accompanying Monk were Johnny Griffin, Ahmed Abdul, and Roy Haynes.

5. In the board game "Monopoly," a "Get Out of Jail Free" card enables a player to get out of jail without paying the usual $200 fine.

6. Charles Lamb (1775–1834). English critic, essayist, and the lifelong friend of poet Samuel Taylor Coleridge. In 1796, his sister, Mary Ann Lamb (1764–1847), in a fit of temporary insanity, attacked and wounded their father and killed their mother with a knife. To save her from a life in an asylum, Charles had himself declared her guardian, and after 1799 they lived together. They collaborated on several books for children.

Chapter Two

1. "Poinciana." Song with lyrics by Buddy Bernier and music by Nat Simon, written in 1936. The poinciana, or flame tree, is an ornamental tree with strikingly beautiful orange and scarlet blossoms that grows in tropical and subtropical climates.

2. Ahmad Jamal (b. 1930). Known for his arrangements for small groups, jazz pianist Ahmad Jamal has been performing and influencing jazz artists for

decades. Jamal's album *But Not for Me*, which included the song "Poinciana," was released in 1958 and became the first gold record album in the history of jazz.

3. Beatrice. Dante and Beatrice met in Florence, Italy, in 1274, when they were both eight years old. Dante fell in love with Beatrice at first sight, viewing her as divine and noble. They first exchanged words nine years later, in 1283. On that occasion, Dante saw Beatrice walking down a street in Florence; she was accompanied by two older women, and she turned and greeted him. Filled with joy, Dante retreated to his room, where he fell asleep and had a dream that became the subject of the first sonnet in *La Vita Nuova*—one of the world's great romantic poems. Dante finished *La Vita Nuova* in 1294, but he was dissatisfied with that poem and became determined to write a poem worthy of Beatrice. Twenty-seven years later, just before his death, he completed *The Divine Comedy*, which he dedicated to Beatrice.

4. "golden age." A reference to the so-called golden age of jazz, which may be generally regarded as the period from the early 1940s (with the rise of bebop) to the mid-1960s. New York was a major center of jazz during this period.

5. Billie Holiday (1915–1959). The great jazz vocalist Billie Holiday was the daughter of guitarist Clarence Holiday, who abandoned his family early on. Billie's mother left Billie to move to New York, leaving Billie to grow up alone. Billie did not go to school but took menial jobs until the age of thirteen, when she went to New York to join her mother.

In New York, Billie was recruited to work in a brothel, and she was briefly jailed for prostitution. At the age of fifteen, she began singing in a small bar in Brooklyn, and a year later was singing in the well-known Harlem jazz club Pods' and Jerry's. In 1933, while singing in Monette's, another Harlem club, Billie was discovered by record producer and talent scout John Hammond. Hammond immediately arranged three recording sessions for Billie with Benny Goodman, and he also found engagements for her in various New York jazz clubs. In 1935, Billie began recording regularly with studio bands that featured the finest jazz musicians of the time, including the great saxophonist Lester Young, who gave her the nickname "Lady Day". The recordings she made from 1935 to 1942 are classic.

Billie joined the Count Basie Orchestra in 1937, and in 1938 moved on to the Artie Shaw Orchestra, becoming one of the first black singers to sing in a white band. In 1939, Billie began singing at the Café Society (Downtown), an interracial nightclub in Greenwich Village that was fashionable with leftist intellectuals and the *haute monde*. During this period Billie recorded "Strange Fruit" (the phrase "strange fruit" is a reference to the bodies of the victims of lynchings); Billie became much admired by anti-racist intellectuals and advocates of social justice, and she began to acquire a popular following.

As her career was moving forward, Billie's personal life was falling apart. She began to drink heavily and became addicted to narcotics; in 1947, she was jailed on drug charges. In addition, she compulsively became attached to men who abused and mistreated her. Despite failing health, Billie continued to record and perform through the mid-1950s. In late 1957, Billie sang "Fine and Mellow" on *The Sound of Jazz* television special. On that classic performance, she was joined by Lester Young, Ben Webster, Coleman Hawkins, Gerry Mulligan, and Roy Eldridge. She died in 1959. The jazz world lamented the loss of its greatest female vocalist. New York poet Frank O'Hara mourned the loss in a poem:

The Day Lady Died

It is 12:20 in New York a Friday
three days after Bastille day, yes
it is 1959 and I go get a shoeshine
because I will get off the 4:19 in Easthampton
at 7:15 and then go straight to dinner
and I don't know the people who will feed me

I walk up the muggy street beginning to sun
and have a hamburger and a malted and buy
an ugly NEW WORLD WRITING to see what
the poets
in Ghana are doing these days
I go on to the bank
and Miss Stillwagon (first name Linda I once heard)
doesn't even look up my balance for once in her life
and in the GOLDEN GRIFFIN I get a little Verlaine
for Patsy with drawings by Bonnard although I do
think of Hesiod, trans. Richmond Lattimore or
Brendan Behan's new play or *Le Balcon* or *Les Nègres*
of Genet, but I don't, I stick with Verlaine
after practically going to sleep with quandariness

and for Mike I just stroll into the PARK LANE
Liquor Store and ask for a bottle of Strega and
then I go back where I came from to 6th Avenue
and the tobacconist in the Ziegfeld Theatre and
casually ask for a carton of Gauloises and a carton
of Picayunes, and a NEW YORK POST with her face
on it

and I am sweating a lot by now and thinking of
leaning on the john door in the 5 SPOT
while she whispered a song along the keyboard
to Mal Waldron and everyone and I stopped
breathing

6. "My Funny Valentine," a standard from *Babes in Arms* (1936), with music by Richard Rogers and lyrics by Lorenz Hart. The lyrics of the song are as follows: My funny valentine/ Sweet, comic valentine/ You make me smile with my heart/ Your looks are laughable,/ unphotographable/ Yet you're my favorite work of art/ Is your figure less than Greek?/ Is your mouth a little weak?/ When you open it to speak/ are you smart?/ Don't change a hair for me/ Not if you care for me/ Stay little valentine stay/ Each day is Valentine's Day.

On February 12, 1964, a charity jazz concert was performed in New York's Philharmonic Hall. The concert was sponsored by the National Association for the Advancement of Colored People (NAACP) in support of voter registration in Mississippi and Louisiana. Performing in that concert was Miles Davis, accompanied by a youthful Herbie Hancock, Ron Carter, Tony Williams, and saxophonist George Coleman. The recording of that concert was released under the name *My Favorite Valentine;* it is considered by many to be one of Davis' greatest albums.

Chapter Three

1. The Twelve Steps program of recovery from alcoholism is utilized by Alcoholics Anonymous, a nonsectarian fellowship of men and women united in their desire to stop drinking. The Twelve Steps to recovery, as practiced by members of Alcoholics Anonymous, are as follows: (1) admitting that one is powerless over alcohol and that one's life has become unmanageable; (2) coming to believe that a Power greater than oneself could restore one to sanity; (3) making a decision to turn one's will and one's life to the care of God as one understands Him; (4) making a searching and fearless moral inventory of oneself; (5) admitting to God, to oneself and to another human being the exact nature

of one's wrongs; (6) being entirely ready to have God remove all one's defects of character; (7) humbly asked Him to remove one's shortcomings; (8) making a list of all the persons one has harmed and becoming willing to make amends to them all; (9) making direct amends to such people wherever possible, except when to do so would injure them or others; (10) continuing to take personal inventory, and when one is wrong, to promptly admit it; (11) seeking through prayer and meditation to improve one's conscious contact with God as one understands Him, praying only for knowledge of His will for oneself and the power to carry that out; (12) experiencing a spiritual awakening as the result of these steps, trying to carry this message to other alcoholics, and practicing these principles in all one's affairs.

2. Floyd Patterson (b. 1935). In 1956, at the age of twenty, Floyd Patterson became the youngest heavyweight world champion of boxing by knocking out Archie Moore in the fifth round. In 1962, Patterson lost by knockout to the great Sonny Liston. Patterson had a lifetime professional record of 55 wins, 8 losses, and 1 draw; 40 of his wins were by knockout.

3. "Moonlight in Vermont," a standard written in 1944, with words by John Blackburn and music by Karl Suessdorf. The song has been recorded by many jazz artists, including Louis Armstrong, Ella Fitzgerald, Gerry Mulligan, Stan Getz, and Sonny Stitt.

4. An allusion to the song, "The Man I Love," by George Gershwin (1898–1937), the first verse of which is as follows: "Someday he'll come along/The man I love/And he'll be big and strong/ The man I love/ And when he comes my way/ I'll do my best to make him stay."

5. John Handy (b. 1933). The great alto saxophonist John Handy has played with Charles Mingus and has performed at Carnegie Hall, the Lincoln Center, the Berlin Philharmonic Auditorium, the San Francisco Opera House, and Davies Hall, among other prestigious venues. He is also a composer and a music educator, having taught music history and performance at Stanford University, University of California at Berkeley, San Francisco State University, and other colleges.

Chapter Four

1. Michael Babatunde Olatunji (1927–2003). Virtuoso of West African percussion. Baba Olatunji was Nigerian; his album *Drums of Passion*, released in 1959, was the first album to bring genuine African music to a Western audience. Over 5 million copies of the album were sold internationally. For forty years, Olatunji traveled the world, spreading African music and culture. He received a Grammy award in 1991 for his collaboration with percussionist Mickey Hart on the album *Planet Drum*. Olatunji was also an educator, and he established the Voices of Africa foundation. The Olatunji concert mentioned here refers to the last public concert given by John Coltrane before his death in 1967. It was held at the Olatunji Center for African Culture in New York City.

2. Earl "Bud" Powell (1924–1966). Bebop pianist and composer whose nimble right-hand melody lines rivaled those of Charlie Parker's saxophone or Dizzy Gillespie's trumpet in speed and inventiveness.

3. Curtis Fuller (b. 1934). One of the all-time great jazz trombonists. Fuller's improvisational style and his wide-interval leaps became important elements in Art Blakey's Jazz Messengers and Benny Golson's and

Art Farmer's Jazztet. Fuller recorded with John Coltrane, Cannonball Adderley, Dizzy Gillespie, Billie Holiday, Bud Powell, and Quincy Jones, among others. Fuller was the only trombone soloist to record with John Coltrane; he can be heard on Coltrane's classic album, *Blue Train*.

Chapter Six

1. Lee Konitz (b. 1927), Warne Marsh. The cool-toned Lee Konitz is one of the most individual of all alto saxophonists. In 1949, while with Lennie Tristano's innovative sextet, he performed the first two free-jazz improvisations ever recorded. His recordings range from cool bop to thoughtful free improvisations. Konitz also performs on the soprano and tenor saxophones. The late Warne Marsh also played alto saxophone with Lennie Tristano. Tristano, Konitz, and Marsh would sometimes play Bach's two-part or three-part Inventions on the bandstand. The novel *Out of Nowhere*, by Marcus M. Cornelius, was inspired by and dedicated to Warne Marsh. The distinctive styles of saxophonists Konitz and Marsh compliment each other beautifully on the album *Lee Konitz, with Warne Marsh*, recorded in 1955, which includes the Count Basie composition "Topsy."

2. "Ysabel's Table Dance" is a jazz composition by Charles Mingus that appears on his album *Tijuana Moods*, released in 1957.

Chapter Seven

1. *Bags Groove*, a classic record by Miles Davis with Sonny Rollins, Milt Jackson, Thelonious Monk, Horace Silver, Percy Heath, and Kenny Clarke, released in 1954.

2. Charles "Hank" Bukowski (1920–1994). Bukowski was a complex, hard-drinking wild man of Beat literature who published more than forty-five books of poetry and prose in his lifetime, mostly in small presses. He identified with the working class, and his literature is accessible to everyone.

3. From the song "A Pretty Girl Is Like a Melody," words and music by Irving Berlin (1919).

Chapter Eight

1. Norman Cousins (1915–1990). Distinguished writer, editor, citizen diplomat, promoter of holistic healing, and author of dozens of books and hundreds of essays and editorials. In the 1960s, Cousins contracted ankylosing spondylitis, a crippling, life-threatening collagen disease. His condition steadily deteriorated, and his prognosis was dismal. He came to the conclusion that the depressing routine of hospital life was actually aggravating his condition, and with the blessings of one of his doctors, he checked out of the hospital and into a comfortable (though comparatively less expensive) hotel, where he began a regimen consisting of high doses of vitamin C and comedy movies. He chronicled his remarkable recovery in the best-selling book *Anatomy of an Illness as Perceived by the Patient: Reflections on Healing and Regeneration*, published in 1979. This autobiographical case history is often cited as the story of how a patient laughed himself out of an illness. The *New England Journal of Medicine* published an article by Cousins describing the role that high spirits and, in particular, laughter brought on by comedy movies played in his recovery of health (*N Engl J Med* 1976 Dec 23;295[26]:1458–63). During the last years of his life, Cousins served as a faculty member of the University of California, Los Angeles, School

of Medicine, where he taught ethics and medical literature and continued his research into the relationship between attitude and health. Norman Cousins was awarded the Albert Schweitzer Prize for Humanitarianism and Japan's Niwano Peace Prize.

2. McCoy Tyner (b. 1938). Legendary jazz pianist who in 1959 spent six months playing in the Art Farmer–Benny Golson Jazztet before joining the John Coltrane Quartet. Tyner remained with Coltrane until 1966, when he started his own trio. Beginning in 1972, his band toured regularly in Europe, Japan, and the Unites States. In 1978 he joined up with Sonny Rollins, Ron Carter and Al Foster in the Milestone Jazzstars. Tyner has released dozens of albums that stretch the boundaries of the jazz piano. "To me," Tyner explains, "living and music are all the same thing. And I keep finding out more about music as I learn more about myself, my environment, about all kinds of different things in life. I play what I live. Therefore, just as I can't predict what kinds of experiences I'm going to have, I can't predict the directions in which my music will go. I just want to write and play my instrument as I feel."

3. Lyrics from the song "Pennies from Heaven," by Johnny Burke and Arthur Johnston. "Pennies from Heaven" was written in 1936 as the title song of the film, starring Bing Crosby. Other songs by Johnny Burke include "One, Two, Button Your Shoe," "Swinging on a Star," and "I've Got a Pocketful of Dreams."

4. Seven Dwarfs. An allusion to the fairy tale *Snow White and the Seven Dwarfs*. The earliest literary versions of the tale may be found in Giambattista Basile's collection of folk tales entitled *Il Pentamerone*, published in 1674. In the Disney version of the fairy tale,

the seven dwarfs are named Dopey, Bashful, Grumpy, Sneezy, Sleepy, Happy, and Doc.

5. Lee Morgan (1938–1972). Hard-bop trumpeter Lee Morgan played with Dizzy Gillespie's big band from 1956 to 1958. From 1958 to 1961 he was a member of Art Blakey's Jazz Messengers. In 1963, he recorded "The Sidewinder," which became a great commercial success (the song became so popular that Chrysler used it in an automobile ad during the 1965 World Series). In addition to his solo success, Morgan recorded many albums with the greats of jazz.

Chapter Nine

1. William Stafford (1914–1993). American poet whose poetry books include *West of Your City* and *Traveling Through the Dark*, which won the National Book Award for Poetry in 1963.

Chapter Ten

1. From the song "Pink Elephants on Parade," a song by Frank Churchill and Ned Washington that appears in the Walt Disney film *Dumbo*.

Chapter Eleven

1. "Delaunay's Dilemma" is a jazz composition written by John Lewis, pianist of The Modern Jazz Quartet, in 1953; it appears on the album *Django*. The other members of the Modern Jazz Quartet are Milt Jackson on vibes, Percy Heath on bass, and Kenny Clark on drums.

2. William Bendix (1906–1964). With his thick features, broken nose, and affected Brooklyn accent, actor William Bendix often played the time-weathered roughneck with a heart of gold. He performed on stage,

radio, film, and television. He is best known for his role in the radio comedy *The Life of Riley*, which aired from 1944 to 1951 and was subsequently made into a film and television program. *The Life of Riley* was originally conceived as a program that was to be called *The Flotsam Family*, with Grouch Marx playing the lead character, but the sponsor of the program did not think Groucho was right for the role. Producer Irving Brecher had seen rugged, blue-collar Bendix on stage in *The McGuerins of Brooklyn*, and he asked Bendix to audition for the program. (Groucho, for his part, went on to do *You Bet Your Life*, first on radio and later on television.) Before joining the New York Theater Guild, Bendix played minor league baseball.

3. Ernie Kovacs (1919–1962). Avant-garde American comedian and television innovator of the 1950s. Kovacs was an iconoclast whose innovative approaches to television comedy would later be reflected in such programs as *Rowan and Martin's Laugh-In* (first aired in 1968), *Saturday Night Live* (first aired in 1975), and *Late Night with David Letterman* (first aired in 1982). At a time when television was treated as an extension of the vaudeville stage, Kovacs would engage in dialog with camera crews or the audience, or he would have the cameramen follow him offstage as he moved through the studio corridors. He pioneered the use of blackouts, teaser openings, improvisations with everyday objects, audio and visual synchronization, and a variety of camera techniques.

4. Coleman "Hawk" Hawkins (1901–1969). Considered the father of the jazz tenor saxophone, Coleman Hawkins was one of the leading jazz saxophonists of the 1920s and 1930s. Hawk joined the Fletcher Henderson Orchestra in 1924 and stayed with Henderson for ten years. He played with a deep tone in an inti-

mate, melodic style. From 1934 to 1939 Hawk lived in Europe, where he played with the Jack Hylton Orchestra in England and traveled and recorded throughout the continent. In 1937, he took part in a famous recording engagement with Benny Carter, Django Reinhardt, and Stephane Grappelli. He returned to the United States at the start of World War II. In 1940, he recorded "Body and Soul," which became his most famous recording. Hawkins was one of the few Hot Jazz musicians who made the transition to bebop in the 1940s. At different times, he hired Thelonious Monk, Miles Davis, and Max Roach to play in his bands. Throughout the 1950s and 1960s he appeared on records by Thelonious Monk, Max Roach, Eric Dolphy, John Coltrane, and Sonny Rollins. He continued to play powerful, emotionally inspired music throughout his life.

5. The phrase "Go West, young man!" was written by John Babson Lane Soule (1815–1891), the editor of the *Terre Haute Daily*, on a bet by Indiana Congressman Richard Thompson. The bet was that Soule could write an article that would be attributed to Horace Greeley (1811–1872), the editor of the *New York Tribune*. The payoff was to be a barrel of flour, which was to be given to a needy person. Knowing Greeley to be a strong advocate of Westward expansion, Soule wrote an editorial in which he said that Horace Greeley himself could not give a young man better advice than to "Go West, young man." Soule won the bet.

6. "Rahsaan's Run" is a jazz composition by the great trumpeter Woody Shaw, which appears on Shaw's album *Rosewood* (released in 1978). Rahsaan refers to Rahsaan Roland Kirk (1936–1977), a highly innovative and unorthodox saxophonist and flutist.

Chapter Twelve

1. "Blues Five Spot" (also known as "Five Spot Blues") is a jazz composition by pianist and composer Thelonious Monk. The song first appears on the album *Thelonious in Action*, a live recording of a 1958 performance by the Thelonious Monk Quartet at the celebrated Five Spot jazz club on New York's Lower East Side. Accompanying Monk were Johnny Griffin on tenor saxopohone, Ahmed Abdul-Malik on bass, and Roy Haynes on drums.

2. "Greetings to Idris," a jazz composition by Pharoah Sanders (b. 1940), which appears on Sanders' album *Journey to the One* (released in 1980). "Idris" refers to drummer Idris Muhammad. The great tenor saxophonist Pharoah Sanders collaborated with John Coltrane on many albums. Pharoah's bluesy intensity complemented Trane's phrasings and melodic inventiveness. "I loved the way he built his solos," says Pharoah of John Coltrane. "He had very well-planned ideas. I always had my own feeling for what I wanted to do, but listening to John made me want to develop my own sound. Even now I'm trying to perfect that." Employing African rhythms and East Asian motifs and modals, Sanders' progressive musicianship is appreciated by jazz artists and listeners around the world.

Chapter Thirteen

1. "Miles ahead" is an allusion to the record *Miles Ahead*, a masterful collaboration between trumpeter Miles Davis and pianist Gil Evans released in 1957. Miles Davis relates how he never listened to any of his records except for *Miles Ahead*, with Gil Evans, and the very early records that he made with Charlie Parker.

2. "Meditation on a Pair of Wire Cutters" is a jazz composition by Charles Mingus. The composition com-

prises several sections and evolved gradually under different titles. It was renamed "Playing with Eric" after the tragic death of Eric Dolphy, who had collaborated with Mingus on several compositions, including "Meditation on a Pair of Wire Cutters." "I heard Mingus explain that Southern racists were once preparing to stop the civil rights marchers by erecting barbed wire barriers, and so he said, 'What we need is a pair of wire cutters.'"—SDG.

3. Antonio Machado (1875–1939). Spanish poet and playwright. In his poem "Portrait," he writes, "In the end, I owe you nothing; you owe me all I've written."

Chapter Fourteen

1. "Misterioso" is a jazz composition by Thelonious Monk, which he wrote in 1948. The song appears on the album of the same name, recorded by the Thelonious Monk Quartet in 1958.

Chapter Fifteen

1. Quoted lines in this poem have been adapted from the lyrics of the song "More Than You Know" (music by Vincent Youmans, lyrics by Billy Rose and Edward Eliscu; first published in 1919). This standard has been recorded by many artists, including Ruth Etting, Sarah Vaughan, Ella Fitzgerald, and Frank Sinatra.

Chapter Seventeen

1. Albert Ayler (1936–1970). One of the giants of free jazz, tenor saxophonist Albert Ayler came to jazz not through bebop but through rhythm and blues bands. In the early 1960s, Ayler played with avant garde pianist Cecil Taylor in Denmark. He returned to the United States in 1963 and led a series of bands while playing a very personal form of free jazz. Ayler's composition

"Ghosts" was first recorded during a live performance of the Albert Ayler Trio on June 14, 1964, at the Cellar Café in New York City.

2. Lyrics from the song "Angel Eyes," written by M. Dennis and E. Brent and recorded by Frank Sinatra on his album *Only the Lonely* (1958).

Chapter Eighteen

1. Zachary Scott (1914–1965). Stage and screen actor who was equally adept playing heroes or rogues. His films include The Mask of Dimitrios (1944), Mildred Pearce (1945), and Jean Renoir's The Southerner (1945).

Chapter Nineteen

1. "Bud's Bounce" is a jazz composition by bebop pianist Bud Powell (see note 1 to Chapter Four, below).

Chapter Twenty

1. Lines in this poem have been taken from the song "Comes Love," written by Lew Brown, Sammy Stept, and Charles Tobias in 1942 and recorded by Joni Mitchell on the CD *Both Sides Now*.

Chapter Twenty-One

1. A reference to Bud Powell (1924–1966). Pianist and composer Bud Powell was one of the key figures in the creation of bebop. Important compositions include "Hallucinations" (which was recorded by Miles Davis as "Budo"), "Dance of the Infidels," "Tempus Fugue-it," "Bouncing with Bud," and the remarkable "The Glass Enclosure."

Glossary

A

Ācārya—a spiritual master who teaches by his personal behavior.

Adhikārī—one who knows the science of Kṛṣṇa and is engaged in His service.

Āgama—authorized Vedic literatures; also, specifically the *Pañcarātras*.

Anartha—unwanted thing; material desire.

Annamaya—(consciousness) absorbed only in food.

Aparādha—offense.

Ārati—a ceremony of worshiping the Lord by the offering of various auspicious articles, such as incense, flowers, water, fans, ghee lamp, etc.

Āśrama—a spiritual order: *brahmacārī* (celibate student), *gṛhastha* (householder), *vānaprastha* (retired), *sannyāsī* (renunciate); living quarters for those engaged in spiritual practices.

Asura—demon or ungodly person.

Avadhūta—a spirtually advanced person whose activities are not restricted by social convention.

Avatāra—lit., "one who descends." An incarnation of the Lord.

B

Baladeva—*see* Balarāma.

Balarāma—Kṛṣṇa's elder brother and His first plenary expansion.

Bhagavad-gītā—lit., "song of God." The discourse between Lord Kṛṣṇa and His devotee Arjuna, expounding devotional service as both the principal means and the ultimate end of spiritual perfection.

Bhagavān—lit., "one who possesses all opulence." The Supreme Lord, who is the reservoir of all beauty, strength, fame, wealth, knowledge, and renunciation.

Bhāgavata—anything related to Bhagavān, especially the Lord's devotee and the scripture, *Śrīmad-Bhāgavatam.*

Bhāgavata-saptāha—a seven day discourse on the *Śrīmad-Bhāgavatam,* usually recited for some material purpose or profit.

Bhāgavatam—*see Śrīmad-Bhāgavatam.*

Bhajana—devotional activities; a devotional song.

Bhakta—a devotee of Kṛṣṇa.

Bhakti—devotional service to the Supreme Lord.

Bhaktisiddhānta Sarasvatī Ṭhākura—the spiritual master of His Divine Grace A.C. Bhaktivedanta Swami Prabhupāda; an *ācārya* in the Gauḍīya-Vaiṣṇava-sampradāya.

Bhaktivedanta—a title conferred upon Śrīla Prabhupāda by the Gaudiya Math, meaning "one who has understood that the conclusion of Vedic scripture is *bhakti* (devotional service)."

Bhaktivinoda Ṭhākura—an *ācārya* in the Gauḍīya Vaiṣṇava disciplic succession; the father of Bhaktisiddhānta Sarasvatī Ṭhākura.

Bhāva—the stage of transcendental ecstasy experienced after transcendental affection.

Brahmā—the first created living being and the secondary creator of the material universe.

Brahmacārī—a celibate student living under the care of a bona fide spiritual master.

Brahmacāriṇī—feminine variant of *brahmacārī.*

Brahman—the impersonal aspect of the Absolute Truth; spirit.

Brāhmaṇa—one wise in the *Vedas* who can guide society; the first Vedic social order.

Brahma-saṁhitā—Lord Brahmā's prayers glorifying the Supreme Lord.

C

Cādar—shawl.

Caitanya (Mahāprabhu)—lit., "living force." Kṛṣṇa who appeared in the form of a devotee to teach love of God through the *saṅkīrtana* movement.

Cāmara—a yak-tail whisk.

Chaukīdār—a security guard.

D

Dakṣiṇā—a disciple's gift to his spiritual master upon initiation, collected by begging and given as a token of gratitude.

Daṇḍa—a staff carried by *sannyāsīs.*

Daṇḍavats—lit., "like a stick." To offer prostrated obeisances, extending one's limbs in a straight line.

Darśana—vision; audience.

Dāsa—lit., "servant" (masculine). An appellation which along with a name of Kṛṣṇa or one of His devotees is given to a devotee at the time of initiation.

Dāsī—feminine variation of *dāsa.*

Dhāma—abode; the Lord's place of residence.

Dhotī—a garment wrapped on the lower body of men, commonly worn in India.

Dundubhi—a type of drum.

Dvārakā—the city where Kṛṣṇa ruled in His later pastimes as a king.

G

Gambhīrā—a room in Jagannātha Purī where Śrī Caitanya Mahāprabhu would experience intense feelings of separation from Kṛṣṇa.

Gamchā—a thin cotton towel, commonly used in India.

Gaṇeśa—the demigod in charge of material opulence and freedom from misfortune.

Ganges (Gaṅgā)—a sacred river in India that washed the lotus feet of Lord Viṣṇu.

Gauḍīya Vaiṣṇavism—the practice of Kṛṣṇa consciousness as taught by Lord Caitanya, who appeared in Gauḍadeśa (West Bengal), and who is accepted as being nondifferent from Lord Kṛṣṇa.

Gaura—a name of Lord Caitanya Mahāprabhu, meaning "golden."

Gaurakiśora dāsa Bābājī—the spiritual master of Śrīla Bhaktisiddhānta Sarasvatī Ṭhākura.

Gaura-Nitāi—Lord Caitanya (Gaura) and Lord Nityānanda (Nitāi).

Gāyatrī—a prayer chanted silently by *brāhmaṇas* at sunrise, noon, and sunset.

GBC—Governing Body Commission, ISKCON's board of directors.

Gītā-nagarī—a spiritual farm community established by Śrīla Prabhupāda in central Pennsylvania.

Goloka—Kṛṣṇaloka, the eternal abode of Lord Kṛṣṇa.

Gopī—a cowherd girl; one of Kṛṣṇa's most confidential servitors.

Gosvāmī—one who controls his mind and senses; title of one in the renounced order of life. May refer specifically to the six Gosvāmīs of Vṛndāvana, who are direct followers of Lord Caitanya in disciplic succession and who systematically presented His teachings.

Govardhana Hill—a hill in Vṛndāvana, the site of many of Kṛṣṇa's pastimes.

Govinda—a name of Kṛṣṇa, meaning "one who gives pleasure (*vinda*) to the cows (*go*) and senses (also *go*)"; may also refer to Lord Caitanya's personal servant.

Gṛhastha—a married person living according to the Vedic social system.

Grāmya-kathā—talk concerning family life.

Guṇas—the modes of material nature, *sattva-guṇa* (goodness), *rajo-guṇa* (passion), and *tamo-guṇa* (ignorance).

Guru-dakṣiṇā—a gift made to the spirtual master as a token payment for his teachings.

Gurukula—a school headed by the spiritual master.

Guru Mahārāja—title of respect given to one's own spiritual master.

H

Hare—the vocative form of Harā, another name of Rādhārāṇī; refers specifically to the internal spiritual energy of the Lord.

Haribol—"Chant the holy name."

Hari-nāma—lit., "the name of the Lord."

Hiraṇyakaśipu—a demoniac king killed by Lord Nṛsiṁhadeva.

I

Indra—the chief of the administrative demigods and king of the heavenly planets.

ISKCON—acronym for the International Society for Krishna Consciousness.

Īśopaniṣad—one of the 108 principal Vedic scriptures known as the *Upaniṣads*.

J

Jagannātha—lit., "the Lord of the universe"; may refer specifically to the Deity of Lord Jagannātha in His temple at Purī.

Jagannātha Purī—place of pilgrimage on the east coast of India where the Deity of Jagannātha is worshipped.

Japa—individual chanting of the Hare Kṛṣṇa mantra while counting on beads.

Jaya—an acclamation meaning, "Victory!" or, "All glories!"

Jīva—the individual, eternal soul or living entity; part of the Supreme Lord.

Jñāna—the process of approaching the Supreme by the cultivation of knowledge.

Jñānī—one who approaches the Supreme by cultivation of knowledge.

K

Kali-yuga—the present age, which is characterized by quarrel and hypocrisy.

Karmī—one engaged in karma (fruitive activity); a materialist.

Kaṁsa—a demoniac king who tried to kill Kṛṣṇa during His childhood pastimes.

Kaniṣṭha—neophyte.

Kathā—talks.

Kicchari—a nutritious stew made with Indian beans, rice and vegetables.

Kīrtana—chanting of the Lord's holy names.

Kṛṣṇa—the Supreme Personality of Godhead.

Kṛṣṇa-Balarāma—the presiding Deities of the ISKCON temple in Vṛndāvana, India.

Kṛṣṇa-kathā—topics spoken by or about Kṛṣṇa.

Kṛṣṇaloka—the eternal abode of Lord Kṛṣṇa.

Kurtā—a tuniclike men's shirt commonly worn in India.

Kurukṣetra—a holy place where the war between the Pāṇḍavas and the Kurus took place and where Lord Kṛṣṇa spoke the *Bhagavad-gītā* to Arjuna.

L

Laḍḍu—a traditional Indian sweetball, made with chickpea flour, butter, and sweetener.

Loka—planet.

M

Madhyama-adhikārī—a devotee whose advancement in spiritual life is midway between the neophyte (*kaniṣṭha*) and advanced (*uttama*) levels.

Mahā-bhāgavata—a devotee in the highest stage of devotional life.

Mahābhārata—the history of ancient India, compiled by Śrīla Vyāsadeva; includes the *Bhagavad-gītā.*

Mahā-guṇa—great qualities.

Mahā-mantra—the great chant for deliverance: Hare Kṛṣṇa, Hare Kṛṣṇa, Kṛṣṇa Kṛṣṇa, Hare Hare/ Hare Rāma, Hare Rāma, Rāma Rāma, Hare Hare.

Mahāprabhu—supreme master of all masters; refers to Lord Caitanya.

Mahārāja—great king. Also used as a title of respect for a *sannyāsī.*

Mahātmā—great soul.

Mahā-vākya—a principal Vedic mantra or verse.

Mālā—string of beads used for chanting.

Mandira—temple.

Mañjarī—an intimate *gopī* maidservant of Rādhā and Kṛṣṇa.

Mantra—sound vibration that can deliver the mind from illusion.

Mātājī—mother.

Māyā—the external, illusory energy of the Lord, comprising this material world; forgetfulness of one's relationship with Kṛṣṇa.

Māyāpur—a town in West Bengal, India, where Lord Caitanya appeared.

Māyāvādī—an impersonalist or voidist who believes that God is ultimately formless and without personality.

Mṛdaṅga—a two-headed clay drum, traditionally used in *kīrtana.*

Mūḍha—fool, rascal.

Mūrti—a form, usually referring to a deity.

N

Nāma—the holy name.

Nārada Muni—a great devotee of Lord Kṛṣṇa who travels throughout the spiritual and material worlds singing the Lord's glories and preaching the path of devotional service.

Nityānanda—the incarnation of Lord Balarāma who is a principal associate of Lord Caitanya.

Nṛsiṁha(deva)—the half-man, half-lion incarnation of Lord Kṛṣṇa who appeared to save Prahlāda Mahārāja from Hiraṇyakaśipu.

P

Pānihāṭī—a village in East Bengal, India, made famous for a chipped rice festival during the advent of Lord Caitanya. Also refers to ISKCON New Pānihāṭī in Atlanta, Georgia, where annually they hold a festival of the same name.

Paramparā—the disciplic succession of bona fide spiritual masters.

Parikrama—a walking pilgrimage.

Parīkṣit Mahārāja—the emperor of the world five thousand years ago who heard *Śrīmad-Bhāgavatam* from Śukadeva Gosvāmī and thus attained perfection.

Pāriṣada—a liberated associate of Kṛṣṇa.

Prabhu—lit., "master." Added to a devotee's name by another devotee to show respect.

Prabhu-datta-deśa—the geographical location assigned by the spiritual master to the disciple for service to his mission.

Prabhupāda, A.C. Bhaktivedanta Swami—founder-*ācārya* of ISKCON and foremost preacher of Kṛṣṇa consciousness in the Western world.

Prabhupādānuga—one who follows the teachings of Śrīla Prabhupāda.

Praṇāmas—an offering of respect shown by joining ones hands.

Prajalpa—foolish, idle, or mundane speech. Talks unrelated to Kṛṣṇa consciousness.

Pramāṇa—evidence or proof.

Prasādam—lit., "mercy." Food that has been spiritualized by offering it to Kṛṣṇa and that helps purify the living entity; also referred to as *prasāda*.

Prema—love of Kṛṣṇa.

Preyas—activity which is immediately beneficial but not ultimately auspicious.

Pūjārī—a priest, specifically one engaged in temple Deity worship.

Pukka—a Bengali term used to define someone or something as "first class."

Purāṇa—Vedic histories of the universe in relation to the Supreme Lord and His devotees. The phrase "spotless *Purāṇa*" refers to the *Śrīmad-Bhāgavatam*.

R

Rādhā-kuṇḍa—the bathing place of Śrīmatī Rādhārāṇī, a sacred pond near Govardhana Hill in Vṛndāvana that was created by Rādhārāṇī and her *gopī* companions.

Rādhā(rāṇī)—the eternal consort and spiritual potency of Lord Kṛṣṇa.

Rāgānugā-bhakti—devotional service following the spontaneous loving service of the inhabitants of Vṛndāvana.

Rajas—passion.

Rāma—as part of the Hare Kṛṣṇa *mahā-mantra,* refers to the highest eternal pleasure of Lord Kṛṣṇa; may also refer to Lord Balarāma or Lord Rāmacandra.

Rāmacandra, Lord—the *avatāra* of Kṛṣṇa who appeared as the perfect king and whose full history can be found in Vālmīki's *Rāmāyaṇa.*

Rāmāyaṇa—the epic history of Lord Rāmacandra, written by Vālmīki Muni.

Rasa—the spiritual essence of a personal relationship with the Supreme Lord.

Rasika—person or thing absorbed in *rasa.*

Ratha-yātrā—an annual chariot festival celebrating Kṛṣṇa's return to Vṛndāvana in which the Deity of Lord Jagannātha is pulled in procession on a *ratha* (chariot).

Rūpa Gosvāmī—one of the six Gosvāmīs of Vṛndāvana.

S

Śabda-brahma—transcendental sound, considered by Vedic philosophy to be self-evident proof of knowledge.

Sādhaka—one who practices regulated devotional service.

Sādhana—regulated spiritual activities meant to increase one's attachment to Kṛṣṇa.

Sādhu—saintly person.

Sahajiyā—a class of pseudodevotees who take the conjugal pastimes of Kṛṣṇa and the gopīs cheaply and who do not follow the proper regulations of *vaidhī-bhakti.*

Śakti—potency.

Sampradāya—a chain of disciplic succession through which spiritual knowledge is transmitted.

Sanātana Gosvāmī—one of the six Gosvāmīs of Vṛndāvana.

Saṅga—association.

Saṅkīrtana—the congregational chanting of the holy name, fame, and pastimes of the Lord; preaching.

Sannyāsa—renounced life; the fourth order of Vedic spiritual life.

Sannyāsī—one in the renounced order of life.

Śāstra—revealed scripture.

Śāstra-cakṣus—one who sees through the eyes of the authorized scriptures.

Sattva—goodness.

Sevā—service.

Siddhānta—the perfect conclusion according to Vedic scriptures.

Śikṣā—instruction.

Śikṣā-guru—an instructing spiritual master.

Śloka—a stanza of Sanskrit verse.

Siṁhāsana—altar or throne.

Smaraṇam—the devotional process of remembering the Lord.

Smṛti—scriptures further explaining the four original *Vedas* and the *Upaniṣads.*

Śraddhā—firm faith and confidence.

Śreyas—activities that are ultimately beneficial and auspicious.

Śrī—a prefix used an an honorific.

Śrīla—a term of respect given to a spiritual master.

Śrīmad-Bhāgavatam—the *Bhāgavata Purāṇa,* written by Śrīla Vyāsadeva, which specifically points to the path of devotional love of God.

Śrīmatī—a term of respect given to women or female Deities.

Śrutī—the original Vedic literatures: the four *Vedas* and the *Upaniṣads;* scripture received directly from God.

Subhadrā—Lord Kṛṣṇa's sister; Yogamāyā.

Śukadeva Gosvāmī—the sage who originally spoke the *Śrīmad-Bhāgavatam* to King Parīkṣit just prior to the king's death.

Supersoul—an expansion of the Supreme Lord as an all-pervading personal presence in the universe and in the heart of every living entity.

Swami—one who controls his senses; a title of one in the renounced order of life.

Swamiji—lit., "great master." A common term of respect addressed to *sannyāsīs.*

T

Tantra—minor scriptures describing various rituals, mostly for persons in the mode of ignorance.

Tapasya—austerity.

Tattva—truth.

Tilaka—auspicious clay markings that sanctify a devotee's body as a temple of the Lord.

Tulasī—a great devotee in the form of a plant; her leaves are always offered to the lotus feet of the Lord.

U

Upaniṣads—108 philosophical treatises that appear within the *Vedas.*

Utsāha—enthusiasm.

Uttama-adhikārī—a topmost devotee.

V

Vaikuṇṭha—the spiritual world.

Vaiṣṇava—one who is a devotee of Viṣṇu or Kṛṣṇa.

Varṇa—the four occupational divisions of society: intellectual (*brāhmaṇa*), administrator (*kṣatriya*), merchant (*vaiśya*), and laborer (*śūdra*).

Vedānta—the conclusion of Vedic philosophy.

Vibhūti—opulence.

Viṣṇu—a fully empowered expansion of Kṛṣṇa.

Viṣṇudūta—the messengers of Lord Viṣṇu who take perfected devotees back to the spiritual world at the time of death.

Vraja—Vṛndāvana.

Vrajabhūmi—Kṛṣṇa's personal abode; another name for Vṛndāvana.

Vrajavāsī—a resident of Vṛndāvana.

Vṛndāvana—Kṛṣṇa's personal abode, where He fully manifests His personal qualities.

Vyāsāsana—a special, elevated seat reserved for the speaker of *Śrīmad-Bhāgavatam.*

Y

Yajña—sacrifice.

Yamadūtas—the agents of Yamarāja, the superintendent of death and karmic justice.

Yamarāja—the superintendent of death and karmic justice.

Yamunā—a sacred river in India, which Lord Kṛṣṇa made famous by performing pastimes there.

Yaśodā—Kṛṣṇa's mother in Vṛndāvana.

Yuga—an age. There are four *yugas,* which cycle perpetually: Satya-yuga, Tretā-yuga, Dvāpara-yuga, and Kali-yuga.

www.ingramcontent.com/pod-product-compliance
Lightning Source LLC
Chambersburg PA
CBHW051842300426
44117CB00006B/243